MILTON FRIEDMAN

MILTON FRIEDMAN

ECONOMICS IN THEORY AND PRACTICE

Abraham Hirsch

and

Neil de Marchi

THE UNIVERSITY OF MICHIGAN PRESS

Ann Arbor

First published in the United States of America in 1990
by the University of Michigan Press

First published in Great Britain in 1990 by
Harvester Wheatsheaf
66 Wood Lane End, Hemel Hempstead
Hertfordshire, HP2 4RG
A division of
Simon and Schuster International Group

Printed and bound in Great Britain.

Library of Congress Cataloging-in-Publication Data

Hirsch, Abraham
    Milton Friedman, economics in theory and practice / Abraham Hirsch
and Neil de Marchi.
        p.   cm.
    Includes bibliographical references.
    ISBN 0-472-10175-7
    1. Friedman, Milton, 1912–   . 2. Economics—Methodology.
I. De Marchi, Neil.   II. Title.
HB119.F84D4   1989
330.1—dc20   89-20266
                                                                      CIP

1993 1992 1991 1990   4 3 2 1

CONTENTS

ACKNOWLEDGEMENTS

This book has been in progress since a 1977 exchange of ideas on Friedman. Over so long a period of time one incurs a large number of obligations. Our greatest debt is to Friedman himself for having created the challenging, exciting and worthwhile materials of which we have been able to make use. We are also grateful to some of his critics – particularly Ernest Nagel, Lawrence Boland and Eugene Rotwein – who have forced us to think out our basic position more carefully than we otherwise might have. We learned a great deal from both Friedman and his critics and it has been a thoroughly enjoyable learning experience. We are also indebted to many friends and critics for reading and commenting on various versions of parts of our work. Milton Friedman took the trouble to read virtually the whole manuscript. Portions have been commented upon by George J. Stigler, Anna J. Schwartz, Eugene Rotwein, J. Daniel Hammond, William F. Barber, E. Roy Weintraub, Benjamin Klebener, A. W. Coats, Nancy and Joe Brenner, Dan Hausman, Michael McPherson, Richard A. Gonce, Lawrence A. Boland, Donald McCloskey, Melvin Reder, Jeremy Shearmur, Royall Brandis, Margaret Schabas, David Laidler, Andrea Salanti, Phillipe Mongin, John H. Wood, Tony Lawson, Uskali Maki, Nancy Wulwick, Mark Blaug, Y. Shionoya and Warren Samuels. Our grateful thanks to them all.

Mark Blaug, as one of the editors of this series, both initiated this particular project and provided us with encouragement and useful advice over a long period.

To Eva Hirsch, and to Thomas Mayer and Kevin Hoover, we are particularly grateful: to the former for research, editorial and critical help at every stage of the work, and to each of the latter for detailed and very challenging comments on the penultimate draft. The book has been substantially improved because of their help.

Thanks are also due to Tom Rosenbaum of the Rockefeller Archive for help in tracing pertinent materials, and to Forrest Smith for expert word-processing of the text.

Portions of Chapter 10 have appeared in *Economics and Philosophy* (April 1986) and are used here by permission of Cambridge University Press.

21 March 1989

INTRODUCTION

Most economists pick up notions about the philosophy of science somewhere along the way which they then use in talking about their own methodology. This gives economic methodologists an easy way to find the 'key' to what they take to be economists' thinking, since philosophy supposedly reaches down to the most fundamental level. But all too often it amounts to labeling in lieu of detailed analysis. Thus economist A is dubbed a falsificationist, B an instrumentalist, C a conventionalist, and so on. If we add a few more labels – like realist, sceptic, descriptivist, positivist, pragmatist, essentialist – the game really becomes fun! On the one hand it enables the methodologist to show that from the philosophical point of view every eminent economist who has been foolish enough to say anything about economic methodology is terribly inconsistent if not downright silly, and on the other hand to concentrate on one or another of the economist's comments which reveals, or so we are to believe, the very heart of the individual's way of thinking. A good bit of the debate generated by Friedman's famous essay has followed this pattern, increasingly, it seems, the closer one gets to the present. One of the reasons we decided to write this book is the belief that much of this sort of analysis is not very enlightening.

These remarks are not meant to imply that recent attempts to relate basic ideas in economic methodology to developments in philosophy have had no contribution to make. Quite the contrary. Our reference is not to economic methodology *per se* but rather to attempts to interpret the methodological views, explicit and implicit, of major contemporary economists. In this area, it seems to us, there has been at least as much retrogression as advance. Eminent economists are used as mere grist for the mill of philosophical analysis to illustrate philosophical positions. Whatever this may reveal about economic methodology generally, it does not reveal much about the views of particular economists. When working economists, particularly innovative ones, write about economic methodology they are probably trying to tell us something about their way of doing economics and not to make a contribution to the philosophy of science. Thus, a study of the economic writings of economists of interest is likely to be a prerequisite of grasping their methodological views. Correspondingly, we should ask of them, for example, not 'How do you believe that the problem of induction should be handled?' but rather, 'What are you trying to tell us about your work?'[1] Our convictions about this provide one of the principal reasons that a project which began as an article wound up as a book.

As historians of economics we were not surprised to find as we worked growing evidence that an understanding of the historical context of the debate leading to and provoked by Friedman's 1953 essay on methodology could shed light on the nature and significance of his contribution. A felt need to take account of this has shaped our treatment. Two particulars may be mentioned. On the one hand Friedman's views deviate so markedly from those which have been dominant in economics from Senior, Cairnes and Mill to J. N. Keynes and Lionel Robbins that it would not be an exaggeration to call them revolutionary. This has not generally been noticed, however, and the neglect has contributed to some of the confusion which Friedman's famous essay generated. To clarify matters we have chosen to refer often to mainstream methodology, mainly using the views of John Stuart Mill as (contrasting) representative, but we have also taken a whole chapter (Chapter 5) to draw the contrasts in detail. A second example is this. Friedman's monumental *Monetary History of the United States* (1963a, with Anna Schwartz) and some other research products like it, were done under the auspices of the National Bureau of Economic Research, an organization that has been called 'the lengthened shadow' of Wesley Clair Mitchell. Mitchell was a heterodox critic of neoclassical economics and, as shown in our second chapter, there are interesting traces of Mitchell's heterodoxy in Friedman's views about methodology. To be judged adequate, one's own views about Friedman's methodology must be capable of incorporating this important aspect in his work. It turns out that a significant portion of the criticism that has been levelled at Friedman simply fails to acknowledge this heterodox strand of his thinking. We have tried to give due place not only to Mitchellian but to other typically neglected characteristics of Friedman's work. Another of these is a striking similarity to views held by the American philosopher John Dewey. We devote the sixth chapter to showing some major characteristics of Dewey's way of thinking to enable readers to judge our contention that ignoring Dewey makes suspect any characterization of Friedman's underlying philosophy as 'instrumental', conventionalist, positivist or falsificationalist. In introducing Dewey, however, we encountered two problems.

The first is a problem of labels, similar to the problem noted at the outset. Dewey's philosophy has been referred to as 'pragmatic', 'experimental' and 'instrumental'. The term pragmatic is unfortunately associated with an a-theoretical practicalism on the one side and a particular theory of truth on the other. Both of these associations are misleading for our purposes. The designation 'experimental' is perhaps even more misleading when talking about a largely non-experimental field like economics. We would have preferred to use the term 'instrumental' which, understood as problem solving, conveys a lot about Friedman's approach to positive economics. Unfortunately, the term has been pre-empted by the modern philosopher Karl Popper, and his disciple in economics Lawrence Boland, and used to stand for something very different from the central ideas in Deweyan thinking. Because of this we feel that there is less risk referring to Friedman's approach in economics as 'pragmatic', though as will be seen, there is no direct relationship between this approach and William James' pragmatic theory of truth; nor is this the pragmatism of J. S. Mill's 'practical man' or of Popper's (and Boland's) engineer/repairman. We devote a good bit of attention to the differences in the sixth chapter but in addition comment on it in passing where it is an issue.

A second problem in drawing the lines connecting Friedman and Dewey is that economists interested in methodology today tend to think in terms of positivist philosophy, Popperian falsificationism, Lakatosian research programs or Kuhnian revolutions. When Dewey and pragmatism are mentioned in passing it is invariably in an uninformed way and for the purpose of showing Dewey's thinking to be naïve. This conditioning may mean that we lose some readers before we get to the sixth chapter, where the issues involved are explicitly considered. We toyed with the idea of an introductory chapter dealing with this problem but rejected it because our purpose is to understand Friedman's economics, and to feature Dewey so prominently would have unnecessarily fuzzied the picture. Nonetheless some readers might prefer to turn first to Chapters 5 and 6 and then go back to Chapter 1. For those, however, who are not especially concerned to place Friedman in relation to the orthodox economics and Deweyan traditions this would not be the best way to proceed. We hope that most will want to see how the various issues arise in the course of dealing directly with Friedman's ideas about economics. The first four chapters are designed to show this.

The book is in three parts. The first introduces Friedman the methodologist with, as indicated, a good deal of attention given to context broadly understood. Part II takes the reader through his economics, though with rather more emphasis being devoted to Friedman's earlier than to his later and better known work. Chapter 7 is designed to supply a link between these two parts. It brings together what Friedman said and what he did. This chapter can be read on its own. It is meant to provide a convenient summary of our findings in these two parts, and is offered in lieu of a concluding chapter.

Any neat conclusion to the book as a whole was rendered virtually impossible by two recalcitrant loose ends, which we have pursued but not tied off in Part III.

Friedman's insistence on prediction as 'the only relevant test' seemed to demand a closer look at what he actually did in the way of prediction and checking. At once a choice presented itself. Option 1 was to pursue this in the context of Friedman's positive economics (treated in Chapters 8 through 10), following in detail the steps Friedman took in moving from theory and theoretical models to empirical models and numerical estimates. These steps are familiar to every working economist and econometrician, involving as they do issues of specification and choice of functional form, testing for such things as exogeneity and identification, the addition of simplifying auxiliary hypotheses and data preparation. One needs to set out these steps and understand them before pronouncing on a result. Recent work on experimentation in other disciplines suggests that much further discussion and even 'negotiation' must take place once results are announced before an experiment can be said to be over (Collins, 1985, Galison, 1987). This is a fascinating area of inquiry, but for our purposes there are several reasons for not pursuing it in this book. First, working econometricians do not need to set out all their choices explicitly in order to communicate with their own research cohort. That means that the job has to be done by historians of economics and methodologists. However, this work is only just beginning (see especially Kim, 1989 and De Marchi and Kim, 1989). Second, it is not clear from preliminary explorations that discussion of results does in fact center on these steps in quite the way one would hope. It may be that there is much more production of non-overlapping alternative results than there are attempts to encompass alternative hypotheses within one empirical model, which is what testing requires. Third, in the nature of the case it is difficult to keep the goal − testing predictions − clear in the mass of technical detail that must be discussed if these steps are taken seriously (for confirmation of this see Desai, 1981, and Hendry and Ericsson, 1985). All these points argued against our attempting to pursue Option 1 here.

Option 2, which we have adopted, was to take relatively direct predictive links between theory and observation and explore them further. Such links are most likely to be found in Friedman's popular writings; and these are anyway the sorts of predictions for which he is best known. Chapter 11 takes the closer look we spoke of earlier, but it examines Friedman's popular rather than his research-related predictions. Even at the popular level it turns out that it is no simple matter to determine just what is taken as given in making a prediction; hence most of our discussion turns on this and not on direct confrontations between theory and observation. As the reader will see, matters are sufficiently complicated to make such simple confrontations of questionable value. We are left, though, with a category of work and its associated problems that simply does not sit easily with what we have tried to do in the rest of the book.

So too with Friedman's political economy. We planned initially to consider only Friedman's positive economics but became aware before very long that something would have to be said about his approach to political economy. One reason is that critics do not always distinguish between the two. Since the differences are sharp, as we show in Chapter 12, this can create a lot of confusion. For instance, there is a difference in *political views* between Dewey and Friedman. Hence to some the notion that these two hold common ideas about *the methodology of positive economics* is simply incredible.[2] (To readers who incline to such a view we suggest reading the last chapter first.) We might have preferred to refer readers to the literature on Friedman's methodology of political economy rather than adding a chapter; unfortunately we could find no such commentaries. Because Friedman's ideas raise intriguing questions about the methodology of political economy, we felt an additional chapter warranted. Also arguing for a separate treatment was the following. Some of Friedman's views about the methodology of political economy are almost diametrically opposed to what he believes about how positive economics should be done. This leads to a curious result: the more regard one has for his work in positive economics the more negative are one's reactions to the methodology of his political economy. Nonetheless, a careful examination of the former does shed some light on the latter. All of these considerations seemed to argue for a separate chapter. We have made no more than a beginning, however. Chapter 12 is not an extensive examination of a statement of Friedman's views on political economy but treats only its methodology, and then only the issues in this area which are related in one way or another to positive economics.

Something needs to be said here about problems of interpretation, particularly those that face would-be interpreters of a living writer's work. The main issue is whether one seeks the subject's judgments on his own work. Friedman has been aware of this project during much of its gestation. He has seen drafts of the first ten chapters and Chapter 12 and has offered encouragement and help on factual matters. At the same time, since this is not a biography nor is it an attempt to identify 'true' origins, motivations, or the like, we saw no reason to interview him; nor did we seek his approval.

In the matter of approving judgments, however, we cannot avoid offering a brief statement of position; for Friedman has made approving statements about the work of others whose interpretations we happen to dispute. Friedman's comments are in the public domain. Thus Lawrence Boland has reported that 'Friedman has commented to me and other methodologists [that] I was "entirely correct" in my characterization of his essay' (Boland, 1984, p. 795; also 1982 and 1987, pp. 382–3) and this has led him and others (for example, Wible, 1982 n. 15; 1985, p. 990) to suggest that nothing more remains to be said on the subject.[3] We think it appropriate to observe that there is at least reason to question this conclusion.

Three points may be made. First, Friedman has said other things which leave a different impression. For example, in a more recent letter Friedman has written (to Donald McCloskey, 10 January 1984, a copy of which was sent to Hirsch by Friedman):

> One minor indication of my difficulty is that you cite Dewey as if he were not a 'modernist' in my sense, yet some recent papers I have read [early drafts of ours setting out parallels with Deweyan pragmatism] have persuaded me that my own methodological views are almost identical with those of John Dewey.

As we make clear in Chapter 4, there are significant differences between the ways of a Popperian instrumentalist, as Boland characterizes Friedman, and one who thinks as a Deweyan. Boland, however, does not make the distinction, and so long as there is confusion on this point it is not improbable that Friedman could read elements of Deweyan instrumentalism into Boland's account and accept the (undifferentiated) designation 'instrumentalist'.

Second, unless comments are detailed enough they can easily be misinterpreted. For example, in a letter written to Hirsch (5 December 1983) Friedman writes that 'I regard my own methodological views as entirely consistent with Popper's'. This statement is at first sight startling since, as we have seen, Friedman was also prepared to see his way of thinking as close to Dewey's. Yet Dewey's orientation is in important respects quite anathema to Popper (see Chapter 6). The puzzle is resolved when Friedman adds 'The key thing of course which I got from Popper was the notion of falsification versus verification . . .'!

Third, one has to read comments like these in the context of what Friedman has said in his published work. We would not deny that there *is* a sense in which Friedman's approach is 'instrumental' in the narrow Popperian meaning, since anyone who appeals primarily to implications as a criterion for accepting theory can be said to be an 'instrumentalist' almost by definition. Moreover, it is not difficult to see why Friedman should have been enthusiastic about the fact that someone at last had recognized this characteristic of his approach after a whole series of interpretations had appeared whose main point was that he had violated the simple laws of logic. Yet Friedman's comments about Dewey – and a whole lot of evidence besides, as we will show – suggest that he may not have meant to subscribe to all aspects of this interpretation.

All this said, we should stress again, however, that we have not quoted from Friedman's correspondence to demonstrate that it is *our* interpretation that has his seal of approval. Our only purpose is to alert readers that no simple or 'obvious' conclusions should be drawn from comments of the sort we have cited.

Hirsch has had the primary responsibility for Chapters 1 through 6 and 12, and De Marchi for Chapters 7 through 11. But this book is more than the sum of separate contributions made by the two authors. Over an extended period we have thrashed out every idea, both on general points and more specific formulations and argued about every page of every draft. As a result, though on some matters we started rather far apart, we are now close to agreement even in those few areas where we may not fully agree. This has thus been a very thorough collaboration, with the result that we can both take responsibility for every aspect of the work.

NOTES

1. How great a difference focusing on the one question rather than the other can make is shown very vividly when one compares Coddington's first article on Friedman's methodology (1972) with his second (1979). Unfortunately, Coddington's second article did not come to our notice until we were so far along that we could not comment on it in the body of the text. We should say here generally that what we have tried to do seems to be equivalent to applying Coddington's 1979 approach to the details of Friedman's work and to showing its underlying rationale. While in his later article Coddington manages to get closer to an understanding of Friedman's methodology than has any other critic, in our view, he does not quite succeed in working through to the pragmatic foundations which underlie his approach.
2. For an example of running the two together see James Webb, 1987.
3. A number of critics, including Wible, but also Caldwell (1980, 1982, pp. 178 and 185) and Maki (1986, p. 142, n. 9) have leaned rather heavily on Boland's information in interpreting Friedman.

PART I

METHODOLOGY

1 • EARLY VIEWS ON METHODOLOGY

It has been said that Friedman has little interest in methodology (Boland, 1970). In a sense this is true. There is no evidence that Friedman ever delved very deeply into the literature of the philosophy of science or even into the major works in economic methodology. Yet there are few well-known economists who were as much concerned with methodology during the course of their careers as Friedman has been, particularly during his earlier years. Again and again Friedman has pondered the nature and significance of some current work in economics, to make manifest its shortcomings from the standpoint of what he considered the proper tenets of scientific methods, and to suggest the proper path economics should follow. In this chapter we consider the published record of these deliberations which took place prior to, or at about the same time as, the publication of the famous essay, 'The methodology of positive economics' (hereafter 'Positive economics').

THE REALISM OF ASSUMPTIONS AND THE QUEST FOR TESTABLE THEORY

Formalism, empiricism and the 'in-between'

Friedman's earliest published comments on methodology contain a hint of the dissatisfaction about the state of economics which he would later express quite openly. In a joint article with Allen Wallis (1942a) on the possible usefulness of indifference curve analysis for factual investigation the authors distinguish between 'deductive analysis' and 'quantitative analysis', or the approach that 'states premises ... in a form that materially facilitates the correct deduction of rather intricate conclusions' versus that which helps with 'the organization and analysis of empirical data' (1942a, p. 767). Friedman and Wallis admit, even emphasize, that some concepts which appear in deductive analysis, such as 'the "natural rate of interest", "pure profits", "entrepreneurial expectations", and, for that matter, "general equilibrium"' are 'utterly incompetent for quantitative analysis'. But they do not express any concern about this state of affairs. And while they call these concepts 'schizoid', the authors do not seem to imply that they are therefore of no value. On the contrary, they give the impression that even where concepts integral to traditional theory are not directly relevant to empirical work, they still may be valuable and useful in their own right. In other words, there are two quite distinct types of theory in economics – the formal and the operationally useful – each legitimate in its own sphere and having no necessary connection with the other.

The term 'schizoid', however, gives us reason to pause. It denotes the absence of wholeness, implies deficiency, and suggests that an approach yielding non-schizoid concepts might be worth looking for. Whether Friedman and Wallis meant to imply all this in using the term is not clear. What we can say is that in subsequent years Friedman has repeatedly found fault with much of contemporary economics because he felt that the science had fallen into an inappropriate polarization of methods; that he has tried to figure out how this came about; and that he has sought ways to close the gap.

The culprits, as Friedman has portrayed it, were formalism and empiricism. As he put it in one place (1952a in Haley, 1952, p. 457) – though without using those very terms – formalism on the one side and empiricism on the other

> have produced real and valuable improvements in the formal 'language' available for describing economic interrelationships and in our detailed knowledge of the phenomena to be explained by economic theory. But they have left something of a vacuum in the equally vital intermediate area of theories of hypotheses that have implications about important phenomena susceptible of contradiction through observation.

The same conviction, as will be seen in Chapter 3, is expressed a year later in his methodological essay ('Positive economics') but in an altered form.[1]

'Realistic' (plausible) assumptions are not sufficient

How was this vacuum created? Friedman has not addressed himself directly to this question in any one place but in a number of articles has said things bearing on it. Thus, in an important review of Lange's *Price Flexibility and Employment* (1944) he argues that economists have adopted a way of reasoning in which theory is judged on the basis of how plausible its assumptions are (Friedman, 1946b, reprinted in Friedman, 1953e, p. 283). Such a procedure makes observation almost irrelevant.

Lange, for example, asks what 'assumptions' (suppositions) are needed to be able to conclude that something will or will not happen; in this instance, that a cut in wages will or will not alleviate unemployment. At the next stage he shows that it is more reasonable to accept one set of suppositions than others; in the case in question, that under modern conditions the 'monetary effect' is such that a fall in wages will not alleviate unemployment. This way of reasoning, Friedman points out (1953e, p. 285), 'has no solid basis in observed facts and yields few if any conclusions susceptible of empirical contradiction'. One who adopts it is thus likely to wind up at the abstract or formal extreme. Friedman is not critical because Lange appeals to theory whose assumptions are *true*; that at least would imply some connection with observed or observable facts. He is critical because Lange rests his case merely on an appeal to *plausibility*, where the connection between what appears reasonable and what is factually correct is vague and remote.

In light of what Friedman later wrote about 'realistic' assumptions and the fact that the term 'realistic' is generally taken to mean 'true' (see Chapter 3), it is rather surprising to find that in this book review Friedman agrees that empirical evidence about assumptions has a bearing on the acceptability of a theoretical argument. He notes that in analyses such as Lange's, where a large number of theoretical possibilities are raised, it is tempting 'to rule out possibilities that on one ground or another can be judged "unrealistic" or "extreme"'. He adds (p. 289): 'There is nothing wrong with the procedure if the evidence on which the possibilities are judged to be unrealistic is convincing'.[2] But he goes on to show that Lange does not present any real evidence and he expresses the view that *in general* economists who argue in the same way as Lange rarely, if ever, do.

Realistic (plausible) assumptions are not necessary

It is fairly obvious that plausible assumptions, which embody a direct appeal to common wisdom or stylized 'facts', may not be sufficient for a theory to be judged valid. The claims of science are first and foremost that appearances may be deceptive; and that layers of analysis may have to be interposed between a 'why' question and some directly observed phenomenon. It is less obvious that plausible assumptions are not *necessary*. This latter notion is one of Friedman's distinctive contributions. He seems to have arrived at it initially not by way of criticism, but rather in the process of defending one of his unorthodox excursions.

In 'The utility analysis of choices involving risk', written with L. J. Savage (1948c, in Boulding and Stigler, 1951), Friedman faced the problem of rationalizing deliberately risky choices within the framework of standard utility theory. Since diminishing marginal utility makes even a fair gamble seem irrational, it is not surprising that Friedman found that he could explain gambling only on the basis of a utility function which would generally not be considered plausible (i.e. did not look 'right'). (See Chapter 8 for further details.) In the orthodox tradition of economic inquiry, most clearly formulated by John Stuart Mill, motives are strictly discoverable by introspection and have to be in line with *common* sense. (See Chapter 5.) Hence Friedman was faced with maintaining the traditional view that gambling could not be explained by economic theory or rejecting the traditional methodological prejudice which required that assumptions be plausible. He chose the latter course. One element in his procedure was an argument that it is not essential that individuals are *aware* that they actually prefer risk but rather that their observed behavior is 'as if' they do in some instances.

Reflect for a moment on Friedman and Savage's procedure. They started with data rather than introspection;[3] they did not introspect or ask people about their motives and then 'reason out'; nor did they use as the premises of an argument information gathered in this way. By failing to do these things they were violating at stage one the rules of traditional economic methodology, for they were using what J. S. Mill called 'the inverse deductive method', of reasoning back to supposed causes from observed instances (1973, VI, IX, 4). Mill deemed this inappropriate in economics (*ibid.* VI, IX, 5) because so many influences are operating at once that there is no way we can be sure that we have correctly ascribed causes. If it is to be trusted, the inverse deductive method requires that ascribed causes be verified by linking them to *known* laws of human behavior. (See Chapter 5.) This is, in effect, checking them for their plausibility. Thus Friedman and Savage violate another of Mill's (and traditional) tenets. What they did was to suggest that one should look at behavior from the 'outside', or study it the way the psychologist studies animal behavior or an anthropologist a tribe. In other words, they were implying that instead of reasoning out what people would do, assuming we possessed 'inside' (or introspective) knowledge of their motives, we should observe the actual consequences of their motives in overt behavior and then hypothesize as to what kind of mechanism *may* have given rise to such results. Having got this far Friedman and Savage, consistent with this point of view, conclude that introspective or questionnaire evidence has no direct bearing on the validity of a theory by way of testing its assumptions; what is pertinent is the predictive power of the theory or hypothesis in further application.

In his methodology essay ('Positive economics'), as we shall see in Chapter 3, Friedman gives a more general argument in justification of this procedure, but since the analysis in Friedman and Savage is clearer in some ways, and less mixed with broader purposes (such as the defense of standard competitive analysis), it is well to consider this point further in the context of the expected utility theory. We may ask whether the arguments used by Friedman and Savage involve the belief that since the assumptions of theory are inferred 'upwards' as a rationalization of observed behavior, they may but need not be true. In 'Positive economics' we encounter the phrase, used of assumptions, that they are necessarily descriptively false; but that is because all abstractions are descriptively incomplete, hence false in that trivial sense. More to the point, people tend to rationalize and what they tell us about why they do things may not be very reliable. They are often not even aware of the why and how of their behavior. As Friedman and Savage put it (in Boulding and Stigler, p. 86): 'Indeed, it is not at all clear what such an assertion [that individuals explicitly or consciously calculate and compare expected utilities] would mean or how it would be tested'. Since people rationalize and are often unaware, how are we to determine how they do in fact make choices?[4] Might they not actually choose in risky situations the way the Friedman and Savage utility function postulates without being aware of it? In this view, it can never be said that assumptions *are* false, but only that they *appear* to be. Awareness of this sort of complication may explain Friedman's evident desire in his 1953 essay simply to avoid discussing assumptions much at all, and certainly to avoid basing his position on assertions about the truth of assumptions.

The final portion of a methodological digression in the Friedman and Savage article throws further light on their position. After admitting that many people deem it 'patently unrealistic to suppose that individuals consult a wiggly utility curve' they go on to argue that, while the shape of their suggested utility function does look strange, it can be given a 'plausible interpretation'. Presumably they did not consider their hypothesis to be outright false, since then it would make no sense to search for an acceptable rationalization. But neither are they making the same appeal as their opponents to self-evident or stylized common sense. They are making a contextual argument: in the context of a suitably extended utility theory the shape makes sense, though it is a different sense than that bound up with the standard principle of diminishing marginal utility. In other words, assuming that a theory gives good predictions as it continues to be applied, a novel element in it which can incorporate previously inexplicable facts of behavior may render plausible what previously had been implausible. The *appearance* of falseness (meaning implausibility) simply does not matter. The message here is, do not be blinkered by that which has always been taken as normal. Note that *in this context* the argument that 'the more significant the theory the more unrealistic the assumptions (in this sense)' (1953e, p. 14) makes good sense. Truly revolutionary theories, like those of Galileo and Einstein, were exceedingly implausible when they were first proposed. Now, of course, they seem quite plausible, but that is only because we are used to them. Such theories have completely changed our notions of what is plausible. Less revolutionary theories, too, have some effect on our notions of what is plausible, but they affect such notions to a lesser degree than those which are more significant.[5]

The methodological arguments adduced by Friedman and Savage are not used to defend traditional price theory, in early versions of which the assumption of diminishing marginal utility might have been taken as given, but rather that *extended* version of it which their work makes possible. In 'Positive economics' by contrast, Friedman follows the same line of argument, only there he uses it to defend price theory – especially the competitive model – itself. The difference, as will be seen (Chapter 4), is a significant one.

The limitations of empiricism

Returning to our concern with how Friedman's views on the methodology of positive economics evolved, recall that the other way to end up at one extreme, with a vacuum at the center of one's science, as Friedman observed in the remark quoted above (in Haley, 1952), is to be overly concerned with 'detailed knowledge of . . . phenomena'. Whereas the proponents of plausible assumptions may abstract so heroically as to wind up in rarefied air and out of touch with all but highly stylized facts (see Lange, 1944), those concerned only with descriptive detail anchor their work in the facts but do not get very much beyond them. They amass a great deal of factual information but little, if anything, that can be related to economic theory. As Friedman observed (1952*a* in Haley, 1952, p. 457), descriptive realism 'was the battle cry of institutionalism and the closely related emphasis on extensive statistical studies of economic phenomena . . .'.[6] This approach fell as far short in one direction, he implies, as the approach of Lange did in the other.[7] Although no reference is given, it seems safe to take Frederick C. Mills' *The Behavior of Prices* (1927) as an example of what Friedman had in mind. Viner's review of that work (1929, pp. 37–52) expressed disappointment at its distinctly a-theoretic character, and could as easily have been written by his future student, Friedman.[8]

The problem of unobservables when introspection is ruled out

In the risk article co-authored by Savage (1948*c*) the major role is played by a postulated utility function which was not even conceivably observable; only its *implications* could be observed. Friedman does not cite the opinions of authorities in support of this procedure; one rather has the impression that the notion came to him in the course of trying to bring within the compass of theory a problem which had defied solution for a very long time. In the process Friedman had come upon a way of dealing with unobservables which he continued to make use of for the rest of his professional career. In a very real sense it is the key that enabled him to get to the 'intermediate area' between fact-gathering and pure theorizing.

We say this because it seems to us that, on the one hand, to derive theory which has any chance of being able to give reliable predictions (and retrodictions) requires extensive observation. Yet, on the other, direct evidence for the key variables we are interested in is often not available. So far as motives are concerned, the basic class of variables with which one is involved in studying how individuals behave, objective observation is impossible. One could appeal to introspection, but Friedman rejected this course, as we have seen. How then might one theorize about behavior? One must *guess*, or so Friedman suggested in the risk article. But this did not mean cutting oneself off from objective observation as a test of theories. Objective evidence is needed, for one thing, to help make guesses which had a chance of moving inquiry along in the right direction. And, second, it is the *implications* of theory which are observable and which have to meet the objective test.[9]

'Unrealistic' assumptions and unobservables

Returning to the Friedman-Wallis article (1942*a*) considered earlier we note that it dealt with an issue which was a major topic of discussion in economics at the time and touched upon the problems of 'unrealistic' assumptions and unobservables. As Joseph Schumpeter has shown (1954, pp. 1053–69), beginning towards the end of the last century and continuing on past the time when this article was written, 'orthodox' economists had begun to ask troubling questions about the methodological adequacy of marginal utility theory. One objection was that the basic assumption of the theory was not 'realistic' because the notion of measurable utility was implausible. A related objection was that the behavioral assumption was not observable; since people did not seem capable of measuring utility, it was impossible *even in principle* to be able to observe them making choices on the basis of marginal utility calculations.[10]

Ordinal utility theory gets around these objections. One can in principle observe consumers making choices as between different goods under given conditions and then use these data with the indifference function type of analysis. But could one in fact use this analysis to try to derive reliable predictions about consumer behavior from the available data? Schumpeter observed (1954, p. 1067):

> ... if [the ordinalists] use nothing that is not observable *in principle*, they do use 'potential' observations which so far nobody has been able to make *in fact*: from a practical standpoint we are not much better off when drawing purely imaginary indifference curves than we are when speaking of purely imaginary utility functions.

Yet Schumpeter winds up on an optimistic note. Citing Abraham Wald's article (1940), which presents a technical means for deriving empirical demand curves, Schumpeter concludes that 'here again one should never say never' (1954, p. 1067). Wald's article suggested to Schumpeter that in the future it might well be possible to account for the available data using indifference function analysis. Friedman and Wallis in their article raise doubts about this conclusion. [11] They argue that since taste factors and opportunity factors are not independent of one another the possibilities for using indifference analysis for making meaningful order in the available data were simply not very good.

But then what was one to do? The authors suggest that one had best work *back* from the available data, without constraining oneself with categories dictated by a priori analysis, thus leaving oneself free to choose those categories (or assumptions) which offer promise of being able to account for the data. What they were suggesting, in effect, was that one use what Charles Peirce called an 'abductive' procedure. [12] This is the notion that a theory which accounts for or 'explains' given data is worth considering. [13] While such a theory is not very likely to be true, the possibilities it opens up for testing its implications with further data, and for revising, retesting and reformulating again and again, appear to be an effective means by which one might derive theories which in time get closer and closer to the truth.

In the risk article co-authored by Savage (1948c), which we considered earlier, Friedman went on to follow this rationale. But in the process he ran into a formidable obstacle. He was trying to derive a theory which explained the paradox that individuals bought both insurance policies and lottery tickets, and any such attempt ran into the problem of implausibility since, on the face of it, such behavior seems contrary to the principle of diminishing marginal utility (or diminishing rate of substitution). Thus Friedman was faced with a choice, as we noted above, of either rejecting the criterion of (conventional) plausibility or giving up the attempt to formulate a theory. By choosing the former he in effect brought back the problems of implausibility and unobservability which had generated the flurry of debate about consumer theory to begin with. In a sense all that happened was that the old problems now appeared in a different light.

But methodologically Friedman had moved a long way. According to the traditional notions of economic methodology (see Chapter 5) abduction was most inappropriate in economics, even if appropriate in other areas. [14] The reason was that if the economist is able to use introspection as a source of completely reliable data, then the kind of speculation that is involved in abduction is neither necessary nor appropriate. [15] It is thus the rejection of introspection as a source of reliable knowledge that distinguishes Friedman's approach from the traditional one. This is the basis for his thesis about 'unrealistic' assumptions. Further, since Friedman rejected what to an introspectionist is directly observable, he was forced to find a way of dealing with the problem of unobservables. The rationale he worked out very early in his career, as we shall see in Part II, is essentially the one he followed in much of his most important work as a positive economist.

MARSHALLIAN AND WALRASIAN ECONOMICS

Having identified something of the sort of 'realism' that Friedman felt we could do without, we need to look more closely at the early distinction Friedman and Wallis drew between analysis which is formally valid and analysis which is a characteristic of substantive hypotheses. [16] Friedman himself explores this further in an important but obscure paper on the Marshallian demand curve (1949c in 1953e) and an extended footnote to this paper on taxation (1952a in 1953e), in a comment on early efforts at building macroforecasting models (1951a), in a review article (1955e) of Jaffé's translation of Walras' *Elements*, and in portions of the review of Lange (1946b in 1953e), which we have not yet taken up. Since Friedman associates the type of work which concerns itself primarily with formal analysis with the approach of Leon Walras and that which concerns itself primarily with substantive hypotheses with that of Alfred Marshall, we will refer to this aspect of Friedman's work in methodology as the Marshallian-Walrasian thesis. In this section we examine the main points of the thesis, while in the appendix to this chapter we indicate why this aspect of his work is difficult to interpret and explain why we favor the particular interpretation that we do.

The derivation of Marshallian and Walrasian theory

Friedman identifies himself as a Marshallian and tells us that the Marshallian uses 'the approach that is standard in the physical sciences' which is 'to use theory to derive generalizations about the real world' (1946*b* in 1953*e*). Here is what this approach consists of in broad outline, according to Friedman (*ibid*. pp. 282–3):

> The theorist starts with some set of observed and related facts, as full and comprehensive as possible.[17] He seeks a generalization that will explain these facts; he can always succeed; indeed, he can always find an indefinitely large number of generalizations. The number of observed facts is finite, and the number of possible theories can therefore be found that are consistent with the observed facts. The theorist therefore calls in some arbitrary principle such as 'Occam's razor' and settles on a particular generalization or theory. He tests his theory to make sure that it is logically consistent, that its elements are susceptible of empirical determination, and that it will explain adequately the facts he started with. He then seeks to deduce from his theory facts other than those he used to derive it and to check these deductions against reality. Typically some deduced 'facts' check and others do not; so he revises his theory to take account of the additional facts.[18] The ultimate check of deduced against observed facts is essential in this process.[19]

Thus in Friedman's view, Marshallian inquiry involves a *continuous process* where theorizing and observation go hand in hand at every step of the investigation and the check of deduced against observed facts is 'ultimate', but only because it is logically the later phase of a repeated sequence.[20,21]

The Walrasian works differently. According to Friedman (1953*e*, p. 283):

> [He] largely dispenses with the initial step – a full and comprehensive set of observed and related facts to be generalized – and in the main reaches conclusions no observed facts can contradict. His emphasis is on the formal structure of the theory, the logical interrelations of the parts. He considers it largely unnecessary to test the validity of his theoretical structure except for conformity to the canons of formal logic. His categories are selected primarily to facilitate logical analysis, not empirical application or test.

In another place (1955*e*) Friedman points up a different aspect of what he considers a mark of 'a true Walrasian in methodology'. What this amounts to is that:

> One *first* constructs a pure theory, somehow on formal considerations without introducing any empirical content;[22] one *then* turns to the 'real' world, fills in the empty boxes, assigns numerical values to constants, and neglects 'second-order' effects at this stage. [Emphasis added.]

The latter are taken into account only when the theory is applied. In other words, as Friedman sees it, for the Walrasians theorizing is separated from observation – and from application – and the kind of interactive process between observation and theorizing which is the hallmark of the Marshallian process of theory derivation, is lacking.[23]

'Language' versus substantive hypotheses as end products

Since Marshallians and Walrasians work so differently, on this view, it is not surprising that the end products they come up with are not the same. The end product of Marshallian work Friedman calls 'substantive hypotheses'. These results are given this name, partly, because they are testable. But in Friedman's scheme they are not only *testable* but *tested* to some degree in the very process of derivation. This is because, first, a hypothesis is initially designed to be consistent with some aspects of observed experience. Then, as we saw above, it is tested and retested with additional data. Thus, there is no stage at which we can say that the hypothesis is 'true', in the sense that we are certain that there is no falseness in it. But at the same time it is legitimate to say at any stage that hypotheses are tested, the degree depending on the stage the research or inquiry has reached at that point. Such is the product of the Marshallian approach, as Friedman tells the story.

The theory of the Walrasians Friedman characterizes as 'language'. By language he means an analytic system derived with the aid of casual observation. Such a theory does not give us much in the way of predictive power, but Friedman does not deny that it can be exceedingly useful. He points to Walras' theory as an example of such 'language' and he is as effusive in his praise of this great achievement as many general equilibrium theorists. But he argues that we need more even than a superb language; we need substantive hypotheses, both for the growth of economic science and for practical purposes. As he puts it (1955e), 'We need the right kind of language; we also need something to say'.

'Language' and prediction

Friedman is as much concerned that Walrasians tend to use 'language' badly as he is that Walrasian methods do not yield substantive hypotheses from which reliable predictions derive. This emerges clearly as a concern in 'The "welfare" effects of an income tax' (1952a), which Friedman calls an 'extended footnote' to his article on the Marshallian demand curve (1949c).[24] What he shows is 'that an alleged "proof" of the superiority of the income tax [over an excise tax] is no proof at all, though it has repeatedly been cited as one'. He does this by arguing that for society as a whole what the consequences will be depends on a whole host of factors, that no *general* conclusions can be reached; it is necessary to know the specifics in a particular situation in order properly to assess it. More generally, Friedman concludes (1953e, pp. 112–13) that 'formal analysis can seldom if ever give easy answers to hard problems. Its role is quite different: to suggest the considerations relevant to an answer and to provide a useful means of organizing analysis'.

'Language' as wholly abstract

In one place (1953d, p. 7) Friedman says that as 'language' theory is 'a set of tautologies', and it has been asked whether theory in this sense can be of use in an empirical science like economics (De Alessi, 1965). Examination of what Friedman says when he applies the term 'language' shows that the notion of empirical content, while very useful in other contexts, is not very serviceable in this one. What matters in this usage is not whether or not theory has empirical *content* but rather that it makes the right kind of *empirical reference*. Friedman shows this when talking about Walras' contribution. He writes (1955e):

> I have described this analysis as involving emphasis on pure form, which I think in a meaningful way it does. Yet I do not mean thereby to imply either that it lacks importance for economics as a substantive science, or that empirical considerations play no role in its construction and use. Quite to the contrary.

The usefulness of 'language'

But that leaves open the question as to what criterion or criteria to employ in deciding whether a 'language' is useful or not. Friedman grapples with this question. He tells us that the quality of the mathematics of a particular model is *not* a proper criterion to use in judging it and suggests that Walras' limitations as a mathematician may have helped him rather than served as a hindrance.[25] He tells us further (*ibid.*):

> Walras' picture . . . was constructed to provide a framework for organizing substantive material of an economic character; the classifications it employs reflect a judgment about the empirically important characteristics of the economic structure; the usefulness of the picture . . . depends upon the extent to which this judgment is confirmed by experience.

But how has Friedman determined that Walras' 'language' results from choosing the empirically important characteristics of the economic structure? How, more generally, should one make such a choice? Friedman does not give an answer nor, as far as we are aware, has anyone else, although this certainly seems an area worth exploring.[26]

This leads to a related question. In what way or ways is such a 'language' useful? The most coherent response that Friedman gives is that its role is 'to suggest the considerations relevant to an answer [in working on a particular problem] and to provide a useful means of organizing an analysis' (1953e, p. 113). On this view one envisages Walras as asking why a particular price has changed, and not only suggesting a wealth of possibilities but, more important, carefully showing how these possibilities are logically related. Once one has such a system one could try to derive testable hypotheses from it. Friedman refers to one such attempt, as we show below (pp. 24–6) and finds that it has not succeeded in yielding what he considers substantive hypotheses.[27]

The two demand curves

In comparing two demand curves, one of which he calls Walrasian (the conventional one) and one of which he refers to as Marshallian (constant real income) Friedman gives us an example of how he applies the Marshallian-Walrasian distinction in a specific case. Unfortunately the exposition is not without ambiguities, if not contradictions, which we will have to look at more closely later on (see Appendix to this chapter). At this point we note only those aspects of this example pertinent to, and consistent with, the account we have given so far of Friedman's position. In a Marshallian view, on this interpretation, in order to derive a theory of demand we would first have to account for the fact that price and quantity generally move inversely. This means that the Giffen phenomenon – assuming that it really exists (see Stigler, 1947) – would not be taken into account by such a theory. From a logical point of view this is an almost fatal weakness, since a theory is false if it is not *entirely* true. But if it is substantive hypotheses that we want then that is something we have to learn to live with. One can hardly expect a theory to account for everything within its own range of reference, particularly in a field like economics. Even in the physical sciences, if it were true that theories explain everything within their ranges of applicability, what Thomas Kuhn (1970) calls 'normal science' would not exist.[28] The Giffen paradox, in this view, poses a challenge for further development of theory, which would involve careful observation to determine, for example, under what conditions it occurs, what precisely its features are, and so on. If instead of such detailed inquiry we merely extend the theory so that it can *logically* account for the phenomenon, we transform it from a substantive hypothesis into 'language' with little, if any, empirical content. The conventional 'explanation' of Giffen goods is of precisely this sort.

Walras' way of working

Friedman suggests that in fact this is the way Walras came up with his 'language'. He observes that Cournot (1963 [1838]) was aware of general equilibrium aspects of market system experience but did not attempt to tackle his problems this way because he felt that it 'would surpass ... our practical methods of calculation' to achieve such a theory. Walras looked at the problem differently. As Friedman views it (1955e):

> It is clear from Cournot's references to 'practical methods of calculation' and to the assignment of numerical values to constants that the 'rigorous solution' he had in mind was not a solution 'in principle', but a numerical solution to a specific problem. His goal was an analysis that would, given the relevant statistical material, yield specific answers to specific empirical questions ... Walras solved a different, though no less important, problem. He emptied Cournot's problem of its empirical content and produced a 'complete and rigorous' solution 'in principle', making no pretense that it could be used directly in numerical calculations. His problem is the problem of form, not of content: of displaying an idealized picture of the economic system, not of constructing an engine for analyzing concrete problems.

'Language' and prediction

Thus, if one tries to cover a wider area of economic experience than is needed to formulate substantive hypotheses then, according to Friedman, the most that one can hope for is a Walrasian type of solution. In other words, if we want substantive hypotheses we must limit our first attempts to relatively small areas of economic experience. As our knowledge grows, these bits and pieces might come together and eventually, via multiple applications of this Marshallian process, we might derive enough knowledge to predict reliably even on a macro scale.[29] Looking at this same idea from another angle, Friedman tells us that if one tries to theorize about the economy *as a whole* without having a great deal of knowledge about the *parts*, and tries to derive testable hypotheses from such theory, even if one succeeds in deriving testable hypotheses they will not check out, that is, such hypotheses will not in fact be substantive.[30] Friedman considers such a result Walrasian as well.

In remarks he made at a conference sponsored by the National Bureau of Economic Research (1951a) at the same time as he was developing his argument in 'The Marshallian demand curve' he tried to explain the reasons for this belief. Carl Christ, at the time a Cowles Commission researcher, had presented the results of an attempt to test an early Klein macro-model of the US economy and Friedman was asked to comment. In his eyes Klein's type of econometric work showed the weakness of what he had begun to regard as the 'Walrasian' approach. Not, we should stress, that he disagreed with the basic intent. For, as he noted (1949c, p. 112):

> The fundamental premise underlying work in this field is that there is order in the processes of economic change, that sooner or later we shall develop a theory of economic change that does abstract essential elements in the process and does yield valid predictions. When and if such a theory is developed, it will clearly be possible to express it in the form of a system of simultaneous equations of the kind used in the econometric model.

Nonetheless, he disagreed strongly with the means proposed for reaching this end and that for a very definite reason. Macro-modellers were attempting to come to grips with the underlying structure of the economy through a priori knowledge, to a large extent bypassing the tedious process of minute factual investigation – the kind of research that one could interpret Marshall to have been suggesting, if one reads between the lines – where theorizing and observation are closely interwoven. As Friedman put it (*ibid*. pp. 112–13) in words which would be echoed a decade later by Adelman and Adelman (1959):

> Granted that the final result will be capable of being expressed in the form of a system of simultaneous equations applying to the economy as a whole, it does not follow that the best way to get to the final result is by seeking to set such a system down *now*. As I am sure those who have tried to do so will agree, we now know so little about the dynamic mechanisms at work that there is enormous arbitrariness in any system set down. Limitations of resources – mental, computational, and statistical – enforce a model that, although complicated enough for our capacities, is yet enormously simple relative to the present state of the world we seek to explain.[31]

Friedman's special twist was to add:

> ... until we can develop a simpler picture of the world, by an understanding of interrelations within sections of the economy, the construction of a model for the economy as a whole is bound to be almost a complete groping in the dark. The probability that such a process will yield a meaningful result seems to me almost negligible.

But how then was one to proceed? Friedman again (*ibid*. p. 114):

> The direction of work that seems to me to offer most hope for laying a foundation for a workable theory of change is the analysis of parts of the economy in the hope that we can find bits of order here and there and gradually combine these bits into a systematic picture of the whole. In the language of the model builders, I believe our chief hope is to study the sections covered by individual structural equations separately and independently of the rest of the economy.

To repeat, in this view, if one tries to generalize about the economy as a whole without having extensive knowledge about the parts, one must end up either with mere 'language' (formal models that are of little use for making predictions) or with hypotheses that are so general as to lack substance. In the absence of knowledge of the fine structure of the economy, as Lange's work and the Klein model showed, we do not get into the 'intermediate area' of substantive hypotheses which was Friedman's chief interest. [32]

Substantive hypotheses as engines for discovery

There is another major ingredient in Friedman's conception of Marshallian economics which we have not considered. It is the notion that theory as substantive hypotheses is an 'engine' that helps generate new theory. It does this by giving us a framework for deriving new theoretical insights with the help of lengthy and careful investigation of the data. Friedman does not develop this point anywhere in detail, but he does illustrate it in his work. He seems to view theory as a paradigm or overall theory, that is, a very broad conjunction of propositions derived via the interactive process of observation and hypothesis formation, which explains a good deal in its area of reference but leaves some observed experience within its domain unaccounted for. Rather than the latter being considered 'falsifications', on this view they constitute challenges. We have seen one example of this pattern in the Friedman–Savage article on risk considered in the last part, where an attempt was made to account for gambling behavior which could not be explained by Marshall's price theory. The extended theory did not eliminate the old; it merely added to it. [33] Its general character is the same, that is, behavior is formulated in utility function (optimizing) terms. And without the original broad theory it seems very unlikely that the more special theory would have been derived at all. As we will see in Part II, a good deal of Friedman's work as a positive economist follows this pattern.

The 'realism'-of-assumptions thesis and the Marshallian–Walrasian distinction

Friedman also tries to show that there is a relationship between economists' concern with 'realistic' assumptions on the one hand and a tendency in recent times to move away from the Marshallian and towards the Walrasian way of doing economics. He argues that concern with the 'descriptive accuracy' [34] of the assumptions of theory, both on the part of the imperfect competition theorists and general equilibrium analysts, moved economics in a Walrasian direction. This suggests that for him the 'realism'-of-assumptions argument is merely one part of a broader thesis which postulates that there are two very different approaches to doing economics involving different conceptions of the process of inquiry or research, of the kind of theory that is created, and so on. As we have seen, given the way the Walrasian works, according to Friedman, the Walrasian either must leave his theory wholly abstract and formal or try to relate it to concrete circumstances via 'realistic' assumptions. Thus, Friedman's 'realism'-of-assumptions argument, as we showed in the first part of this chapter and will further demonstrate in Chapter 3, is part of an attempt to show why he considered the Walrasian approach inadequate. The Marshallian, in this view, need not appeal to the 'realism' of the assumptions of his theory because he relates the theory to empirical reality via its implications. It is not just that these implications can be empirically tested, which makes 'realism' or plausibility a very secondary consideration. Even more important is the fact that in the process of research empirical reality is involved at every step, both in formulating the theory and in the ongoing interactive process whereby hypothesizing becomes one controlled component, and not an unconstrained conjecturing. As we will show in Chapters 3 and 6, in such a process of inquiry assumptions which are not entirely true can be useful in leading to amended versions of theory which attain a higher and higher degree of verisimilitude.

Before going on to look at this matter further, in the Appendix to this chapter we consider some of the problems we encountered in trying to derive a consistent interpretation of Friedman's Marshallian–Walrasian thesis. In Chapter 2 we confront the unusual mix of heterodox and orthodox elements discernible in Friedman's position and try to show how this blend gives his approach its unusual cast.[35]

NOTES

1. The importance of this tripartite conceptual framework in Friedman's thinking, where the 'scientific approach' is taken to be neither formal nor empirical but as falling between the two, has generally been overlooked because it is not related to any of the philosophies which have been popular in recent years. We find this kind of conceptual framework at the center of John Dewey's philosophy, as we show in Chapter 6.

2. We find the same kind of ambiguity here in the use of the term 'realistic' that was to cause so much confusion later on (see Chapter 3). Friedman in effect is referring to *plausibility* on the one hand and *being supported by* evidence on the other, and calling them by the same name. Lange's argument depends on its *plausibility* for its acceptance; Friedman says he would be more receptive if its premises *were supported with specific objective evidence*. There are other grounds for plausibility than evidential support.

3. Though not 'as full and extensive' as possible. We consider the significance of this observation later.
4. In an early comment (Friedman, 1949*a*) on a paper which mapped out an agenda which involved asking businessmen how they would make decisions in hypothetical situations Friedman gives a more direct and explicit statement on why he is suspicious of data which are derived from introspection and questionnaires than he does anywhere else. The comment ends with the observation: '... it is important to remember that *Homo sapiens* is distinguished from other animals more by his ability to rationalize than by his ability to reason'.
5. Klant (1974 and 1984) shows how badly one can be misled if one concentrates on a single phrase and overlooks the remaining evidence. First, he insists on defining the term 'realistic' to mean 'true' (1974, p. 143). Second, he argues (*ibid.* p. 155) that general economic theories can only be judged on the basis of their plausibility. But can such theories be 'specialized', as Friedman suggests? Third, he argues (1984, p. 149) that it does not matter to Friedman if businessmen behave differently than his theory postulates, or even if somehow we learn to carry out experiments that showed Friedman's assumptions to be wrong (1974, pp. 151–2).
6. It was, of course, primarily the empiricists (in Friedman's tripartite classification scheme) who were the severest critics of orthodox theory on grounds that it was 'unrealistic'. In 'Positive economics', as is well known, Friedman uses the 'realism'-of-assumptions argument to disarm such critics. But at the same time, as will be shown in Chapter 4, he destroyed the most effective argument that had traditionally been used in defense of the theory.
7. See Friedman's later remarks about the institutionalists in Kitch, 1983, p. 172.
8. Viner was later Friedman's influential teacher, Mills was later Friedman's colleague at the National Bureau of Economic Research. In a sense Friedman's approach lies somewhere between the two. We say this because like Mills, in his most important work (1963*a*, 1982*b*) he collected masses of data. But like Viner, and unlike Mills, he was always looking for the theoretical relevance of the data he dealt with. (We see this already in his 1945 publication.) In a very real sense, as we hope to show (in the next two paragraphs of the text, in Chapter 2, and in Part II), it was the 'realism'-of-assumptions way of thinking which enabled him to make a link between the two. (It should be added that when Mills talked generally about methodology his views did not sound very different from Friedman's – see Mills, 1928, pp. 28–9.)
9. It is often argued (e.g. Klant, 1984, p. 153) that 'Economic subjects in contrast to electrons are observed daily by curious spectators in multiple states and situations'. But are their *motives* observable? When members of the Vienna Circle philosophy group recognized this problem in the physical sciences they changed their name from Logical Positivist to Logical Empiricist.
10. In traditional economic methodology we confirm theory of the form 'if p then q' ($p \supset q$) by *observing* that the implications of the theory (q) follow from the premises (p). Thus, if p cannot be observed, the theory can neither be corroborated nor falsified and therefore cannot be said to have empirical content.
11. Although Schumpeter cites the Wallis–Friedman article he apparently

overlooked the fact that the authors cited Wald's (1940) but felt that Wald's *technical* feat was not sufficient to enable one to derive an interpretation from available data that was meaningful in the *economic* sense.

12. See, for example, Peirce (e.g. Thomas, 1956, Chapters 6 and 13). The philosopher John Dewey, while not using the label 'abduction', took over this idea from Peirce and made it a basic tenet of his logic. (See Dewey, 1938, and Chapter 6, below.)

13. We put the term 'explains' in quotes to show that we are not referring to its essentialist meaning.

14. John Stuart Mill, whose overall logic of science is the one to which economists generally have adhered, at least till very recently, in effect rejected abduction for *any* science (see Chapter 5, below).

15. See, for example, Cairnes (1875, Sections 3 and 4), Robbins (1949, pp. 104–5), Knight (1944, p. 307).

16. The 'empirical' category of the tripartite classification scheme (empirical, formal, and in-between) now drops out and the comparison is made between the last two. Friedman probably dropped the empirical because the standing of the empiricists was not such as to pose much of an obstacle in the way of developing the in-between area which he championed. The real struggle was between the formalists and the in-between group, with the formalists, in Friedman's view, very much the dominant group.

17. We do not take this to imply that one starts from *scratch*. Were any problem *totally* unfamiliar one would hardly be able to deal with it at all, let alone learn in the process. In facing a problem, whether everyday or scientific, one brings one's knowledge to bear in many areas, which includes theories both formal and informal. But to bring one's knowledge to bear one has to begin to find out the nature of the problem since this is not known to begin with but is only discovered as the process of inquiry proceeds, as is implied in Friedman's statement. One begins, or rather breaks into, this continuous process of inquiry with observation because the inquiry would not be properly directed if we were to make contact with empirical reality only by chance, just as the process would be undirected if we had no theory or ideas when facing the problem. Ideas are automatically carried over from one investigation to another; when we begin an investigation we begin by noticing things which do not fit and try to explain them. The Friedman–Savage article illustrates this process.

18. As will be seen in what follows, 'he revises theory' does not mean that he throws out one theory and replaces it with another. The process is more like normal science puzzle-solving in Thomas Kuhn (1970) than what most economists take to be the 'falsification' of Karl Popper (1965).

19. On the face of it such a conception may seem unexceptionable but if one reads it in light of the teachings of mainstream methodologists, whether John Stuart Mill or Robbins from the past or Koopmans, Machlup and Samuelson from more recent times (see Chapter 5), the approach is seen to be most unusual.

20. We will argue in Chapter 3 that this process not only tends to bring the implications closer to what actually happens but also very generally tends to move the premises closer to the truth as well.

21. Concerning the inquiry process, this way has something in common with Popper's 'conjectures and refutations' (1972) except that the conjectures are less random and the process is conceived to have a positive rather than a

negative objective. Dewey argued a long time ago, as has Popper more recently, that the 'quest for *certainty*' (Dewey, 1929) is futile. But while no logical basis for induction may be available, it does not follow to most of us that we cannot learn in a positive way from a process which includes induction.

22. Note that this does not necessarily imply that there is no observation at all in the initial stages but only, as the last quote suggests, that there is very little. It is hard to conceive of an economist who neither does casual observation himself nor relies on the casual observation of others.

23. As we show in Chapter 5, mainstream economic methodology follows Walrasian lines in this regard.

24. See also 1949c and 1946b, where the same concern is expressed.

25. Friedman hastens to add that 'I do not mean to be urging that bad mathematics is better than good but only that each task requires its own tools'.

26. He does, however, illustrate in actual controversy how good 'language' functions; see Bailey (1954) and Friedman (1954c).

27. He considered another such attempt (in 1955f), also in his view unsuccessful.

28. Kuhn shows very clearly the difference between the process involved in normal science and that in falsification, in P. A. Schilpp, 1974, pp. 798–819.

29. According to Kevin Hoover (1984a, p. 66), Friedman's Marshallianism amounts to the insistence that 'whatever the economic problem, any practically significant analysis of it requires that reality be partitioned', or that one aspect of economic reality be analyzed in detail at one time, the rest being given but cursory attention. On this interpretation, Friedman's argument that 'the more significant the theory the more unrealistic the assumptions' says that the more partitioned the better. Hoover properly recognizes that there is a connection between Friedman's 'realism'-of-assumptions thesis and the Marshallian–Walrasian distinction. We feel, however, that his analysis falls short because: (a) he deals with only one aspect of the Marshallian–Walrasian distinction as Friedman develops it in various places; and (b) he forces the meaning of 'realism' into the narrow framework that results from this. As we show here and in Chapter 3, both in making the Marshallian–Walrasian distinction and in his 'realism'-of-assumptions thesis, Friedman has much more in mind than Hoover recognizes. Hoover's very interesting comparison of Friedman's monetary economics with that of the new classical variety would have shed even more light on the comparison than it does had he conceived of the Marshallian–Walrasian distinction more broadly.

30. We get some insight into this matter by considering the arguments of Paul Samuelson, who probably more than any other has helped steer economics in a Walrasian direction. In the *Foundations* (1965a [1947]) he tells us that his objective is testable theory and he tries to clarify what he intends by this, using the following argument (p. 12): 'We may [via deduction] bring to explicit attention certain formulations of our original assumptions which admit of possible refutation (confirmation) by empirical evidence'. Note that Samuelson says '*may* bring to attention ... formulations ... which admit of *possible* refutation'. Surely on the face of it this seems a chancy procedure, like the monkey left long enough in front of a typewriter typing out all of Shakespeare's plays. Of course, had this Walrasian approach succeeded

brilliantly in generating substantive hypotheses we would imagine that Friedman would have changed his mind. Samuelson *did* succeed brilliantly, but in the area of 'language'. When the attempt was made to derive testable hypotheses from Samuelson's qualitative comparative statics in order to actually test them (Archibald, 1965), it was found that little in the way of testable hypotheses could be derived using only the minimal information Samuelson wanted to use. Of course, if the theory were testable, it would still have to be tested and be corroborated to be considered a body of *substantive* hypotheses. In light of Samuelson's own position it is not surprising to find him devastatingly critical of Alfred Marshall (see Samuelson in Kuenne, 1967).

31. Note that the statement is revealing of how Friedman got into the 'black box' problem. If one refuses to speculate about the whole because one lacks knowledge about the parts, one becomes vulnerable to 'black box' criticism because one does not have an overall theory with which to answer some obvious questions about the phenomenon one deals with. Harry Johnson, in his famous lecture (1971, p. 13), did observe that Friedman was trying to fill in the gaps through further research. Given Friedman's methodological position it would have been most surprising had Friedman not proceeded this way.

32. It can be argued that Friedman's partial approach works better, in the absence of extensive knowledge of the parts, in studying a smaller segment of the economy than a larger one. This may be the reason that Friedman's work in the area of permanent income is more universally and unreservedly acclaimed and appreciated than his work in money. See, for example, Walters' (1987) comparative evaluation which we take to reflect the views of the profession generally at the present time.

33. As a result Friedman has been accused of fitting facts to theory rather than testing theory with facts. See Diesing, 1985.

34. Hoover points out (1984b, n. 7) that there is 'a contradiction between a theory being completely general and photographically exact'. This is right in general and at one time we, too, were troubled by what looked like a contradiction. But further reflection on the passage in Friedman to which Hoover refers suggests that when he talks about assumptions being 'photographically exact' Friedman means the same thing as when he refers to assumptions which are 'realistic'. Since it is not contradictory to refer to general theory which has 'realistic' assumptions we conclude that what is involved here is a bad use of terms rather than a contradiction.

35. During the early period Friedman made a large number of technical contributions having to do with the interpretation of data (see Bibliography). From a methodological point of view what stands out about this work is, as Walters has noted (1987, p. 423): 'His excursions into statistics were utilitarian rather than speculative, and he could see little to be gained by the endless sharpening of statistical knives . . .' Since 'the endless sharpening of statistical knives' falls into the area of 'language' ('tool building' taken almost as an end in itself), it can be said that as a statistician Friedman revealed the same pragmatic bent from an early age as he did as an economist.

Appendix to Chapter 1

DIFFICULTIES IN INTERPRETING THE MARSHALLIAN–WALRASIAN THESIS

Having said all that we have in the second part of the chapter about what we take to be the main meaning and significance of the Marshallian–Walrasian thesis, it is necessary to add that here, as in 'Positive economics', Friedman does not give us much help. In the body of the chapter we have only noted our conclusions, without commenting on the difficulties or explaining how we dealt with them. Here we consider the problems, and give some account as to why we dealt with them as we did, for those who might be interested in these details.

References to the Marshallian–Walrasian distinction

In only one of the articles that deal with methodology does Friedman speak explicitly of the Marshallian–Walrasian distinction (1949c), and that piece is marred at a crucial juncture by what looks like a *non sequitur* (see below, this Appendix). However, as we showed in the chapter, Friedman is very explicit about the fact that the 'realism'-of-assumptions issue is an integral part of the Marshallian–Walrasian thesis, so that one might expect to find some help in trying to understand the latter by considering what Friedman says in articles where his major concern is the 'realism'-of-assumptions issue and no specific reference is made to the Marshallians or their adversaries. We found that this was indeed so – the Lange article (1946b) was particularly useful in this regard – and this helped us to use a wider range of materials in deriving our interpretation than just the one very confusing article. But this still left us with a whole host of other problems.

The two demand curves again

With regard to Friedman's arguments about the demand curves, note that he does not tell us explicitly that the two are derived differently. That they are, however, seems an integral part of his argument. It may be acceptable in the constant-money-income curve approach to do only cursory observation, since that is all it takes to devise a usable formal 'language'. But if the constant-real-income curve is to have any greater substance as a hypothesis, extensive observation should have been done to 'ground' it. After all, we cannot take it for granted that p and q will move inversely, on condition that the impounded items remain the same; we can do so only if we have actually observed this to have happened in a large number of instances in actual experience. Friedman seems to assume that this has been done but does not tell us about it.

A second confusing element in Friedman's presentation is that the major *explicit* argument he gives for the constant-real-income demand curve is that it makes for more consistent analysis. As an example he discusses the granting of a subsidy on a product offset by an income tax to cover the cost. In that particular case other things would have to change since the subsidy results in greater sales of this commodity, requiring greater output, so that if there had been full use of resources to begin with other changes would have to take place in the economy. This means an almost certain shift in the demand curve with which one begins. Thus one cannot work through a consistent analysis with a given demand curve. But is it more consistent analysis that makes the Marshallian approach superior to the Walrasian? Friedman's arguments about the two demand curves give that impression. But if this is all the difference there is, why in other places does Friedman lead us to believe that there is a very fundamental difference which involves the matter of how these two carry on their inquiries, the products resulting, and so on?[1] If one argues that the two curves were derived differently, as we have tried to show, then the basic difference in approach is seen to be clear and important and consistent with the 'language'-substantive hypothesis distinction which seems to be at the heart of Friedman's broader message. But in this light his failure to be explicit on the matter of derivation is particularly unhelpful.

A related problem with Friedman's formulations results from the fact that if it is 'language' (or analysis) that we are concerned with, the matter of which demand curve will give the more consistent results would seem to depend on the kind of problem at hand, as one critic (Yeager, 1960) has observed.[2] In fact, it is Friedman here who seems Walrasian because he gives the impression that he is looking for a *general* solution to a complex problem and that he believes that by doing the formal *analysis* consistently (or using 'language' more thoroughly) one can come out with a substantive hypothesis. This seems counter to all that he seems to want to maintain; his own words contradict him in print (see above quote from 1952*a*, in 1953*e*, pp. 112–13).

The reason this problem is generated, it seems to us, is that Friedman is concerned with what looks like two very different issues which however he calls by the same name. On the one hand he tries to distinguish between the Marshallian and Walrasian approaches. This has to do with broader issues, such as how results are derived, the nature of the results achieved, etc. On the other hand he wants to distinguish between what he considers the proper use and the misuse of 'language' or analysis. Thus, in the article comparing the welfare effects of an income and excise tax (1952*a* in 1953*e*) and in portions of the demand curve article (1949*c* in 1953*e*) he tries to show us that unless we consider indirect effects, our use of 'language' (or formal analysis) is not very adequate because we then do not take into account all factors which, even on casual observation, seem *conceptually* pertinent. Since Friedman tells us, as we have seen, that it is the role of (formal) 'language' 'to suggest the considerations relevant to an answer' to a problem, the question as to whether we do this job well or ill would seem to fit into the formal 'language' or Walrasian realm as he seems to conceive it. Yet he calls the more adequate use of (formal) language Marshallian and the less adequate use Walrasian. What basis is there for giving this difference the same name as that for the difference in basic approach to the way economics is done?

Both issues that Friedman deals with are important ones but dealing with them under the same heading only confuses things. For example, it leads to the questionable argument that one type of demand curve is generally superior (for example, for the purposes of formal analysis), as we have seen. Further, it does a great deal to blur his major objective, which we take to be to argue for what he calls the Marshallian way of doing economics. What we mean by this is what Friedman argued is the scientific approach in economics (in the article on Lange, 1953*e*, pp. 282–3). In this context the 'realism'-of-assumptions thesis is very pertinent. But so far as the use of 'language' (or formal analysis) is concerned, the rationale runs the other way because, first, we do not have prediction to appeal to as arbiter as we do when we work from data, as implications, to premises which are sufficient.[3] Second, what is involved here is *reasoning out*, and where reasoning out is concerned *any* 'unrealism', whether of the actually false or the merely implausible sort, is a distinct detriment. Obviously, if one bases one's case on the adequacy ('realism') of assumptions, as Friedman does when he attacks the Walrasians for omitting assumptions which casual observation suggests to be relevant, and then argues that the 'realism' of the assumptions does not matter, as he does in many places in his general attacks against 'Walrasians', one follows a confusing if not contradictory argument. We do not know how much this inconsistent way of arguing in one of Friedman's two best-known methodological articles contributed to the confusion that abounds about the meaning of his methodological message but we suspect that it may have been substantial. We say this because readers who believe that 'realistic' assumptions are necessary see in the Marshall article that Friedman seems to agree. They do not see the broader Marshallian–Walrasian thesis because they are not prepared to see it. But then finding Friedman arguing that the 'realism' of assumptions does not matter, such readers can only conclude that Friedman is being illogical. (We deal further with this matter in Chapter 3.)[4]

Labeling one demand curve Marshallian

There is a problem of a different sort with Friedman's characterizing of one demand curve as 'Marshallian'. Has he properly characterized Marshall's analysis of demand? Critics have questioned whether he has (Alford, 1956). We need not try to determine who is right since our interest is not in Friedman as historian of economics. However, Friedman admits that Marshall had actually used both demand curves, and he tries to explain this by arguing that since the evidence suggests that Marshall held the conventional view only in later years, he might have forgotten his own earlier analysis. This is very much a guess, of course, and since we do not have specific evidence, that is all that we can do. But how we guess depends to some extent, at least, on the way we view Marshall's basic approach. It seems to us that though Marshall was less exclusively concerned with the kind of formal 'language' that only clarifies than was Walras, and more concerned with substantive hypotheses, he certainly must have been concerned with 'language' as a device for clarifying ideas as well, *as all theorists have been*. In that case it seems less speculative, and more reasonable, to guess that in some instances Marshall may have favored the traditional curve, when his main concern was with clarifying ideas, whereas in other instances he favored the constant-real-income curve because he was more concerned with substantive hypotheses. The fact that among economic methodologists a clear distinction between using theory merely to clarify ideas and using theory to help make predictions is rarely made, and that some, for example Marshall's contemporary and one-time protégé, J. N. Keynes (1955, pp. 143–4), argue that no such distinction *should* be made, would seem to support this line of explanation.

Use of the label 'Marshallian'

We have so far taken it for granted that the Marshallian label which Friedman uses is an appropriate one, but we must now question whether Marshall's methodological position is correctly represented, since the way we answer this question makes some difference as to how we interpret what Friedman is saying. Friedman gives citations from Marshall to support his interpretation and some of these certainly seem to fit. Thus, he quotes Marshall to the effect that economic theory is an 'engine for the discovery of concrete truth', and further:

> Man's powers are limited: almost every one of nature's riddles is complex. He breaks it up, studies one bit at a time, and at last combines his partial solutions with a supreme effort of his whole small strength into some sort of an attempt at a solution of the whole riddle.

However, these passages are not unambiguous. The 'engine' Marshall talks about may not be the 'engine' that Friedman has in mind, and in talking about breaking up problems and studying them one bit at a time Marshall may very well have had in mind the Millian notion (see Chapter 5) that we break up effects into their separate causes, a notion that is far removed from the position Friedman seems to hold.

We encounter the same problems in interpreting other passages in Marshall. Thus Friedman quotes further from Marshall to the effect that (p. 90):

> Facts by themselves are silent .... The most reckless and treacherous of all theorists is he who professes to let facts and figures speak for themselves, who keeps in the background the part he has played, perhaps unconsciously, in selecting and grouping them, and in suggesting the argument *post hoc ergo propter hoc*.

Few economists, whether Marshallian or Walrasian, would question such a statement. The crucial question rather, from the standpoint of whether Marshall's own approach coincides with what Friedman calls Marshallian, is whether he believed that *theories* by themselves are silent because they must be *fact*-impregnated. On this question Marshall is not nearly so clear. Our purpose in bringing this up is not to show that Marshall was not a Marshallian in Friedman's sense – we believe that to a large extent he was – but rather to suggest that just what he was is not easy to determine.[5] As a consequence, use of the Marshallian label can be confusing.[6] At least on the surface it is hard to see in Marshall's *Principles* (1961 [1890]) and, say, Friedman and Schwartz' *Monetary History* (1963*a*) a completely common methodology. Yet both apparently fall into Friedman's Marshallian category. Thus while we may get some help from Marshall himself in trying to understand what Friedman meant by the term 'Marshallian', with no more specific reference than Friedman gives us, looking to Marshall for help is just as likely to confuse.

Deriving an interpretation

We could go on pointing out obstacles encountered in trying to understand what Friedman wanted to convey, but enough has been said to show that these obstacles are perhaps no less formidable than are those which confront us in trying to fathom the meaning of 'Positive economics'. Given this state of affairs, what should one do? A possible reaction, and a common one to 'Positive economics', is to conclude that Friedman in this work is illogical, inconsistent, incoherent; or that he was not really trying to formulate a methodological thesis at all but rather had an ulterior purpose or purposes, so that what on a superficial view may look like ideas that have to do with methodology, on a more careful reading all seem to have little if anything to do with that subject.

One can conceive of the possibility of methodological writing about which no other conclusion is possible. But before concluding thus about the pieces we are reviewing, it seems reasonable to consider whether, in spite of all of these difficulties, and considering Friedman's work as a whole and its basic rationale rather than concentrating only on bits and pieces of what he said here and there, one might not be able to derive an interpretation which makes sense and which is consistent.[7] Thinking along theses lines leads us to conclude that most of the difficulties we encounter arise from the fact that Friedman generally presents as a dichotomy – the Marshallian–Walrasian distinction – what are in effect the two extreme points on a continuum. Where one ends up on the scale depends, firstly, on whether one is interested only in conceptual analysis; and, secondly, on how much pertinent data are available to work with.

If one is interested only in conceptual analysis observation is not directly pertinent; hence the kind of work one does holding this objective falls towards the pure or Walrasian end of the scale. But even if one wants to do the kind of inquiry from which one hopes to derive substantive hypotheses, if data are not available the best one can do is to reason out on the basis of plausible assumptions and thus land fairly close to the Walrasian end. Friedman himself illustrates this in 'The "welfare" effects of an income tax and an excise tax' (1952a), where his argument relies entirely on casual observation and reasoning out. The thesis in that piece, recall, is that it is worth thinking through a problem to determine whether all of the factors which casual observation suggests might be pertinent are taken into account. There is little opportunity here for starting with 'some set of observed and related facts, as full and comprehensive as possible', and after formulating a hypothesis there is little opportunity 'to check these deductions against reality'. Yet with reference to the Marshallian–Walrasian distinction, it is not difficult to see why Friedman should feel that his analysis is (more) Marshallian and the analysis he criticized more Walrasian, since Friedman does attend more to the details of what goes on in the world in his formulation.

In fact, if we look at the work Friedman has done as positive economist we see that some of it is far more Marshallian and correspondingly less Walrasian than other pieces. Thus as we have noted, in the article on tax effects (1952a) there is some casual observation and a lot of reasoning out. The article on risk co-authored with Savage (1948c) includes more observation but not very much. Friedman's *A Theory of the Consumption Function* (1957c) includes considerably more observation than does the Friedman–Savage article and is closer to the rationale which Friedman calls Marshallian than is that earlier work. *A Monetary History* (with Anna Schwartz, 1963a) is still further towards the Marshallian end of the continuum. And looked at this way we have little difficulty with the Marshallian and Walrasian designations because we become aware that the real Alfred Marshall himself need not be envisaged as falling at the very end of the continuum in the one direction and the historical Leon Walras at the very end in the other to make the comparison meaningful. It is undeniable that there is a very significant difference as between the approaches of these two eminent economists and it seems reasonably clear that it was this difference that Friedman was trying to get at.

From what has been said so far it would appear that there is no exclusiveness between the two approaches as Friedman sees it. Whether it is more appropriate to be on one part of the scale or another in a particular instance depends, first, on whether data are pertinent (they would not be in dealing with a problem which is entirely conceptual) and second, the extent to which the pertinent data are at hand (or can be made available). There is, however, a sense in which what Friedman calls the Marshallian and Walrasian approaches are competitive, namely, in the matter of choosing an ideal for economic inquiry. The fact that data are pertinent, and even readily available, does not mean that an economist will necessarily choose to use them. Economists might still rely on the most meagre of casual observation and devote almost all of their energies to reasoning out. That in every age there have been economists who have operated this way, there can be little doubt. To express his disagreement with such an approach Marshall argued that 'there is no room in economics for long trains of deductive reasoning' (1961 [1890] p. 781). Friedman expresses himself even more strongly. He argues, as we have seen, against those who take 'abstractness, generality, mathematical elegance' as the ends of economic theorizing. His message in this respect, it seems to us, is not very different from Marshall's.[8]

It is in the competitive sense that the Marshallian–Walrasian thesis relates to the 'realism'-of-assumptions thesis. Where implications cannot be observed, as where one compares 'welfare' effects of different taxes, the 'realism' (or plausibility) of assumptions is obviously important in judging theory, as Friedman shows by his own practice. The matter is different where data on implications are available or can be made available, as in the monetary area. Yet in this view, in the short run it might still be defensible to reason out on the basis of relatively scanty data (as Friedman does in the risk article co-authored with Savage); for even where more data could be made available[9] with additional effort because research is a continuous process, any one researcher need not go through the whole process himself.

Marshallianism seems to be an ideal in the inquiry process, as Friedman sees it, but need only be imperfectly fulfilled at any point in time.[10] What is important is that research be done in such a way that the continuity is not broken as it would be, for example, if results are not testable or tests are conceived not as a process leading research along but rather as discrete one-shot ventures whose only purpose is to identify 'true' theories. As will be seen in the next chapter, this point of view leads Friedman to interpret the rationale of economic theory quite differently than either orthodox or heterodox economists generally do.

NOTES

1. Surprisingly Friedman cites Knight's publication of 1944, which supports his choice of demand curve, though on Knight's view its superiority rests on introspective considerations. Knight explicitly rules out the possibility of using either analysis to derive substantive hypotheses capable of being tested with the evidence.
2. Blaug (1978, p. 389) tells us that Yeager 'raises *the* methodological issue inherent in the Friedman interpretation' of demand curves (emphasis added). The point Yeager raises, however, is not the only methodological issue nor even the most important one about Friedman's analysis.
3. Sufficient but not necessary. This is a process which Peirce called 'abduction', as we have seen, which is an integral part of Dewey's logic. (See Chapter 6.)
4. Samuelson's famous 'F-Twist' argument (1963) may very well have been provoked this way. The 'F-Twist' merely assumes that 'reasoning out' is the way to deal with such problems, a point of view Friedman seemed to support in his demand curve analysis and in other places. And, indeed, had Friedman appealed to 'reasoning out' in his 'realism'-of-assumptions thesis then Samuelson would have been right. The problem arose because Samuelson failed to see that there was a different rationale involved; Friedman probably invited such misreading by not making clear that there were two legitimate ways of arguing, one for the area of 'language' and the other for substantive hypotheses, and that in the 'realism'-of-assumptions thesis the case was made entirely in terms of the latter.
5. Among many other bits of evidence there is the following from J. N. Keynes (1890, p. 240, n. 1): 'The function of a pure theory', says Professor Marshall, 'is to deduce definite conclusions from definite hypothetical premises. The premises should approximate as closely as possible to the facts with which the corresponding applied theory has to deal'.
6. The attempt to determine whether Knight was a Marshallian shows up another basic difficulty. Knight was as critical of the 'pure mathematics' type

of economic theorizing as Friedman is, and in this sense is Marshallian. But the foundation on which he rested the substance of his analysis was introspection. (For the most pertinent reference, see Knight, 1944.) But if we reject introspection as a basis for judging theories, Knight winds up without substantive hypotheses and therefore in the class of the Walrasians. Nonetheless, a follower of Knight could argue with some justification that in certain basic respects Knight is closer to Alfred Marshall than is Friedman.

7. One must, of course, consider what he says in specific instances in order to begin to understand; we do not think that there is any other way to derive a meaningful general interpretation than by considering specific instances. But in considering the parts one must have ideas about the general rationale, which ideas are revised as the work proceeds. In this respect the process is no different here than it is in economic inquiry itself.

8. One gets the impression that Friedman favors the Marshallian approach, too, because he feels that it is more practical. But he does not say this explicitly nor − even though this would not be obvious to everyone − does he stop to argue it.

9. A considerable amount of research has been done on this subject (see Schoemaker, 1982). Ironically, some of the evidence that has turned up (pp. 553−4) suggests that when subjects played with real money the results were the same as when they merely hypothesized, evidence that runs counter to one of Friedman's basic beliefs.

10. Our conclusion is thus very different from that of Frazer and Boland (1983), who consider Friedman a short-run instrumentalist and a long-run Popperian. We would say that, to the extent to which a meaningful distinction can be made between Friedman's approach to the short and the long run, Friedman is more tolerant of the Walrasian approach in the short run than in the long run. Since the Walrasian is the less instrumental (see Chapters 3 and 5) this makes our result just about the opposite of Frazer and Boland's.

2 • FRIEDMAN'S UNORTHODOX POSITION

One tends to classify economists as either orthodox or heterodox. Over the years a whole structure of related concepts has evolved which is helpful in getting to the core of meaning of an economist's work; they save us the trouble of having to formulate new points of reference with every new subject. But where an economist falls on both sides of the divide in basic orientation, as Friedman does, there is difficulty in interpreting him because the very categories needed to analyze his position are not readily at hand.[1] Some, of course, would challenge this characterization of Friedman since he is generally taken to be a leading defender of neoclassical economics, the hard core of orthodoxy. How can an acknowledged leader of one group be said to belong partly to another? We grant that there is a puzzle here but point to Friedman's very critical comments (considered in the last chapter) – criticism that is quite basic in nature – to support the contention that the difficulty is not of our making. Nevertheless, we must confront this puzzle squarely if we are to come to grips with Friedman's methodological position.

In the first part of this chapter we will deal with Friedman's anti-orthodox side, since that has been generally overlooked.[2] We will reinforce what has been said already by showing that, in important respects, the methodological views which we ascribed to Friedman in the last chapter are very close to those of Wesley Clair Mitchell, an economist whose anti-orthodox credentials are well established.[3] There is, of course, the other side of Friedman; this we attempt to fit into the whole by showing, in the second part, in what ways in his early writings Friedman disagreed with aspects of Mitchell's anti-orthodox stance. In the last part of the chapter we compare Friedman's views with those of Jacob Viner, an economist wholly in the orthodox tradition.

It is not our purpose to show how much Mitchell 'influenced' Friedman. It would be hard to determine just how influential Mitchell actually was as teacher and senior colleague at the National Bureau of Economic Research (hereafter NBER), or through the teachings of

Arthur F. Burns, Mitchell's disciple and Friedman's undergraduate teacher and friend. The same can be said about the effects of Viner's teachings. But there is no reason for us to speculate about this. Whether the influences were great or small has little bearing on the point we are trying to make. We introduce Mitchell, first, because one aspect of the type of criticism he levelled at orthodoxy remained an integral part of Friedman's methodology, and second, because Friedman's type of defense of orthodoxy can be understood as an implicit criticism of another facet of what Mitchell objected to in orthodox economic theory. In other words, we use Mitchell to help us deal with the puzzle to which we pointed in the last paragraph. We use Viner in the same way.

SIMILARITIES BETWEEN FRIEDMAN'S VIEWS AND MITCHELL'S

Theory and empirical work

Friedman's criticisms of aspects of the orthodox approach to economics sound very much like Mitchell's. An example is Friedman's comment that some theoretical concepts are of little help to economists who do empirical work. As Friedman and Wallis put it at the beginning of the article we considered in the last chapter (1942*a*, p. 175):

> Although the indifference function has become the keystone of the theory of consumer choice, empirical workers in the field, even those most thoroughly familiar with the niceties of indifference analysis, have ignored it or, in a few instances, dragged it in as a more or less irrelevant afterthought.

This raised the question whether 'the indifference function might be useful' at all for 'the organization and analysis of empirical data on consumer expenditure' (p. 176). The authors answer in the negative; this very important piece of orthodox theorizing does not enable its users 'to obtain exact knowledge of the quantitative relation of consumer expenditures to prices and income for the purpose of predicting the effect of changes in economic conditions on the consumption of various commodities and services' (p. 188). They add:

> Indeed, an investigator with his gaze firmly fixed on the objective of relating consumer expenditure to prices, income, and tastes or needs would probably not seriously consider using the indifference function as an intermediary. Only if he were steeped in theoretical analysis to the point of oblivion [*sic*] to the real problem and the data available for its solution would he mistake the scaffolding set up to facilitate logical analysis for the skeletal structure of the problem.

Mitchell also makes the charge that orthodox concepts are not useful to empirical workers, but his criticism is more sweeping than Friedman's. Consider, for example, Mitchell's comments in his presidential address, delivered at the American Economic Association (hereafter AEA) meeting in 1924. After noting Marshall's belief '"that qualitative analysis has done the greater part of its work" in economic science, and that the "higher and more difficult task" of quantitative analysis "must wait upon the slow growth of thorough realistic statistics",' Mitchell observes (1950, p. 23):

> ... despite all the gains it has made, quantitative analysis shows no more promise of providing a statistical complement of pure theory than it showed when Dr. Marshall pronounced his dicta .... Indeed, I incline to go further and say that there is slight prospect that quantitative analysis will ever be able to solve the problems that qualitative analysis has framed, in their present form. What we must expect is a recasting of the old problems into new forms amenable to statistical attack. In the course of this reformulation of its problems, economic theory will change not merely its complexion but also its content.

Picking theoretical concepts useful for empirical work

If we grant that some orthodox concepts are not useful for empirical work, what kind of concepts does the empirical worker need? On this matter Friedman and Mitchell seem to agree. Friedman and Wallis tell us (1942a, p. 176) that what the empirical workers need are concepts that have 'material value for the organization of empirical data'. And Mitchell, in talking about the role of theorizing in business cycle research, his life's work, tells us (1927, pp. 469–70): 'The methods employed must be methods which make it possible to weave these diverse materials [historical and statistical] into a single fabric ...', that is, help to organize it.

The derivation of such concepts

How are such organizing concepts to be derived? Here, too, we find Friedman and Mitchell in agreement. Friedman and Wallis say (1942a, p. 189) that 'empirical workers have adopted the direct approach of isolating factors correlative with consumer demand and measuring the relationships'. Thus (p. 189):

> Whether these are taste factors or opportunity factors is irrelevant. If, for example, the food expenditures of families of a certain group uniformly increase by 45 per cent when income increases from $1,000 to $2,000 and decrease correspondingly when income declines from $2,000 to $1,000, what does it matter whether the changes reflect responses to fixed

indifference functions or a concomitant alteration of tastes? The important issues in interpreting studies of this type are the extent to which the adjustment of given families to changes in circumstances can be inferred by comparing the contemporaneous behavior of families in different circumstances, and the extent to which the observed relations are stable through time. These questions are subject to direct empirical investigation.

It is very doubtful whether later in his career Friedman would have put it this way, but the notion that the empirical worker must go to the data as part of the process of deriving the concepts he needs in his empirical work remained with him. As we have seen, in the review of Lange which we considered in the last chapter Friedman argues (p. 282) that 'the theorist starts with some set of observed and related facts, as full and comprehensive as possible.' Friedman's objection was precisely that Lange had not done this.

Mitchell in his presidential address (1950, p. 26), put the point succinctly:

> ... quantitative workers derive their data directly from these real markets. They start with the mass phenomena which the qualitative analysts approached indirectly through their hypothetical individuals.

In other words, if we want theory which is useful for dealing with empirical data we have to use data gathered from real markets as an element in the process of derivation.

Friedman argued in the indifference function article that theory which has been derived with the aid of but casual observation is of little direct use to those who work with extensive data. We find Mitchell arguing that the same is true in the field of business cycles. He noted (1927, p. 2):

> The more intensively we work, the more we realize that this term [business cycles] is a synthetic product of the imagination – a product whose history is characteristic of our ways of learning. Overtaken by a series of strange experiences our predecessors leaped to a broad conception, gave it a name, and began to invent explanations, as if they know what their words meant. But in the process of explaining they demonstrated how inadequate their knowledge was. From their work we can learn much; *the first lesson is that we must find out more about the facts before we can choose among the old explanations, or improve upon them.* [Emphasis added.]

The interplay of observation and theorizing in the inquiry process

Mitchell believed that not only must the economist first carefully examine what there is to explain before getting very far with theorizing but also that he must keep observing as he theorizes because theorizing which runs too far ahead of observation leaves us somewhat up in the air.

The process of inquiry, as conceived by both Mitchell and Friedman, involves the interplay of fact-gathering with hypothesis formation at every step. In fact, the failure of contemporary economists to do this was a major reason for both Friedman's and Mitchell's criticisms. We have seen how this lack of interplay in Lange's work irked Friedman. Mitchell was even more forceful in arguing the need for this interactive process and also more explicit about the fact that its absence is a serious weakness. As he put it in a letter (in Burns, 1962, p. 98):

> Very likely what I try to do is merely carrying out the requirements of John Stuart Mill's 'complete method.' But there is a great deal more passing back and forth between hypotheses and observation, each modifying and enriching the other, than I seem to remember in Mill's version. Perhaps I do him injustice as a logician through default of memory; but I don't think I do classical economics injustice when I say that it erred sadly in trying to think out a deductive scheme and then talked of verifying *that*.[4]

Plausibility as the criterion for judging theory

Still another point at which both Friedman's and Mitchell's visions intersect is in their rejection of plausibility as a basis for accepting theory. Thus, the criticism Friedman levelled against Lange's work, which most would consider 'orthodox', was, as we have seen, that Lange substituted plausibility for objective evidence in judging whether an hypothesis has merit. This type of criticism lies at the very heart of Mitchell's way of thinking. It is, for example, the reason for his dissatisfaction with Irving Fisher's arguments in support of the quantity theory in *The Purchasing Power of Money* (Mitchell, 1912). Fisher had not theorized in a general equilibrium framework the way Lange did, so the theoretical possibilities he considered were fewer. But his analysis, like Lange's, consisted in formulating theoretical possibilities and rejecting most of them because they were implausible: for example, that changes in the velocity of money might be inversely correlated with changes in the quantity of money or that prices might be the active factor and the quantity of money the passive one. Mitchell made an additional observation which reinforced this point. Having made his case a priori, Mitchell noted, Fisher went on to show that in reality, during 'transition' periods, the relationships between the variables were very different from those postulated in the a priori analysis. To Mitchell it was the latter part of the work that was the more important because it was based on observation of what actually happened rather than on what was merely plausible.

Mitchell took note of the fact that Fisher had tried to give an inductive 'proof' of his theorizing – which Lange had not – and this makes Mitchell's criticism of Fisher look different from Friedman's objections to Lange's work, but this difference is negligible. As Mitchell noted, the statistical proof was a work of supererogation because the equation of exchange was an identity, so that if the facts did not fit the theory it was the facts that were in error and not the theory. Fisher admitted that whether one accepts the theory or not depends on whether one considers the arguments plausible rather than on whether the evidence supports one's position. (See also Hirsch and De Marchi, 1986).[5]

An 'inside' versus an 'outside' view of behavior

Still another area in which Friedman's approach is different from the orthodox, and basically the same as Mitchell's, is that of beliefs about how behavior should be conceived. Orthodox methodologists, as J. S. Mill clearly shows (see Chapter 5), took it for granted that economists had to view behavior from the 'inside', that is, they asked: 'How would I behave if I were in this situation?' One could also watch others around one, but that was primarily for the purpose of learning in what ways one's behavior might be idiosyncratic. Mitchell judged that this approach did not carry one far. He proposed a more objective 'outside' view. As he put it in one place (1950, p. 171, n. 70; see also p. 254): '. . . an economic theory might be worked out concerning the way in which a species of animals or a tribe of lower hunters get their living . . . . But such a theory would be a descriptive analysis of behavior written by an outsider.' Mitchell did not discuss this point anywhere in detail, but it is reasonably certain that he was as distrustful of accepting what people thought their motives were or how they thought they made decisions as Friedman and Savage showed themselves to be in their 1948 article. He tells us (in Burns, pp. 94–5) that he had learned from John Dewey while still an undergraduate that people rationalize and that the way to find out how they behave is to observe what they actually do.[6]

The extent of our knowledge

Friedman as well as Mitchell believed that non-NBER economists, like those who theorized about business cycles, and the econometricians at the Cowles Commission, thought that they knew far more about the economy than they really did. We have already seen evidence of this in Mitchell's remarks about how economists had approached the subject of business cycles (see above, p. 44). We found (in Chapter 1) the same sentiments expressed in Friedman's criticism of Carl Christ (1951a). But there is a difference. Mitchell felt that economists overestimated what they know because they thought they had solid knowledge that was incorporated in neoclassical theory; in fact such 'knowledge' was not solid at all because it was not supported with evidence. Friedman, on the other hand, felt that the Cowles Commission people were unduly optimistic because the knowledge of micro and monetary theory on which they built – which Friedman felt *was* solid knowledge – had to do with statics and comparative statics, whereas the problem of business cycles was fundamentally a dynamic one. The significance of this important difference will be explored in the next section.

Before moving on, however, we should stress that the general areas of agreement which we have noted are not a random set of beliefs, neither for Friedman nor for Mitchell, but rather part of a general philosophy about how one should approach economic questions. Both want more than what Friedman calls a 'language', that is, an analytic scheme that helps us to communicate but is not directly useful for finding reliable regularities.[7] The reason for their holding this belief is also the same for both of them, which shows how fundamental is the agreement. After all, the reason many economists opt for 'language', or something very close to it, is that they believe that nothing more is attainable (see, for example, Keynes, 1938). The question of whether the logic of economics is the same as that of physics is an open one and the same economists and logicians of economics have come down firmly on both sides of the issue. Mill, for example, in some places (1973, VI, I, and III) argues forcefully for the unity of sciences thesis, yet in others says things that can be interpreted to mean that economic theory is not much more than a 'language' (see, for example, Hollander, 1985).[8] Mitchell and Friedman are almost unique among major economists in both believing strongly and very explicitly that the logic of the physical sciences *without qualifications* applies to economics.

The evidence for this leaves very little room for doubt. Thus Mitchell tells us in a revealing letter (in Burns p. 96):

> There seemed to be one way of making real progress, slow, very slow, but tolerably sure. That was the way of natural science.

In another letter (*ibid.* p. 66) he tells us:

> In the latest fraction of human history we have made rapid industrial progress because we have learned how to formulate our knowledge of physical and chemical phenomena in these [scientific] terms. But in all matters of social organization we remain backward; we don't know how to recast our inherited ways of treating each other with anything like the success we have had in recasting our inherited ways of treating materials ... [Progress in medicine] has come from the laboratories, where the issues of life and of death in individual cases are replaced as the immediate object of attention by little problems of chemical reactions and bacteriological detail for which the busy practitioner had neither time nor patience. So must it be in other subjects [including economics].

Friedman expresses the same view when he tells us (1953c, p. 10):

> The inability to conduct so-called 'controlled experiments' does not, in my view, reflect a basic difference between the social and physical sciences both because it is not peculiar to the social sciences – witness astronomy – and because the distinction between a controlled experiment and an uncontrolled experience is at best one of degree.

Not unexpectedly Friedman and Mitchell also agree, though Mitchell is much more explicit about this, that the objective of deriving theory which yields reliable predictions cannot be achieved by following the suggestions of methodologists of the orthodox tradition, from Mill through Robbins. This still leaves open the question whether the more innovative major economists had in fact derived their results the way the methodologists had suggested, or rather whether what they *did* was something of which both Mitchell and Friedman could approve. We show in the next section that in regard to this matter Friedman's views diverge sharply from Mitchell's.

DIFFERENCES BETWEEN FRIEDMAN'S VIEWS AND MITCHELL'S

Friedman's views about Mitchell

In a laudatory but not uncritical analysis of Mitchell's approach written shortly after Mitchell's death, Friedman sets out what he took to be Mitchell's views about how a theory of economic change could best be derived. As Friedman saw it the following is a fair representation of Mitchell's basic position (in Burns, 1952, pp. 242–3):

> Granted that our objective is a theory of economic change that will explain observed phenomena and correctly predict phenomena not yet observed; granted, too, that, when attained, such a theory will abstract essential elements from the complex of economic phenomena and in that sense will be 'unrealistic'; it does not follow that the best way to derive such a theory is to proceed directly to its formulation. In the study of any class of phenomena, it is necessary first to examine the phenomena themselves, to describe them, and to find empirical regularities, in order to provide a basis for generalization and abstraction; and at this stage the orderly organization of empirical data is more important than the elaboration and refinement of abstract hypotheses.[9]

Friedman agreed with Mitchell 'In his judgment [that] the theory of economic change was at this stage' and also 'that economists were treating it as if it were not, as if the phenomena were already sufficiently well known to provide a basis for generalization'. It was Mitchell's view, too, according to Friedman, that:

> in consequence, they were excogitating numerous theories 'both suggestive and perplexing.' He [Mitchell] would be better occupied, [Mitchell] felt, in using these theories to suggest the empirical phenomena to be investigated, and then devoting the major part of his attention to describing these phenomena, only afterward formulating a rationalization of them.

Where Friedman disagreed was with Mitchell's 'applying [these same notions] to economic theory as a whole rather than to the theory of economic change alone'. Friedman adds: 'I do not think the same judgment is valid for orthodox relative price theory, as Mitchell recognized on occasion.'

How economic theory had been derived

What Friedman does not say explicitly but what is clearly implied in the above passage is his belief, first, that orthodox price and monetary theories had already gone through the early stage; and second, that economists had done this part of their job well, that is, that the pertinent phenomena had been thoroughly examined and described and the empirical regularities found, providing a solid basis for generalization and abstraction.[10] This same belief is implied, too, as we have seen, elsewhere in Friedman's early work. Friedman was rejecting the notion of methodologists that economists had derived economic theory, not by using careful and extensive investigation of what there was to explain at an early stage, but rather by first building up a structure on the basis of introspection and casual observation. This conventional view was agreed to by orthodox methodologists without exception, and defended (for example, by Mill) as entirely appropriate. It was also accepted as a correct historical account by anti-orthodox critics like Veblen and Mitchell. Mitchell was very critical of orthodox price theory, at least partly because he accepted this orthodox account of how the theory had been derived (see, for example, Mitchell, 1950, pp. 349–52, 399–400); Friedman rejected this account and therefore, though he shared Mitchell's notions about the way one should approach economics, he could still consistently believe that orthodox price theory met the standards that Mitchell had proposed and he, Friedman, had accepted.

Abstraction and the 'unrealism' of assumptions

Friedman's comments on Mitchell reveal something else which is important. Note the remark that an acceptable theory 'will abstract essential elements from the complex of economic phenomena and in that sense be "unrealistic"'. And that he adds to this that 'it does not follow that the best way to derive such a theory is to proceed directly to its formulation'. These comments are particularly interesting because they show Friedman attempting to mark out an independent position which is, in some respects, different from the orthodox, but in others, different from Mitchell's. What Friedman seems to be saying, in part, is that because theory must be abstract it does not follow that it can be pulled out of one's imagination; an extensive process of observation is necessary if the imagination is to be given a chance of putting together the right elements. This is Mitchellian. But that is not enough, according to Friedman. The theory must 'extract essential elements from the complex of economic phenomena and in that sense be "unrealistic"'. We run into a problem here. How are we to determine what is 'essential'? And what does Friedman mean by the term 'unrealistic'?

The first question is relatively easy to answer. It seems reasonably clear from what Friedman has said elsewhere that a theory is taken by him to include the 'essential' elements if it is able to predict reasonably well. But why characterize such a theory as 'unrealistic'? The fact that one leaves things out in abstracting does not necessarily make such a theory 'unrealistic', in the sense of making it an inaccurate descriptive represent-ation of reality (see, for example Katouzian, 1980, pp. 80–1). It merely takes one to a higher level of generality, as when one talks about a 'tree' rather than a birch, a beech or an elm. There is nothing 'unrealistic' about the notion of a tree when it is included as an element in a theory. Further, if Friedman is using the verb 'to abstract' in the conventional way, it is hard to see what point he is trying to make if he is merely telling us that theorizing necessarily involves abstracting.

To understand this part of Friedman's thesis, we believe, it is necessary to read it in the context of the argument as a whole. As we have seen, Friedman gives Mitchell his due in agreeing that lengthy and careful investigation of what there is to explain is a necessary first step in economic inquiry. But in opposition to Mitchell, as we have also noted, he believed that such investigation may give rise to just the kind of theory which makes up Marshallian economics. Mitchell, though, contrasted the kind of inquiry he favored with the work of those who theorized in the neoclassical manner, and he argued that as long as there was a great deal of data available which showed how *real* people behaved in *real* markets, it did not make sense 'to retain a keen interest in *imaginary* individuals coming to *imaginary* markets with ready-made [*imaginary*] scales of bid and offer prices' (Mitchell, 1950, p. 26, emphasis added).[11] If Friedman was reacting to such views, as we think likely, then the 'realism' involved referred to what could be found in the data. When one theorized, on Friedman's view, one had to go beyond the data,[12] which

Mitchell was very reluctant to do, [13] and *imagine* a simple pattern that could account for the data; such a simple (abstract) pattern was not 'real' because it was not in the statistics, even though it might be interpreted as implied by them. [14]

Similarities and differences

Thus, while Friedman rejected the contention of orthodox methodologists that theory could be defended by pointing to plausible assumptions, he at the same time rejected criticism, such as Mitchell's, which attacked theory because its premises were implausible. It turns out, then, that while accepting just about all of Mitchell's criticism of normative economic methodology, a methodology which to a large extent rejected orthodox economic theory at least partly on the grounds that its assumptions were not supported directly by the data, Friedman still winds up favorably disposed towards orthodox theory because he feels that different criteria should be used to judge it. It is also his hunch that the theory so judged does meet the test, namely, it gives reasonably good predictions in economic experience. [15] Thus, Friedman can at one and the same time be scathingly critical of an orthodox economist like Lange, who he feels practiced what orthodox methodologists preached, but sympathetic to Alfred Marshall, who he feels followed in practice a more defensible methodology. The difference is in how, as Friedman saw it, economists had derived their results, and their basis for accepting them.

Orthodox methodology and the derivation of economic theory

This is worth explaining further because it is a subtle point to grasp. We have suggested that a major point of difference between Friedman and Mitchell arose out of their respective views on how economists such as Marshall had *derived* their theories. Mitchell took it for granted that methodologists had correctly reported this: Marshall – and others – had proceeded from plausible assumptions. But after criticizing economists for not interspersing observation with theorizing, he added (in Burns, 1952, p. 90):

> Of course, there is a good deal of commerce between most economic theorizing and personal observation of an irregular sort – that is what has given our theories their considerable measure of significance. But I must not go into that issue.

Unfortunately, Mitchell never did go into 'that issue'. That leaves us to wonder whether he might not have modified his views had he pursued this question. On the other hand, as far as we are aware, Friedman did not go into 'that issue' either. In Friedman's case the omission is of particular importance because if he had, he might have made his position clearer, and perhaps less controversial.

The heart of the difference

From what has so far been said it might appear as if a major difference between Mitchell's view and Friedman's was that Mitchell was concerned with the 'realism' of the assumptions of theory whereas Friedman wanted to focus on tests of implications. To a very limited extent this is true; as we have noted, in some places Mitchell seems critical of economic theory because its assumptions are 'unrealistic', particularly in his earlier writings. But there is a more important side. As Paul Homan argues in a very perceptive study where he compares Mitchell's views with Veblen's (1928, p. 409):

> Veblen's method of demolishing systematic theory is to cast doubt upon its *postulates*. Mitchell appeals to his mass of facts and distills them into a convincing picture of economic processes which lends no support to the *conclusions* of systematic theory.

As we have seen, Friedman felt that Mitchell's evidence on dynamics tells us little about whether the implications of *static* theory are borne out by the facts. Mitchell seems to have taken it for granted that they were not.[16] As we show in Chapter 4, Friedman takes it for granted that they *are*, but without offering evidence.[17] The difference for the most part is thus not whether one should appeal to assumptions or implications but rather lies in the empirical judgment about whether the implications of static (and comparative static) theory are or are not generally borne out by the facts. Friedman was associated with the NBER team attempting to derive dynamic theory, not the institutionalist Mitchell's criticism of static theory.

FRIEDMAN'S POSITION AND JOHN DEWEY'S LOGIC

Friedman's position

Summing up, we note that Friedman on the one hand is unorthodox because, like Mitchell, he rejects mainstream methodology as a guide for trying to understand how economic theory can best be derived in the future. But he disagrees with Mitchell in not believing, as Mitchell did, that earlier methodologists had correctly rationalized the process that had been used by the major economists in deriving their theory. Rather he feels that important work in economics, such as Alfred Marshall's, had been derived in a manner quite in conformity with the way Mitchell felt that it should be. But from this it followed that how well the implications of the theory accord with what actually happened and how wide is the realm to which the theory applies are the criteria to apply to it, and not how 'realistic' or plausible are its assumptions.

Dewey's position

This is indeed an unusual position. Few if any economists, either before Friedman wrote 'Positive economics' or since, have held such views. A non-economist who comes close is the philosopher John Dewey. In his *Logic* Dewey argued (1938, pp. 504–5):

> Classical political economy, with respect to its logical form, claimed to be a science in virtue, first, of certain ultimate first truths, and secondly, in virtue of the possibility of rigorous 'deductions' of actual economic phenomena from these truths . . .. The members of this school, from Adam Smith to the Mills and their contemporary followers, differed of course from the traditional *rationalistic* school. For they held that first principles were themselves derived inductively, instead of being established by a priori intuition.[18] But once arrived at, they were regarded as unquestionable truths, or as axioms with respect to any further truths, since the latter should be deductively derived from them.

Dewey's criticism:

> From the standpoint of logical method, the conceptions involved were not regarded as *hypotheses* to be employed in observation and ordering of phenomena, and hence to be tested by the consequences produced by acting upon them.

In other words, Dewey had no objections on logical or methodological grounds to accepting orthodox economic theory so long as it was viewed within a different methodological perspective than the one from which orthodox methodologists themselves viewed it. That does not mean that Dewey believed that economic theory should be accepted as is, but rather that it should not be rejected merely because its assumptions do not appear plausible, any more than that it should be accepted merely because they do. If the theory were viewed in a Deweyan perspective it would then be judged on the basis of how well its implications accord with what actually happens. Implied in all of this is the belief that economic theory had in fact been derived via a process of inquiry which Dewey had earlier outlined in his *Logic*, which is essentially the one Friedman ascribed to in criticizing Lange. We say this because, to Dewey, merely testing the implications of a theory without regard to how the theory was derived is not a very meaningful procedure. We have tried to show above, and will further support in the next part, that Friedman shared these views.

A further look at Friedman's position

Thus, Friedman rejects the *logic* of economic theory, as formulated by the economic methodologists – deduction from plausible premises – just as Dewey does. And he seems to have a notion of what the appropriate logic should be, which is essentially the logic that Dewey formulated.[19] But it does not follow from this for Friedman, any more than for Dewey, that orthodox *theory* must be rejected. For he believed the methodologists misrepresented the way the theory had actually been arrived at, at least in certain instances, notably Marshall. It is Friedman's position, as it was Dewey's, that 'the concepts involved [should be] regarded as hypotheses to be employed in observing and ordering of phenomena, and hence ... [should] be tested by the consequences produced by acting upon them'. Theory should be judged according to how helpful it is when one uses it to try to understand past economic experience and to predict future occurrences, and especially, by whether it leads to new insights as the process of further inquiry proceeds.

In light of the fact that Friedman started with such unusual notions, it is not surprising that when he came to formulating his ideas in the famous essay 'Positive economics' he should have come up with results that startled the profession, provoking equally the defenders of orthodoxy and its heterodox critics. The fact that he did not very effectively communicate his ideas in the essay makes it even more difficult to understand a message which, even if very clearly presented, would have been difficult to come to grips with by economists whose way of thinking followed to a large extent the rationale that John Stuart Mill formulated in his *Logic*.[20] Mill's *Logic* will occupy us in Chapter 5, Dewey's in Chapter 6. First, however, we look briefly at the views of another of Friedman's teachers, one who was quite orthodox but whose views on methodology at first glance look rather close to Friedman's.

VINER'S VIEWS ON METHODOLOGY IN RELATION TO FRIEDMAN'S

We said that few if any economists have held the kind of methodological position that Friedman does. A possible exception is Jacob Viner, Friedman's teacher at Chicago, to whom he has expressed a great debt.[21] We say the *possible* exception because Viner's views on methodology are not at all easy to determine. Most of what Viner had to say directly is contained in an essay on methodology that he published as a very young man (1917). There is the question whether the views there expressed are entirely representative of the ones he later held. Further, the views in this early piece are not very clearly expressed; the more carefully one reads the essay the more ambiguous it becomes. There are later references but these give a very different impression. Fortunately for our purposes we need not try to derive a definitive interpretation of Viner's views. Our purpose is to use Viner, as we did Mitchell, to help shed light on Friedman's position and for that purpose the evidence that is available is probably adequate. It turns out that Viner is more helpful by way of contrast rather than agreement.

Viner's early essay

Beginning with the early essay (1917), we note that if one does not read the work very carefully one gets the impression that Viner's views and Friedman's just about coincide. Its main purpose is to criticize very severely John Stuart Mill's views – much more so than Mitchell did, for example – and to argue that induction should be given a larger role than Mill allows. [22] This surely is in the same spirit as that which characterizes Friedman's work. And Viner goes on to make specific points which sound very Friedman-like.

One point he makes is that the great economists got their results primarily through 'inductive inference from observation' (1917, p. 248). This, as we saw, looks close to the position that Friedman holds, which is one of the elements which contributes to making his views so unusual. Viner goes on to criticize Mill for the view that verification is not a part of science and points out that this eliminates from economic science an area in which induction plays a very large role. As a further part of this argument Viner suggests that the way to find out about economic phenomena is to look and see rather than to introspect. As he puts it (*ibid*. p. 250):

> In order to learn how men act in a given situation, or how a change in the situation will modify their behavior, it is surely more practical to observe their behavior than to attempt to discover by introspection or otherwise what they might be supposed to do if actuated by a certain motive operating alone.

Explaining further why he felt that less attention should be paid to introspection Viner tells us (*ibid*. p. 250):

> The modern trend in psychology is decidedly away from introspection and the attempt to explain behavior by rational motives revealed by introspection. The psychologist looks rather to the systematic observation of

behavior as the source of psychological generalizations, and uses the inductive method – experimental only in part – as a means of obtaining his general principles. The part which consciousness plays cannot be so revealed, of course, and here the method of inference from specific observation fails, but the economist as such is only concerned with the external aspects of human psychology, and can well afford to leave the analysis of motives to the speculative psychologist. The bonds which tie political economy to an out-of-date rational hedonistic psychology and its appropriate logical method of investigation are not indissoluble.

This point is highly significant because, as we tried to show (see also Chapter 5), faith in introspection is undoubtedly a major reason that methodologists argue on the basis of 'realistic' assumptions, which Friedman was opposed to, rather than from observed implications to premises as Friedman recommended. As the quote from Viner suggests, the link between reliance on introspection and reasoning on the basis of 'realistic' assumptions (that is, method) is very strong.

Another point that Viner makes and which make his views appear to be like Friedman's is that Mill had underestimated the importance of the method of concomitant variation (or correlation) for economics. This method is very useful for trying to uncover meaningful relationships when working with large amounts of data, and it is for this reason that we say that the point is in line with Friedman's position. It is when 'The theorist starts with some set of observed and related facts, *as full and comprehensive as possible*' that this method comes into its own. Note that the points that have been made so far are related, that they seem to be part of a general orientation, and that this orientation seems to have a lot in common with Friedman's.

So close do Friedman's methodological views seem to Viner's that unless one looks very closely one is tempted to conclude that all that Friedman did was to follow his illustrious teacher. But to do so would involve overlooking some subtle but very important differences. Thus while Viner wanted to shrink the role of introspection, the context was his reading of Mill whom he took to be arguing that introspection was the *only* source of data for the economist. Having attacked this extreme view Viner ends up saying that the data of the economist are not 'entirely' or 'even predominantly obtained by introspection' (*ibid.* p. 260). But this is a long way from dethroning introspection. The significance of Viner's criticism of Mill for ruling verification out of science should also be questioned. Granted, Mill is vulnerable on this point. Yet there is no question that Mill believed that verification was important and that the way to verify was to use induction. What the disagreement amounts to therefore is whether to call this aspect of research 'scientific', a not very substantive issue in this context.

Returning to Viner's recommendations about using the method of concomitant variation or correlation, note that he tells us that when using this method we need to use 'keen insight' or 'direct knowledge' in order to distinguish true (or 'necessary') relationships from spurious ones (1917, p. 257). Viner does not tell us what he means by 'keen insight' or 'direct knowledge'. The most likely sense of 'direct knowledge' is introspective knowledge about the assumptions of the theoretical explanation one gives for the 'necessity' of a relationship; and of 'keen insight', that the correlations 'make sense'; hence, that the reason we give for the belief that a relationship is a necessary one is that it be plausible. We suggest these meanings because they are commonly held beliefs about correlations and because it is difficult to conceive of any other way to interpret Viner's terms. In any case this view is very different from Friedman's. Unlike Viner, Friedman does not refer to relationships as 'necessary', and it is not hard to see why. In the abductive process which is basic in his approach the appeal is to the evidence of implications. So long as one feels that one must *prove* the necessity of the relationships one uncovers, one cannot possibly hold Friedman's going-beyond-the-data point of view (see p. 50–1). A major reason Mill rejected this position, as we show in Chapter 5, is that he insisted on proving the 'necessity' of relationships.

That in Viner's view assumptions had to be 'realistic' seems reasonably clear from other things that he says in his 1917 essay. Thus in one place Viner tells us (*ibid*. p. 237) that 'Unless a science is wholly abstract or hypothetical, it must therefore rely on inductive inferences for its fundamental general propositions ...' The reason this was necessary, it would seem, was that otherwise the assumptions would not be known to be 'realistic'.[23] And in talking about the derivation of the 'postulates' of classical political economy, he argues that they were derived directly via induction. He adds that they are not hypothetical but real.[24] All of this would seem to suggest that basically Viner is accepting the traditional methodological position (properly interpreted and stripped of Mill's extreme statement about science not involving verification) and not at all accepting the heterodox position favored by Friedman. Viner, like Senior before him (see Senior, 1966 [1852] Lecture IV) was reacting to Mill's notion that the premises of political economy are 'hypothetical', misinterpreting this term to mean unreal or unsubstantiated. He therefore emphasized that the premises must be derived 'inductively'. In fact then Viner's position is further from Friedman's than is Mill's.

Remarks about quantitative economics

Eleven years after publishing the methodology piece Viner appeared as discussant at an AEA session to discuss quantitative economics. The general impression one gets from his remarks is very different from that arising out of a reading of the earlier essay. Viner appears almost to be under attack and the tone of his remarks is very defensive.[25] Whereas in the earlier comments he had talked about 'more scientific and productive methods' than Mill's (1917, p. 252), he now advises (1928, p. 42) that 'methodological analogies from physics should not be applied to economics as a whole without the most serious qualifications and reservations'. Without naming names he is devastatingly critical of 'American exponents of new methods, including the quantitative method . . .' (*ibid.* p. 42). He argues (*ibid.* p. 44) that 'There is an important distinction between statistical enumeration, classification, compilation, on the one hand, and economic analysis on the other.' And he urges us not to blur this distinction. But he agrees that theorists should be trained in statistical techniques and foresees an important contribution being made by such people. Thus (*ibid.* p. 49):

> The great achievement of the future in general economic theory, and one which American statistical economists who are also masters of the old techniques seem to me most likely to attain, will be by lessening the generality of the mathematical economics [of the Lausanne school] and widening that of neoclassical [Marshallian] economics to bring these into a harmony of such a character as to make the new product susceptible in some degree of statistical verification and of concrete applications.

It looks very much as if Viner is here pointing to input–output and not Friedman and Schwartz' *Monetary History* (1963 a).

In what looks like a sort of summing up Viner observes (*ibid.* p. 45):

> Where the mind unaided by statistical analysis sees complexity everywhere, and statistical analysis unaided by the mind finds beautiful simplicity, I am reactionary enough to place my faith in the intelligence of my predecessors.

It is likely that Viner's 'statistical analysis unaided by mind' is a reference to Mill's 'practical man' (see Chapter 5) – though it could as well be Mitchell – and the one who sees 'complexity everywhere' is Nassau Senior, or one who can generate an infinity of patterns by playing with the lens. 'The intelligence of my predecessors' seems to refer to teachings not very different from those of John Stuart Mill. Viner may have been inclined to give observation a more important role than do many other economists, but for the rest his position seems to be solidly traditional.[26]

Later comments

In later work, as in the earlier, Viner's pleas that work in economics has links with reality in some places sound startlingly like Friedman's phrases, as when he tells us (1955, p. 107):

It is only for the universe of discourse in which economic theory is primarily an area of intellectual play that the criteria of 'good' theory are primarily 'demonstration,' 'rigor,' and 'elegance.'

But for the most part the main substance of Viner's remarks is quite different from Friedman's. Such, for example, is Viner's response to Schumpeter's suggestion (1954, p. 1031) that it is proper for economists to operate with 'unrealistic' assumptions because physicists do, where he questions whether what is right for physics is in this respect necessarily right for economics (1954, p. 896). He responds the same way in another place (1955, pp. 104–5) to a related suggestion. He tells us:

Much of the achievement of the natural sciences, I am told, has consisted in the discovery of stable empirical regularities in advance of the discovery of intellectually satisfying theoretical explanations for them, and the empirical regularities have in most cases proved more enduring than theories that purported to account for them.

While admitting that:

If we relied on analogy, the same experience could be anticipated for economics, and some of the members of our discipline who most concern themselves about its claims to recognition as a 'science' tend to work this analogy hard.

Viner refuses to go along with this. He tells us:

The social order is in these respects [with regard to changeableness] different in kind, or different to so high a degree as for most practical purposes to be equivalent to difference in kind, from the physical or even from the biological order of nature

Viner may have interpreted the phrase 'stable empirical regularities' to mean universal constants and this may well be part of the reason he responds the way he does. It is very likely that Friedman and Mitchell would have agreed with him on this point. But this is not the whole story, because Viner uses these statements as part of an argument leading to a comment (p. 106) that one should 'use statistics as a drunkard uses a lamp-post, for support rather than illumination'. He adds to this that 'The usefulness and indeed essentiality of empirical research, including systematic statistical research . . . is not an issue'. But this assent is given only on the condition that empirical research is 'carried out *in subordination* to abstract theorizing' (emphasis added). Within this context what sense is there in Friedman's need-to-go-beyond-the-data view on assumptions (see pp. 50–1 above)? If it is theorizing alone that yields illumination and empirical research is the handmaiden, as Viner (and Mill) suggest, if one *starts* with theorizing and calls in the empirical worker only after the theoretical structure is more or less set, then the assumptions of theory *must be* 'realistic' – meaning *either* plausible *or* supported with evidence – for otherwise the process simply does not make sense. Viner apparently agreed with this and therefore had little use for 'unrealistic' assumptions (see, for example his publication of 1940). It is the abductive process which gives meaning to Friedman's position. To get useful theory one must go beyond the data. Nonetheless, as we showed in the last chapter and will argue further in what follows, observation is an *equal* partner with theorizing, and while the researcher ideally should have all the best theoretical knowledge always available while he investigates in the Deweyan manner, when he starts the investigation it is *observation* which comes to the forefront. Mill rejected such a notion and so does Viner. Therefore to both of them it would follow that Friedman's approach merits Samuelson's 'F-Twist' characterization (Samuelson, 1963).

As a final example we cite Viner's question about the 'adequacy [of classical international trade theory] as a [general][27] theory to guide policy in the present-day world' (1955, p. 100). Viner begins by pointing out (p. 124):

> Superficially at least [the fundamental assumptions on which the classical theory rested] seem radically different from the actual conditions under which international trade is carried out today.

He goes on to note that the fundamental question then becomes:

> Is the classical theory sufficiently elastic to be able to withstand, perhaps with some minor amendment, this apparent change in the nature of the world it purports to describe?

Viner concedes that 'we should expect [theories] to have some give in their assumptions'. But he adds:

> ... there must be a limit somewhere. A theory elastic enough to withstand any degree of subversion of its premises must be a theory so good in general that it is not much good for anything specific.

He winds up mourning the obsolescence of the theory. In all of this there is reference neither to judging the adequacy of assumptions on the basis of how well the theory predicts nor to whether the theory might lead to a growth of knowledge – Friedman's criteria.[28]

Viner's views compared to Friedman's

The overall impression we get from reading Viner is that he was essentially a methodological conservative.[29,30] In many ways, of course, Friedman is a conservative too. Like Marshall (and Viner) he wants to conserve the theoretical framework (or paradigm) he has inherited and not change it until the evidence is clear beyond a reasonable doubt that it has to be changed.[31] But in the area of methodology, in arguing his peculiar 'realism'-of-assumptions thesis, as in his general methodological approach, he is a revolutionary. It is a revolution of which Viner would not have approved. Of course Mitchell might not have approved either. But note that the reasons for their disagreement would have been different. Viner might have disapproved, because Friedman strayed too far from traditional moorings.[32] Mitchell, had he disapproved,[33] would have done so because Friedman's position is not empirical enough and in this respect was therefore altogether too much like the traditional one.[34] These departures from both his teachers help show up what is most distinctive about Friedman's position.

NOTES

1. Every economist is unorthodox in some ways and orthodox in others. There is no problem, however, where the proportions are either very uneven or the heterodoxy is of a familiar kind. Friedman's is of an unfamiliar kind and, while as an economist he certainly is more orthodox than heterodox overall, in the area of methodology he is decidedly heterodox.
2. One reason Friedman's position presents problems is that one expects that an economist who is orthodox would defend economic theory in an orthodox way. There is, of course, no logical necessity for such consistency. To see the coherence in Friedman's position it helps to see it in the context of an established heterodoxy.
3. A number of commentators have referred to Mitchell when talking about Friedman − Wood (1981), Hammond (1987a, 1987b), Breit and Ransom (1982), Frazer and Boland (1983) − but they have done very little to show how Mitchell might help us to understand Friedman's position.
4. Burns also emphasizes this aspect of the National Bureau program. For example, he tells us (1948): 'This process of constructing an analytic framework, seeking out observations, processing them, reshaping the framework, seeking out new observations, and so on, is the continuous and well-tried method of science'.
5. Friedman of course, had a different view of the *substance* of Fisher's work than Mitchell did. But he could no more be in agreement with Fisher's *methodology* than Mitchell was without being inconsistent.
6. More recently M. Foucault (1974) has argued for an archeological approach. Foucault is concerned with the way people communicate − not in how they behave in their economic dealings − but his purpose, like Mitchell's, is to allow observation to contribute to understanding the details of behavior, rather than feeling constrained, as Mill suggests that one should be (see Chapter 5, below), to fit the facts into predetermined conceptions about 'human nature'.
7. 'Language' could be useful without enabling us to discover reliable regularities since it could help us to avoid inconsistency. Thus, one who has a good 'language' and does no more than the casual or everyday kind of

observation would be a better guide, *ceteris paribus*, than one who does not have this 'language'. The *ceteris paribus* is necessary because if it is possible to derive knowledge about regularities in social, as in physical science, the role of 'language' may well shrink in importance.

8. In arguing that one cannot in economics reason from effects to causes as one does in the physical sciences Mill in effect destroyed his professed unity of science thesis. He was able to slur over this by arguing that introspection was an *empirical* process. If we reject this contention then Mill's moral sciences, like Aristotelian science generally, are seen to rest in a fundamental way on everyday or common-sense knowledge. It will be shown in Chapters 5 and 6, below, that Mill's logic of the physical sciences also contributes to hiding this facet of Millian (and traditional) economic methodology. Thus Hollander offers a 'language' interpretation because he finds no (universal) causal laws in Mill's logic of economics. (See below, Chapter 5.)

9. Compare with Friedman's comments on Christ's paper noted in the last chapter.

10. We say this because if Friedman believed, as we showed in the passage just quoted, that 'it is necessary first to examine the phenomena themselves, to describe them, and to find empirical regularities', and he accepted Marshallian theory, then he must believe that this theory had gone through the same process.

11. Georgescu-Rogen (1966, p. 103–4) in response to this passage pointed out that its effect was to wipe out abstraction. Like Friedman he takes for granted that the 'unrealism' of such abstraction is not a problem.

12. See Friedman's much later remarks (in Kitch, 1983, pp. 171–2), where he contrasts his own approach with that of Mitchell and the institutionalists. His point is essentially the same one as he had made much earlier.

13. See Burns' essay in Burns, 1952.

14. As we pointed out in the last chapter, this was a process which Peirce referred to as 'abduction'.

15. The reason we say that it was his 'hunch' is shown in Chapter 4.

16. James D. Black (1928), at an AEA session attended by Mitchell, suggested that Mitchell had done harm by saying that the newer quantitative workers will not take the trouble to refute old results but will merely ignore them.

17. In later years Friedman could have pointed to the results of his own research in support of his position but oddly enough, he never has.

18. Rather surprisingly here Dewey seems to accept Mill's notion that introspection is an inductive process. He does not do so elsewhere (see Chapter 6, below); nor do Mitchell or Friedman.

19. We do not mean to imply that Friedman had studied, or was even acquainted with, Dewey's logic. Our point is that the thinking revealed by Friedman in this respect – and as we show elsewhere, in many others – is close to that which Dewey explains and defends.

20. As will be shown in Chapters 5 and 6 below, Popperian logic, as interpreted by economists, which has become so popular in recent years, is in some respects similar to Mill's, so that it is unnecessary to stop to argue whether it was really Mill's logic or Popper's which accounts for the challenge that Friedman's point of view presents to the average economist (and philosopher too for that matter).

21. See for example, Friedman (1972*d*, pp. 939–41), Breit and Ransom (1982, p. 226 n. 3), Kitch (1983, p. 211).

22. See Mitchell (1949).

23. 'Realistic' in this instance means 'true'. As we saw in the last chapter, Friedman felt that if one had convincing evidence that assumptions were true this did add value to the theory, yet reasoning this way was only a second-best procedure because there was still a large chance that predictions would be off the mark since in most instances not all pertinent factors will have been taken into account. Classical economics (e.g. Cairnes, 1875, pp. 39–47) recognized this difficulty but felt that reliance on 'realistic' assumptions (meaning by this either plausible or true ones) was still the wiser course.

24. Viner also says (1917, p. 259): 'The premises of a deductive inference may be verified by specific inspection of some of the instances covered by those premises.' But this appears at the end of the article, where a long list of examples is given, this being one of them, to illustrate that 'the methods of induction and of deduction are co-essential to any science dealing with concrete facts'. In the body of the article, where his main thesis is developed, Viner argues for 'concrete' premises derived directly via induction.

25. Perhaps the reason for this was that Mitchell, who on occasion speculated about the 'older' methods (in which Viner placed his main trust) eventually fading out, was on the same program. At this session, however, Mitchell was very conciliatory.

26. Especially if he continued to hold the views earlier expressed, that assumptions be derived inductively. But as far as we are aware neither Viner nor Senior asked for specific inductive evidence to support the traditional notions about behavior.

27. Viner tells us: 'By "general theory" I meant a comprehensive theory that embraces all the variables recognized as having major significance, which tries to account for all identified and significant mutual interrelations, and dependencies of these variables, which operates with considerable degree of analytic rigor, and which reaches conclusions that, if true, would be of some consequence.'

28. As part of an answer to Edgeworth's remark that the absence of perfect competition would put the theorist out of business, Viner remarks (p. 104): 'An empirical theory may seem absurd in the light of an abstract theory, but the embarrassment is for the abstract theorist, not for the empiricist, if the empirical theory works.' It is difficult to understand how this sudden burst of instrumentalism fits with the more consistent components of Viner's methodology. Standing alone unrelated, and coming just before Viner's argument that economics cannot be as empirical a science as its physical and biological relatives, it looks as if Viner is merely considering a hypothetical possibility whose probability he considers to be close to zero.

29. Our conclusion is not inconsistent with Friedman's comment in a letter: 'without question one of the greatest intellectual experiences of my life was the first-quarter course in economic theory with Jacob Viner. This opened my eyes to a world I had not realized existed. I was made aware of both the beauty and the power of formal economic theory' (quoted in Breit and Ransom, 1982, p. 226, n. 1). Viner's strong inductive bent coupled with his great enthusiasm for the classical tradition and his skill in using economic theory to shed light on what goes on in the world were obviously very attractive. But it does not follow from this that Friedman followed Viner in *methodology*. As we have tried to show, there is little evidence that he did and quite a bit that he did not.

30. It is difficult to avoid the impression that Friedman was one of the chief targets of Viner's methodological criticism, as also were Mitchell and other members of the NBER. It should be added that other than his dissertation (1924), which he referred to as a verification of theory, Viner did not do any extensive empirical investigations. On the basis of his expressed views on methodology, it is not difficult to see why.

31. For an interesting examination of this tendency among Chicago economists see Reder (1982).

32. The traditional mooring was John Stuart Mill's logic of science, not just his logic of economics. This distinction is important because on the basis of the more general logic, deriving the premises of theory inductively is recommended. For the rest, all remains the same. This is shown by the criticism directed against Friedman's methodology by Eugene Rotwein, a student of Jacob Viner's at Chicago. It is hard to find anything in Rotwein's devastating critique (1959) which is inconsistent with Viner's teachings in his published work.

33. There is some doubt on this score because, on the one hand, Mitchell wanted evidence for *everything*, and it does not appear likely that assumptions would have been considered an exception. On the other, he strongly rejected not only introspection but conventional (plausible) beliefs that were considered self-evident as well. He wanted to learn from the data *of economic activity* how people behaved. This meant reasoning back to premises from implications. Whether he would have been willing to take this last step to Friedman's version of the 'realism'-of-assumptions thesis, and go beyond the data, there is no way of knowing.

34. Perhaps Mitchell might have argued the way Leontief did (1971, p. 5): 'True advance can be achieved only through an iterative process in which improved theoretical formulation raises new empirical questions and the answers to these questions, in their turn, lead to new theoretical insights ... this ... makes untenable the admittedly convenient methodological position according to which a theorist does not need to verify directly the factual assumptions on which he chooses to base his deductive arguments, provided his empirical conclusions seem correct'. (Note that the second part of the quote does not follow at all from the first.)

3 • THE METHODOLOGY OF POSITIVE ECONOMICS: I

Every one of Friedman's works which we have considered so far was written for a special purpose: the work with Wallis to show the limitations of indifference curve analysis; the articles on Lange and Jaffé's translation of Walras' *Elements* as reviews of important recent work; the work with Savage as a theoretical contribution; the Marshallian demand curve article as a contribution to Marshall interpretation; the comments on Carl Christ's testing were made in the role of assigned discussant at a meeting. Friedman's interest in certain issues of economic methodology no doubt had a lot to do with his undertaking at least some of these assignments, but none of the contributions concern themselves *primarily* with economic methodology *per se*. The methodology comments are secondary to the main business at hand; it is apparent that the methodological ideas were generated in the process of doing economics.

'The methodology of positive economics' ('Positive economics') is different from the earlier work in two important respects. First, 'Positive economics' is more ambitious. One of the things Friedman tried to do was to show that the type of criticism commonly levelled against neoclassical economics, of which samples were appearing at the time in the *American Economic Review*, was invalid.[1] He also tried to show that some developments that had occurred in economics in relatively recent times were not very constructive. All of this involved methodology and Friedman shapes the discussion, as in earlier contributions, so as to make it possible to highlight substantive issues. Both subjects − methodology and neoclassical economics − are very broad, so that even if Friedman had tried to do no more in 'Positive economics' than invalidate the criticisms, it would have been more difficult for him to make his points as well as he had in the earlier work.[2] But in addition, as the title shows, Friedman had another still broader purpose in view. This was new. He wanted to present a *general* position on the methodology of economics; all of which adds up to quite an agenda for a comparatively brief paper. Even if the author had taken a great deal of time to formulate his ideas carefully, which it is clear he had not done, and even if his ideas were less original, the paper would not have been easy to understand, particularly for a reader unfamiliar with the earlier work. The bewilderment which 'Positive economics' has elicited comes as no surprise once one recognizes how great was the potential for misunderstanding.

The crowding of topics creates one set of problems: none of the themes of 'Positive economics' is developed very fully. The general context creates another. It is not obvious to the casual reader who comes directly to this piece that the ideas presented are those of an economist who came upon them in the process of doing economics.[3] Yet it was now possible to see Friedman in the role of philosopher of science, with the result that he became a target for broadly philosophical criticisms.[4] Then, too, the broader context tempted Friedman into areas where he was not an expert, and this dilutes the force of his argument. Thus his examples from physics and botany have caused a great deal of confusion to those who read them as contributions to the philosophy of science.[5] Because they do not enlighten we will ignore them here.[6] Further, Friedman drags in notions and phrases from philosophy of science, here and there, and this creates additional difficulties. One can find evidence that Friedman is a logical positivist,[7] a Popperian falsificationist,[8] an instrumentalist,[9] and so on.[10] Some of these imported notions not only mislead with regard to Friedman's general philosophical orientation, they appear also to contradict some of his most important methodological insights. The borrowings, then, are not very helpful.

Recognizing that there are difficulties, what is the best way to proceed? It is our view that 'Positive economics' can best be understood in relation to the earlier methodology statements which we considered in the first chapter. When making those remarks Friedman generally took more time to develop specific points, and he seems not to have been concerned with how his formulations related to the prevailing views in the philosophy of science. Not surprisingly, his meaning is easier to grasp in the earlier work.[11] Because of this, as a point of departure in the next section, we compare some of the earlier methodological statements with certain formulations of 'Positive economics' and note in what ways knowing the former helps resolve some problems in interpreting the latter. In later sections we deal with additional problems which are encountered in trying to understand 'Positive economics'.

'POSITIVE ECONOMICS' IN RELATION TO THE EARLIER ARTICLES

The pattern in the earlier work

There is a pattern in the arguments that Friedman and his collaborators develop in all of the work we considered in the first chapter. First, they are quite specific about the objective they are concerned with. In the indifference curve article it is 'predicting the effect of changes in economic conditions on the consumption of various commodities and services' (1942*a*, in 1953*e*, p. 188). In the article on Lange it is the derivation of theory which has 'the ability to deduce facts that have not yet been observed, that are capable of being contradicted by observation, and that subsequent observation does not contradict' (1946*b*, p. 300). In 'The utility analysis of choices involving risk' it is 'to suggest that an important class of reactions of individuals to risk can be rationalized by a rather simple extension of orthodox utility analysis', where the rationalization or hypothesis is such that it has 'implications for behavior, in addition to those used in deriving it, that are capable of being contradicted by observable data' (1948*c* in Boulding and Stigler, 1952, pp. 57 and 96). In the article on the Marshallian demand curve the purpose is to devise an interpretation of Marshall's demand curve that 'is more useful for the analysis of most economic problems' (1949*c* in 1953*e*, p. 48), and more generally, to show that this interpretation gives us theory which has greater value 'in explaining facts, in predicting the consequences of changes in the economic environment' (*ibid*. p. 91). [12] In his comment on Carl Christ's work, the objective is to 'develop a theory of economic change that does abstract essential elements in the process and does yield valid predictions' (1951*a*, p. 112). In the review of Walras it is to show that 'We need the right kind of language [in economics]; we also need something to say'. The objective noted in the invited comment on methodology in the AEA volume *A Survey of Contemporary Economics* is 'theories or hypotheses that have implications about important phenomena susceptible of contradiction through observation' (1952*c*, p. 457).

Second, Friedman and his collaborators are very explicit about how the objectives postulated could *not* be achieved. In the indifference function article we are told that one cannot succeed in using indifference curve analysis to illuminate actual budget data. In the Lange article Friedman tells us that we will not achieve the objective by formulating very general theories which suggest myriad hypothetical possibilities, enough of which are then eliminated as implausible till we are left with some acceptable result. In the risk article, the wrong procedure is to insist that all acceptable theory has plausible premises or assumptions. In the Marshall article it is striving to derive theory which, above all, is highly abstract, very general, and mathematically elegant, as in the standard approach to consumer demand theory. [13] In the comment on Christ what is mistaken is the attempt to write down the structure of the whole economy before having detailed knowledge about the interrelationships within sectors of the economy. In the Walras review it is focusing entirely on the 'language' aspects of theory. In the *Contemporary Economics* volume it is theorizing in the abstract or collecting a great deal of data that merely describes what goes on.

Third, Friedman and his collaborators are explicit about the means they think must be used to *actually achieve* the postulated objective in each case. In the indifference curve article it is 'by concentrating some heavy theoretical artillery on the logical structure implicit in practical work' (1942*a*, p. 189). In the Lange article, as in the Walras review (1955*e*, n. 6), it is 'that the theorist starts with some set of observed and related facts, as full and comprehensive as possible . . .' (1946*b* in 1953*e*, p. 282). In the risk article it is to try to account for observed empirical regularities, even on the basis of theory which rests on premises which at first glance appear to be implausible, and to keep testing the implications of such theory to determine whether it continues to be helpful. In the Marshallian demand curve article it is to follow Marshall and try to derive the kind of theory which he did. In the Christ comment it is to derive detailed knowledge about the relationships in particular sectors of the economy. Only in the *Contemporary Economics* discussion is this last component lacking, a result of the very general nature of this comment.

The objectives of economic inquiry

Still looking at work Friedman did before 'Positive economics', we note that in a number of places he and his collaborators observe that there are other worthy objectives in economic science than those they postulate.[14] Thus, in the very early article on indifference curve analysis Friedman and Wallis, while arguing that this analysis cannot achieve the objective they postulate, concede (1942*a*, p. 176) that:

> The indifference function has proved fruitful in theoretical economics because it states premises about consumer choices that materially facil-itates the correct deduction of rather intricate conclusions. Thus, it has improved our understanding of competitive and complementary relations among goods and of interrelated effects of prices and income on quantities purchased, and it has led to important substantive results in the economics of welfare and in the theory of index numbers.

In the discussion in *Contemporary Economics*, written just before 'Positive economics' was published, Friedman expresses the view (1952*c*, p. 457) that 'these tendencies [of separate high theorizing and close observation] have produced real and valuable improvements in the formal "language" available for describing economic interrelationships and in the detailed knowledge of the phenomena to be explained by economic theory'. And he goes on to talk about 'the *equally* vital intermediate area' which he champions (emphasis added). In the Walras review Friedman argues that creating a good 'language' is a very important aspect of economic theorizing though not the whole of it. From such statements one does not get the impression that Friedman was trying to *narrow* the way economics is studied but rather that he was trying to *widen* it by adding a new dimension, the 'intermediate area'.

The rationale of the Friedman–Savage article

Since the matter of the 'realism' of assumptions has become such an important issue among critics of 'Positive economics', it is worthwhile to look more closely once again at the one article where Friedman presents the same thesis in a narrower context, the Friedman–Savage contribution on choice under uncertainty. What Friedman does, first, as we saw in Chapter 1, is to develop a hypothesis on the basis of certain observations. This is not quite consistent with the recommendation in the Lange article that one start with observations 'as full and comprehensive as possible' (1946b in 1953e, p. 64). Yet empirical observation is taken as a point of departure for his theorizing, not conjecture about motives, and after formulating his hypothesis he notes that this hypothesis can and should be subject to extensive tests. Friedman lays out what he considers to be the appropriate process of inquiry and it is the same process he has talked about elsewhere. It is only after he has derived a hypothesis which was consistent with known facts, and which he tells us must be tested with further data — that is, in the context of a particular view of the inquiry process — that he turns to defend this hypothesis whose premises do not appear to be plausible. He does *not* argue for a hypothesis pulled out of the air, or one that is somehow given within a static concept of inquiry. Further, after deriving a theory with assumptions which do not appear at once as plausible, he goes on to argue that if one shifts one's focus somewhat, what appeared at first as improbable becomes plausible. The rationale in all of this, as we have seen in Chapter 1, rests on the belief that plausibility at any moment is a function of past discoveries. Rather than allowing past discoveries to keep us locked into unchanging conceptions of plausibility, Friedman implies, we should allow new discoveries to revise our conceptions. Thus, in this article Friedman gives us the whole picture of the inquiry process as he sees it, from the facts to be explained to the reorientation of notions about what is plausible.

The concept of methodology

These observations about the Friedman–Savage article on risk point up another important characteristic of Friedman's position. Friedman has quite a bit to say about 'methodology' in this piece, but it is not 'methodology' as it has generally been conceived by philosophers of science and economic methodologists who have followed their teachings. Thus, Fritz Machlup, quoting from Karl Popper, the philosopher who probably has had more influence in economics in recent times than any other, tells us that a distinction has to be made 'between the *psychology of knowledge*, which deals with empirical facts [sometimes referred to as the context of discovery], and the *logic* [or methodology] *of knowledge* which is concerned only with logical relations' [sometimes referred to as the context of justification] (Machlup, 1978, p. 54). It should be evident from what has been said that there is no such sharp distinction in Friedman's view. Friedman's conception is much broader than Popper's or Machlup's, and closer to that of John Dewey (1938), to whom logic or methodology is a *theory of inquiry*, which *does* concern itself with facts − the facts about inquiry − and which hypothesizes about what *procedures* hold the greatest promise for solving the particular problems that one brings to an investigation. [15]

Similarities and differences

When one turns from Friedman's earlier work to 'Positive economics' one finds some familiar ideas. Thus, at the very outset Friedman tells us that the task of positive economics is 'to provide a system of generalizations that can be used to make correct predictions about the consequences of any change in circumstances' (1953e, p. 4). The only new element is the name given to this, 'positive' economics. Very prominent in 'Positive economics' is the argument that 'realistic' assumptions are neither necessary nor sufficient for theory to be considered adequate. Repeated, too, are Friedman's ideas about the inquiry process. Friedman tells us (pp. 12–13):

> Full and comprehensive evidence on the phenomena to be generalized or 'explained' by a hypothesis, besides its obvious value in suggesting new hypotheses, is needed to assure that a hypothesis explains what it sets out to explain − that its implications for such phenomena are not contradicted in advance by experience that has already been observed. Given that the hypothesis is consistent with the evidence at hand, its further testing involves deducing from it new facts capable of being observed but not previously known and checking these deduced facts against additional empirical evidence.

Further, Friedman notes again that theory is partly a 'language' and partly 'a body of substantive hypotheses designed to abstract essential complex reality' (p. 7).

But as noted earlier, we also find a new element in 'Positive economics'. Friedman now talks *generally* about what are right and wrong views about 'positive *science*'. One result of this is that notions are introduced that in some respects appear to be inconsistent with earlier views. Thus, while admitting that theory has a role to play as 'language', Friedman adds (p. 12) that 'the usefulness of tautologies themselves ultimately depends ... on the acceptability of the substantive hypotheses that suggest the particular categories into which they organize the refractory empirical phenomena'. This sounds different from what had been said in the early indifference curve article and the Walras review where the derivation of complex implications from hypothetical premises is taken to be a legitimate end in itself. And it is different, too, from the comments in *Contemporary Economics* where, as we have seen, Friedman talked about three approaches to economics – the formal, the empirical and the in-between or predictive – and said that they were 'equal'. Now the predictive seems to be *the* only legitimate one. It does not seem to us that Friedman had changed his mind – particularly so since the Walras article appeared after 'Positive economics' – but rather that he was now more intent on arguing for *his* approach.

Another example of where the wider context creates some problems for an interpreter is in Friedman's analysis of the structure of theories in science. He tells us (p. 24):

> We can regard the hypothesis as consisting of two parts: first, a conceptual world or abstract model simpler than the 'real world' and containing only the forces that the hypothesis asserts to be important; second, a set of rules defining the class of phenomena for which the 'model' can be taken to be an adequate representation of the 'real world' and specifying the correspondence between the variables or entities in the model and observable phenomena.

This is obviously the logical empiricist (or Positivist) analysis which was popular at the time, analysis which was formulated to show the structure of theories in science (see Suppe, 1977). This group, whose views on the respective roles of logic and psychology coincided with Karl Popper's, was not interested in the *process* of inquiry; for them this fell into the realm of psychology because it dealt with facts. In Friedman's case, as we have seen, notions about how inquiry should be carried out were of major importance; even though in the closing section of 'Positive economics' he falls in with the Positivist distinction and writes as if there is not much that can be said about the process.

The theory (unobservables)-correspondence rules distinction creates a further problem because it further conflicts – so it appears – with Friedman's conception of the inquiry process. We say this because the Positivist analysis gives the impression that there are two distinct processes involved in theorizing, abstract modelling and correspondence rule formulation, where the two types of activities can be separated from one another and only come together at one point, that is, in a final act of verification. But if one takes it for granted that the abstract model and its interpretation evolve together as the process of inquiry proceeds then they are connected at every point. If one has such a conception of inquiry, as Friedman does, based both on what he has said and even more in what he has done as a positive economist, we do not see what purpose is served by dragging in the Positivist distinction. It surely suggests that Friedman agreed with the Positivists. Even more important, it has given readers the impression that his underlying methodology is that of the logical positivists (or empiricists), a view which we argue is erroneous. [16] In judging the significance of the allusion we are inclined to say that it is in the nature of excess baggage, borrowed to draw attention to the very important problem of domain – where, and how, a theory properly applies, which is one type of correspondence problem – so plainly at odds with Friedman's broad process-view of inquiry as to be really nothing more than an unfortunate borrowing. [17]

New problems in 'Positive economics'

Those problems which creep into Friedman's formulations in 'Positive economics' that we have considered so far are not too troublesome because it is enough to point to Friedman's earlier statements to straighten out the record. The wider context of 'Positive economics', however, generates other problems which cannot be so easily dealt with. Friedman now uses the term 'realism' in a number of different senses, as we show in the next section. In the third section (held over to Chapter 4), we consider why Friedman puts such heavy stress on prediction, a characteristic which led to him being called an 'instrumentalist' (while also being characterized as a Popperian). Further, in trying to defend neoclassical theory *generally* against criticism, Friedman gets into a logical difficulty and gives the impression that his methodology is a tool for its defense, perhaps even ideologically motivated. We address this in the fourth section. Finally in the last section (also in Chapter 4), we focus on Friedman's attempt to explain *why* economists in the past tended to concentrate on the 'realism' of assumptions rather than on how well the implications of theories accord with what happens, and we try to show that because he was not as knowledgeable about the history of economic methodology as he might have been, he missed an opportunity to convey clearly his own thesis, a thesis which is consistent with the way he feels that economics should be done and is revealed in much of his work as positive economist. Putting Friedman's thesis in historical perspective also reveals how his views about methodology are related to those which have been dominant in economics for most of its history.

THE MEANING OF REALISM

Going beyond the data

In the last chapter we showed that in talking about Mitchell, Friedman argued that a theory must be 'unrealistic', which we took to mean that to derive theory requires that we go beyond the data used as a point of departure in the initial stage of the inquiry process. If one could find *other* data to support one's assumptions one could fit such a procedure into the confines of traditional inductive logic, as Mill showed in discussing physical science (see Mill, 1973, III, 14, 4 and Chapter 5, below). A problem arises where introspection is rejected as evidence for behavioral postulates and it is recognized that the best, if not the only, objective evidence that one can find to support one's theory is *additional* evidence of implications.[18] Friedman developed some of the implications of this insight,[19] as we have seen, in an article co-authored by Savage and published five years before 'Positive economics'.

'Realism' as plausibility

In discussing the Friedman–Savage article on risk in the first chapter we noted that in their argument in defense of a theory with 'unrealistic' assumptions, the term 'unrealistic' was used to mean *implausible*. We showed that it is clear in that article that by 'unrealistic' the authors do not mean *false* because, after deriving a hypothesis resting on 'unrealistic' assumptions they proceed to give a 'plausible interpretation' for their initially strange-looking utility function. Obviously it would have made little sense to give a 'plausible interpretation' for propositions which the authors believed to be false. What they were arguing for was that one should not reject a theory merely because initially it looks false – that is, because it is implausible – if it does indeed account for the facts of experience one wishes to explain. That leaves open the question whether the premises or assumptions of the theory are indeed false, which they may be, a matter which we consider presently. At the moment we wish merely to remind the reader what was said in the first chapter about the usefulness of this analysis for interpreting a phrase in 'Positive economics' that has created a storm of controversy. There Friedman tells us (p. 14):

> Truly important and significant hypotheses will be found to have 'assumptions' that are wildly inaccurate descriptive representations of reality, and, in general, the more significant the theory, the more unrealistic the assumptions (in this sense).

The characterizations of the assumptions as 'wildly inaccurate *descriptive* representations of reality' (emphasis added) confuses the issue, because if the assumptions were really wildly inaccurate representations they would be false,[20] for example, if the wiggly utility curve in the Friedman–Savage risk article were descriptively inaccurate of the way people behave,[21] then the hypothesis would be false. Even though it happens to rationalize the facts we have at hand, the chances that it will account for additional facts looked at in the future is not very good.[22] Thus, in *truth*, the assumptions only *appear* to be descriptively inaccurate, just as in important theoretical innovations in the physical sciences, especially, for example, the Bohr conception of the atom, initially some assumptions *appeared* to be 'wildly inaccurate descriptive representations of reality'. Yet curved space is today taken to be an *accurate* descriptive representation even if not unproblematic. By the same token, if the wiggly utility function that Friedman had come up with had continued to give good predictions and retrodictions, we would have come to recognize that it is in fact an accurate descriptive representation. The question then is not whether premises or assumptions *are* descriptively *false*, for if they are we have a defective theory on our hands, but rather whether they appear to be false at first sight. Though Friedman couches this part of his argument in terms of assumptions being descriptively inaccurate, here, as in the risk article, it is implausibility that he has in mind.

The role of introspection

Of course, there is a difference when we deal with a behavioral science like economics, as compared with physics. Since in the behavioral sciences we deal with people like ourselves, and we have the power to introspect about our own behavior, we tend to believe that we can account for how other people behave on the basis of such 'inside' observations. We can always ask 'What would I do if I were in this position?' and by this means derive hypotheses about the way people generally behave that appear to be 'obviously' true.[23] That this process – which orthodox methodologists from Senior to Robbins have relied on very heavily – is one means of deriving knowledge about the world is undeniable. The question is how reliable such knowledge is. There is some doubt about this, so that the need to use 'outside' information would seem to be in order, as Wesley Mitchell had argued earlier. This does not mean that what introspection brings to the fore is useless and should be disregarded. By the same token, information from questionnaires can also be useful but it, too, is of dubious value. As Friedman notes (p. 31, n. 22), questionnaires

> may be extremely valuable in suggesting leads to follow in accounting for divergencies between predicted and observed results ... but they seem to

me almost entirely useless as a means of *testing* the validity of economic hypotheses.[24]

Thus, while the phrase characterizing 'unrealistic assumptions' as 'wildly inaccurate descriptive representations of reality' is unfortunate, the idea Friedman was trying to convey with this argument is both interesting and important. It represents an unorthodox way of judging theory, not on the basis of 'inside' information derived from introspection, but on the basis of 'outside' objective observation bearing on the implications of theory. We will argue in Chapter 5 that while the more orthodox logic of J. S. Mill, as it applies to economics, should not be rejected out of hand, its superiority over the pragmatic approach, which underlies Friedman's position – manifested in such shocking arguments as that theory with implausible assumptions should not be ruled out on that account – is not so obvious that Friedman's arguments can be lightly dismissed.

Realism and abstraction

In some places in 'Positive economics', as in the earlier risk article, Friedman uses the term 'unrealistic' to mean implausible; in other places in 'Positive economics' he uses this same term in other ways. In some places the term 'unrealism' is used to mean 'abstract', and here Friedman takes it for granted, as he had in the article on Mitchell considered in the last chapter, that if we are to theorize at all we need to leave things out. No one disagrees with this. What concerns Friedman is how to determine *what* to leave out. As he puts it (pp. 32–3):

> What is the criterion by which to judge whether a particular departure from realism is or is not acceptable? Why is it more 'unrealistic' in analyzing business behavior to neglect the magnitude of businessmen's costs than the color of their eyes? The obvious answer is because the first makes more difference to business behavior than the second; but there is no way of knowing that this is so simply by observing that businessmen do have costs of different magnitudes and eyes of different color. Clearly it can only be known by comparing the effect on the discrepancy between actual and predicted behavior of taking the one factor or the other into account. Even the most extreme proponents of realistic assumptions are thus necessarily driven to reject their own criterion and to accept the test by prediction when they classify alternative assumptions as more or less realistic.

In this argument Friedman overlooks that orthodox methodologists have traditionally answered the question he poses about how to abstract very differently from the one he espouses. In effect he ignores the possibility of using introspection and casual observation to determine how to abstract. If we ask ourselves why we behave the way we do in economic dealings, for example, we could answer as Mill (1967, p. 329) does that 'the materials of this knowledge [about motives] everyone can principally collect within himself . . .'

Thus, Friedman's argument about abstraction is not as trite as it has often been taken to be (e.g. Nagel, 1963). Friedman is not only arguing that we must abstract, which is obvious, but he is telling us also to abstract in the way physical scientists do and not, as economic methodologists have urged, to reason from ('true' but partial) causes to effects (in Mill's terms). What Friedman is arguing for is what we have called an 'outside' approach to studying economic behavior. In other words, his argument against rejecting theory with 'unrealistic' assumptions, in the sense that they leave things out or are abstract, and his argument considered earlier, against rejecting 'unrealistic' assumptions (in the sense of implausible), have a common source, namely *the rejection of introspection as a basis for either rejecting or validating assumptions of economic theory*. And without introspection the direct test of the behavioural assumptions becomes questionable.

Further evidence for the thesis that Friedman's is this 'outside' view is found in a number of other places in 'Positive economics'. Thus, he argues (p. 19) that a theory should not be considered false because its premises or assumptions appear to be false but rather − exactly the other way around − that assumptions can be said to be false if the implications of the theory which uses these assumptions are not borne out by the empirical evidence. This, of course, reverses the epistemic order presumed in orthodox methodology where one reasons from 'true' causes to implications; Friedman is telling us to reason from observed implications to possible premises (or causes in Mill's sense) which we tentatively believe to be true because they account for what happens.[25] Further supporting this contention is Friedman's argument in 'Positive economics' about the use of assumptions as an indirect test of theory. As he puts it (p. 28):

> . . . in the absence of other evidence, the success of the hypothesis for one purpose − in explaining one class of phenomena − gives us greater confidence than we would otherwise have that it may succeed for another purpose − in explaining another class of phenomena.

In other words, the premises of a successful theory, in this view, are taken to have truth value, but not because they are plausible or because we can show directly that they are 'true', but because evidence of successful prediction creates a presumption that the theory has some measure of truth.[26,27]

'Unrealism' and reasoning from effects to causes

This still leaves us with the question of why assumptions derived by reasoning from effects to causes (or implications to premises) should be referred to as 'unrealistic'. The reason, *particularly in economics*, is that when we reason this way we very soon wind up with unobservables and attempts to reason about them may well appear, at least to some, as implausible, or purely notional. Remember Mitchell's observation that traditional economic theory concerns itself with 'imaginary individuals coming to imaginary markets' as indeed it does. An indifference curve, and even the demand curve as a part of theory is not observable, and diminishing marginal utility is even less so. Of course if, with Mill, we conceive of introspection as an empirical process, we eliminate the need for these unobservables. Even if we do not do this it is possible for unobservables not to be troublesome because they appear plausible, as do the assumptions of utility theory to many, for example. After all, what introspection does is to give us a means of determining what is plausible. Thus, in effect, Friedman's 'abstraction' argument for 'unrealism', and his 'plausibility' argument boil down to one and the same protest – against the use of 'inside' knowledge to validate theories.

The role of abduction

The question arises whether Friedman's point of view is not an irrational one. Its rationale seems to be 'if *p* then *q*, and *q*; therefore *p*', which is, of course, impermissible in logic. Note that the rationale of orthodox economics seems to be the logic of *modus ponens*: 'if *p* then *q* and *p*, therefore *q*' (that is, truth passes forward from the premises to the implications). But first, if the behavioral assumption of economic theory is merely plausible, then the deductions we derive will also be no more than that. Second, if *q* is taken to be not only an implication but a prediction as well, then *p* must be the *whole* truth and not just part if it; for example, even if we agree that the economic motive is empirically true, deductions derived from this premise alone may not give good predictions. Third, the rationale of the orthodox approach is thus not 'if *p* then *q*', but rather the closer *p* is to the truth (and the more of the pertinent *p*s we have succeeded in discovering), the greater the chance that *q* will be a good prediction.[28] To reason this way seems reasonable, but it does not have the force of logic, as is sometimes assumed.[29] Fourth, and most importantly for grasping Friedman's view, in the pragmatic approach one does not argue 'if *p* then *q* and *q*, therefore *p*', but rather that, if *p* can account for *q*, a weak presumption in favor of the truth of *p* is made in the early stages of an investigation.[30] When in the process of further inquiry other implications are deduced and tested with other data, and false predictions (or retrodictions) are discovered, we face the question as to why our theory has ceased to function properly. If we can revise the theory so that it can now account for both sets of data, it is probable that we have eliminated some of the false premises. The rationale of the process of inquiry, where this step is taken again and again is that by the elimination of false qs we generally bring our revised theory closer to the truth. This process does not have the force of formal logic behind it but as we have just seen, neither does the deductive or a priori approach recommended by Mill.[31]

'Realism' as falseness

There is still a fourth meaning that the term 'realistic' seems to have in 'Positive economics'. We refer to Friedman's argument that where the assumption of perfect competition gives good predictions and retrodictions for the cigarette industry, we should use this assumption even though it is 'unrealistic'. Here the term 'unrealistic' obviously means *false*. This use has caused a great deal of confusion, which is not surprising. How can one reconcile this use with the others we have considered? The answer is that once again it has to do with the preference Friedman entertains for working from effects to causes and not, as traditional economic methodologists recommended, from causes to effects.

In the Millian mode one picks premises which are presumed to be 'true', for example, that there are few firms in an industry or that they produce a differentiated product, and then proceeds to reason out to implications, for example, that the demand curve for the firm in such industries will not be horizontal. When one comes to apply such analysis, it is crucial to determine whether the premise is true, for example, that there are in fact few firms in the industry being considered. If not, that is, if the premise or assumption is false, application of the analysis in this instance makes little sense. On the other hand, in the pragmatic mode, if one begins with the Marshallian theory of the firm as paradigm, as Friedman does, and where the first step is 'some set of observed and related facts, as full and comprehensive as possible', one looks for empirical regularities which can serve as a point of departure for the inquiry. (In contrast, in the Millian mode it is introspection and casual observation which serves as the point of departure.) The observation of empirical regularities shows what there is to explain. In this early stage of inquiry we might find, for example, that cigarette companies seem to act as if the demand curves for their product were horizontal in some circumstances (in responding to price controls, for example) and downward sloping in others (in determining advertising outlays, for instance), and one reports this as a matter of both practical and research interest.

What does this show? Conclusions here are not the result of reasoning out but only of observation. Moreover, they enter at a relatively early stage in the inquiry process.[32] The reasoning comes in when we ask 'why'? If we assume the existence of a horizontal demand curve for an industry with a differentiated product and few sellers, it looks as if we are working with a false assumption. It *is* false if one gives as the reason for Marshall's competitive theory giving good predictions in this instance that there are many firms in the industry. But Friedman does not argue this way. He does not take this reason as the last word on the matter since there could be other reasons, for example that businessmen in an oligopolistic industry perceive the demand curve for their product to be horizontal in some instances. What he does is to take the puzzling observation as a problem to be dealt with; he is well aware that there is the need to search for a broader theory – one that can account for even such observations. He concludes this part of his argument with the observation (p. 38):

> It would be highly desirable to have a more general theory than Marshall's, one that would cover at the same time both those cases in which differentiation of product or fewness of numbers makes an essential difference and those in which it does not. Such a theory would enable us to handle problems we now cannot and, in addition, facilitate determination of the range of circumstances under which the simpler theory can be regarded as a good enough approximation. To perform this function, the more general theory must have content and substance; it must have implications susceptible to empirical contradiction and of substantive interest and importance.

Note that Friedman is not willing to accept an unexplained correlation as an *end-product* of investigation but only as *point of departure*.

Directly improving the 'realism' of the assumptions

While the pragmatist believes that the greatest promise for deriving theories of which the premises are closer to reality, is to concentrate on trying to formulate theories, the implications of which accord with what there is to explain, he does not necessarily resist attempts to improve premises directly. It is merely that, as Friedman shows, he does not *without exception* accept as an advance any change that supposedly brings a premise closer to reality. The reasoning behind this, as Friedman shows, is something like the following. Granted that to the extent to which we can bring the premises of a theory closer to reality the theory is improved, this holds only if the new theory gives at least as good predictions with the supposedly 'better' premises as with the seemingly worse ones.[33] It is because he feels, rightly or wrongly, that this does not hold that he is critical of imperfect competition theory, as he shows in 'Positive economics'. For this reason, too, he prefers 'Marshallian' to 'Walrasian' economics (which is more complete, hence more 'correct'), as we showed in the first chapter.

The centrality of the 'realism' issue

If one cuts through the verbiage about 'realistic' assumptions, both Friedman's and his critics, and gets down to the bedrock of differences in methodological beliefs, one finds that this matter shrinks into insignificance. Almost all critics, if not all of them,[34] take 'realistic' to mean 'true'.[35] But the real question is how to gauge the extent to which the assumptions of a theory are adequate. The traditional approach is to rely on premises which are plausible, as determined by introspection and/or very casual observation. Friedman's way is to try to find premises which, under 'similar'[36] circumstances, have tended to give reasonably good predictions or retrodictions. He does not deny that the closer the premises are to the 'truth' the better the prediction will be. We do not think that there is any disagreement on *this* issue.

But having said that, we are left with two very basic problems. First, one cannot often even roughly determine by direct inspection just how close assumptions are to the 'truth'; in some areas we cannot judge at all. Second, there are generally far more factors (or 'causes') determining any outcome than can possibly be taken into account in any one theory. How is one to determine which of them can be neglected and which not? The pragmatic way of dealing with these questions is to try to find out which premises are best in particular circumstances at an early stage of inquiry by testing which give the best predictions (or have implications that are closest to what actually happens). Of course it is partly practical interests that suggest this course. To deal adequately with real problems one must be able to predict and surely retrodictive ability is a major way, if not the major one, of gauging a theory's predictive potential.[37] But it is not only practical concern that suggests this course. It is also that the pragmatist believes, as we have seen, that the inquiry process if properly carried out will tend to bring assumptions themselves closer and closer to the truth. There is no guarantee of this of course, but neither is there a guarantee that introspection and casual observation will give us 'truer' assumptions (overall) and thereby more scientific (explanatory) theory, let alone more reliable predictions.[38]

NOTES

1. See 'Positive economics' (1953e), n. 13.
2. As we have seen in the Appendix to Chapter 1, it is not easy to derive a consistent interpretation of Friedman's meaning even of the narrower articles once one goes beyond each individual piece and tries to figure out Friedman's *general* thesis.
3. Of course all readers know that Friedman is a distinguished economist so

that one might have expected that readers would try to determine what relationship there is between what Friedman did and what he said, but the evidence shows that this connection is not very readily made by critics without encouragement from the author.

4. Anyone who writes on the philosophy of economics is subject to philosophical criticism. But when the main subject of an article is an economic one and the methodology comments seem only incidental, as is the case with Friedman's work heretofore considered, these contributions are generally not taken to be worthy of one's attention, let alone seen as a basis for extended philosophical criticism. Thus, not atypically, Walters (1987, p. 424) discusses the Friedman–Savage article (1948c) without observing that there is a good bit of methodology in it. Not atypically, too, he goes on to interpret 'Positive economics' as if it were a philosophy of science tract, attributing to Friedman the general view (p. 423) that 'even if one could specify empirical correlates for the assumptions ... that is irrelevant for judging the usefulness of the theory'. (The methodology portions of the Friedman–Savage article – see above, Chapter 1 – surely raise questions about this interpretation of Friedman's position in 'Positive economics'.)

5. For example, Dennis (1986), Katouzian (1980), McLachlan and Swales (1982), Rosenberg (1976), Rotwein (1959).

6. The examples from physics and biology may best be understood by reversing the order in which one would normally consider them, that is, by considering *first* the rationale Friedman uses to argue against imperfect competition theory (discussed later in this chapter) and *then* interpreting Friedman's examples from outside economics in this context. This means, of course, that Friedman's examples from outside economics are not very helpful. It does not follow from this, however, that Friedman is wrong about economics, nor even that the rationale he favors is necessarily wrong even for his outside examples, assuming they were more carefully formulated. What Friedman was trying to show is that the observation of regularities is needed as a point of departure in the early stages of research in different areas in every science in order to guide the process of inquiry in the right direction.

7. For example, Caldwell (1982), De Alessi (1965), Helm (1984), Hollis and Nell (1975), Maki (1986), Rosenberg (1976). Rather surprisingly Caldwell has argued recently (1988b, p. 538) that 'after the publication of Friedman's famous essay, "The methodology of positive economics", various positivist doctrines became part of the official methodology of positive economics'. He adds, even more surprisingly: 'This is all the more paradoxical given that Friedman's position is closer to instrumentalism than it is to positivism'. Such paradoxes come about, it seems to us, because of the slippery nature of these terms.

8. For example, Blaug (1974), Dennis (1986), Salanti (1987).

9. For example, Boland (1979, 1980, 1982, 1983), Frazer and Boland (1983), Caldwell (1980, 1982), Helm (1984), Nagel (1963), Samuelson (1963), Seligman (1969), Stanley (1985), Webb (1987), Wong (1973).

10. Some see Friedman as taking more than one position. Frazer and Boland (1983) see Friedman as both instrumentalist *and* Popperian; Maki (1986) sees Friedman as positivist, pragmatist-conventionalist and realist; Katouzian (1980) sees Friedman as positivist, pragmatist, and instrumentalist; Hollis and Nell (1975) see Friedman as positivist and pragmatist; Latsis (1976) sees Friedman as an anti-falsification conventionalist.

11. Though the Walras review was published after 'Positive economics', we consider it with the pre-'Positive economics' writing because, as noted in Chapter 1, it has the same characteristics as the earlier pieces.

12. No reference is made in this section to 'The "welfare" effects of an income and an excise tax' (1952a) because, being an 'extended footnote' to the Marshall article, its essential features are those of the broader piece.

13. In the 'extended footnote' (1952a) Friedman further tries to show that by using logical adequacy as the only criterion in choosing theory one can easily be misled when drawing conclusions about the real world.

14. And the Walras review.

15. We examine the issues involved in these different conceptions in Chapter 6.

16. There are other reasons, of course, as Klant (1974, p. 145) shows. Since the term 'positive' is part of the title of this essay, less informed readers could be expected to be prepared to find confirmation that the author is a 'Positivist' on that ground alone. Friedman makes clear that, like J. N. Keynes, he uses the term to distinguish between 'positive' and 'normative', and no more than that. But this is easy to overlook, particularly since the normative-positive distinction is today sometimes (wrongly) taken to be a sure sign of adherence to the Vienna Positivist doctrine.

17. Part of the problem is caused not by Friedman but rather by his interpreters, some of whom seem to consider as Positivist anyone who believes that objective evidence should play an important role in judging theories. The essentialists Hollis and Nell (1975) are the extreme case of this but others sometimes go almost as far.

18. Rosenberg (1976, pp. 148–52) argues that 'economic agents are as observable as human beings are' and that 'the desires are not unobservable (at least to the persons who have them)'. The latter assumes, if we are to apply this observation to economic theory, not only that people know what their desires are, but that they know as well how their desires translate into action. Friedman, as we have seen, questioned this. Caldwell (1982, p. 177) rejects the notion that Friedman is concerned with unobservables because, in his view, Friedman does not say that assumptions are not directly testable, but rather that the 'realism' of a theory's assumptions is immaterial. If one looks at more than particular phrases surely this distinction vanishes.

19. In referring to this discovery as an 'insight' we do not, of course, mean to imply that it is necessarily the 'right' view. In matters of this sort what is 'right' must always remain an open question. But it can be said that it was an 'insight' because it clearly moved Friedman ahead in the direction in which he was trying to go.

20. Critics have pointed this out, for example Katouzian (1980, pp. 80–1), Rotwein (1959, pp. 564–5).

21. What Friedman means is that people are not necessarily aware of what they are doing or why they are doing it. But this does not make it descriptively false.

22. See, for example, Rotwein (1980, p. 1553), Melitz (1965, p. 46), Hoover (1984b). Boland seems to recognize this, too (1979, p. 513), but glosses over its significance.

23. Not surprisingly, critics of Friedman have brought in the possibility of introspection in their criticisms. See, for example, Rotwein (1973, p. 145), Coddington (1972). As Helm (1984), referring to Hicks' approach argues (p. 131): 'A principle of charity is typically invoked, whereby the reasons an

agent gives are taken to be *the* reasons for that act, unless the observer has good reason himself to think contrarily'.

24. There is a subtle but important difference between using data to test a theory on the one hand and, after it has been tested and found wanting, using data as an aid in the process of trying to determine how the theory should be revised. Data that may be useful for one purpose need not necessarily be useful for the other.

25. Piron (1962), referring to Braithwaite (1953), points out this difference in epistemic order in Friedman's approach. But he does not show the significance of this with the result that the point is easy to miss, as shown by Rotwein's reply (1962).

26. The significance of the difference between arguing on the basis of assumptions or of implications is generally overlooked. Thus Klant (1974, p. 143) argues: 'If the predictions prove to be valid we may also say that the assumptions are realistic, *or*, *the other way around*, that the validity of the predictions depends on the validity of the assumptions' (emphasis added). This gets rid of the problem by definition.

27. There are obvious difficulties here with the use of the word 'truth'; there is general agreement today that empirical generalizations cannot be proven to be true. What is generally meant when economists talk about assumptions being 'true' is either that there are no falsifying instances – this is rare – or that what is postulated sometimes happens or often happens or almost always happens. An even more common meaning historically is that the generalization will occur (often? generally? almost always?) in the absence of other causes acting at the same time.

28. See, for example, Rotwein (1959).

29. Boland (1983) points this out.

30. Hollis and Nell (1975) come close to recognizing this (p. 198) but do not see its significance.

31. The role of abduction in the pragmatic way of thinking will be examined more fully in Chapter 6.

32. McClelland (1975, p. 137) argues that while this mode of reasoning can be used legitimately, it should be used only where there is no theory with 'realistic' assumptions which gives predictions almost as good as this theory. We think that Friedman would agree, but only if by 'realistic' we mean 'backed by evidence' and not 'plausible'.

33. 'Better', of course, meaning not only that the premises are nearer to the truth, but also that we have the pertinent ones. (Note that Friedman's position here sheds some light on the 'black box' controversy referred to in Note 31 of the first chapter.)

34. Even those like Caldwell (1980, 1982) who admit that they are puzzled by Friedman's use of the term 'realism', and even suggest other possibilities for the meaning of the term, wind up taking it to mean 'true'.

35. As we saw in considering Friedman's approach to imperfect competition theory, in the early stages of research one sometimes works with notions that look false from the standpoint of an implication of a popular theory which rests on plausible assumptions. But this is only a derivative issue which results from reasoning back from observed implications rather than forward from plausible premises. It is the *former* issue which is central.

36. Friedman admits that there is vagueness in this conception of 'similarity' but expresses the view that little can be done about this (pp. 25, 26–30). The

admission of such uncertainty is consistent with his pragmatic orientation. It is anathema to the rationalist.

37. Mill agreed with this. But he felt that this had little if anything to do with the scientific standing of a theory (see below, Chapter 5).

38. Musgrave (1981) suggests that we distinguish between negligibility, domain and heuristic assumptions and offers this taxonomy as a key to understanding the ambiguities in Friedman's methodology. We do not find Musgrave's analysis very helpful for this purpose because, while it sheds light on Friedman's *non-economic* examples, these examples, as we have noted, are not at all revealing about Friedman's methodology of positive *economics*. For example, one could say that in the imperfect competition example Friedman is introducing an assumption that limits the domain because he knows that perfect competition theory often gives bad predictions when there are few sellers in an industry. But that is not the main point. His main message is that we are at an early state in the inquiry; as research progresses, the domain of the improved theory should expand and become more definite. But in Musgrave's more traditional philosophical analysis one moves in the other direction, i.e. one begins with a belief about the world such as Aristotle's observation that the quantity of money and its value move inversely. Then as exceptions are discovered one finds reasons for this which give the domain-limitation assumption of a rational theory. What Friedman is looking for is empirical knowledge about the differences as between domains so that at the same time that one extends the domain of the theory one is able to make better predictions, and make improvements in theory in a Kuhnian normal-science framework (see Chapter 1).

4 • THE METHODOLOGY OF POSITIVE ECONOMICS: II

THE ROLE OF PREDICTION AND EXPLANATION IN SCIENCE: FRIEDMAN AS INSTRUMENTALIST AND/OR POPPERIAN, OR DEWEYAN

Why does Friedman put such heavy stress on prediction? Why does he infrequently refer to explanation and when he does, put the word in inverted commas? One possible answer is that he is an 'instrumentalist'. We consider this interpretation first. We then examine the notion that he is a Popperian and, in what follows, that he is both 'instrumentalist' and Popperian. Having cleared away a good bit of underbrush, we will be in a position in the last section to deal with the question posed at the outset. In the process of trying to answer it we will discover why Friedman was so anxious to do battle with those who relied on the 'realism' of assumptions to validate theory. A glaring weakness in all interpretations that have been proposed – 'instrumentalist', Popperian or any other – is that none of them attempts to account for what is unique about Friedman's methodological stance. We will try to fill this void at the end of this section.

Evidence for the instrumentalist interpretation

If one focuses on one famous passage in 'Positive economics' it looks as if Friedman is unquestionably an instrumentalist for he tells us (pp. 8–9) that 'the *only* relevant test of the *validity* of a hypothesis is comparison of its predictions [and retrodictions] with experience' (first emphasis added). From such a statement one might easily conclude that Friedman is interested in neither truth nor explanation. The label 'instrumentalist', which Boland has pinned on him,[1] would thus seem appropriate since 'instrumentalism' 'says that theories are convenient and useful ways of (logically) generating what have turned out to be true (or successful) predictions or conclusions' (Boland, 1979, pp. 508–9). But if one is familiar with what Friedman has said elsewhere in other contexts doubts arise immediately.

Theory as 'language'

Friedman's views are more complex. Thus in 'Positive economics' (p. 7) he tells us (as he had earlier, 1949c):

> ... a theory is, in general, a complex intermixture of two elements. In part it is a 'language' designed to promote 'systematic and organized methods of reasoning'. In part it is a body of substantive hypotheses designed to abstract essential features of complex reality.

Friedman sees *two* components of theory, substantive hypotheses being only one. In the previous quote he refers only to hypotheses. And since he goes on to tell us what he considers the criteria for a good 'language' to be, he does not seem to mean that the only relevant test of a 'theory' (which includes both hypotheses and 'language') is in how well it predicts.

Yet Friedman also says that the 'language' aspects of theory are subsidiary:

> the usefulness of ... tautologies themselves ultimately depends ... on the acceptability of the substantive hypotheses that suggest the particular categories into which they organize the refractory empirical phenomena ('Positive economics', p. 12).

This seems to reinforce the notion that after all Friedman is interested only in prediction. He will theorize, if need be, but simply for the purpose of getting better predictions. The verdict that he is an instrumentalist seems to stand.[2]

The role of theory

But then why is Friedman interested in theories at all? Why not just find correlations on the basis of which one can make predictions? Some critics have come to the conclusion that Friedman is in fact primarily interested in correlations (for example, Caldwell, 1980, p. 370 and 1982, p. 175; Coddington, 1972; Blaug, 1980; Seligman, 1969; Stanley, 1985; Cyert and March, 1963; Boland, 1979), and not interested in explanation (Rotwein, 1959; Boland, 1979; Wong, 1973; Klant, 1974).[3] This follows directly from the notion that he is unconcerned about the truth of the assumptions of theory. After all, if theory with false assumptions is just as good, and prediction is the only goal, then one could always dream up assumptions that turn correlations into theories. For example, suppose we find that the prices of pickles and astrological charts have moved together for a period of time. To make a legitimate theory out of this correlation one need only formulate the assumption that merchants of astrological equipment closely watch the price of pickles and set their prices accordingly. In other words, if one is truly unconcerned about the truth of assumptions one winds up in effect relying on correlations.[4]

Friedman as Mill's naïve 'practical man'

Our examination of Friedman's use of the term 'unrealism' in the last chapter raises questions about this interpretation. Granted that Friedman feels that when very little knowledge is available, acting on the basis of correlations may be wiser than on the basis of theories for which there is little evidence.[5] But nowhere does he argue, nor even hint, that this is *generally* the case. The basis of the instrumentalist interpretation is rather the belief that by 'unrealism' Friedman *always* means 'false'. However, we saw in the last chapter that this is not the case. Further, it is not consistent with Friedman's notion of the inquiry process since the instrumentalist would need only to look for correlations so that the interactive process of observation and hypothesizing would not be necessary.

There is a yet more important reason for not accepting the 'instrumentalist' interpretation. We saw early in Chapter 1 that Friedman envisaged three approaches, where at the one end were the empiricists who produced 'detailed knowledge of the phenomena to be explained by economic theory', at the other were the formalists who produced improvements 'in the formal "language" for describing economic inter-relationships', and there was also a 'vital intermediate area' which Friedman took as his territory, 'where theories or hypotheses have implications ... susceptible of contradiction' (1952*a*). The instrument-alist interpretation puts Friedman not where he put himself but at the empiricist end.[6] In terms of traditional economic methodology (see Chapter 5), the interpretation of Friedman as instrumentalist makes him out to be a 'practical man', an investigator whose kit of tools includes only simple induction from a few instances and nothing more; one who observes correlations but is not interested in going further and asking *why* they occur (Mill, 1967, p. 324). As Nagel has observed (1963, p. 219), such a position not only removes all reason from science but denies a role to theory in the dynamic process of inquiry. Nagel pointed out that because of clumsiness of expression one might be tempted to interpret Friedman's position this way. But on the basis of 'Positive economics' *alone* Nagel concluded that to attribute such a position to Friedman would be unwarranted; in Nagel's view 'the main thesis [Friedman] is ostensibly defending is [in spite of very clumsy formulation] nonetheless sound'. There is perhaps room for disagreement with

Nagel if one judges only on the basis of this one essay. But beyond it, the evidence against the instrumentalist interpretation is also very strong, as we shall see presently.

An alternative instrumentalist interpretation

There is a broader sense in which Friedman can be said to be an 'instrumentalist'. In this view an 'instrumentalist' is one who feels that valid explanations can be derived from the empirical interactive process of reasoning and observation only and not in any other way. The non-instrumentalist, in this view, does not accept such a limitation. Coddington (1972, p. 4), for example, is critical of Friedman for 'denying that in economics, we can ever explain anything in any deep and satisfying sense, and therefore concluding that we should set ourselves the more modest task of finding generalizations which "work" (in the sense of having good predictive performance)'.[7] Just what such critics mean by phrases like 'deep and satisfying sense' is not clear.[8] But we know that some find the explanation that 'God wills it' more deep and satisfying than that the heavenly bodies can be accounted for by Newton's laws. The latter is too 'external'. In economics, it can be said one achieves more deep and satisfying explanations by extensive reasoning fitted on to plausible assumptions (see Cairnes, 1875, pp. 74–7; Robbins, 1949, p. 105).

Thus Friedman can be said to be an 'instrumentalist', if we mean by this that he does not look for 'deep and satisfying' (essentialist?) kinds of explanation but is content with finding matter-of-fact cause and effect relationships. It seems to us, however, that to use the term in this way is confusing.

The Popperian connection

Can Friedman then be said to be a Popperian? So it seems when he tells us:

> The hypothesis ... is accepted if its predictions are not contradicted; great confidence is attached to it if it has survived many opportunities for contradiction. Factual evidence can never 'prove' a hypothesis; it can only fail to disprove it, which is what we generally mean when we say, somewhat inexactly, that the hypothesis has been 'confirmed' by experience ('Positive economics', p. 9).

Such passages have led some observers to conclude that Friedman is a 'falsificationist'[9] (for example, Blaug in Latsis, 1976; Salanti, 1987).[10] Claims Friedman has made that he was influenced by Popper (see, for example, Boland, 1984) serve to strengthen this view. But *how* might

Popper have influenced him? Our view is that the best way to decide this, as noted in the introduction, is to consider what Friedman did as positive economist and to examine as well the *role* the above remark plays in the essay. We consider the former in Part II below; we will be concerned with the latter in this section.

Note, first, that the meaning and significance of falsificationist logic is somewhat different from what it is often taken to be by economists. The reason we cannot prove an empirical hypothesis to be true is that it requires us to go beyond the data and, as Hume argued, one cannot then be *certain* that one's expectations will be borne out. One cannot, in other words, prove deductively that an empirical generalization is true. This is a consequence of the logician's definition of 'truth' which leaves no room for exceptions; one falsifying instance makes the hypothesis false. Falsification, on the other hand, does not involve conjecture. When truth is defined this way, one falsifying instance is enough to show for *certain* that a hypothesis is 'false'.[11] But what does this show? In science our objective is to derive hypotheses which hold beyond a specific set of observations, and this involves taking risks, risks which we cannot avoid by substituting falsification for verification.[12] Thus, while Hume's observation, on which Popper's falsification doctrine rests, has value in showing that we must always leave some room for doubt,[13] it is counter-productive, particularly for a practical field like economics, because it leaves no basis for *any* measure of confidence in any empirical theories we might derive from our research.[14] Friedman certainly seems sensitive to this.

For one thing, he is not ready to throw out a theory on the basis of falsifying evidence. Rather, he argues that a theory is rejected only if its predictions are contradicted '"frequently" or more often than predictions from an alternative hypothesis'. He also says that one should not give up a theory until one has a better one. But once we do that we are out of the narrow Popperian realm,[15] because we have no more logical reason for accepting a hypothesis which has been falsified less frequently than for accepting one that has been verified more frequently. While paying lip service to falsification, then, Friedman obviously adheres to a position which is quite different. Even Boland (1984), who argues that Friedman was influenced by Popper, tells us (1979, p. 511) that for Friedman 'testing always means "testing for truth" (in some sense). It never means "testing in order to reject" ....' If Friedman was influenced by Popper it clearly was not in being converted to the falsificationist way of thinking.

There is further evidence in 'Positive economics' against the thesis that Friedman is a Popperian. Friedman is very explicit that specifying 'the rule for using [a] model', an essential ingredient of the process of formulating testable theory as he conceives it, is not a completely determinate affair. He observes (p. 25):

> In seeking to make a science as 'objective' as possible, our aim should be to formulate the rules explicitly in so far as possible and continually to widen the range of phenomena for which it is possible to do so. But, no matter how successful we may be in this attempt, there inevitably will remain room for judgment in applying the rules. Each occurrence has some features peculiarly its own, not covered by the explicit rules. The capacity to judge that these are or are not to be disregarded, that they should or should not affect what observable phenomena are to be identified with what entities in the model, is something that cannot be taught; it can be learned but only by experience and exposure in the 'right' scientific atmosphere, not by rote. It is at this point that the 'amateur' is separated from the 'professional' in all sciences and that the thin line is drawn which distinguishes the 'crackpot' from the scientist.

But it is just such a view on Thomas Kuhn's part which has led Popper and his followers to accuse Kuhn of 'irrationality, relativism and defence of mob rule'. Kuhn argues in defense of this kind of indeterminateness against his Popperian critics (in Lakatos and Musgrave, 1974, p. 234):

> To say that, in matters of theory-choice, the force of logic and observation cannot in principle be compelling is neither to discard logic and observation nor to suggest that there are no good reasons for favouring one theory over another. To say that trained scientists are, in such matters, the highest court of appeal is neither to defend mob rule nor to suggest that scientists could have decided to accept any theory at all.

It seems to us that, had Friedman become involved with the Popperians, as he very well might have had he responded to the critics of 'Positive economics', he might very well have used some such argument as Kuhn's.

That Friedman's way of thinking is very different from that of the falsificationists is shown in still another way.[16] We see this best when we examine in some detail what Friedman did as a positive economist. But one catches a glimpse of it in a work we have already dealt with, the joint article with Savage on risk (1948c). There, as we have seen, Friedman deals with evidence that contradicts neoclassical consumption theory. He does not take this as a falsification but rather as an opportunity for trying to extend a theory which he takes to be useful because, he feels, it gives reasonably good predictions over a broad range of economic experience. In other words, there is a lot of support for it. He therefore leaves the main lines of the theory intact, that is, he models choice under an assumption of diminishing marginal utility. But he introduces the notion of a utility function made up of two parts, both characterised by diminishing marginal utility. Tentative acceptance of this hypothesis does not necessitate rejecting Marshallian theory, only extending it. We find this same kind of rationale deployed widely in Friedman's work. There is no 'falsificationist' methodology here in the sense in which the term is generally used in economics.

Judging by what Friedman did, his conception of the role of theory looks rather more like the one held by John Dewey, [17] who argued (1916, p. 186) that theory is tested by reference to experience:

> ... not, however, as if a theory could be tested by directly comparing it with facts – an obvious impossibility – but through use in facilitating commerce with facts. It is tested as glasses are tested; things are looked at through the medium of specific meanings to see if thereby they assume a more orderly and clearer aspect, if they are less blurred and obscure. [18]

Earlier we touched on one further difference between Popper's views and Friedman's (Chapter 1). It has to do with whether the experience of past inquiry can help to formulate criteria for judging theories. Popper answers with a resounding negative as we have seen, [19] because this would involve induction which Popper rejects. Friedman feels that what has been learned from successful past inquiry can be helpful for making judgments about the potential usefulness of theories that had been derived in different ways. For example, it is on this basis that he separates Marshallians from Walrasians. [20] Though Friedman does not repeat this analysis in 'Positive economics' [21] it is clear that he had not changed his mind in the short time since he published the earlier articles. This distinction, as we showed in the first chapter, is related in an integral way to the 'realism'-of-assumptions thesis that is so central in 'Positive economics'.

The instrumentalist/Popperian paradox

Karl Popper is not only responsible for the conception of 'instrumentalism' as it is currently used, he is also its most severe critic (see, for example, Popper, 1972). As a result it comes as something of a surprise to find Friedman characterized in a recent article as *both* an instrumentalist *and* a Popperian (Frazer and Boland, 1983). How can the two be reconciled? To understand the problem involved in trying to answer this question it is necessary to recognize the role that the 'instrumentalist' plays in Popper's way of thinking.

The very austere logical Popperian world has been judged too ethereal to be related to practical everyday reality so that an *ad hoc* addition has been added to make the connection. The *ad hoc* addition is the 'instrumentalist', an inferior type like Mill's 'practical man' who serves as a link with the world of practical reality. This is necessary because of Popper's rejection of induction, which is central in Popper's view of things. This means that one takes very seriously the fact that having counted a large number of white swans or black crows one cannot be certain that all swans are white or all crows black. But it means a lot more. What philosophers such as John Stuart Mill are concerned with under the heading of 'induction' is primarily ways of distinguishing between more and less reliable sequences, both for practical purposes and for science. Mill, who was in the same tradition as Hume, was well aware that counting black crows alone is not the best way to find reliable sequences; and he tried to find more sophisticated ways (Mill, 1973, IV, 4, 2). Popper will have none of this. The observation of regularities is rejected as a basis for acceptable belief in empirical regularities in any shape or form because that does not make a good *argument*. [22] That is why in the Popperian system it is illegitimate to make any (positive) theoretical knowledge claims that have empirical reference. But this rather leaves us hanging in the air.

Were it not for the existence of regularities life could not go on. Moreover, with regularities we need a way of distinguishing the more from the less reliable ones. Popper has been forced to recognize this but the rejection of induction prevents him from somehow fitting this elementary fact into his system of thought. He himself shows this very well. He tells us (1972) that when involved in practical affairs we should choose 'the best tested theory [because it] is the one which, in light of *critical discussion*, appears to be the best so far, and I do not know anything more "rational" than a well-conducted critical discussion'. [23] But in practice we are interested in what works, and unless we can make a bridge between rationality and effectiveness, Popper's philosophy is not much help in this regard. Can such a link be made? Absolutely not, Popper tells us, because 'in spite of the "rationality" of choosing the best-tested theory as a basis of action, this choice is *not* "rational" in the sense that it is based upon *good reasons* for expecting that it will in practice be a successful choice: *there can be no good reason in this sense* . . .' (emphasis in the original). [24]

Thus useful knowledge cannot be integrated into Popper's system. That is why he is forced to go outside to postulate a special technological (or instrumental) realm to allow for the obvious fact that in everyday life a basis has to be found for making decisions, and these decisions cannot be made without a knowledge of reliable regularities. [25] The technologist in Popper's view deals with such problems. His thinking is entirely different from the scientist's. He is a crude kind of pragmatist who will do anything that 'works'; he thinks that finding what 'works' depends on induction, but induction of the crudest sort. [26] It is this kind of instrumentalism which is implicit in Frazer and Boland's claim that Friedman is a short-run instrumentalist but long-run Popperian.

Our disagreement with this scheme of things, as a framework into which to fit Friedman is, first, that there is no evidence in any of his published work, neither in what he did nor in what he said,[27] to suggest that he has any interest in *a Popperian type* of economic science. Hence, to call him a short-run 'instrumentalist' and a long-run Popperian, as Frazer and Boland do (1983), makes little sense.[28] In Boland's account (1980, pp. 166–8), a long-run Popperian is a Socratic perpetual questioner, never content with *any* answers, and never feeling the need to go beyond the immediate facts of everyday observation. It is a little difficult to envisage such a Socratic type number-crunching at the NBER. Second, Popper's (and Boland's) instrumentalism is a terribly crude position because Popper offers no way of distinguishing between a sophisticated inductivist and a very unsophisticated one. In this view technologists cannot see beyond correlations. Friedman simply does not fit into this category even in the short run. Third, there is no link whatsoever in the Popperian scheme between pure and applied science, other than the observation that the applied science might use obsolete theories because they work (Frazer and Boland, 1983, pp. 141–2). But a clear relationship between pure and applied science is necessary if we are to understand where Friedman stands.[29]

A dynamic process viewed in a static framework

We are now in a position to state why we feel that one cannot understand the rationale of Friedman's work within the static Popperian framework. Popper refuses to consider as part of the philosophy of science the *process* of inquiry, because it deals with facts. This means that in setting up criteria for judging science one is not allowed, strictly speaking, to learn from the facts of scientific investigation. This leaves Popper in the rarified domain of formal logic, where the difference between verification and falsification is a simple dichotomy and the impossibility of proving *deductively* any inductive inference – meaning that it is *certain* – completely dominates the landscape. Popper does not stay within these confines; he subtly moderates his position into a positive methodology or applied logic, as well he must to hold his audience.[30] For example, he is well aware through his very extensive knowledge of actual scientific investigation that finding one, or even more, falsifying instances often cannot sensibly be taken as the basis for rejecting a theory (see Blaug, 1974, and the references to Popper on p. 151, n. 10). And certainly he has succeeded in clarifying some very important issues.[31] But he goes beyond clarification to lay down the law, which invariably gets him into the psychology of research, as Kuhn (in Lakatos and Musgrave, 1970, pp. 235–6) shows. And the effect of this trespassing into the psychology of research[32] is to neutralize, on the one hand, the significance of his logical formulations, involving falsification, which his economist followers have found so significant;[33] yet, on the other hand, it has not enabled him to bring into focus the inquiry process which, as we have tried to show, is so necessary to understand the rationale of Friedman's way of thinking. Friedman's is neither the way of an (ethereal) pure Popperian scientist long-run nor a crude Popperian instrumentalist nor a sophisticated (methodological) falsificationist short-run.[34] It is 'pragmatic', but not in the very crude Popperian sense.[35]

Why the heavy stress on prediction?

We return to the question we posed at the beginning of this section: why did Friedman put such heavy stress on prediction in arguing his case?[36] Interestingly, we find Dewey saying pretty much the same thing though somewhat less unguardedly. Dewey tells us (1916, p. 198):

> What makes the essential difference between modern research and the reflection of, say, the Greeks, is not the absence of 'mere thinking', but the presence of conditions for testing the results; the elaborate system of checks and balances found in the technique of modern experimentation.

The testing Dewey is appealing to has to do with implications or predictions, and he seems to be telling us that what distinguishes modern science is making predictions and testing them.

Dewey seems concerned only with predictions, because he is arguing not just *for* a particular view of inquiry but *against* an alternative. What he finds objectionable in the alternative, which he takes to be typified by Aristotle's logic, is that it 'assumes certain first and fundamental truths unquestioned and unquestionable, self-evident and self-evidencing, neither established nor modified by thought, but standing firm in their own right' (*ibid.*). Such 'truths', of course, are plausible beliefs embedded in the assumptions of theory. In other words, it is Dewey's fight *against* a way of thinking which rests upon 'self-evident' premises that leads him to single out the test of implications to such an extent that one could interpret him to be concerned *only* with prediction. Once one goes beyond limited phrases one finds that this is not Dewey's position. Much the same can be said of Friedman, though because he is less guarded and more forceful in expressing himself, it takes more effort to recognize this.[37]

The Deweyan growth of knowledge thesis

It is rather surprising that at a time when the growth of knowledge has come to the forefront among economic methodologists (for example Caldwell, 1982, Chapter 5) the connection between Friedman's ideas about the 'realism' of assumptions and his ideas about the growth of knowledge should have been overlooked. It is Friedman's view, as it is Dewey's, that one must concentrate on implications because, as the era before modern science and much in the history of economics show, concentration on the 'realism' or plausibility of assumption leads to stagnation. Even what may look like advance in this mode, substituting more 'realistic' assumptions for those that are less so, has often meant changing one set of dogmas for another which has somehow lost its plausibility. Of course, this thesis on the growth of knowledge is not as well worked out in Dewey as in more recent works (for example Kuhn, 1970; Lakatos, 1974*b*; or Krige, 1980). But it can be argued that for *economics* Dewey's cruder (and broader) analysis has more significance because the appeal to the 'realism' or plausibility of assumptions, so popular with economic methodologists, is a variant of Aristotelian thinking.[38] That does not necessarily make it wrong, since it can be argued that the subject matter of economics is so different from that of physics that Aristotelian logic is more appropriate than modern varieties. But once one denies that there are any basic methodological differences between these subjects, as very many economists do today, then Dewey's thesis which contrasts the testing of implications with reliance on plausible assumptions becomes pertinent. One must recognize this to understand where Friedman's methodology fits in relation to the traditional kind.

DEFENSE OF THE MAXIMIZATION-OF-RETURNS HYPOTHESIS

After making the point that a theory should be judged on the basis of how well its implications accord with what actually happens, and not on the 'realism' of its assumptions, Friedman goes on to say, quite consistently, that the way to judge the maximization-of-returns hypothesis of neoclassical economics is to examine the evidence bearing on the implications of the theory. He draws back, however, noting that while he thinks that the evidence is there, he does not have it at hand. He offers arguments instead which rest on a very different kind of rationale than that which is in evidence in other parts of 'Positive economics' and the earlier work that we considered in previous chapters. He tells us (pp. 22–3):

> Confidence in the maximization-of-returns hypothesis is justified by evidence of a very different character. The evidence is in part similar to that adduced on behalf of the billiard-player hypothesis – unless the behavior of businessmen in some way or other approximated behavior consistent

with the maximization of returns, it seems unlikely that they would remain in business for long ... [Further,] the continued use and acceptance of the hypothesis over a long period, and the failure of any coherent self-consistent alternative to be developed and be widely accepted, is strong indirect testimony to its worth.

The nature of the arguments

There are three separate components in this defense. The billiards-player analogy sheds little light on the maximization-of-returns hypothesis itself. It is merely one example of many that could be given to show that people do a lot of things without being able to explain how and why they do them. It suggests that a certain measure of scepticism may be in order in interpreting questionnaire data derived from businessmen's responses on how they make decisions. This bears on the criticism of those who object to maximization-of-returns hypotheses but it tells us nothing about the ability of the hypothesis to predict.

The survivor argument

The Darwinian argument about the survival of firms is more positive. It tells us that the rules of the market-game are such that winners can be expected to have certain traits; for example, in a game requiring great physical strength it would be reasonable to believe that those who win would be physically strong. We have three problems with this line of argument. The first is that, while it is of the form 'if p then q and q, therefore p', which is the abductive kind that Friedman generally favors, in this instance Friedman does not give us any *evidence* to support the claim that firms actually *do* maximize returns (that is, the implied result). His 'facts' are stylized and merely plausible. Were he to have the data, the theory could be taken as a hypothesis to account for them and to give us a valid basis for future predictions and *tests*. Without the data this argument does not have the abductive form and Friedman at best is open to the charge that he has committed the logical fallacy of affirming the consequent.[39]

A second problem we have with the firm-survival argument is that it misses its purpose. The major reason the 'unrealism' thesis makes sense is that once introspection is ruled out as a source of certain knowledge, directly testing behavioral assumptions becomes very difficult if not impossible. We therefore start by observing that the pattern in the available data – e.g. price and quantity movements – is consistent with the assumptions and then, as Friedman argued elsewhere, we test the implications with further data. But Friedman destroys the very foundations of this way of reasoning by suggesting that we *do* have a 'satisfactory' basis for directly judging assumptions. The basis is plausibility, or 'realism'; precisely what he argued against in most other places.

A third problem we have with the firm-survival argument is that even if firms do in fact maximize returns, the theory might still not give good predictions,[40] and whether it does is the question at issue. The reason that predictions could very well turn out to be wrong is that the theory is too simple. For example, on the basis of the maximization-of-returns hypothesis one could argue that there cannot be employment discrimination in a market system because discriminating employers would wind up with less qualified workers overall and be unable to compete with those with less prejudice. The fact that discrimination does exist, of course, does not refute the maximization-of-returns hypothesis and, in fact, by using Friedman's type of approach a variant of neoclassical theory could be formulated to account for what actually happens (Becker, 1971). But to argue that the theory *in general* could be expected to give good predictions based on the firm-survival argument is inconsistent with both the letter and the spirit of the methodology-of-positive-economics thesis. Friedman could have argued consistently that the maximization-of-returns hypothesis is an integral part of a good paradigm or guide in research, but to do this adequately would have required him to give the very kind of evidence which he admitted he did not have.

The theory-survival argument

Little need be said about the Darwinian survival argument as applied to the maximization-of-returns hypothesis itself. It is plain that it rests entirely on plausibility. Critics (for example Archibald, 1959, cited by Rotwein, 1959; Blaug, 1980, pp. 115–19 and references there cited) have pointed out that there are problems with the argument,[41] but from our point of view such questions are a minor concern; they are the kind which invariably arise when one argues on the basis of the plausibility of assumptions. Our major interest is not whether the basis of Friedman's argument is plausible, as he argues, or not, as his critics claim. It is rather that he is *using* plausibility at all, rather than evidence bearing on the implications of the theory he is defending, to make his point. Friedman's tacit assumption is that neoclassical theory has survived because of its scientific usefulness, rather than because of its ideological or 'ceremonial' value, and this assumption is as difficult to prove or disprove as is the assumption of rational behavior. Its 'truth' certainly is not self-evident.[42]

The surprise twist and possible reasons for it

The significance of this aspect of the essay is thus that Friedman has reverted to the very mode of argument which he criticizes in others, criticism which, on the face of it, seems to have been the *raison d'être* of 'Positive economics'. In effect we are told that it is more reasonable to believe this hypothesis than not to believe it; the very pertinence of specific evidence about implications is shunted out of sight. One may ask of this aspect of Friedman's approach to economic methodology, as he did of Oscar Lange's approach to economics:

> What observed facts would contradict the generalization suggested, and what operations could be followed to observe such critical facts? (1953*e*, p. 283).

One is tempted to argue in defense of Friedman that he is using here a second-best strategy. The test of implications may be the best way to judge a hypothesis, but if such evidence is not available we are forced to look for another way. Such a defense will not do, however, since in effect it destroys the very rationale of Friedman's basic position; it is a variant of the type of argument that John Stuart Mill (and other major mainstream methodologists) gave in defending the plausibility-of-assumptions approach. Mill had argued that we could not even get started in trying to formulate economic theory of the kind Friedman champions because the complexity of social phenomena and the very limited ability we have to experiment make it impossible to derive premises or assumptions by reasoning back from effects to causes (see below, Chapter 5). In fact, Friedman himself expresses the view that it is because of the difficulty of meaningfully testing theory through its implications that economists had turned to the plausibility-of-assumptions argument. He rejects this second-best alternative in very strong terms. But is there any better reason for Friedman using it himself?

That he should have felt the need to defend neoclassical economic theory is not surprising. As a student of both Arthur Burns and Wesley Mitchell, and their colleague at the National Bureau, Friedman must have heard a lot of criticism of neoclassical economics; some of this criticism he accepted, as we have shown in Chapters 1 and 2 above. But he was also a student at Chicago where, he tells us (Breit and Ransom, 1982, p. 226, n. 3) Jacob Viner had revealed to him how useful neoclassical theory could be in empirical work. And perhaps even more important, he was finding the theory useful in his own research. Thus it is not surprising that he should have argued *for* economic theory, conceived a certain way; just as earlier, in the work considered in the first part of Chapter 1, he argued *against* economic theory looked at in another way.

And essentially the same rationale which was used in the critical arguments could be used in the defense. Thus if Lange could not be trusted because he rested his case on plausible assumptions, neither could critics of economic theory, who argued that economic theory was not reliable because its assumptions were not plausible.

This line of thinking blunts the thrust of the critics, but it leaves the theory undefended. The critic's arguments might be questionable, yet the substance of their criticism could still be correct. As Friedman seemed to be aware, if one argues that what matters is how well the implications test out, rather than how plausible the assumptions are, one cannot very well avoid the matter of evidence. He could have reacted to this challenge in a number of different ways. First, he could have noted the need for evidence, as in fact he does, but left the matter there. Second, he could have referred to the way he himself found theory to be useful, and to the work of others. Had Friedman taken this course, and offered a compelling argument, he would have had to show that he was defending the theory, not as a reliable guide to policy in *general*, but rather as a good starting point − a paradigm, so to speak − for research in positive economics. The defense then would not have sounded so very partisan. The third course was the one that he actually took. It is a way of arguing that Friedman has followed when he has not been directly involved with work in positive economics. In his work in political economy, as we show in Chapter 12, below, it is the dominant mode. (There are elements of it, too, in his own predictive activity, as we show in Chapter 11, below.)

The consequences

While one can only speculate as to why Friedman chose to defend Marshallian theory the way he did, the consequences of the choice are very apparent. It has been argued that *the* purpose of Friedman's venture into methodology was to defend neoclassical economics (for example Blaug, 1980; Caldwell, 1980; Mason, 1980; Maki, 1986; Rotwein, 1959; Samuelson, 1963). One critic (Webb, 1987) has taken the purpose of the piece to be the refutation of institutional economics. Some have argued (Mason, 1980; Samuelson, 1963) that the essay is an ideological tract,[43] and still others in the same vein feel that the article is a mere polemic and cannot be taken seriously as a methodological contribution.[44] These reactions are understandable. Friedman uses the implications type of argument against the critics, it may be held, because it wipes out the substance of their criticism. He uses the assumptions type of argument in support of the theory because it is by this means that the strongest case can be made. In this view it is futile to try to find a consistent point of view in Friedman's methodology because his objective of attacking critics on the one side, and supporting defenders on the other, makes consistency an impossibility. Secondly, Friedman's strong and inconsistent defense of neoclassical economics in 'Positive economics' has tended to throw off even critics who have read 'Positive economics' very carefully. Weaknesses in his formulations which otherwise might have been brushed aside as difficulty with details which affect the exposition rather than the substance of the thesis – a position taken, for example, by the philosopher Ernest Nagel (1963), who ignored the defensive aspects of the essay – are blown all out of proportion in the hands of those who focused on the defensive aspects. Given such a response, though it is understandable as a reaction to the way Friedman argues, it is easy to lose sight of the fact that he has something very interesting and original to say in 'Positive economics' about economic methodology.[45]

POSITIVE ECONOMICS IN HISTORICAL PERSPECTIVE

Reasons for the importance given to assumptions

In his comments in a session at the annual meetings of the AEA, just before he wrote 'Positive economics', Friedman observed (1952c, p. 456):

> One manifestation of the difficulty [of testing the implications of tentative hypotheses in the social sciences] has been the attempt to find an easier test of hypotheses, to suppose that hypotheses have 'assumptions' whose conformity to reality is a test of validity different from and additional to the test of implications or predictions.

In 'Positive economics' (pp. 11–13) he says the same thing in a more roundabout way.

These comments can be very helpful in pointing to the central vision that seems to lie behind Friedman's views about economic science and how it fits within the history of economics. But before we can put this material to good use an impediment has to be removed. Friedman talks about the difficulty of *testing* the implications of theory as being the catalyst which led economists to look to the realism of assumptions. To what extent he is right about this need not concern us since we are not trying to judge him as a historian of economics. What is significant for our purposes is that economic *methodologists*, whose job it is to explain what economists are doing and why they are doing it, held a different view on the matter, and this certainly made economists *sound* as if they looked to assumptions in judging theory even where they might in fact have judged the theory differently.

According to methodologists, of far greater importance than the difficulty of *testing* hypotheses in drawing attention to assumptions has been the problem of *deriving* theory in an area as complex as economic experience. From Nassau Senior to Lionel Robbins, it was agreed that theory could not be derived in economics as in physics, by working back from detailed observation, viewed as implications, to assumptions or premises.[46] The possible causes were too many, the resultant of their interactions all one can see. Hence, it was argued, one must rely on commonly held generalizations – the major one derived from introspection – to furnish premises for theorizing. If questions were raised about the empirical basis of the theory thus derived the prevailing view was that it could not be taken for granted that the implications of such a theory would always, or even generally, coincide with what actually happens.[47] How then does theory so derived relate to empirical reality? The answer given was that the theory was empirically grounded because it rested on 'true' assumptions.[48]

Our point then is that, as methodologists saw it, the reason economists came to appeal to the 'realism' of assumptions is that they believed that one could not hope to derive economic theory by working back from detailed observations, implications or effects, to general premises, assumptions or causes; one had to go directly to premises or assumptions and then work out their implications. Since the implications of such theory could not be relied on to coincide very well with what actually happens, the theory could not be related to empirical reality primarily through its implications. Instead, economic methodologists argued, it was the 'truth' of the assumptions which made the theory empirically valid (see below, Chapter 5). This is the background against which Friedman's position can best be understood.

If one looks at it this way one grasps many elements at once. First, that what is most basic about Friedman's stance is that he rejects the negative heuristic of the orthodox, as Mitchell did, regarding extensive investigation as an aid in *deriving* theory. Had he not done so it seems unlikely that he would have got tangled up with the matter of 'unrealistic' assumptions to begin with. Second, one understands why, though Friedman is primarily a theorist, he turns out works like *The Monetary History of the United States*. Third, one becomes aware that once involved with extensive observation of the facts of economic experience, an 'outside' approach to the study of behavior seems more appropriate than an 'inside' (or introspective) one. After all, a major objective, if not *the* major one, is to predict and retrodict. Does it not then make sense to try very hard to find the patterns in behavior which are to be accounted for? Introspection is not a reliable guide in this work, though once one knows what there is to explain it could be useful in suggesting reasons for patterns found, which are then checked out with further data.

Fourth, the evidence suggests that those who get involved in observing what actually happens tend to lose interest in the 'realism' of assumptions. Thus, as we have noted, Wesley Mitchell in the early days was very much involved with the 'realism' of assumptions, as Veblen had been. He urged economists to go to psychology, sociology and anthropology, for help in finding true assumptions (see Mitchell, 1910). But after he got deeply involved in empirical work he argued instead that we could not rely on others but had to derive our own premises by studying the data of economic experience (1950, p. 408; 1949, p. 298). Mitchell did not entirely give up his concern about 'realistic' assumptions, but what came to interest him much more, as we saw in Chapter 2, was implications. This raises the question, fifth, as to how extensive investigations can best be used to help derive the right assumptions. As far as we are aware Mitchell did not concern himself with this question, nor did other empirical economists; Cowles Commission econometricians, for example, relied for the most part on time-honored economic theoretical notions (see Chapter 5, below). Friedman's contribution here was to opt for speculation guided by extensive observation, using a procedure Mill had forbidden, and relying entirely on the test of implications to try to weed out assumptions that were faulty. Mitchell was wary of speculation, as were most of his empirical-minded contemporaries. The orthodox did not need to speculate, or so they believed, because they had introspective information. For Friedman, in the 'in-between' area, such speculation was unavoidable.

Sixth, once one has come this far it also becomes apparent that while the logic of Friedman's approach is far closer in basic ways to Mitchell's and Arthur Burns' than it is to orthodox methodology, it *looks* much closer to the orthodox. This appearance is because, since Friedman does not insist on evidence for his premises, he can theorize about 'imaginary individuals coming to imaginary markets' just as the orthodox do. This is where 'unrealistic' assumptions come in, the kind the truly orthodox would consider very damaging to the validity and usefulness of a theory if they were to think about them as 'unrealistic' or implausible.[49]

Friedman's specific targets

Friedman was interested in showing more than that economists appealed to assumptions because it was so difficult to test the implications of tentative hypotheses. He wished to single out certain work in economics for having gone astray as a result of concern with descriptive realism. As he put it in one place (1953c, p. 457):

The associated desire for descriptive realism indirectly fostered mathematical economics, with its emphasis on Walrasian general equilibrium analysis as an escape from the *ceteris paribus* of partial equilibrium analysis; it explicitly motivated monopolistic competition analysis and explains its popularity, which derived from a belief that the 'assumptions' of the previous analysis were 'unrealistic', rather than from any recognized contradiction of its predictions; it was the battle cry of institutionalism and the closely related emphasis on extensive statistical studies of economic phenomena . . .

How could one single out these particular groups when it was not only the 'bad guys' who made such an appeal but the 'good guys' as well – Ricardo, Mill, and even Marshall? It seems to us that what concerned Friedman was not primarily that his target groups had used realism as a *test* of theory but that they tried to use it as a basis for directly *deriving* theory. As we saw earlier, in Chapter 2, Friedman seemed clearly to have felt that economists of whom he approved, whom he called Marshallian, derived theory via an interactive process of theorizing and observation. One does not derive theory this way if the desire for descriptive realism is uppermost because there is then an easier way which saves much tedious work, namely picking realistic assumptions and working out ingenious implications. There is no need to pore over extensive data. Friedman rejected this short cut because his notions about the kind of research process that was most likely to be fruitful were different. One way of getting at this difference was to argue that others were concerned with the 'realism' of assumptions. Another way was to argue 'that the only relevant test of the validity of a hypothesis is comparison of its predictions with experience'. Still another was the argument that 'the theorist starts with some set of related facts, as full and comprehensive as possible'. As we have seen, Friedman put it in other ways as well. In all of this there are definite ideas about the inquiry process which rest on notions unusual for economics.

The uniqueness of Friedman's approach

Friedman in later years has had a great deal of difficulty in explaining in what ways his approach differed from others (see, for example, 1972*d*). We suggest that it is his somewhat out-of-focus historical perspective which contributes to this difficulty. About the need for testing the implications of theory – at least in principle – few of Friedman's adversaries would disagree, but about the need for extensive investigation as an essential aid in deriving theory there is as much difference between Friedman and most contemporary economists as between Friedman and Mill. It is this difference which is at the heart of the 'realism' controversy.

NOTES

1. Actually others had made this observation earlier (Nagel suggests the possibility in 1963; Wong uses the label without qualification in 1973), but it was undoubtedly Boland (1979) who was most convincing and made the label stick.
2. We say 'it seems' because what language does in effect is to lead toward explanation in which the 'instrumentalist' is supposed not to be interested. This will occupy us again later in the chapter.
3. Caldwell tells us only that '*instrumentalists*' prefer correlations to explanations. Since he designates Friedman an 'instrumentalist', however, it would follow that Friedman, too, prefers correlations.
4. This interpretation of Friedman as 'instrumentalist' had led to a great deal of light-hearted criticism of which Samuelson's 'F-Twist' (1963) is the best known.
5. It is only in this situation that Friedman can be said to prefer correlations to theories. If one takes the position that theories in economics never give reliable predictions then Friedman's position reduces to that of the 'instrumentalists'. Even there, however, since Friedman wants to keep trying to derive theory that predicts, the instrumentalist label does not fit. Friedman himself, of course, believes that Marshallian economic theory gives reasonably reliable predictions.
6. That empiricists are very critical of Friedman is further evidence against this interpretation. See, for example, Gordon's argument (1984, p. 374) that 'instrumentalists in the Dewey tradition [by which is meant institutionalists] have a genuine concern with the validity of their assumptions'. (See below, Chapter 6, for Dewey's actual position.)
7. In a note to this passage Coddington suggests that this may be the reason Friedman uses the word 'explain' only in inverted commas. It seems to us rather that he is trying to avoid the kind of essentialist association of this term, which we find, for example, in Hollis and Nell (1975).
8. Coddington later refers to 'causation', a term which has essentialist associations that Friedman tries, but does not succeed, in avoiding, just as he tries to avoid use of the term 'truth', which is also imbued with essentialist connotations. If 'cause' for Coddington is the kind of thing that we identify in theories, then the accusation that Friedman is not interested in causes is wrong. (On this matter see Hammond in Samuels, 1986.)
9. Walters, 1987, p. 423, says very directly that 'This approach [of Friedman's] applied the new philosophy of science, developed by Karl Popper, to economics ...'
10. Blaug has since changed his mind (see Blaug, 1980). Salanti (1987, pp. 383–4) speaks of Friedman's 'own peculiar falsificationism (perhaps accidentally suggested to him by his contacts with Popper ...)'. He also refers to Hirsch and De Marchi (1984), which he takes to demonstrate Friedman's 'peculiar (pseudo) falsificationism'. It seems that for Salanti anyone who believes in testing implications is a 'falsificationist', and if his way is different from Popper's, as Salanti interprets him, then he is a 'peculiar' (pseudo) 'falsificationist'.
11. If we change the convention and define the term 'false' to include only falseness and reserve to truth all the rest, as is more often than not done in everyday life, then the way scientists talk might change somewhat but what

they do and what they mean would not. If we define 'truth' the way Charles Peirce did (quoted in Dewey, 1938, p. 345) as 'The opinion which is fated to be ultimately agreed to by all who investigate' then we avoid this asymmetry and the certainty trap.

12. Popper is concerned that if we refer to a theory as 'verified' when it is not certain, we will stop looking for better theories. Were this true, science would have been at a standstill until Popper came along to shock scientists out of their complacency with his change of vocabulary. It seems to us rather that the central question has to do with why knowledge in the Aristotelian sciences did not grow but in modern science does. We do not see how logic can begin to answer this question.

13. In his 1929 publication, as well as in other works, Dewey tries to show the implications that follow from the fact that we can never be certain about empirical generalizations. Where Popper wants to hold on to tradition and retain certainty as an attribute of 'truth', Dewey opts for giving it up (see n. 10, above). This matter is pursued further in Chapter 6.

14. We return to this problem later in this section.

15. As we observe below, Popper himself does not adhere to the strict ('naïve') falsificationist doctrine, but in economics it has generally been the strict version which has held sway, certainly until very recently. For example, one gets the distinct impression from Boland (1982) that for Popper falsification means rejection; Caldwell (1982) holds this to be true only of the earlier Popper, but on the whole one gets the same impression from him generally as from Boland.

16. From those, that is, who take falsification to be a criterion of theory choice. Popper does not claim that the falsification idea derived from experience. In fact, when criticized because scientists do not act the way they should if they were falsificationist, he responds (1983, Introduction, Section IV) that the falsification analysis is intended only to help make our ideas clear. Likewise, when criticized by A. J. Ayer (in Schilpp, 1974) because his concept of verisimilitude did not help to assess progress towards truth, Popper answered (*ibid*. p. 1101) that his purpose was simply to clarify what is meant by the phrase 'progress towards truth'.

17. Lakatos and Kuhn are closer to Friedman's point of view in this respect than Popper. Dewey, however, fits more closely still.

18. If *this* is what we mean by 'test' then the falsification thesis is not very pertinent. What is pertinent is whether one theory is better or worse than another, the criterion Friedman suggests. Note that in trying to determine what is better and what is worse one cannot say *precisely* why, as happens when one tries on glasses. *Use* of the glasses over a period of time generally settles the matter much better than *arguing* about it.

19. The shift in the philosophy of science in recent years to concern with the growth of knowledge has somewhat moved philosophers away from this position. (See, for example, Kuhn, in Schilpp, 1974; Agassi, 1983; Krige, 1980.) As far as we are aware Popper has not moved with this trend.

20. Otherwise why would he concern himself with the fact that the Walrasians theorize without having 'some set of observed and related facts as full and comprehensive as possible'? Why does he not content himself with just falsifying the results? Whether Friedman is right or wrong about what he thinks has been learned from the past experience of inquiry is, of course, another matter, one to which little attention has been paid because

methodologists have generally been more concerned with how we *talk* than with what we *do*.

21. He does repeat it later in defending his methodological position (1972*d*, pp. 920–91).

22. Blaug (1980, p. 16) argues that 'Popper's assertion that "induction is a myth" refers [only] to induction as a demonstrable logical argument ...' Since deduction is the only type of demonstrative argument, Blaug attributes to Popper the thesis that induction is not deduction. Did we really need Popper to teach us this?

23. We run into difficulty here because, as we have seen, in some places (e.g. 1965) Popper sees 'instrumentalism' to be the proper mode for practice, although the 'instrumentalist' does not argue about theories. In another place (Lakatos and Musgrave, 1970) Popper suggests that the applied scientist operates in the manner of a Kuhnian normal scientist. We are not aware of Popper's ever having reconciled these three not entirely compatible conceptions. Frazer and Boland (1983) perhaps wisely refer only to the 'instrumentalist'.

24. This passage, considered in relation to the ones cited in n. 15, above, shows up what looks to us like a contradiction. The references in n. 15 suggest that all that Popper wants to do is to clarify. But in the passage here he is telling us *what not to say*. Perhaps what Popper means is that we cannot say certain things if we want to be perfectly clear or coherent. But this interpretation creates further difficulties because Popper goes on to argue (in Lakatos and Musgrave, 1970) that unless we have good arguments in support of a position it has to be wrong. Popper seems to consider any of the facts in a case, other than the most general and available ones, as of little pertinence in this regard. This is evident in his exchange with Kuhn (*ibid.*).

25. In science one has to make 'practical' decisions, too, as to how to set up one's equipment and which equipment to use, for example. Popper sweeps such issues under the rug again, perhaps because he is interested in how scientists talk rather than what they do.

26. See Popper, 1965, pp. 111 and 113. Popper allows the technologists to use obsolete theories. This is consistent because using obsolete theories is on the same level as using correlations.

27. See Introduction for mention of correspondence to which Boland and Hirsch refer.

28. Frazer and Boland tell us (1983, p. 142): 'Deciding what we ought to do is considered a practical problem of choosing between alternative theories. Thus, for those who choose to extend the instrumentalism of Friedman's essay on methodology, explanation is not entirely cast aside for mere prediction.' But by (Boland's) *definition* the 'instrumentalist' is interested only in prediction. Thus it would appear that Friedman is not a full-fledged 'instrumentalist'. Is he then a 'Popperian' scientist? Of course not, long-run no more than short-run, as Boland himself makes abundantly clear. Is he then a 'conventionalist', as Boland tells us in other places (1970)? This is not very helpful either because according to Boland *everyone* is a 'conventionalist' except for Karl Popper, and even he trangresses (Boland, 1982, pp. 170–1) when he develops notions like the demarcation criterion and degrees of corroboration, so we only have a part-Popper left avoiding the conventionalist 'trap'. The part of Popper that thus remains is the (early) Socratic Popper who simply asks questions (*ibid.* Chapter 10). It is hard to

imagine anything further from Friedman's point of view than this purified Popperianism.

29. We have commented in greater detail on the Frazer and Boland argument in Hirsch and De Marchi (1984).

30. According to Newton-Smith (1981, p. 46), 'What makes Popper plausible to many is that they do not take him seriously. They do not think within the constraints of his system.'

31. Lakatos (Schilpp, 1974, Part II, 5) tries hard to push Popper out of this 'pure' area but gets rejected by him (*ibid*. Part III, 2, 12).

32. A student of Popper's, J. Agassi (1983), has come to question Popper for the same reason a Deweyan would. Popper does not draw the full implications of his recognition that certainty does not exist.

33. This does not include Boland (see 1982, Chapter 10).

34. For the meaning of the last terms see Lakatos (in Lakatos and Musgrave, 1970).

35. We find the cavalier way in which pragmatism is treated in the economic methodology literature rather remarkable, for example Coddington (1972), Boland (1982, pp. 142–4), Katouzian (1980, pp. 78–83).

36. See n. 7, above, for a comment on Friedman's putting the word 'explain' in inverted commas.

37. Where Popper is arguing against Karl Marx he almost sounds like John Dewey (and Friedman) in what he says about the history of science. Thus he tells us (1966, Section II, p. 12, emphasis added) that in modern science 'our scientific theories will always remain hypotheses, but that, in many important cases, we can find out whether or not a new hypothesis is superior to an old one. For if they are different, then *they will lead to different predictions, which can often be tested experimentally* . . .' Thus, the test of implications would appear to be the *crucial* element in distinguishing modern from Aristotelian science for Popper, as for Dewey. However, there is a good bit in Popper's work which contradicts this interpretation.

38. One has no difficulty in applying *modus ponens* in the Aristotelian mode because one does not need to solve the induction problem when reasoning from *plausible* premises, and one arrives via the use of Aristotelian logic at conclusions which are as certain as the plausible premises are believed to be. This avoids the kind of problem that Boland gets into in trying to apply Aristotelian logic to questions that arise about modern science, as Dennis (1986 and 1987) shows. See also Boland's reply (1987).

39. At best, because he merely takes it for granted that firms maximize returns. Even if they do, the Darwinian thesis would not necessarily be a good one unless it were the kind of hypothesis from which a whole host of interesting implications could be derived which were borne out by further tests. But the attempt to bypass such tests is the very purpose of this kind of argument.

40. Archibald (1959) makes this point.

41. Others, however, have found merit in the argument. See Koopmans (1957), Gordon (1955), De Alessi (1971).

42. None of the critics to our knowledge has pointed out the inconsistencies in Friedman's position that result from his use of the Darwinian arguments, although Koopmans implies it.

43. Koopmans (1957) reacts to the essay by speculating whether methodological conservatism is associated with political conservatism.

44. See Maki (1986) and Webb (1987). This view is often expressed in unpublished pieces and in conversations among economists.
45. A cursory examination of what Friedman has to say about methodology in places where he is not defending neoclassical theory or a political position should be convincing on this point, even to those who do not share his point of view.
46. Mill (1967), Senior (see Bowley, 1937, p. 58), Cairnes (1875, p. 63), J. N. Keynes (1955 [1890], pp. 209–11), Robbins (1949, p. 82). Part of the reason they came to this conclusion is that as far as they were concerned if one started by doing extensive observation one could not go beyond the data to formulate theory; this was called the a posteriori method. Perhaps more important was that they had introspection to rely on.
47. Senior (1966 [1852], pp. 62–3), Mill (1967, p. 326), Cairnes (1875, pp. 99–100), J. N. Keynes (1955 [1890], pp. 221–2). Robbins (1949, Chapter 5) looks like an exception since, without using this word, he seems to be telling us that economic theory does give reasonably good predictions. But he does not feel that any tests of implications are necessary and he does not tell us why, if there are reliable regularities, such as the relationship between the quantity of money and the price level, one cannot use these regularities as a starting point for theorizing.
48. Here there is complete unanimity without even any subtle deviations. See Mill (1967, p. 327), Cairnes (1875, p. 55), Senior (1966 [1852], Lecture IV), J. N. Keynes (1955 [1890], pp. 223–4), Robbins (1949, p. 105).
49. Neither, of course, will most of the empirically minded heterodox.

5 • FRIEDMAN'S METHODOLOGY IN THE CONTEXT OF JOHN STUART MILL'S LOGIC

Up to this point we have tried to show what Friedman has said about economic science in his writings. We have in passing referred to the methodology of John Stuart Mill as representative of the orthodox tradition in order to highlight one feature or another of Friedman's unusual methodological position. While such references are of some help, in order to grasp fully the nature and significance of Friedman's views it is necessary to make a more systematic and extensive comparison. For that reason, in this chapter we consider Mill's views in some detail. While in some respects other methodologists of the orthodox tradition – Senior, Cairnes, Robbins – show up the contrasts which are of interest even more clearly, we choose Mill because he delves more deeply into basic issues.

In this chapter we will consider not only Mill's views about economic science, but also what he says about the moral and physical sciences. We do this, first, because in order to understand the differences between Friedman's position and that of the traditional economic methodologists it is necessary to go beyond economic methodology to consider questions that arise in the broader area of the logic or philosophy of science. Second, methodologists of economics, as Mill illustrates, have often gone beyond economics in arguing their methodological positions and this tendency has markedly increased in recent years. In fact, a good bit of the criticism that has been levelled against Friedman's methodology has drawn support from the broader area of the philosophy of science.[1] As a consequence, if we were to neglect this area we would be bypassing some of the most interesting issues that 'the Friedman problem' has brought to the fore.[2] For the same reason we consider, in the next chapter, pertinent aspects of John Dewey's views. While it is helpful to understand the implicit views of science that Friedman holds as they relate to those of traditional orthodox economic methodology, it is even more important to understand how the different aspects of Friedman's position hang together. Dewey's logic helps to show this. It helps us to see how one whose thinking is pragmatic, as Friedman's is, would deal with the kind of broader issues which interpreters have raised. In earlier chapters we have referred to Dewey here and there to try to clarify one point or another; in the next one we systematically show his relevance for understanding Friedman's views.

We can hardly hope to paint a comprehensive picture of Mill's logic in this chapter or of Dewey's in the next. We therefore confine ourselves to those views of both philosophers which are most directly pertinent for our purposes. We begin here by looking at Mill's logic of science;[3] in the second section we deal with his views on moral science; and in the third we turn to economic science.

THE PHYSICAL SCIENCES

The deductive and hypothetical methods and the role of specific experience

As Mill saw it, we are required to sort out causes when what we see around us are 'complex effects, compounded of the effects of many causes' (1973, III, X, 5). That is why the a posteriori method, which attempts to work back from effects to causes, is generally inappropriate (*ibid*. III, X, 5). What is appropriate is the a priori method, which goes from causes or premises to effects or implications.[4] The basic causal laws can be found and 'proved' to be 'true' (*ibid*. III, IX) according to Mill, by the four methods of experimental inquiry (*ibid*. III, VIII), namely, the methods of agreement, of difference, of residues and of concomitant variation. This is done before a science reaches the advanced stage. Once in the latter, however, we have to grapple with the complex mixture of causes and effects which are behind everything we see around us. Even were we to know all of the effects of all of the causes, we would still have to determine which causes apply in a particular situation and how they interrelate with one another to produce the effects. For that reason, the first stage of the method of the advanced sciences – what Mill calls the deductive, or a priori, method – is the 'ascertainment of the laws of separate causes by direct induction' (*ibid*. III, XI, 1). This involves, as he explains, identifying the pertinent causal laws, which are already generally known from previous investigations using the four methods. The second stage (*ibid*. III, XI, 2), involves 'ratiocination from the simple laws of the complex cases', where the implications of the combination of what are taken to be the causal laws are worked out. In the third stage (*ibid*. III, XI, 3), called 'verification by specific experience', the implications are compared with direct observation.

Mill's particular conception of 'verification' derives from his general view of the process of scientific investigation. Since, as we have seen, an important part of the process of scientific investigation is finding which causal laws apply in any area, it is conceivable that pertinent causal laws may be overlooked, or that the way they combine with one another might be miscalculated. The process of verification shows up such errors.[5] Mill goes on to argue that even though 'the simple laws into which we ultimately analyze such phenomena' cannot be discovered from complex instances, verification of a theory of which a causal law is a part 'helps to confirm' the simple causal law. But if the theory is not confirmed that has no bearing on the truth of the causal laws. The reason is that the causal laws have been 'proved' to be invariable and unconditional *before* the deductive method is used; what happens at the *advanced* stage of a science is that they begin to be combined (*ibid.* III, IX, 1).[6]

After he has considered the deductive method Mill considers the 'hypothetical method'. This method 'suppresses the first of the steps, the induction to ascertain the law, and contents itself with the other two operations, ratiocination and verification, the law which is reasoned from being assumed instead of proved'. This, of course, means working from effects to causes. He is unenthusiastic about this method and one gets the impression that he considers it primarily to show its limitations. These are severe. Mill considers its use legitimate only 'provided that the case be such that a false law cannot lead to a true result, provided no law except the very one which we have assumed can lead deductively to the same conclusion which that leads to' (*ibid.* III, XII, 4).[7] Mill lays down this condition because otherwise *necessity* would not be demonstrated. It follows from this that a popular belief must be rejected. As Mill tells it (*ibid.* III, XII, 6):

> ... it seems to be thought that an hypothesis of the sort in question [one whose premises have not been 'proved'] is entitled to more favorable reception if, besides accounting for all of the facts previously known, it has led to the anticipation and prediction of others which experience afterward verified .... Such predictions and their fulfillment are, indeed, well calculated to impress the uninformed, whose faith in science rests solely on similar coincidences between its prophecies and what comes to pass. But it is strange that any considerable stress should be laid upon such a coincidence by persons of scientific attainments.[8]

The deductive method in the hands of an empiricist

It seems strange that an empiricist like Mill, who argued that deduction cannot yield empirical truth but is capable only of passing it on in reasoning, should have put his trust in the *deductive* method. This can be explained by the fact that he assumed that most of the inductions will have been done already in an *advanced* science which is what Mill was primarily concerned with. What then remains is to relate the simple causal laws to the complex reality that we see around us. The latter can be viewed as the implications and the former the premises or assumptions of the theory of interest to us. A consequence of this is that the observation of specific experience plays very little role in Mill's conception of advanced science.

An example that Mill gives (*ibid*. III, IV, 1) is revealing in this regard. First he outlines the conceptual basis of his argument. He tells us that if A is always accompanied by D, B by E, and C by F, we could legitimately conclude that ABC is accompanied by DEF. He then tries to make this analysis concrete with an example from the history of science. Thus if we take A to be the 'law' that air has weight, B the 'law' that pressure in a fluid is propagated in all directions, and C the 'law' that pressure in one direction if not opposed by equal pressure in the contrary direction produces motion which does not cease until equilibrium is restored, it follows that: 'From these three uniformities we should be able to predict ... the rise of mercury in the Torricellian tube'. The lesson Mill derives from this is that 'we should thus come to know the more complex uniformity, *independently of specific experience*, through our knowledge of the simpler ones from which it results ...' (emphasis added). He does add that '*verification* by specific experience would still be desirable and might possibly be indispensible', but in spite of this it should be apparent apparent how limited a role specific experience plays in his way of thinking, even for the advanced *physical* sciences.

Thus, while 'verification' is said to be one of the major components of Mill's deductive method, the role he gives to it is in fact very limited. First, as we have seen, 'verification' is generally not essential. Second, if our theory is disconfirmed, what it suggests for the most part is merely that pertinent causal laws have been left out of account. That is a limited role. And this limited role given 'verification' is not an aberration but follows directly from Mill's vision of science. There is an implicit growth of knowledge theory in his logic, whereby mankind starts out by intuitively using the four methods on simple phenomena – for example 'that food nourishes, that water drowns or quenches thirst, that the sun gives light and heat, that bodies fall to the ground' (*ibid*. III, IV, 2). When the stage is reached where complex phenomena become the center of attention the deductive method comes into its own.[9] In all of this the core of 'truth', which resided primarily in the phenomena we see around us to begin with, is transferred over time into causal laws or 'tendencies'. Ultimately, then, in the progress of science, sensations (or specific experience) are important only at the periphery of science. As Mill puts it in one place:

The really scientific truths, then, are not these empirical laws [embedded in the implications of theory] but the causal laws [embedded in the premises or assumptions] which explain them. [10] The empirical laws of those phenomena which depend on known causes and of which general theory can therefore be constructed have, whatever their value may be in practice, no other function in science than that of verifying the conclusion of a theory.

Note the process again. The causal laws of one theory are brought under the umbrella of another as science advances, and as this goes on we get to the 'ultimate' causal laws or 'laws of nature'.

According to one mode of expression, the question, 'What are the laws of nature'? may be stated thus: What are the fewest and simplest *assumptions*, which being granted, the whole existing order of nature would result'? (*ibid.* III, IV, 1, emphasis added.)

The dualism in the system

It should be apparent that there is a subtle dualism in the Millian system. Empirical laws are explained, and made a true part of science, by causal laws from which they can be deduced as implications. These causal laws in turn are explained by simpler – or more general – causal laws from which they themselves are deduced. And so on, until laws of nature are arrived at which, in combination with initial conditions, explain everything there is to explain in the universe. On this vision, it seems correct to suggest, as Mill does, that the *real* science is in the fundamental premises or assumptions. Yet in one place (*ibid.* VI, IX, 1) we are told that 'the grounds of confidence in any concrete deductive science is not the a priori reasoning itself but the accordance between its results and those of observation a posteriori'. It looks very much as if 'the grounds of confidence' and 'scientific truth' are not the same thing at all in Mill's system. (Had Mill insisted that the grounds of confidence must give support to the scientific truths for us to continue to hold that they are scientific truths, there would not be dualism, but then Mill would in effect have been arguing a pragmatic position – see Chapter 6. But in the Millian system the evidence may be inconsistent with the implications of the theory, thus giving us little in the way of grounds of confidence, yet our belief in the scientific validity of the causal laws underlying the theory remains unaffected. Further, even if there are excellent grounds of confidence, because the implications of our theory are borne out by the facts, but if the truth of the assumptions of the theory have not been established – with plausibility being at least one of the ways this can be done – then we have no basis for even suspecting, in Mill's way of thinking, that the theory may have scientific validity. Here is where the dualism occurs.)

The way in which Mill's approach to logic is deductivist

In classical logic it is assumed that one can somehow determine that some general statements, like 'all men are mortal', are true. Once we agree on this, the laws of deductive logic enable us to *prove* that implications derived from such premises are true. Mill accepted this scheme as far as it went but felt that it was not sufficient for science. He felt that the premises on which this whole structure rested had also to be proved to be true. Thus, 'knowing therefore accurately the properties of the substances concerned [in economics as in any other science], we may reason with as much certainty as in the most demonstrative parts of physics, from any assumed set of circumstances'. But, adds Mill, 'This will be mere trifling if the assumed circumstances bear no sort of resemblance of any real ones . . .' (1967, p. 329). We must therefore prove that our assumptions are true and for this purpose Mill's four methods of induction are needed in the physical sciences.

This analysis shows why Mill was unable to accept his opponent Whewell's 'consilience of inductions' criterion (see, for example, Whewell, 1847, vol. 2, p. 85),[11] one component of which is the notion that a hypothesis whose assumptions had not been proved should be accepted if, 'besides accounting for all the facts previously known, it has led to the anticipation and prediction of others which experience afterward verified . . .'. To have agreed with Whewell would have meant to Mill violating Aristotelian (deductive) logic by affirming the consequent. Mill is obviously working within the classical framework of deductive logic where deductive inferences must be proved. Induction fits into this framework by providing premises more reliable than Aristotle's. But Mill's view is basically deductivist.[12] The criteria Mill proposes for judging a theory in an advanced science are not defended as being derived from experience. They are proposed because they enable us to be certain that truth has been attained by inspection, just as inspection showed Mill that Whewell's proposal had to be rejected on logical grounds.[13]

Did Whewell really violate the rules of deductive logic? Not at all. He did not mean that he had *proved* a hypothesis supported by consilience the way Mill felt that it had to be proved. His argument was inductive in that it appealed to experience. The basis of his confidence in 'the consilience of inductions', as he called the phenomenon where a hypothesis is borne out for a wide range of data, was that there is a great deal of evidence to support it. His study of the history of science showed, he felt, that hypotheses which met this test turned out not to be disconfirmed later. In fact, he felt that the evidence showed that hypotheses which met this test were the ones which led to scientific *advance* (see Losee 1983,

p. 116). Note the subtle difference in the criteria that Mill and Whewell appeal to. Mill wants criteria to help judge whether theory is *true*. He does not even try to show that use of this criterion will lead to the growth of knowledge. His logic is *static*. Whewell's approach on the other hand is *dynamic*, in the sense that what we believe to be valid today depends on the results of a process of inquiry which has taken place over time, and not primarily on logical demonstration. But he has no way of proving that theories which he felt should be accepted are true.[14] This is what made him vulnerable at a time when it was taken for granted that theories, to be scientifically acceptable, had to be proven true. In our time, now that it is recognized that theories cannot be proven to be true and that all that we can hope to do is to get closer and closer to something that seems for the time being to be 'right', Whewell's position looks considerably stronger and Mill's, for the same reason, weaker.

At around the turn of the century, beginning with Peirce and Dewey, it began to be recognized that theories in empirical science cannot be *proved* to be true.[15] And if the truth of theories could not be proved, a more concrete or operational objective was needed as a substitute. Growth of knowledge was generally taken to be the new objective; it actually seems to have been the implicit goal for Whewell. While others may have seen this first, there is little doubt that Karl Popper in our own time has done more than anyone else to convey this notion. But whereas Peirce and Dewey adopted an inductivist approach like Whewell's, because they believed that one had to learn from experience (induction) how science has created growth of knowledge, Popper elected to retain Mill's deductivism,[16] rejecting deductive *proof* but insisting on deductive *disproof*, or falsification.[17] Thus methodologists who had been influenced by Popper could not be expected to be any more sympathetic to Friedman's inductivism than could those who adhere to Millian logic.

Within this context a fundamental disagreement about Friedman's methodology becomes more meaningful. Millians like Rotwein (1959) reject Friedman's position because it would lead us to accept theories which are not proved to be true. Boland (1979), a Popperian, catches a glimpse of the truth by recognizing that Friedman was not trying to prove anything the way one proves a theorem in geometry. He therefore was not guilty, in this view, of logical error. But to a Popperian a true scientist must try to falsify and therefore Friedman can be certified only as a technician or 'instrumentalist'. Neither Rotwein's nor Boland's conclusions are anything other than we would expect. To a deductivist, any inductivist can be no more than a 'practical man' or 'instrumentalist'. That is so because the inductivist does not rely on deductive proof (for the Millian) or deductive disproof (for a Popperian). The interesting question is what kind of 'instrumentalist' or 'practical man' Friedman is.

THE MORAL SCIENCES

The role of specific experience

We saw in the last section that the observation of specific experience plays a very small role in Mill's view of the advanced physical sciences. In his conception of the moral sciences in some respects it plays an even smaller role, but for somewhat different reasons. For one thing, Mill considered the a posteriori method, which in discussing the moral sciences he refers to as the chemical method, even less appropriate for them than for the physical sciences (1973, VI, VII, 1). Second, he argued (*ibid*. VI, VII, 1):

> The laws of the phenomena of society are and can be nothing but the laws of the actions and passions of human beings united together in the social state. Men, however, in a state of society are still men; their actions and passions are obedient to the laws of individual human nature.

It followed that the moral sciences are deductive, since if detailed observation of specific experience were needed to derive premises for theorizing it had already been done by the psychologist before the social scientist set to work. But even the psychologists, because of the way Mill conceived the subject of psychology, did not do any real observation of specific experience. To Mill psychology studies 'the uniformities of succession ... according to which one mental state succeeds another, is caused by or, at least, is caused to follow another' (*ibid*. VI, IV, 3). This means that psychology is an introspective science in which the observation of the ways people actually behave plays little if any role. [18]

This does not mean that the observation of specific experience plays *no* role in the moral sciences. In fact one gets the impression that for Mill there is no less need for observation of specific experience in the moral than in the *advanced* physical sciences. (Remember that in talking about the advanced sciences Mill takes it for granted that the observation which leads to the discovery of the basic causal laws had already been done.) But the way observation fits in differs in a significant way.

The inverse deductive method

Mill tells us that the deductive method has to be modified when applied to sociology or what he calls the social science. Thus (*ibid*. VI, IX, 4):

> In statistics, it is evident that empirical laws may sometimes be traced, and the tracing then forms an important part of that system of indirect observation on which we must often rely for the data of the deductive science .... The process of the science consists in inferring effects from

their causes, but we have often no means of observing causes except through the medium of their effects. [19]

As a consequence, the deductive method is here used inversely according to Mill. Instead of first deducing implications from causal laws and then verifying these implications with specific experience, the empirical generalizations are derived first from specific experience and then are 'verified' by being related to *known* causal laws. It is while talking about this inverse process that Mill almost seems to go so far as to put the observation of specific experience on a par with deductive theorizing; he tells us that what is involved in sociological inquiry is a 'twofold logical process and reciprocal verification'. But to interpret him this way would be wrong because Mill also tells us:

> The experimental process is not here to be regarded as a distinct road to the truth [any more than in any other science], but as a means (happening accidentally to be the only, or the best, available) for obtaining the necessary data for deductive science.

In other words, this is *not* abduction (or even the hypothetical method). We do not work back from implications to find causes and forward to derive implications and then test them. Nor is there in Mill's formulation a continuous process of observation of specific experience and theorizing back and forth. Rather one starts with the causal laws already in hand and with data, and tries to match the two. To make the match involves theorizing and therein lies the core of this method. Thus in the Millian system one either begins with causes, derives implications and then verifies the results with specific experience, as one does in the physical sciences; or one begins with implications in the form of specific experience and tries to relate these observations to known causal laws, thereby giving the facts meaning and scientific significance, as one does in some moral sciences. The purpose of the inversion is not to derive premises or causal laws. We make the inversion because in some of the moral sciences 'the immediate causes of social facts are not open to direct observation . . .' (*ibid.* III, IX, 4). Are they open to direct inspection in others, like economics? How one answers this question, as we have seen in earlier chapters, has a lot to do with the approach one adopts to economics.

The moral sciences as inexact and predictive

Early in the sixth book (Chapter 3) of the *Logic* Mill defends the thesis that the moral disciplines are sciences. He points out that in the exact sciences the implications deduced from causal laws correspond exactly with observation but in sciences which are not exact there is divergence.

The reason these sciences are not exact, we are told, is that not all pertinent causes, causal laws and/or antecedent circumstances are known. As an example Mill points to meteorology, a science which is not exact, 'from the difficulty of observing the facts on which the phenomena depend . . .' Since he takes it for granted that meteorology is a science though its predictive power is very poor, he thereby deflects the argument that the moral disciplines should not be considered sciences because their predictions are not as good as those of physics or geometry. That establishes the *scientific* claims of the moral sciences.

But Mill was also interested in the *practical* aspects and for this purpose meteorology is not a good model; tidology was better because:

> . . . not only . . . is tidology a science, like meteorology, but it is, what hitherto, at least, meteorology is not, a science largely available in practice . . . General laws may be laid down respecting the tides, predictions may be founded on these laws, and the result will in the main, though often not with complete accuracy, correspond with the predictions.

In the course of the argument Mill explains how an inexact science becomes an exact one, using astronomy as an example. He tells us:

> It [astronomy] has become an exact science because its phenomena have been brought under laws comprehending the whole of the causes by which the phenomena are influenced, whether in a great or only in trifling degree, whether in all or only in some cases, and assigning to each of these the share of effect which really belongs to it. But in the theory of the tides the only laws as yet accurately ascertained are those of the causes which affect the phenomenon in all cases and in a considerable degree . . .

Mill goes on to explain how tidology and the moral sciences are related.

> Inasmuch . . . as many of those effects which it is of most importance to render amenable to human foresight and control are determined, like the tides, in an incomparably greater degree by general causes than by partial causes taken together, depending in the main on those circumstances and qualities which are common to all mankind, or, at least, to large bodies of them, and only in a small degree on the idiosyncrasies of organization or the peculiar history of individuals, it is evidently possible with regard to all such effects to make predictions which will *almost* always be verified and general propositions which are almost always true. [20]

What Mill seems to be telling us is that we can rely on theory resting on general causal laws in the moral sciences to give us reasonably good predictions, and this without verification. The position can best be understood when read in the context of Mill's interpretation of the Torricellian experiment mentioned in the last section. This does not mean that verification did not have a role to play in Mill's logic of moral science. Its role, as Mill shows in later chapters, is to help improve forecasts in specific instances by taking account of *minor* causes. The major causes and their effects we know from the 'science'. Mill's recipe is reasonably clear:

> By combining ... the exact laws of the greater causes and of such of the minor ones as are sufficiently known with such empirical laws or such approximate generalizations respecting the miscellaneous variations as can be obtained by specific observation, we can lay down general propositions which will be true in the main, and on which, with allowance for the degree of their probable inaccuracy, we may safely ground our expectations and our conduct.

Looked at from this angle one sees again how very small is the role given to specific experience in this scheme. Its purpose is taken to be merely to find empirical laws or approximate generalizations respecting miscellaneous (smaller) variations that are specific to different times and different places. This is not calculated to encourage an agenda of detailed factual investigation in the moral sciences.

ECONOMIC SCIENCE

No twofold logical process possible

In the *Logic* Mill tells us relatively little about the logic of political economy as he perceived it. There are, however, a number of comments which are revealing. For instance (1973, VI, IX, 5):

> ... in those more special inquiries which form the subject of the separate branches of the social science, this twofold logical process and reciprocal verification is not possible; specific experience affords nothing amounting to empirical laws.

Thus, even if we were to conclude that in the social science or sociology Mill allowed a role for the observation of specific experience equal to or almost equal to deduction – a possible but improbable interpretation, as we noted – it is clear that he *does not hold such a position with regard to political economy*.

Mill makes another interesting comment about political economy in the *Logic*. He tells us (*ibid*. VI, IX, 3):

> There is ... one large class of social phenomena in which the immediately determining causes are primarily those which act through the desire of wealth, and in which the psychological law mainly concerned is the familiar one that a greater gain is preferred to a smaller.

But how do we *know* that the immediately determining cause in this large class of social phenomena derive from this one motive? No answer is given in the *Logic*. Mill does comment that 'the ascertainment of the effect due to the one class of circumstances alone is a sufficiently intricate and difficult business . . .'. That may be, but by what means can we figure out that this class of phenomena does indeed result from this motive? Mill might have answered that the implications of this hypothesis are better borne out by the observation of specific experience than any other, but that would have been inconsistent with the basic foundations of science as he formulated them in the *Logic*. He had however tried to answer the question in 'On the definition of political economy' (hereafter referred to as Essay) published seven years before the *Logic*, and not surprisingly, the answer he gave was consistent with the framework which he had laid out in the later and more extensive work.[21]

Introspection versus extensive observation

In the Essay, Mill explains (in Robson, 1967, p. 329):

> The desires of man and the nature of the conduct to which they prompt him are within the reach of our observation. We can also observe what are the objects which excite these desires. The materials of this knowledge everyone can principally collect within himself, with reasonable consideration of the differences of which experience discloses to him the existence, between himself and other people.

Thus it is introspection primarily which gives us the basic causal law on which the science of political economy rests.

The question arises as to whether detailed observation of specific experience might not be a more reliable basis for deriving the causal law (or laws) which are needed in economics; Mill, like all the other mainstream economists of his time and since, answered in the negative. His reasons were that economic phenomena are exceedingly complex and experiment is all but impossible in this area; or, to put it somewhat differently, the four methods of inductive inquiry which he recommended as the means for deriving the causal laws (or premises) for the physical sciences are not available to economists. Thus he is very clear about what we should *not* do in economic inquiry, namely, we should *not* try to derive the behavioral premise (or premises) for theorizing from detailed observation of specific experience. He is also unambiguous about what we should do, namely, through introspection and (casual) checks of our own behavior against that of our neighbors, derive the economic behavioral premise. This, notice, is a different way than what he had recommended for the physical sciences. There the four methods of inductive inquiry were said to be the means by which the causal laws or premises of theory are generally derived.[22]

Economics, physics and geometry

Since, on Mill's view, the way causal laws are derived in economics differs from the way they are derived in physics, one might have expected him to conclude that the nature of the theory that the economist derives is different from theory in the physical sciences, but this is not his conclusion. He argued rather that, aside from the fact that political economy is not as exact a science as physics or astronomy, there is no further difference. The model of Euclidean geometry played a key role in leading Mill to this conclusion, as is shown in the Essay, where he argues (*ibid*. pp. 325–6):

> It [political economy] is built upon hypotheses strictly analogous to those which under the name of definitions are the foundations of the other abstract sciences. Geometry presupposes an arbitrary definition of a line ... Just in the same manner does political economy presuppose an arbitrary definition of man ... Political economy, therefore, reasons from *assumed* premises – from premises which might be totally without foundation in fact and which are not pretended to be universally in accordance with it. The conclusions of political economy consequently, like those of geometry, are only true as the common phrase is *in the abstract*, that is, they are only true under certain suppositions in which none but general causes – causes common to the whole class of cases under consideration – are taken into account. [23]

That we *know* the general causal law in political economy Mill was certain, as we have noted. [24] 'Knowing therefore accurately the properties of the substances concerned', he observed, 'we may reason with as much certainty [in political economy] as in the most demonstrative parts of physics ...' [25]

Verification and disturbing causes

In Mill's view, if the behavioral causal law embodied in the assumption of the theory of political economy is 'true', and the logic used in deriving implications is correct, then the theory is 'true' and forms part of the corpus of established knowledge. Whether the implications of the theory accord with the facts, on this view, has no bearing on the *scientific* validity of the theory. As Mill tells us (*ibid*. p. 424):

> To verify the hypothesis itself a posteriori, that is to examine whether the facts of any actual case are in accordance with it, is no part of the business of science at all, but of the *application* of science.

Further, an individual 'may be an excellent professor of abstract science [of political economy]' without at all concerning himself with how well the implications of the theory accord with the facts. [26]

There are two problems here. First, as we showed in the last section, Mill had argued in talking about the moral sciences generally that so long as we have the relevant causal laws – in political economy the motive of preferring more to less – we can expect to make 'predictions which will *almost* always be verified and general propositions which are almost always true'. This suggests that theories in all of the moral sciences, including political economy which was the most advanced, give at least reasonably reliable predictions. Yet one gets a different impression from the Essay where a great deal of space is devoted to warning us that 'disturbing causes' – that is, specific factors which are relevant in particular instances – have to be taken into account in making predictions. How can one reconcile the two?[27] One suggestion is that since Mill felt that the implications of theory give us only 'tendencies', caution is in order. But note that in the very confident passage from the *Logic* where Mill acknowledged that we get only tendencies from theory, he still felt that so long as these tendencies are the general and major ones, we *can* trust in our theory, only we will miss *complete* accuracy. Two remarks are in order. It seems to us, first, that Mill was ambivalent about this matter; as, generally, his successors have been. Second, it raises the question on whom we are to rely for making reliable predictions. Surely not on the political economist who, Mill believed, may be an excellent professor of abstract science without knowing much in the way of what goes on in the world. It is the *statesman*, in Mill's view, who plays this role. As he noted (*ibid*. p. 433):

> No one who attempts to lay down propositions for the guidance of mankind, however perfect his scientific acquirements, can dispense with a practical knowledge of the actual modes in which the affairs of the world are carried on, and an extensive personal experience of the actual ideas, feelings, and intellectual and moral tendencies of his own country and his own age. *The true practical statesman* is he who combines this experience with a profound knowledge of abstract political philosophy (emphasis added).

A consequence of this position is that the nature of 'verification' becomes very murky. To confirm this we return one last time to the *Logic* (1973, Book VI, Chapter IX). Mill deals there with verification, 'where the object is to determine the effect of any one social cause among a great number acting simultaneously, in effect, for example, of corn laws, or of a prohibitive commercial system generally'. The problem is that there are so very many variables involved that comparing the implications of a theory with the facts generally does not tell us very much. We have to look at each case separately and when we have predicted very well in a large number of cases and where we have not failed to predict, then we can have confidence 'that our science *and our knowledge* of the particular case render us competent to predict the future ...' (emphasis added). But then are we verifying *the theory* or our ability to locate the pertinent 'disturbing causes' in particular instances?

Note that it is questionable whether in Mill's scheme for economics 'disturbing causes' as a rule become part of the theory.[28] That is the reason that the professor of the abstract science is such an unreliable guide, and also that, as we have seen, he need pay no attention to specific experience. In this view, the theory of political economy takes the form 'if p then q', where $p = p_1 + p_2 + \ldots p_n$ and p_1 is the tendency to maximize which we derive from introspection. One who knows political economy can be of aid with prediction only if $p_2 \ldots p_n$ do not materially affect q.[29]

The 'practical man'

Mill did not dream up the 'practical man' (or 'instrumentalist') the way Popper did.[30] Even before he became involved with logic he had done battle with political pamphleteers who had based their arguments entirely, or almost entirely, on correlations of a few observations. (See Robson, 1973, vol. 4, pp. 19, 127, 130, 190). In the essay the 'practical man' becomes the chief protagonist; one almost gets the impression that Mill's major purpose was to deal this annoying opponent a fatal blow.[31] Yet Mill's decision to reject entirely what the 'practical man' was doing is surely open to question. Granted this approach left very much to be desired. Was there nonetheless not some merit in it? If we find regularities in the data of economic experience, might they not be useful? And might it not be worthwhile to ask *why* the regularities occur? Might this rationale, in fact, have played a role, perhaps an important one, in the work of creative economists like Adam Smith when they were in the process of formulating economic theory? Mill did not consider this possibility. The reason, it seems to us, is that with Euclidean geometry as a model he needed very solid axioms from which to hang his theory. As a result, he insisted on criteria which could hardly be met when working back from implications to premises. Further, in Mill's psychology behavior depends on states of mind and the evidence of specific experience sheds little light on states of mind. In addition, Mill had introspection to rely on to serve as a basis for theorizing and such theory could be very effectively defended. What need was there for exploring new possibilities? Recall that for Mill the '*real*' science was in the premises or assumptions of theory and that he felt that economists had done very well in locating the true causal law in their domain. What remained then for the most part was to develop more thoroughly the implications of the known causal law and to find minor causes which would improve prediction. Note that all this derives from the fact that Mill's approach to logic or the philosophy of science is deductivist, as we showed at the end of the first section of this chapter.

In the next chapter we argue that when one views science through inductivist spectacles not only do one's notions about psychology change, but one tends as well to drop Mill's idea about the 'real' science being in the premises or assumptions. In this very different context, too, one sees that the way the 'practical man' inquires is not so entirely different from the way the scientist does. Only the former is a very superficial thinker; he stops at the first stage of an investigation, an unwise course of behavior not only for science but for practical purposes as well.

MILL'S VIEWS AND FRIEDMAN'S

It should be apparent from what has been said how radically Mill's views differ from Friedman's. The major differences are as follows:

1. Friedman does, but Mill does not, view extensive observation of specific experience as a necessary component in the process of deriving 'good' (meaning both scientifically sound as well as useful) theory in economics.
2. Friedman does, but Mill does not, view inquiry in economics as a continuous process where observation of specific experience and hypothesizing interact at every stage of the inquiry process.
3. Mill does, whereas Friedman does not, regard 'realistic' assumptions or premises – no matter how these terms are defined – as either necessary or sufficient to make theory provisionally acceptable as part of economic science.
4. Friedman does, but Mill does not, believe that the extent to which a theory can predict (and retrodict) should have a bearing on how we judge its premises.

Underlying all these differences is the fact that Friedman's approach to logic is basically inductivist (like Whewell's) whereas Mill's in this respect is deductivist.

Note that we are saying nothing under 4. about 'falsifying' a theory; both Friedman and Mill agree that theory is not falsifiable. It is only the naïve-falsificationist Popperian who is ready to *reject* a theory as soon as an anomaly appears. The difference between Friedman and Mill is that for Friedman the failure of the implications of a theory to correspond as well with the facts as those of another theory is ground for choosing the

latter and questioning the truth of the premises of the former. Not so for
Mill.

A MODERN PERSPECTIVE

Mill to Robbins

Our purpose in this chapter has been to show against the backdrop of
traditional methodology in economics that Friedman's views depart
radically from that tradition. So far we have shown only that Friedman's
views differ sharply from John Stuart Mill's. There is of course the
question of how representative Mill's views are, and here we have to
admit that in some respects Mill is not representative at all. He has, for
example, been much criticized for his notion of the 'economic man';[32] he
has been said to give us an interpretation that makes economics look far
more abstract than it really is;[33] and above all, he has been accused of
not being consistent in practice with his own methodological formulations.[34] Our interest, however, is not in the broad field of economic
methodology in all its many facets but only in those basic respects in
which Friedman's views differ from Mill's. In this respect Mill is
representative almost without exception of a methodological tradition
stretching at least from Senior to Robbins. J. N. Keynes (1890, Chapter
VI, Sections 3 and 4) differs somewhat in that he can be interpreted as
suggesting that specific experience might be useful in deriving theory,
though not in the area of value and distribution. But he is quite alone
on this point. On the other three points that we have noted there is
consensus. Even more importantly, if we look for the preconceptions
underlying the explicit methodological formulations, what we find are
the same general views about science that Mill explicitly formulated. The
major difference is that Mill goes more deeply into the issues and
generally he is more consistent.

We have no space to support this position more fully here, but it may
be illustrated by example. Thus, Mill's views on verification might strike
the reader as unusual but if the views of the others are any less striking it
is only because they are less explicit. For example, J. E. Cairnes says of
political economy (1875, p. 48) that 'its conclusions ... may or may not
correspond to the realities of external nature, and therefore must be
considered as representing only hypothetical truth'. And Lionel Robbins,
after suggesting that 'Economic laws describe inevitable implications'
(1949, p. 121), goes on to argue that these laws hold only if an unspecific
ceteris paribus is granted. Since, 'nobody in his senses would hold that

laws of mechanics were invalidated if an experiment designed to illustrate them were interrupted by an earthquake', so too, we are to understand, the laws of economics hold independent of experimental verification (p. 123).

More current views

We have referred to the tradition running from Senior to Robbins. But Robbins wrote down his views over half a century ago. Have not important changes taken place since? Indeed they have. There has been much ferment in economic methodology, the more so the closer one gets to the present time. Positivism, for example, has come and gone, leaving us in a rather unsettled state (see, for example, Caldwell, 1980). In a sense all of this is true. Specific experience certainly plays a more important role in the work of the economist today than it did a half century ago and more attention is being paid to testing, whether verification or falsification. Yet with regard to those aspects with which we are concerned it is doubtful whether any substantive changes have occurred.

Take prevailing views about methodology expounded and illustrated in introductory textbook in economics. There is typically not much that Mill could not have accepted.[35] There are of course more, and more sophisticated, methodologists in economics, but in terms of the points we have made, contemporary methodologists are in some respects closer to Mill than were some of the earlier ones: compare for example Mark Blaug (1980) with J. N. Keynes (1890) on the feasibility of using specific experience as an aid in deriving theory. The extremely negative response by methodologists to Friedman's 'Positive economics' is also revealing of a basically Millian orientation. There are seeming exceptions, of course, Fritz Machlup being the most conspicuous one. Yet in spite of the approval which Machlup gave to a major aspect of Friedman's position, closer examination reveals that he shared Friedman's general views no more than did any of the other methodologists. The fact that Machlup identified his own methodological position with Mill's (1978, pp. 142–3) suggests that on broad fundamentals – the kind we are concerned with – his way of thinking, like that of most of his contemporaries, was far closer to Mill's than appears on the surface.[36]

The advent of econometrics in recent years has affected the way economists and economic methodologists view their science. It has made plausible, and acceptable, the notion that economic theory can be, and should be, subject to falsification. But as is generally agreed, while falsification is accepted in principle, in practice it is almost universally honored only in the breach (see Blaug, 1980, Part IV). But what then is the empirical basis of this approach? A glimpse at how some pioneers of this movement attempted to answer the question is revealing.

Some of the leaders at the Cowles Commission in the 1940s, notably Tjalling Koopmans and Jacob Marschak, were consciously attempting to introduce an empirical component to theory by adding 'shock' (stochastic) elements to exact models (see, for example, Koopmans and Hood, 1953). This can be considered an extension of the methodological approach of J. S. Mill; the realism of the assumptions of theory or the plausibility of the motives is taken as a given and testing comprises only identifying the size and nature of the error term: that is, seeing how closely an exact formulation fits an inexact world. Some remarks made by Koopmans (1947) in criticism of National Bureau work and in defense of Cowles Commission methods give us an interesting insight into the connection. Using reasoning which could have come from Cairnes or Robbins, Koopmans tells us (1947, p. 220):

> While it was long possible and sometimes tempting for physicists to deny the usefulness of the molecular hypothesis, we economists have the good luck of being some of the 'molecules' of economic life ourselves, and of having the possibility through human contacts to study the behavior of other 'molecules'. Besides introspection, the interview or questionnaire, and even small scale experiments, are available as means of acquiring or extending knowledge about individual behavior. Thus we, indeed, have direct access to information already recognized as essential.

This approach is as much an 'inside' view of behavior as was J. S. Mill's which, remember, rests on knowledge of motives introspectively derived.[37]

In the next chapter, where we consider some fundamental aspects of Friedman's pragmatic way of thinking, the important differences between Friedman's approach and that which could be called 'orthodox', in Mill's time, but also today,[38] should become even more apparent.

NOTES

1. Without question the major criticism levelled against Friedman is that his position is philosophically indefensible (see, for example, Caldwell, 1980). Boland's 'defense' (1979) rests primarily on the argument that Friedman could be philosophically defended if one accepted 'instrumentalism'. But Boland rejects this philosophical position (see Boland, 1984), so that while he rejects Friedman's critics, he also rejects Friedman, for philosophical reasons.
2. Most economists, and certainly economic methodologists, subscribe to the view which Nagel (1950, p. xxvii) attributes to Mill that 'sound theory (whether in the natural or in the social sciences) is a product of sound logic'.

That being the case, it is often hard to avoid questions of logic when arguing about whether one approach – or one theory – is preferable to another.

3. Unless one keeps in mind Mill's general views of science one can easily go astray. As an example we cite Hollander (1985, pp. 112–13), who argues that in Mill's view 'evidence drawn from introspection varies from time to time and place to place'. He reaches this conclusion by running together empirical and causal laws, on the one hand, and assumptions and implications on the other. Such difficulties confront us not only in trying to interpret Mill but also in trying to interpret other methodologists in the classical tradition if their fundamental notions about 'science' generally are not taken into account.

4. We say 'causes or premises' because for Mill causes are embedded in the premises.

5. Hollander (1985, pp. 125–31) argues that Mill felt that results of general significance could be derived from verification. We disagree but it is unnecessary to stop to argue the point here. Our interest is in the tradition, and if one examines what methodologists in this tradition said and what economists did, one cannot but conclude that if Hollander is right about Mill in this regard it merely shows that Mill was very unrepresentative.

6. Conceivably, in Mill's system, one could get a disconfirmation because a causal law which had been thought to be pertinent turned out not to be, though he nowhere talks of this possibility, perhaps because he did not feel that it was of any practical significance. What he stresses, as we have noted, is that a failure may occur because pertinent disturbing causes have been left out or because they have been improperly combined. It cannot be because the causal laws themselves which have been applied are wrong. The causal laws, of course, could conceivably be wrong, but only if they had not been 'proved' before being applied, as the correct application of the deductive method mandates. This last point shows why Mill was so unenthusiastic about what he called 'the hypothetical method' which is considered in the next paragraph of the text.

7. As Losee (1983) shows, this almost deprives the hypothetical method of any conceivable usefulness. Mill was also willing to accept the results derived via the hypothetical method if the guessed premises could then independently be shown to be true. What this does is to get us back to the deductive method with more tolerance for the sequences of operations. It does not get us to abductive logic as the next quote in the text shows.

8. Perhaps Mill expressed himself so strongly because his adversary, William Whewell (1847), had made the concept which Mill here condemns – Whewell called it 'consilience' – a central tenet of his philosophy of science (see Losee, 1983). Further comments on Mill–Whewell differences will be noted in passing.

9. This shows why Mill's method is called a priori (by Mill himself as well as by others). In the advanced stage of science one starts by thinking out a scheme or theory. The observation of specific experience, as in Popper, is posterior. In the early stages, on Mill's view, all sorts of causal laws are discovered. But this does not enter into the scheme because at the *advanced* stage the causes have to be combined and this can be done only by reasoning out; otherwise there would be no direction.

10. There are, of course, no unobservables (or theoretical terms) in Mill. As we show in the next section, Mill did feel that in the moral sciences we often

(generally?) cannot 'see' the causes at work in the data of experience so that we have to reason inversely. But this did not lead him to consider abduction as an alternative to the deductive method. Neither, of course, have any of the other traditional methodologists to this day.

11. For an excellent treatment of the role of this concept in Whewell's way of thinking, see Laudan, 1971.

12. It is only in this broad sense that Mill can be characterized as a deductivist. Since Mill insists on grounding any theory on inductively derived causal laws he can, in this other (more usual) sense be called an inductivist. (With regard to the latter see Buchdahl, 1971.)

13. Losee (1983) deals with this difference between what he calls Whewell's 'historicism' and Mill's 'logicism'.

14. In fact, as Laudan shows (1971, pp. 375–84), Whewell argued unsatisfactorily that theories which met the consilience test were necessarily true. He was aware that from the standpoint of deductive logic he had failed but suggested: 'Induction is inconclusive *as reasoning*. It is not reasoning; it is another way of getting at truth' (cited by Laudan, 1971).

15. Hume knew this a long time ago but the full implications of this knowledge were generally not recognized until much later.

16. This is somewhat surprising since, as Laudan (1971, pp. 388–9) points out, there is striking similarity between (the sophisticated falsificationist) Popper's views and those of Whewell on the matter of criteria for theory choice.

17. The differences between Popper and Kuhn are instructive in this regard. See Popper (in Lakatos and Musgrave, 1970) and Kuhn ('Reflections on my critics', *ibid.*).

18. Mill was a very diligent observer of social phenomena but his view of psychology prevented him to a large extent from making use of such observations in formulating social *theory*. Since the basic causal laws of the moral sciences were taken to be known through introspection alone, all that observation could do was illustrate how the laws worked themselves out. As we show in the next section, this is the way he rationalized the inquiry process of the moral sciences.

19. Some of Mill's successors have argued that the physical scientist can reason from effects to causes *only* because introspection was not possible in this area (see Cairnes, 1875, III, 3; Robbins, 1949, p. 105; also a quoted passage from Koopmans later in this chapter). Robbins felt that the *economist* thereby had the advantage.

20. It seems reasonably clear that Mill's practical interest affected his judgment here as it has that of many other economists.

21. We say 'not surprisingly' because it seems to us that his notions about the logic of economics had considerably more to do with the way he formulated his logic of science than his ideas on science generally had on his notions about the logic of economics.

22. But in another sense it is not so different because the discovery of causal laws by the four methods was done before sciences reached the advanced stage. As an *advanced* science, then, economics was like physics.

23. To Mill, of course, geometry was an empirical science.

24. The mistake is often made of concluding from the quoted passage that because he said that the behavioral premise was 'assumed' it must mean that he did not think that it was true, or was relative to time and place (see, for example, Senior, 1966, no. 4 of 1852 Lectures; Hausman, 1981; Hollander,

1985, p. 110.) Note, first, that the premises of geometry are also said to be 'assumed' and surely Mill did not mean – this being in the days before non-Euclidean geometry – that they were relative or shaky. Second, as we showed in the first part of this chapter, to Mill causal laws (as opposed to empirical generalizations) were invariable and unconditional. The *implications* of the conjunction of a number of such causal laws could be uncertain or relative because they applied exactly only where no other causes were at work, but that is quite another matter.

25. What we are certain of are the implications that follow logically from any one causal law. Such an implication Mill called a 'tendency' (1973, III, X, 4). It is given this name because since the effect of one law could always be deflected by others it is necessary to be aware of all of the causal laws in any situation to be able to derive reliable predictions.

26. This is the one tenet that later traditional methodologists rejected (for example, Robbins, 1949, p. 150), but as is clear from Robbins, the reason for the change is that the 'political economist' or 'economist' has broadened to include part of the function Mill gave to the 'statesman'. This represents no basic change in methodology as such.

27. In some places in the *Logic*, too, Mill shows great caution (for example, 1973, VI, IX, 2), so change of mind over time cannot be a reason.

28. We say this because disturbing causes are said by Mill to be *minor* and *specific as to time and place*. Hollander (1985, pp. 122–4) minimizes the distinction between major and minor causes but his reasons seem to us unconvincing. For our purposes it is unnecessary to argue here again about what Mill might or might not have meant since it is the *tradition* we are interested in and for others in this line there is no such ambiguity.

29. But recall what was said above about Mill's seeming ambivalence on this point. Therefore to conclude, without qualification, that Mill believed that economics was not a predictive science, as Hollander does (1985, pp. 131–4), seems to us questionable. As we have noted, other methodologists in this tradition were also ambivalent on this point.

30. The Popperian 'instrumentalist' category is also a more mixed bag which includes the philosopher Bishop Berkeley, physicists such as Mach, and the local TV repair man (see Popper, 1968, III, 3 and 4; 1965, p. 111; Frazer and Boland, 1983, pp. 141–2). It is doubtful if any of these figures, other than perhaps the last, is adequately represented.

31. Mill tells us in his *Autobiography* (1957 [1873]) that Macaulay's criticism of his father's paper on government led him to write the piece. What Mill objected to in Macaulay was the empirical approach, essentially what he objected to in the arguments of the 'practicals'.

32. See, for example, Alfred Marshall's comments in a letter quoted by Whitaker (1975, n. 32).

33. See, for example, Viner (1917).

34. See, for example, Marshall (1961, V. I, Appendix B).

35. 'Falsificationism' ostensibly entered the introductory economics course with Lipsey (1963). But even here the philosophy seems to have had far greater effect on what Lipsey said than on the way he presented his material. With the second edition (1966), where Lipsey makes the transition from 'naïve' to 'sophisticated' falsificationist, there is not much left to which a Millian could object. When we arrive at the more recent American edition of this same text (Lipsey, Steiner and Purvis, 1984), just about every trace of methodological heterodoxy has been removed.

36. In his publication of 1964 Machlup, responding to Samuelson's of 1963, argues that 'the bulk of economic theory ... contains only theoretical constructs and no operational concepts, and yields results which, we hope, point to elements of truth present in complex situations'. In the context in which this statement is made it is essentially Millian since it makes Mill's point that we cannot judge the scientific acceptability of a theory by how well it predicts, since theory merely points to *elements of truth* (i.e. *some* true *causes*) present in complex situations. It should also be noted that Machlup nowhere argues that 'The theorist starts with some set of observed and related facts, as full and comprehensive as possible'. Nor, so far as we are aware, does he envisage inquiry as a continuously interactive process of observation and hypothesis formulation. In fact, there is some evidence (for example, 1964, p. 735) that he would reject such a notion.

37. Thus it is not at all surprising to find Koopmans (1957) giving a reasonably standard (Millian) criticism of Friedman's position. Though in a sense Koopmans is closer to Senior in rejecting the notion that the assumptions of economic theory are hypothetical. This difference, however, results only from misunderstanding.

38. In a forthcoming volume Daniel M. Hausman argues that today economic theorists still apparently subscribe to Mill's methodology regardless of what they might say when they discuss methodology.

6 • PRAGMATIC FOUNDATIONS

In the last chapter we examined Mill's logic of science as a background against which to consider how, in some fundamental respects, Friedman's approach to economic science differed from Mill's, and to show, too, that this difference applied to their approaches to science generally. In this chapter we show how Friedman's approach coincides with that of John Dewey on a number of basic points. To make the analysis meaningful it is necessary to show, at least in a very general way, how Dewey's logic relates to Mill's. For that reason we will in most instances note the issues that Mill's logic brings to the fore and show how Dewey's logic – the logic implicit in Friedman's approach – deals with these issues. In the fourth section we consider Dewey in a more contemporary context, using Karl Popper as representative of more traditional ways of thinking in philosophy. Our purpose in doing so is not to show that Dewey is right and Popper (and the mainstream tradition) wrong. It is to make clear the basic issues which determine whether one tends to look at Friedman's approach sympathetically even while recognizing severe difficulties with his exposition, as for example Nagel (1963) does, or whether one tends to reject this approach to science entirely, as for example does Rotwein (1959), Boland (1984), Wong (1973), and Caldwell (1982), among others.

DIFFICULTIES WITH MILL'S WAY OF THINKING

The problem of unobservables

We saw in the preceding chapter that for Mill the core of science resides in causal laws and that these causal laws are embedded in the premises or assumptions of theory. This is true of his view of science generally as well as of social science and economics in particular. It is not an arbitrary notion on Mill's part for the essential characteristic of science for him was that it explains, and explanation on this view involves deducing implications from true premises which embody causal laws. Since deduction merely passes on the truth from premises to implications, on Mill's view, we must have true premises to get true implications. But the premises of one theory can be the implications of another, right on up to the basic laws of nature, so that ultimately it is in the laws of nature that the basic truths are embedded and thence passed down to all lower level theories.

There is a problem with this line of reasoning. For Mill causal laws are established empirically by induction and the question arises whether this is possible in any or most instances. In economics as in other moral sciences, as we have seen, Mill admitted that causal laws could not be derived from specific experience; he recommended introspection instead. This is not an innocent switch, as will be seen presently. But even for the physical sciences there is a problem because the hooks that are needed on which to hang theories are generally not available. For one thing, we run into the problem of unobservables, which have come to be recognized since Mill's time, but which were of course there all along. Thus, we have Newton's forces acting at a distance and electrons spinning in planetary-like systems. Nor are the moral sciences free of this problem. It is not any easier to see a motive than it is a force or an electron; all are constructs. What we see are the *effects* or consequences of motives, as of forces and electrons. We see the effects and reason backwards to hypothetical causes that are provisionally taken to be true.

Finding true universal premises

A second problem we run into is that even where we are dealing only with observables it is impossible to prove, as Mill requires, that the universal generalizations embodied in the premises are true, a dilemma Popper has referred to as the Hume problem. Mill, as we have seen, seemed to feel that Hume's argument applied only to empirical generalizations, but Hume's insight applies as well to theories, as Dewey (and Karl Popper) have argued. We will consider this argument in what follows.

The need to appeal to true premises

It is not very difficult to see why Mill argued the way he did and, in fact, how this same way of thinking created the grounds for the rationalist type of argument.[1] As Dewey points out (1938 p. 142), Mill's reasoning

> ... has been used ever since the time of Aristotle, and is still current today. It is argued that inference must rest upon something known from which it

starts, so that unless there are true premises which serve as such a basis it is impossible, no matter how adequate inference and discursive reasoning may be, to arrive at true conclusions. Hence the only way of avoiding *regressus ad infinitum* is said to be the existence of truths immediately known.

It is not by chance that Mill came to call his preferred method for science the a priori. As Dewey saw it, we can establish a genuine empirical basis for theory by switching from the a priori to the a posteriori, that is, from looking back to premises to looking forward to implications, and relying primarily on the test of implications in judging theory.

The problem with introspection

Mill seems to escape the problem in economics which we have been considering by substituting introspection for the observation of specific experience, but in the process he generated a problem just as serious.[2] As Dewey pointed out (*ibid*. pp. 144–6), introspection is a vastly more complicated process than Mill allowed. Even such a simple statement, used by Mill as an example, as 'I was vexed yesterday', involves a complex process of inference and, as Dewey observed (1938, p. 145), 'Mill's whole doctrine of immediate knowledge is itself *an inference* from a psychological theory which is itself inferential.' Dewey adds: 'In its strictly logical bearing it rests upon the uncritical acceptance of the old notion that no proposition can be "proved" unless it follows from "truths" already known.'

The Euclidean model

Many philosophers today would probably agree with this criticism of Mill but this leaves open whether we try to patch up Mill's system or to substitute a new system for it, in which case, what new system? Dewey opted for a new system because he felt that the Euclidean model which Mill used was not appropriate for empirical science. Dewey tells us (*ibid*. p. 141):

> For centuries, the axioms of and definitions of Euclidean geometry were regarded as absolute first principles which could be accepted without question. Preoccupation with the new order of problems disclosed that they were both overlapping and deficient as logical grounds for generalized geometry. The result has made it clear that instead of being 'self-evident' truths immediately known, they are postulates adopted because of what follows from them.

As we showed in the last chapter, in formulating his logic of economics, as in his logic of science generally, Mill relied very heavily on Euclidean geometry as model.[3]

AN ALTERNATIVE APPROACH

A Euclidean versus a process view

If we try to replace Millian logic, as well as Euclidean geometry as a model, we run into a serious problem. We seem to lose our basis for 'proof'. How are we to distinguish between mere correlations and genuine theory for which we have 'proof'? This question has been asked by some of Friedman's critics and his methodology found wanting by them because it seems to run the two together.[4] To Dewey this is not a problem because the difference in *reliability* can be explained if instead of comparing the one against the other *at any one point in time* we consider the function that both have in the process of inquiry which takes place *over time*. On this view the difference between a correlation and a theory is that the former comes at the earliest stage of the inquiry process; it is therefore less reliable, and merely tentative. For example, knowledge of day following night does not derive from any very extensive process of inquiry; Newton's theory does. This being the case, there is a much better basis for predicting that day will follow night on the basis of Newtonian theory than there is on the basis of the mere correlation derived from observation alone. There is, of course, very considerable evidence for the correlation but there is definitely more for predictions made on the basis of the theory because it is supported by a considerably wider range of evidence. In the Deweyan system the difference between correlations and theory is acknowledged; but it is a difference to be viewed within the context of the inquiry process and not as one involving the matter of 'proof'.

Uncertainty and lack of proof

Dewey rejects the notion of 'proof' for empirical generalizations. The notion of proof to Dewey implies certainty and building upon David Hume's profound insight which Mill interpreted very narrowly, Dewey spent considerable energy arguing against what he called a futile 'quest for certainty'.[5] One consequence of giving up the quest for proof or certainty in empirical work is that Mill's objections to what he called the hypothetical method drops away. Dewey, in a way, turns Mill upside down. As Friedman shows, in this anti-Millian way of thinking the implications of a theory are not taken to be true because the premises are known to be true but rather the premises are provisionally taken to be true because the implications of a theory coincide with facts. On this view Mill's 'hypothetical' (experimental) method takes on the central role in inquiry, whether scientific or common sense.[6] Thus, in this perspective it can be said that the weakness in Mill derives from the fact that he confused modelizing with theorizing – form with substance – and chose the model over the theory as the basic component of science.[7]

Two different rationales

Yet Mill's objection to what he called the hypothetical method cannot be so easily dismissed. A theory, after all, has the form 'if p then q' ($p \supset q$). The hypothetical method, as we showed in Chapter 3, above, seems to rest on the notion that p is true because q is observed to be true, a logical *non sequitur*. The problem with this result, on a Deweyan view, is that it overlooks the fact that theories result from inquiry and inquiry is a *process*. A way around this difficulty is to be had, within the confines of logic, but only if p and q are treated as equivalents. This shows even more clearly the gap between the logic of demonstration and Dewey's process of inquiry. As Dewey notes (1938, pp. 318–19):

> It is a familiar principle that affirmation of the consequent does not warrant complete affirmation of the antecedent. Denial of the consequent grounds, however, denial of the antecedent. When, therefore, operations yield data which contradict a deduced consequence, elimination of one alternative possibility is effected. Recurrent agreement of the indicative force of data, provided they are secured by independent experimental operations, gives cumulative weight to the affirmation of the antecedent whenever we can affirm the consequent. The affirmation of any given hypothesis proceeds in this way.

The role of specific experience

Once one accepts the hypothetical method for science, as Dewey does, Mill's rational basis for limiting the role of specific experience disappears. Specific experience comes into its own. Its role on this way of looking at things transcends the mere verification of the implications of theory, theory which on Mill's view is derived in economics – as in all the moral sciences – without the aid of specific experience, and in the physical sciences without such aid in the advanced stage. It becomes a fully equal partner with theorizing at *every* stage of scientific investigation.

In fact, it may well appear even to one who is not a Millian that Dewey goes *too far*, as not a few consider that Friedman does, giving specific experience too *large* a role. Consider, for example, the following passage from a work of Dewey's where he summarizes his main ideas (1950, p. 118):

> The first distinguishing characteristic of thinking then is facing the facts –
> inquiry, minute and extensive scrutinizing, observation. Nothing has done

greater harm to the successful conduct of the enterprise of thinking (and to the logics which reflect and formulate the undertaking) than the habit of treating observation as something outside of and prior to thinking, and thinking as something which can go on in the head without including observation of new facts as part of itself. Every approximation to such 'thinking' is really an approach to the method of escape and self-delusion ... It substitutes an emotionally agreeable and rationally self-consistent train of meanings for inquiry into features of the situation which cause the trouble.[8] It leads to that type of Idealism which has well been termed intellectual somnambulism. It creates a class of 'thinkers' who are remote from practice and hence from testing their thought by application – a socially superior and irresponsible class.

We have shown in Chapter 1 that Friedman considered some economists to be such thinkers.

Preference for the 'intermediate' area

Note that Dewey is as opposed to piling up facts as he is to detached theorizing. In fact, as he shows in such passages as the following, he sees a connection between these two equally one-sided approaches. He tells us (p. 119):

The isolation of thinking from confrontation with facts encourages that kind of observation which merely accumulates brute facts, which occupies itself with mere details, but never inquires into their meaning and consequences ... Thinking which is a method of reconstructing experience treats observation of facts, on the other hand, as the indispensable step of defining the problem, of locating the trouble, of forcing home a definite, instead of merely a vague emotional, sense of what the difficulty is and where it lies. It is not aimless, random, miscellaneous, but purposeful, specific and limited by the character of the trouble undergone ... When the scientific man appears to observe aimlessly, it is merely that he is so in love with problems as sources and guides of inquiry, that he is striving to turn up a problem where none appears on the surface: he is, as we say, hunting for trouble because of the satisfaction to be had in coping with it.

There is a striking closeness of Dewey's thinking here to Friedman's, who argues for 'the equally vital *intermediate area*' (1952c, p. 457, emphasis added).

Note, too, that when Dewey says that 'the *first* distinguishing feature of thinking ... is facing the facts', he does not mean to imply that one can do meaningful observation without ideas, any more than does Friedman when he argues that 'The theorist *starts* with some set of observed and related facts, as full and comprehensive as possible ...' The reason for facing the facts (or for careful observation) is primarily that we never begin any investigation from scratch; our problem is to determine how the matter being studied is different from that which the theory which we hold when we start the investigation can adequately deal with. In everyday practice we often find after very cursory examination that the theory enables us to deal with the case very well, though not infrequently some adjustments have to be made. The researcher, however, is not interested in such dull cases. To determine whether a particular problem is worth working on, there must be rather extensive investigation to find out which aspects of the problem are familiar ones and which are not (1938, Chapter VI). Observation is thus first only in the context of the process of inquiry as usually practiced. Were we to start from scratch, as philosophers often assume, it makes no sense to argue that observation comes first. But then neither does it make sense to argue that one must start with theorizing – that is, that the facts are theory-impregnated – since unless theory is fact-impregnated as well, it is fantasy and not theory.

The 'realism' of premises

It is because Dewey visualizes inquiry as a process that he argues that to insist on the 'realism' of premises, to use Friedman's way of putting it – which in this sense means precise truth – would actually hold back research. As Dewey puts it (*ibid*, p. 142):

> It is notorious that a hypothesis does not have to be true in order to be highly serviceable in the conduct of inquiry. Examination of the historical progress of any science will show that the same thing holds good of 'facts': of what has been taken in the past as evidential. They were serviceable, not because they were true or false, but because, when they were taken to be provisional means of advancing investigation, they led to discovery of other facts which proved more relevant and more weighty .... The history of science also shows that when hypotheses have been taken to be finally true and hence unquestionable, they have obstructed inquiry and kept science committed to doctrines that later turned out to be invalid.

The logic of economics

These remarks are directed at logicians like Mill, as Dewey makes clear in a comment on the history of economics. He tells us (*ibid*. p. 504):

> Classical political economy, with respect to its logical form, claimed to be a science in virtue, first, of certain ultimate first truths, and, secondly, in virtue of the possibility of rigorous 'deduction' of actual economic phenomena from these truths ... The members of this school, from Adam Smith to the Mills and their contemporary followers, differed of course from the traditional *rationalistic* school. For they held that first principles were themselves derived inductively, instead of being established by a priori intuition. But once arrived at they were regarded as unquestionable

truths, or as axioms with regard to any further truths, since the latter could be deductively derived from them.

Dewey's criticism:

> From the standpoint of logical method, the conceptions involved were not regarded as *hypotheses* to be employed in observation and ordering of phenomena, and hence to be tested by the consequences produced by acting upon them.

These quotes, it seems to us, point to the heart of the difference between Mill and the orthodox tradition, on the one side, and Friedman and Dewey, on the other. Much more is involved than merely the 'realism' of assumptions, no matter how the term 'realism' is defined. There are two very different conceptions of science confronting each other, the one Euclidean and the other process. The two are not compatible with each other even though the objective of the work of both ways of thinking is taken to be the same.

Dewey was greatly concerned with this difference and he described it in a number of different ways. In one place, as we have seen, he tells us:

> What makes the essential difference between modern research and the reflection of, say, the Greeks, is not the absence of 'mere thinking,' but the presence of conditions for testing its results; the elaborate system of checks and balances found in the technique of modern experimentation.

The role of prediction

Note how central is the notion of prediction (and retrodiction) in Dewey's way of thinking as revealed in this passage. Friedman, as we have seen, argues that 'the only relevant test of the *validity* of a hypothesis is comparison of its predictions with experience'. This sounds like an extreme statement, but Dewey voices similar sentiments in an even broader context. Dewey also explains *why* he expresses himself this way. He tells us (1938, pp. 109–10):

> When it is said, as it sometimes is, that science is *prediction*, the anticipation that constitutes an idea is grounded in a set of controlled observations and of regulated conceptual ways of interpreting them. Because inquiry is a progressive determination of a problem and its possible solution, ideas differ in grade according to the stage of the inquiry reached . . . . Every idea originates as a suggestion, but not every suggestion is an idea. The suggestion becomes an idea when it is examined with reference to its functional fitness; its capacity as a means of resolving the given situation.

In other words, a prediction is not a conjecture drawn out of thin air. It derives out of a process, and the process is directed towards solving a definite problem. Predictions are made at every step of a scientific investigation but the prediction referred to in Friedman's statement, as in Dewey's, is the last step (for the moment) in the process. In a very real sense, it sums up everything that has gone before.

Where the 'practical man' fits in

A prediction can also be made, of course, on the basis of an observed correlation and it was this kind to which Mill was so strongly opposed because he felt that the 'practical man' often reasoned this way. In a way the Deweyan approach is that of the 'practical man', though not at all that of the *naive* practical man who is Mill's target. If there are no more extensive results of research available about a problem, then acting on the basis of an observed correlation may be the wisest course to take. In fact, it may have a lot more to recommend it than acting on the basis of a theory which rests upon plausible but not very carefully examined premises. Mill might have at least partly agreed with this and reminded us of his appeal to 'disturbing causes'. But if we take this part of his logic of economics very seriously, would not a great deal of research still be required to find the right disturbing causes (even though that is the kind of interchange between observation and theorizing that Mill felt was *not* appropriate in economics)? So argues a Deweyan; and he asks further, whether it would not be wiser to set out this way to begin with. Of course, one might believe – as Friedman implicitly does, and as we tried to show in the second part of Chapter 2 – that the great economists in fact *did* behave this way, and not, as Mill and the other orthodox methodologists claimed, by building on 'true' assumptions.

The logic of economics judged by what economists have done

This raises again the question, 'what is the rationale or logic according to which economists have achieved their most importants results'? Mill tells us that the logic of political economy that he presents is 'undoubtedly its character as it has been understood and taught by its most distinguished teachers'. If we judge on the basis of what economists have *said*, Mill is probably right. But one must remember, as Dewey urges us to do, how strong has been the hold of the Euclidean model, not only on Mill and other logicians, but on economists as well. Might not economists have intuitively subscribed to one logic while paying lip service to another? This question is not easy to answer. The hint one gets from Dewey on how to go about trying to answer it is that one should try to use aspects of economic theory as hypotheses in dealing with experience and observe whether they help us to see or rather blur our vision. If the former, then the presumption must be that the logic to which economists appeal when they present their theory is not the logic implicit in the way they have actually proceeded (although it is not *certain* that such is the case). This, as we have noted in Chapter 2, is the position that Friedman holds.

THEORY, PRACTICE AND THE ROLE OF DISCONFIRMATION

The role of disconfirmation

There is one point on which Mill and Dewey are agreed. Neither finds inconsistent evidence a signal that theory has to be rejected. We saw that Friedman, too, agrees on this point.[9] There is an important difference, however. To Mill, certainly in economics, disconfirmation meant that pertinent disturbing causes had not been taken into account. To Dewey, disconfirmation in the process of inquiry shows that the theory as a whole needs to be revised, which may mean replacing all of the premises with new ones. Mill and Dewey agree, too, that disconfirmation is not entirely negative; it simply suggests that something has to be done.[10] But here too there is a difference. For Mill disconfirmation merely shows us that something is missing.[11] For Dewey it plays a more positive and directive role. As he has observed (1938, p. 519):

> The history of science, as an exemplification of the method of inquiry, shows that the verifiability (as positivism understands it) of hypotheses is not nearly as important as is their directive power. As a broad statement, no important scientific hypothesis has ever been verified in the form in which it was originally presented nor without very considerable revisions and modifications. The justification of such hypotheses has lain in their power to direct new orders of experimental observations and to open up new problems and new fields of subject-matter. In doing these things they have not only provided new facts but have often radically altered what were previously taken to be facts.

Friedman never said as much, but as we show in Part II, much of what he did as positive economist lends itself to this interpretation.

Theory and practice

Dewey can help us to interpret Friedman's methodological stance in still another way. Friedman's orientation is clearly 'practical', and since science and practice are generally seen to fall into separate compartments, his approach has been said to be more 'short-run', or practical, whereas those who follow the more traditional approach are said to be more 'long-run', or scientific (see above, Chapter 4). It has further been argued, partly on the basis of what Friedman has said in private correspondence, that Friedman is a short-run instrumentalist but long-run disciple of the philosopher Karl Popper (see above, Chapter 4). But once one recognizes the Deweyan nature of Friedman's way of thinking this interpretation is seen to be wide of the mark. We say this because nowhere do we find Friedman sharply distinguishing between theory and practice, as this view implies that he must. The evidence rather suggests that pure science and applied science are thoroughly integrated in his way of thinking; thus, in the essay on methodology the major *raison d'être* of positive economics or economic science is taken to be that it helps us deal with practical social problems. Friedman repeats these sentiments in other places as well. Dewey shows why, in this way of thinking, the separation of pure and applied science (or theory and practice) from each other is one of the most serious errors one can make. In Dewey's works this issue is brought up again and again (see, for example, 1971, pp. 134–7).

On Dewey's view, for example, inquiry in science and in everyday life differ with regard to *subject matter* but *not logic* (1938, p. 79). Further, on this view, the problems the scientist works with are said to derive from experience. Dewey argues that this is true even of mathematics, Euclidean geometry being a good example (*ibid.* p. 397). In addition, to Dewey every application of science is in a very real sense a test of a theory; if the *application* works, it is a confirmation, if not, a disconfirming instance and a sign that revision is necessary (1971, pp. 134–7). Friedman has expressed himself in the same way. For example, in his Nobel Lecture (1977*b*) Friedman has observed:

> Ideological war has raged over these matters [of inflation and unemployment]. Yet the drastic change that has occurred in economic theory has not been the result of ideological warfare. It has not resulted from divergent political beliefs or aims. It has responded almost entirely to the force of events: brute experience proved far more potent than the strongest of political or ideological preferences. (See also 1975*a*.)

One need not necessarily agree with Friedman, or with Dewey, to recognize that the continuity between pure science and application is something that Friedman, like Dewey, takes for granted. In fact, Friedman's preference for Marshallian economics and his rejection of 'abstractness, generality, mathematical elegance' as the ends of economic inquiry derives not just from his practical interest alone but more essentially from his pragmatic views about science. On this view the distinction between theory and practice has no basis: theorizing is directed inquiry to the end of resolving concrete (practical) problems. Or, to put it in the vocabulary Friedman himself has used, without denying the usefulness of 'language', it must be recognized that one must have something to say (see Friedman, 1955*e*). 'Saying' something involves *purpose*, and it is this which makes inquiry meaningful, whether it is 'practical' in the very narrow or some wider sense of the term.

In the next section we will show that this notion of a close relationship between theory and practice (as between pure and applied science) has very deep roots in the Deweyan way of thinking.

TWO TYPES OF INSTRUMENTALISM

Thought as an instrument

Dewey traced the basic problems which he found in modern philosophy to the ancient Greek philosophers (see, for example, 1929; 1950 [1920]; 1938, pp. 33–4, Chapter V). Among such problems was the exalted place given by them to what Dewey considered disembodied 'reason' or 'mind'. To counter this Dewey argued that *thought* was 'instrumental', meaning first, that it was an instrument used to help achieve objectives, and second, that the objectives were as wide as human purpose itself. Because he characterized thought as 'instrumental' he has been taken to be, and at one time he himself claimed to be, an 'instrumentalist'. But note that he did *not* argue that *theories* are *merely* instruments *nor that the purpose of thought is prediction alone.* What this shows is that Dewey's use of the term 'instrumentalism' has little to do with philosophical realism *per se*, one way or the other, [12] and by the same token neither does Friedman's talking about 'unrealistic' assumptions. It is a very unfortunate and confusing coincidence that Friedman's type of Deweyan instrumentalism should have become mixed up with Popper's, with which it has relatively little to do. [13]

The consequences of this view

There follow from Dewey's downgrading of *thought* to instrumental status a whole host of interesting and important consequences. First, it leads to the rejection of the positive/normative distinction. [14] The distinction served the historical purpose, according to Dewey, of marking out a realm of 'truth' – as of 'beauty' and 'goodness' – where the philosopher, who is master of 'reason', could reign supreme. [15] Dewey rejects this dualism (1938, pp. 6–7, 10, 103–4, 177–8). [16] Another of the consequences that follow from this is that observation comes into its own. It brings into prominence something philosophers have generally tried to downgrade, in recent times almost as much as in antiquity. As an example we note the attempt by Karl Popper to disprove the notion that

Newton derived his theory from observations (1965, no. 8). The proof is very simple and what it shows is that Newton did not derive his theory from *observations alone*. Could one not as simply show that he did not derive his theory from *thought alone*? Popper rather gives the impression that Newton did, which he then uses to argue the case against induction. Dewey does not argue the opposite thesis but rather the notion that observation is an *equal* partner with reasoning and that one cannot contribute much without the other. To him the question whether observation (which is theory-impregnated) or thought (which is fact-impregnated) comes first is about as meaningful as the chicken-or-egg controversy.

Once observation is given equal status with theorizing, third, the kind of inductivist approach to logic that Whewell displayed (as discussed in the last chapter) becomes more attractive. This is partly so because once it is recognized that the truth of theories cannot be proved, truth as an immediate objective drops out. What can take its place? This leads to a consideration of *why* truth had been taken to be the proper goal of inquiry and one possible answer is that we do not want *spurious* correlations. Proving that theories were true, to Mill, for example, meant that the regularities discovered were unchanging; we could rely on them. They showed how things *really* were. The loss of certainty changes all of this but leaves us with an alternative, once it is recognized that in spite of the inability to prove theories true, science has displayed persistent growth of knowledge. What is it that has been responsible for this growth? We cannot look merely at theory, according to Dewey, and by the use of intuition determine whether there is or is not advance, as Plato's untutored slave-boy could recognize a true theorem in geometry from mere inspection. We have to examine what scientists have done which has brought about progress, a state of affairs which, were the evidence for it not so strong, would appear incredible in the face of our inability to distinguish which theories are true. Thus, to try to understand acknowledged progress would seem to require induction. Note that in this context the separation between methodology and logic breaks down (1938, pp. 3–6). In the Deweyan view we do not derive criteria in logic by rational means which are then applied in science. It is rather that we have no other way to derive the criteria themselves except by inquiring into science itself. The results of this inquiry we then proceed to apply back to science. But the two are part of the same process.

What Dewey found in the history of science

What do we find when we study science, or as Dewey would prefer to put it, successful inquiry? According to Dewey, as to Peirce, a particular method, that is, a way of carrying on inquiry, is what distinguishes successful inquiry, scientific as well as the inquiring that occurs in everyday life. Now if Dewey and Peirce are right in this, a reorientation is needed of the traditional concepts. While truth might be our ultimate goal − in the words of Peirce, 'The opinion which is fated to be ultimately agreed to by all who investigate . . .'[17] − we need a vocabulary to refer to results inquiry has achieved at a particular time. For that purpose Dewey offered the term 'warranted assertion' (e.g. 1938, pp. 8–9). It is not a substitute for truth but merely a term that can be helpful while we look for it. Note that we cannot appeal to 'true' premises here, as Mill did, because truth will be ours only ultimately. Testing implications holds more promise, but while this is the most important guide that we have it is not the entire answer either. Tests are important because they are part of a process which includes observation and abduction. Even in physics tests frequently do not tell enough to enable us to distinguish advance from retrogression; in economics ambiguity is the norm. What then is to be done when at a particular stage of inquiry no one theory can be said to be better than any of the others?

Dewey's answer, like Peirce's before him is to tell us to inquire further by those means which have brought progress in science in the past.[18] At any point in history there may not be enough knowledge *rationally* to choose one theory over another.[19] But experience from the physical sciences tends to show that in time further inquiry moves us along until the choice is reasonably clear. Economics does not seem to share this characteristic and there is little question but that part of the reason lies with the nature of the materials the economist deals with. But according to Dewey as we have seen, another part is due to the mistaken method of inquiry which has historically prevailed in this discipline.

The Popperian view[20]

For Popper as for Dewey the realization that theories in science cannot be proved plays a central role. But from there on the two diverge sharply.[21] Popper proceeds to reason out the implications that derive from this important insight. Firstly, he argues that induction is irrational and tells us that it has to be thrown out. As Popper sees it, since we cannot with complete coherence argue that all swans are white no matter how many white swans we see, induction has no rational basis (1972, Chapter 1). This seems to leave him without any means of distinguishing better theories from worse ones; but Popper points out that the induction problem leaves *modus tollens* (passing falseness back from a conclusion to one or more of the assumptions) functioning as well as ever. Thus, secondly, while we cannot prove that a theory is true, we can disprove it deductively if one falsifying instance is observed.[22] This leaves us logically with a group of theories which *could* be true. But this is a relatively indeterminate position so Popper goes on to consider hypothetical reasons why one theory might be better than another; for example, it might have more empirical content.

The way Popper goes about his work reminds one of the ways of pure economic theorists. He reasons out a deductive scheme which has empirical reference but makes no empirical claims. He rightly complains, as do economic theorists, when his reasoning is taken to have more empirical content than he intended (see, for example, Schilpp, 1974, p. 1100). Further, he argues that his formulations are not falsifiable (or empirically testable), though he draws what look like empirical results from them, for example, the notion (called the transference principle) that what is true in logic must be true in psychology (see, for example, 1972, p. 24). This reminds one of what certain economic theorists often do,[23] Ludwig von Mises in particular.[24]

All of this is pure theory, or logic, as Popper calls it.[25] It is overly simple, even were it correct as far as it goes, so that 'disturbing causes' have to be taken into account when an attempt is made at application, just as with pure economic theory. It is when he tries to *apply* reasoning that Popper becomes, in the words of Lakatos (1974*a*) the *methodological* falsificationist (naïve and sophisticated).[26] And it is the methodological (applied) falsificationist who has to start taking into account the real problems that are encountered in actually trying to perform falsification tests. For example, Popper now distinguishes between the potential *falsifiability* of a theory, a purely logical affair, and a theory's being *demonstrably* falsifiable, something which has empirical content (e.g. 1983). It is at this point that the analysis becomes more complex and questions arise about the consistency of the whole system. For example, does Popper as methodologist not let in by the back door the same induction that as logician he threw out of the front (e.g. Newton-Smith, 1981, Chapter 3). But these problems need not delay us. What we are trying to show is how close is the rationale of what Popper does as logician to that of an economist of the Millian persuasion. Thus, what little role the observation of specific experience plays in both is either behind the scenes or used to fill in disturbing causes. The theory consists in reasoning out a plausible scheme and the results are not considered vulnerable to empirical test. When there is a discrepancy between theory and practice either the practice is said to be wrong – as when scientists appeal to induction – or disturbing causes are added – as in introducing the concept of demonstrable falsification. The real problems force Popper more and more into metaphysical argument (see Caldwell, 1988a). Metaphysical speculation is not unknown, of course, in the annals of pure economic theory.

What all of this shows, it seems to us, is that a Popperian could no more be expected to be receptive to Friedman's message about economic methodology than a Millian. By contrast, it takes an understanding of the sense in an inductivist approach to the philosphy of science to be able to be aware of what Friedman was trying to do.[27]

FRIEDMAN'S CONTRIBUTION TO THE PRAGMATIC APPROACH

It is one thing to argue generally that one should reject introspection as the major means for deriving economic theory and argue instead that one should work back from observed regularities taken to be implications to hypothetical premises. It is quite another actually to derive such premises. Since Dewey, as philosopher, operates at a high level of abstraction, he does not concern himself with this problem; Friedman does, and thereby gives us some insight into one possible way to deal with this problem which is generally consistent with the fundamentals of Dewey's logic. What we learn from Friedman's working experience is that many of the hypotheses that suggest themselves in the process of inquiry involve unobservables – like permanent income and utility functions – and that it is difficult to make the connection between the hypothesized premises and observed implications and thereby derive theory whose implications can be meaningfully tested with further data. As we will show in Part II, it is one of Friedman's major contributions to have shown how one can come to grips with this problem in a number of different areas. Had Friedman not thought in a Deweyan way, it seems unlikely that he would even have encountered this problem, certainly not in the form in which it did arise.

NOTES

1. One who argues this way claims that unless one accepts his thesis one is led into absurdity. In other words, *reason* compels us to accept the argument.
2. Robbins (1949, p. 105) argues that this gives the economist an *advantage*.
3. Mill was critical of his father for following Euclid in developing his theory of government (Mill, 1957 [1873]) because his father's theory was too simple, that is, it did not include enough causal laws or axioms. But he did not criticize his father for setting up 'true' axioms, the way Euclid had done, and then attempting to derive true implications. On this father and son agreed.
4. As we showed in Chapter 4, they actually accuse Friedman of being interested only in correlations. But since there is evidence aplenty that he *is* interested in theory, the conclusion would seem to follow that he confuses the two.

5. One of Dewey's books is called *The Quest for Certainty* (1929) but this theme is central to just about all of his works.
6. That does not deny the role that the Euclidean type of *presentation* plays in science. As Braithwaite (1946, Chapter 4) has pointed out, after deriving theory by working back from observed implications to premises and testing the theory by checking whether additional implications deduced from the theory are borne out, the scientist often presents the theory as model where, as in Euclidean geometry, the implications *appear* to be accepted because the assumptions are taken to be true. That is, in *modelling* one argues *as if* the implications are true because the premises are true even though the basis for the belief runs the other way.
7. As we noted in Chapter 4, above, Piron (1962) accused some of Friedman's critics of confusing the two.
8. The 'rationally self-consistent train of meanings' is what Friedman refers to as 'language'. One easily gets the impression from statements like this that Dewey – and Friedman – may have underestimated the value of 'language'. But considering that 'language' has often been taken to be the *only* objective of philosophy – as of economic science – it seems to us that a certain one-sidedness can be forgiven.
9. The notion that theory for which there is falsifying evidence must be rejected probably entered economics through the influence of what Lakatos (1974*a*) called the methodological/naïve/falsificationist Popper, or because the teachings of the *logician* Popper (e.g. 1972, Chapter 1) were taken to be statements about what is or should be done in science.
10. Popper, too, suggests that one learns from falsification; in fact, it has been said (Berkson and Wetterman, 1984) that Popper's philosophy rests upon a falsification theory of learning. However, the term 'falsification' surely implies *rejection*, and so it has generally been interpreted by economists. For example, paraphrasing Popper, Caldwell tells us (1982, p. 125), '. . . scientists . . . should reject those [hypotheses] which have been disconfirmed'. Even those, like Boland, who interpret Popper to mean that one learns through falsification, when trying to explain how this occurs manage only to show that it is a means of eliminating error (Boland, 1982, pp. 167–8). But eliminating error is a *negative* process, that is, one of rejection. Learning, after all, is at least partially a *positive* process where one comes out knowing more, not only of what is *not* so, but of what *is* so as well.
11. Hollander argues (1985, Chapter 2, Section 7) that Mill, too, saw in verification a tool for improving theory *generally* but we do not think that the evidence supports him. There is a difference between completing theory – discovering what is missing in specific cases – and improving the general explanatory power of the theory.
12. Wible (1984, pp. 1054–7) has an interesting discussion on this point. However, he is both inconsistent and wide of the mark in saying that 'Dewey's theory of inquiry portrays science as a rhetorical process . . .'.
13. 'Relatively' because, as we showed in Chapter 4, at the first stage of the inquiry process the two coincide. The 'Popperian' instrumentalist stops after stage 1 but the Deweyan goes on.
14. Except for the purpose of pointing out that *for the moment* one is not considering values outside of those which arise within the inquiry process itself. (See below, Chapter 12.)

15. Deduction reigns supreme in this realm according to Dewey. Philosophers choose it because, by providing proof, it gives a feeling of certainty. Induction, on the other hand, shows up very clearly the uncertainty in human existence (see Dewey, 1929, pp. 3–20).

16. In Chapter 12, below, we look further at Dewey's view about the positive–normative dichotomy.

17. Dewey quotes this (1938, p. 345) in a note more than halfway through the *Logic*. This does not mean that he was unconcerned about truth. It was merely that he felt that truth as such has little value as an operational concept in the inquiry process or to one studying that process.

18. Traditional philosophers like Popper are no more able to accept uncertainty as an element of human experience than were neoclassical economists. As a result, the very possibility that scientists might at times make decisions on any other basis than reason stimulates them to lash out with charges of 'irrationalism, relativism, and mob rule' (see Kuhn, 1970, p. 234). Yet there is a weakness, too, in Kuhn's heavy reliance on non-rationalism. Even where there is uncertainty, as economists know, decisions *can* be made rationally though there is then more room for difference of opinion. As research continues, such differences can be expected to narrow. That is the view of Dewey (after Peirce), and of Friedman (e.g. 1968*c*, and 1977*b*).

19. That is, to derive a compelling answer by reasoning out.

20. Popper has formulated a philosophy of social science which in basic ways is different from his general philosophy of science. But this aspect of his work has generally been ignored by economists (see Hands, 1985); as far as we are aware none of Friedman's critics has appealed to the social science Popper. For that reason little need be said about those views of Popper here.

21. We find other similarities, such as the notion both hold that inquiry should center around problems. But these similarities are of little interest for our purposes.

22. Popper is very much in the classical tradition and so insists on deductive proofs or disproofs. For science the former is not possible but for metaphysics, which has come to play a larger and larger role in Popper's philosophy of science, it is, and there one can use as a basis for *modus ponens* whatever seems 'reasonable'.

23. Without using this term, Krige (1980) argues in effect that philosophers of science, Popper among them, content themselves with comparing 'states of equilibrium', e.g. Aristotelian and classical mechanics *after the latter had been fully formulated*. To understand important developments in science, like 'revolutions', according to Krige, it was necessary to understand what went on during the period when the former was crumbling and the latter was slowly being developed. Philosophers of science make this mistake, on Krige's view, because they are held back by the 'context of justification' constraint. Economists very often confine themselves to the context of justification, as when they concentrate on static theory.

24. As Hicks (1946, p. 23) has argued: 'Pure economics has a remarkable way of producing rabbits out of a hat ...'. The same can be said of philosophy of the traditional sort.

25. See the warning, in Popper (1972, Chapter 11).

26. Lakatos also refers to a 'naturalistic falsificationist' (pp. 95–103) who treats logic as if it were methodology. This criticism is similar to the one Friedman

makes (see Chapter 1, above) against those who leap from abstract theory to making statements about the real world (as Lange, for example, is accused of doing).

27. Recall that the inductivist tries to derive standards for judging theories by studying inquiry (that is, inductively), whereas the deductivist relies on criteria which appeal to 'reason' (of which deductive reasoning is the most important ingredient). We need hardly add that one can be an inductivist without being a Deweyan.

PART II

POSITIVE ECONOMICS

7 • ON COMPARING FRIEDMAN'S METHODOLOGY WITH HIS PRACTICE OF POSITIVE ECONOMICS

In the first six chapters we have discussed what Friedman espoused in the way of methodology. Chapters 8 through 10, below, give an overview of his work as practicing economist. Here we construct a bridge, summarizing first the main results of our earlier discussion, then giving a preview of what is still to come.

These two parts of our study were not pursued separately. We used what Friedman did in interpreting what he said, and vice versa, mirroring the iterative and interactive process that we have identified in Friedman's own writings. Yet it is instructive to examine the relationship between the two parts, which we do here, as if each were distinct. Where what he said does not coincide with what Friedman did the reason may lie in our interpretation; or it may be that Friedman was not always consistent. The comparison we pursue in this chapter should help the reader by pointing up the issues which have to be considered in trying to decide whether the reason for incongruities is the one or the other.

THE COMPONENTS OF FRIEDMAN'S METHODOLOGY

Any summary of Friedman's methodological principles is bound to suffer from more than the usual limitations of summaries. The reason lies in his pragmatic approach to economic inquiry. In the pragmatic way of thinking methodology is simply part of the background knowledge with which one proceeds. It is taken for granted and nothing is said about it. Except that sometimes an investigator must question what is considered the best available knowledge in methodology because he or she finds that it stands in the way rather than being helpful. Friedman's methodological comments are made in this spirit. When he says something of a methodological sort he is trying to tell us about the way he does economics and believes that it should be done, usually in opposition to some prevailing alternative, and usually in some specific context. The resulting observations are therefore concrete, directed, partial. To try to make them into general principles may well be attempting to put on them a burden they were not meant to carry and will not bear.

With this caveat, we suggest that the following five major propositions give a reasonable characterization of Friedman's methodological thinking.

Proposition 1: Adopt an 'outside' view of behavior

This is fundamental. It involves a denial that reliable knowledge about the motives of economic subjects can be derived by introspection or through some shared (common) sense; but also a denial that we have enough knowledge of the detailed interrelationships in the economy to build realistic models. We therefore have to make do without 'inside' knowledge about what drives economic agents *and* without the basic materials for an insider's (or knower-of-true-detail's) description of the economy itself. We are obliged to build models that project what might be the case on to agents and on to the economy, to fill the inevitable gaps in our knowledge of what actually is the case. Put differently, to pretend that we are in a position to put together descriptively detailed theory or models is quite false.

The argument from the difficulty of observing motives to opposition to realism of assumptions is straightforward. If motives are unobservable, then the truth or untruth of statements reflecting them cannot be determined. Moreover, direct inquiry of the subjects themselves (or, by implication, introspection on their part) is open to error because subjects rationalise; or they may simply lack awareness; or they may be confused. Friedman acknowledged these difficulties early on (in the joint article with Wallis, 1942*a*, on problems of deriving data-based indifference functions), and his scepticism about survey questionnaire data is still evident in 'Positive economics'.

But not all economic explanation involves motives, and indeed economists had labored hard before Friedman came on the scene to get rid of the last traces of them in the theory of demand. Problems with motives therefore cannot explain Friedman's wholesale opposition to realism of assumptions. The additional difficulty needed to complete the account seems to be our lack of detailed knowledge about economic mechanisms, that is, about the many exact and finely specified reactions to changes in conditions that we must identify and if possible quantify if our theory is to be fruitful. The absence of concern with such detailed mechanisms is the basis of Friedman's early criticism of Keynesian analysis (1943*a*,

1946*b*, 1947*a*, all discussed below, Chapter 9); the pretense that we can go ahead and model as if we had the necessary knowledge is the ground of his attack on Carl Christ (Christ 1951, Friedman 1951*a*).

How should we proceed with insecure knowledge about motives or interrelationships in the economy? One response is to make do with personal introspection (plus the notion that we are enough the same for this self-knowledge to extend to others), and to suggest that stylized facts will do, or that somehow economic theory tells us what the underlying behavioral relationships in the real economy are. These are all appeals to plausibility, and Friedman found them all suspect. One problem with this way of proceeding was that theory developed on the basis of supposed or stylized facts and theoretical knowledge was more likely to be useful in deriving further theoretical results than in analysing actual economic observations. The Wallis and Friedman article (1942*a*) elaborates this view, and the theme is sustained in later criticisms of Lange and of 'Walrasian' economists. For Friedman, the correct focus must be on concrete problems and carefully compiled data: theoretical analysis must use the one in the service of the other.

But if we do not know enough to build realistic theories and cannot hope to analyze real data and to address real problems by speculating, what role is there for theory? Friedman regarded theory as a creative process, introducing potentially useful interjections between broad sets of ideas and the data and problems at hand. This is the abductive process whose roots, we have suggested, lie in Dewey's logic rather than Mill's. For Friedman, motives are beyond our ken and theory for theory's sake was outside his range of interests; but that still leaves a role for theory in spite of our having nothing but general notions, observations and problems to start with. And it is a role for theory that is perfectly consistent with 'as if' accounts of what there is to explain.

That is important, for it strikes many as strange that the same Friedman who seemed concerned to derive observation-based theory in 1942 was happily invoking 'as if' explanations in 1948. But for Friedman these 'as if' accounts are not so many hot-air balloons floated freely aloft. They are firmly anchored by the problems and data one starts with; *and* in the further checks of their implications that one should carry out. Thus theoretical notions (even those difficult to isolate empirically, such as 'true' velocity) have a role as 'carriers' of creative thought. They facilitate the discovery process, but they are always subject to the twin safeguards of data (and problems) and 'predictive' checks.

These safeguards are so crucial that we make them the second and third elements in our summary statement of Friedman's methodological views.

Proposition 2: Start with observation

The quotation from which this heading is adapted has been used several times in our discussion, but it is worth giving it again, in full: 'The theorist starts with some set of observed *and related* facts, as full and comprehensive as possible' (1946*b* in 1953*e*, p. 282; emphasis added). We have italicized 'and related' to emphasize that Friedman is distancing himself, even here, from mere fact-gathering, or statistical descriptivism. As he says in 'Positive economics', 'we cannot perceive "facts" without a theory' (1953*d* in 1953*e*, p. 34). In other words, a problem, and some guiding hypotheses about it, are integral to meaningful observation. But why the stress, as well, on wide and detailed knowledge of the facts themselves? Friedman gives an answer in 'Positive economics' in two parts. Facts help us in deriving hypotheses (*ibid.* p. 12). And, more importantly here, we need comprehensive information on the phenomena we are trying to explain so that we can check in advance that our chosen hypothesis does not have implications inconsistent with what is known (*ibid*). Facts, in this second role, constitute an important check on theorizing, even though they are not invoked to impart realism to assumptions.

Proposition 3: Test implications, continuously, although not in order to falsify

This proposition has three parts, each of them important to Friedman. The first is the idea that empirical observation constitutes a check on theorising via the process of testing the *implications* of hypotheses on 'new' facts (those outside the set used to derive the hypotheses, whether already known or not). This is, of course, the best known of Friedman's positions, and we need not elaborate on it, except to remind the reader that it fits into our overall summary as part of his adoption of an 'outside' (behavioral) stance.

The second part involves tying a loose end deliberately left in our discussion of Proposition 2 (start with observation). On the one hand, facts are observed through the lens of theory; on the other hand, the theorist *starts* from observation. Friedman himself resolves the apparent conflict in 'Positive economics'. He stresses that 'any theory is necessarily provisional and subject to change with the advance of knowledge' (*ibid.* p. 41) and that there is in fact no 'initial stage': 'the so-called "initial stage" itself always involves a comparison of the implications of an earlier set of hypotheses with observation; the contradiction of these observations is the stimulus to the construction of new hypotheses or revision of old ones' (*ibid.*, pp. 13–14). We have to do here, then, with a continuous process of inquiry in which observation, the derivation of hypotheses, the testing of implications and the use of revised hypotheses in generating new, testable implications, succeed each other in a never-ending round.

Third, as this very description of the nature of inquiry suggests, Friedman is not to be fitted into the narrow falsificationist approach to testing, in which the purpose is to identify and eliminate error. He is not so much out to falsify as to find a hypothesis that works; that is, one that 'correctly predicts the consequences of changes in conditions' (1968d, p. 15). In principle, then, even unsuccessful tests may tell us a good deal. They will tell us more, of course, if the hypothesis is 'nested' in some theory, since we will then have some indication as to where to look in order to explain unsuccessful trials. Friedman, we shall discover, is very much concerned with such nesting: he is interested in causal mechanisms, the charge of black-box instrumentalism made by many critics notwithstanding. Popper and Friedman are not so far apart on these things, but there is a vast difference in their respective willingness to regard past confirmations as a foundation for future building. This leads directly to our fourth summary proposition.

Proposition 4: Use the best knowledge available as a framework in doing empirical research

By framework here we mean a very broad mindset (e.g. equilibrium analysis, or the maximization postulate) perhaps taken as 'received' now but originally (or in principle) derived via the process Friedman recommends (Propositions 2 and 3), then specialized (i.e. restricted) through the use of auxiliary assumptions, so as to yield refutable implications. Through trial and error these are refined so as to yield, eventually, reasonably good predictions in a particular area of economic experience. This accords closely with what Friedman himself has to say about the status of his own preferred hypotheses (1953d in 1953e, pp. 22–3), and about a broad hypothesis as an abstract model and its ideal types, on the one hand, and the rules specifying the specific circumstances under which it might be expected to hold, on the other (ibid., pp. 18–19, 24–5, 35–6). In place of framework here we might have used the word paradigm which is not Friedman's term but Kuhn's. Friedman's view of economic inquiry is akin to Kuhn's normal science, even down to the importance he ascribes to tacit knowledge (ibid. p. 25) and the essential role he gives to measurement in accounting a hypothesis successful (ibid., pp. 10, 25). Within a paradigm, for Friedman as for Kuhn, science is cumulative (ibid., p. 40). Friedman, however, believes in the possibility of making comparisons between basic theoretical approaches (e.g. Keynesian versus quantity theoretical), a possibility that Kuhn would question.

Friedman's language on the cumulative nature of economic science is unmistakably clear, as when he identifies with 'the small band of workers who have tried to follow the ideal of a cumulative science built on carefully done and coordinated research on manageable problems [which small band, however,] has tended to be engulfed by the larger body determined to find the complete answer at one fell swoop' (letter to Rockefeller Foundation requesting funding for the Chicago Workshop in Money and Banking: 13 November 1953. Rockefeller Archive, GR, 200S, Box 573, folder 4907).

Once again, there is a sharp contrast to be drawn between this view of inquiry and the Popperian view of progress comprising the elimination of errors. Friedman is more willing to accept tested hypotheses as *usable* knowledge – 'whether it works' is after all for him the 'true test' – even though he shares Popper's conviction that all knowledge is provisional.

One proposition remains on our list.

Proposition 5: Do not look for answers 'in principle', but address concrete problems

Solutions to concrete problems are those which a policymaker can use. They must be based on a good knowledge of circumstances, to make sure the case at hand does indeed fit with the analytical apparatus one brings to bear. That apparatus – hypotheses and their model instantiations – must be manageable, hence simple enough to use, while yielding results that are 'sufficiently accurate' for one's purposes (1953d in 1953e, p. 15). And these results, which may be thought of as predictions about what to expect given certain specified changes in conditions (1968c, p. 15), must be reasonably stable across institutional environments. To give a simple illustration of this last point, money must continue to affect nominal income in stably measurable ways whether there is a Federal Reserve system or not.

We have seen these requirements contrasted with 'Walrasian' economics, where the emphasis is on formal completeness, generality and mathematical elegance. To illustrate: it is Friedman's judgment that to get a *tolerably useful* answer to the question how prices will be affected by a product tax, one does not necessarily need a complete description stressing product and firm differences within the industry in question (1953d in 1953e, pp. 36–7). A common force (the increased tax) outweighs things that differentiate firms, such as brand competition, in this particular case; or 'so far as the specific problem is concerned', as Friedman put it, italicizing the words in the original, in a review of Robert Triffin's *Monopolistic Competition and General Equilibrium Theory* (1941, p. 390). But there is no claim on Friedman's part that such an assumption will be right for *all* circumstances. It is also his judgment that to get tolerably usable insight for policy control in the economy we do not need to wait for detailed, multi-equation models of the whole structure and its internal interdependencies. We can do a great deal with a knowledge of 'bits and pieces of order here and there' (1951*a*, p. 114). Thus, a properly formulated hypothesis on consumption which also fits the data can be used to tell us a good deal about the relative effect of temporary versus permanent fiscal changes; and a detailed knowledge of the dynamics of monetary impulses can tell us whether lags and multiplier effects are constant enough to make manipulation of monetary aggregates a desirable thing to engage in.

By contrast a desire to have some single, universally applicable answer must necessarily drive one to abstract from much that is specific about the problem at hand and from much knowledge of what there is to be accounted for in observed behavior. There is a trade-off between generality of analysis and being able to deal with concrete problems, as there is between descriptive completeness and manageability. Friedman was thoroughly sceptical about departing far from the twin touchstones of the problem at hand, on the one hand – a very concrete concern – and such things as transparency of mechanism, sufficient realism, tolerable accuracy, manageability, on the other. These last four criteria, clearly, are all relative: what is acceptable to the analyst will depend on the problem to be dealt with, and on available alternative analyses.

One way to read this fifth proposition, then, is that it expresses Friedman's opposition to what he disparaged as the search for *the* answer 'at one fell swoop' (see above, p. 158).

We have seen the evolution of this preference: from opposition to Lange's all-too-unspecific (and therefore near-empty) analysis, to the questioning of efforts to develop forecasting models by Cowles Commission workers. Much of 'Positive economics' can be usefully read from this perspective as well. We shall also find that the principle informs his positive economics: witness his well-known concentration on single-equation models (e.g. money demand, consumption function) rather than general equilibrium analyses; and his extended struggle to model the particulars of the dynamics of the monetary transmission mechanism. Even pieces of analysis which we shall discover do not readily fit into the pattern of work defined by the other four summary propositions, such as his exploration of expected utility (1948*c*), his exercise to show that fiscal intervention can be destabilizing (1951*c* in 1953*e*) and his denunciation of Keynesians for having modelled the Phillips Curve trade-off in nominal rather than real (or at least expectations-adjusted) terms (1975*b*); these may be viewed as attempts to show that problem-related inquiry, not general theory, carries one farther, more reliably.

We are done with our summary of Friedman's methodological views, but before turning to see how closely he has followed them in practice, it seems worthwhile pausing to add a slightly different perspective to our summary. We propose to look briefly at Marshall's methods. Marshall was held in the highest regard by Friedman, even though Jacob Viner, if we may judge from Friedman's notes on his lectures in price theory at Chicago, was inclined to criticize Marshall for using real problems as an occasion to put his technical tools to work, rather than letting the problems dictate the selection of methods. If anything, Friedman held exactly the opposite view of Marshall; and it will add to our appreciation of what Friedman himself was about to see just what he so admired in Marshall, the economist.

Our approach will be to look first at the way Marshall tackled the analysis of excise taxes, since Friedman himself made a comparative analysis of income versus excise taxes. Then we take note of the fact that Friedman also praised Cournot. A look at something Cournot did along the same lines as Marshall should disclose more precisely what Friedman found useful in the approach of each. Finally, we describe two general research strategies adopted by Marshall and which seem to capture a large part of the work Friedman did as positive economist.

MARSHALL AS POSITIVE ECONOMIST

Marshall on the effects of excise taxes

There is no explicit welfare comparison of income and excise taxes in Marshall's work, hence no direct comparison with Friedman's 'The "welfare" effects of an income tax and an excise tax' (1952a) is possible. There is, however, much on excise taxes. A Memorandum prepared for the Royal Commission on Local Taxation (1899) contains a discussion of the incidence question for many sorts of indirect taxes, as does a Memorandum on Fiscal Policy of International Trade (1903), both of which are reprinted in *Official Papers of Alfred Marshall* (1926) (hereafter *Papers*). Some relevant material is also to be found in chapters of Book III of *Money, Credit and Commerce* (1923), and in Appendix L of the *Principles* (1890), in which Marshall discusses Ricardo's views on the incidence of a tax on agricultural output.

The closest Marshall comes to a comparative efficiency analysis is when he notes (Memorandum for the Royal Commission on Local Taxation, *Papers*, p. 338) that income 'seems, on the whole, the best basis of a system of taxation', because, or so we may infer, 'taxes are paid by persons, not things' (*ibid.*, p. 334) and the effects of an income tax are confined wholly to the person, with no effects on other persons or things. In other words, an income tax is straightforward in its effects; there are no allocative repercussions.

Despite the absence of a direct comparison with income taxes, we learn a good deal about Marshall's way of doing economics through his discussion of excise taxes. His method of analysis is familiar to students of economics: he uses the apparatus of supply and demand to display the impact effects of tax-induced changes in relative prices. Excise taxes move supply curves. The burden of the tax may be shifted forwards, towards the consumer; or backwards, onto suppliers. If the industry subject to the tax is competitive and demand inelastic, the consumer bears the whole burden; and so on, through the many variants possible among the conditions supposed (see, for example, *Papers* p. 340).

From our point of view, what is most striking about Marshall's analysis of taxes is that these direct incidence effects are only a starting point. More on that in a moment. Not only is this true, but even although he seems to begin with a theoretical framework and looks set to create a taxonomy of possible outcomes, it quickly becomes apparent that even what look like analytical exercises in Marshall are heavily empirically informed. He illustrates 'the general process of shifting' by reference to 'a tax upon the product of a staple trade'. Printing is the trade he selects. After noting that if the tax is passed forward too eagerly demand will fall off, he at once enters into a detailed discussion of the sorts of machinery (printing machines) and workers (compositors) who would be most affected, because of their job-specific capabilities. These are then compared with that plant, those machines (e.g. steam engines) and those workers (porters, engineers and clerks) who would readily transfer to other employments. And with those in subsidiary industries who would feel the effects (paper- and type-makers; authors, publishers, booksellers) (*Papers*, pp. 341–2).

Or, to take another instance, in a letter to Bowley in illustration of the role of statistics in a concrete inquiry, Marshall sets out one and a half pages of detailed questions on the subject of the welfare effects of lowering the price of sugar to British consumers, or of maintaining the current (controlled) price. Some examples:

C. How far is it true that the present distress in those colonies [West Indian islands] is due to physical and moral degeneration as the results of
   (a) climate;
   (b) self-indulgent habits engendered by the abnormal ease of making money in the old time?

    D. Estimate of the probable loss incurred by bolstering up unenterprising capitalists in the employment of degenerating labour, with the prospect of having later on to support that labour.

    E. Pecuniary gain or loss resulting from leaving sugar bounties as they are, and giving a capital sum of £1,000 as a present to each white man, woman and child in the West India islands (see Pigou, 1956, pp. 425–6).

To return to the point that direct impact effects are just a beginning for Marshall, consider his analysis of an import duty in the Memorandum on Fiscal Policy of International Trade. Marshall operates not as a theorist who sets up his assumptions and then 'reasons out' (to some general conclusions for hypothetical categories of cases), but as one who actually has to give advice, or to make the decision in favor of one tax over another, or for no tax at all. He cautions frequently against making direct application of the results of simple first-round impact analysis. A prefatory note in his Memorandum, for example, points out that 'the incidence of import duties is extremely complex' and he adds: 'the indirect are often much more important than the direct effects' (*ibid.*). Marshall also warns that although the exposition to follow is concerned chiefly with 'proximate causes and their effects' a student should actually be 'endeavouring to probe to the causes of causes' (*ibid.*).

A quick sketch of his own treatment confirms the basis for Marshall's hesitancy. He begins with the direct effects of an import duty. As a rule – though 'there is no absolute rule in the matter' (*ibid.*) – exporters will raise the price to the importing country by the full amount of the duty. But he quickly moves on to complications: the value of money may alter in the importing country, confounding predictions; over time improvements in production and increases in incomes may render the effects of the duty negligible. Various additional complications are explored, including assumptions about whether trade is bi-lateral or multi-lateral, the nature of demand for the good in question (both considerations affecting elasticity), and even details such as the bulk of the commodity relative to value, the relative 'power' of the trading partners, and so on. The discussion continues for a total of fifty pages, which Marshall clearly considered too brief a space to do justice to the question.

All of this is in line with Marshall's own very balanced methodological judgment: 'in my view "Theory" is essential ... *the* work of the economist is "to disentangle the interwoven effects of complex causes"; and ... for this, general reasoning is essential, but a wide and thorough study of facts is equally essential ...' (in Pigou, 1956, p. 437). That comes from a letter to Edgeworth which includes a lengthy remonstrance against Cournot for what Marshall judged to be his inappropriate method of treating monopoly and combinations. Thus:

> Cournot's method of treatment is wholly inapplicable to the real conditions of life .... No instance could, I think, be better of the *mischievousness* of an academic education in *abstract* economics not continued into *real* economics [*ibid.*, p. 435].

We also find Marshall favorably comparing Von Thunen with Cournot. He regarded Cournot as the better mathematician; but 'to make up, ... [Von Thunen] was a careful experimenter and student of facts and with a mind at least as fully developed on the inductive as on the deductive side' (*ibid.*, p. 360).

Marshall's judgments on Cournot are interesting and relevant, since Friedman not only held up Marshall as an example of how to pursue economics (see, for example, 1974*b*, pp. 134, 160), but he praised Cournot in comparison with Walras. His particular reasons are worth exploring, since Friedman tended to invoke the distinction between 'Walrasian' and 'Marshallian' economics as a standard of bad and good, as we saw in Chapter 1. In what sense then did he also regard Cournot as being on the side of the angels?

Cournot's un-Walrasian tax analysis

What he liked about Cournot, Friedman said (in a review article on Jaffe's translation of Walras's *Elements*), is that 'his goal was an analysis that would, given the relevant statistical material, yield specific answers to specific empirical questions, such as the effects of a specified tax on a specified product; answers that could be confronted by observation and confirmed or contradicted' (1955*e*, p. 204).

To facilitate comparison with Marshall, and with Friedman's own discussion of income versus excise taxes, we take a moment to see just how Cournot tackled the welfare analysis of a sales tax.

In general, Cournot points out, a sales tax on one commodity reduces the quantity bought and may therefore lower its producers' total revenue. At the same time, those consumers who still buy some of the goods in question are worse off by the tax on that amount. Society as a whole is worse off by the sum of these two effects. This can be measured at base prices to yield an estimate of the real social loss. In Figure 7.1, those who still buy some of the good are in the same position as if they had lost income in the amount $(p_1 - p_0)D_1$. The producers of the good lose revenue equal to $p_0D_0 - p_1D_1$ (assuming $p_1D_1 < p_0D_0$). Hence the diminution of real social income, the sum of those two, is $p_0D_0 - p_0D_1$. Cournot's exploration of the welfare effects of a sales tax versus an income tax consists of the following observations. First, with a sales tax the Treasury will collect tax revenue of tD_1, which can be redistributed in

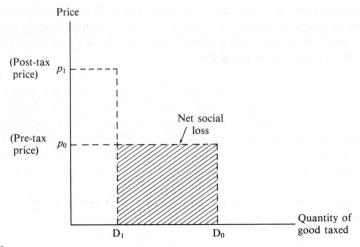

Figure 7.1   Welfare effects of a sales tax on one commodity (Cournot)

the form of transfer payments. Second, a similar redistribution can be effected using an income tax, but without the reduction in real income previously identified.

It is obvious in the case of Cournot's analysis that his conclusions depend on his concentrating entirely on the commodity in question without considering other production possibilities and without asking how the redistribution of tax revenues might affect spending and production decisions. The so-called loss from the sales tax is a very special magnitude, because there is in fact no loss of productive resources to society as a whole.

In Friedman's own treatment of these questions, failure to recognize the last point, and attempts to arrive at a single simple estimate of the welfare effects without considering production possibilities or the effects of the use of the tax revenues on spending, are criticized as reflecting 'an essentially arithmetic and descriptive approach to economic analysis'. This is contrasted with 'an analytical and problem-solving approach' (1952a in 1953e, p. 100). We need not go into Friedman's analysis in detail. For a single consumer and a sales tax on a single commodity, the tax changes the budget constraint, putting the individual on a lower indifference curve than an income tax which yields the same revenue and leaves money income (equal to expenditure) and relative prices unchanged. The welfare effect of the excise tax in isolation may be thought of as consumption possibilities lost. This approach, valid for an individual and a tax on just one commodity, clearly cannot be transferred to society in general, precisely because it says nothing about production possibilities, nor about other commodities or the possible effects on production and consumption of alternative uses of the tax revenue. It suffers, in other words, from exactly the limitations of Cournot's analysis (see 1952*a* in 1953*e*, Sections I and II).

Cournot, then, is praiseworthy because, in contrast to the 'abstractness, generality, mathematical elegance' of Walrasian analysis, things which in themselves 'are all secondary, . . . to be judged by the test of application' (1949*c* in 1953*e*, p. 91), he tries to give a specific answer to a specific concrete problem. But if it comes down to the test of application, Cournot's analysis is altogether too restricted, and Marshall comes closer to matching Friedman's own view of how one should proceed.

We turn now to two research strategies adopted by Marshall and which fit a good deal of what Friedman did in his applied work.

TWO MARSHALLIAN MODELS FOR RESEARCH AS USED BY MARSHALL AND BY FRIEDMAN

The paradigm-stretching model

In this strategy, economic theory is applied to apparently anomalous phenomena and the categories of theory itself are modified, or combined afresh so as to yield a new emphasis. The standard paradigm, or best available 'knowledge', is thereby 'stretched'.

An example in Marshall's writings is his handling of 'Giffen's hint' about a positively sloped demand curve for bread. On the face of it the suggestion that an increase in the price of bread will result in increased purchases flies in the face of the 'law' of demand. In the third edition of the *Principles* (1895) Marshall stretches the paradigm to cope with this awkward suggestion. Consider the budget of the poor to be fixed. A rise in the price of bread, the staple, then leaves less of the budget for allocation to more expensive non-staple foods (e.g. meat), and other things, at previous levels of bread purchases. In effect, the marginal utility of money rises, so if food intake (somehow measured) is more or less fixed the allocation of money shifts in favour of the still-least-expensive food, bread; more bread is purchased, despite the fact that its price has risen (Marshall, 1961 [1890], vol. 1, p. 132).

The now-standard explanation of this anomaly runs in terms of dominant, negative income effects. But because negative income effects are peculiar, the explanation does not sit easily with theorists. As Stigler puts it: 'we must all agree with Edgeworth that experience and common sense are opposed to the idea of a positively sloping demand curve . . .'

(1947, in 1965, p. 384). But this was not Marshall's explanation. Here it is again, though without any mention of the marginal utility of money. With a fixed budget *and* more or less fixed food-intake, somehow indexed, a rise in the price of the staple food causes more of the fixed budget to be spent on the staple, since that is the least expensive way to meet the *given* total food needs. This is more akin to a problem of production or supply than it is to a puzzle in the modern theory of consumer choice. That Marshall thought of it as a 'production' problem can hardly be doubted, because he tried to persuade Edgeworth of the reasonableness of the Giffen hint by using the example of a traveller, needing to solve the problem of going a fixed distance in the least time, but with an overriding budget constraint. The traveller will yield a little on time and travel more of the distance by the slower of two available modes of transportation if the price of that mode is unexpectedly raised but still remains considerably cheaper than the faster, more costly method (Marshall to Edgeworth, 22 April 1909, in Pigou, 1956, p. 441).

Marshall's achievement here lies in his having created a new perspective from which to view the problem – cost minimization rather than utility maximization – without, however, abandoning the standard insights of the paradigm. Once spelled out the solution strikes the reader as ingenious and quite plausible, although from the established perspective, as yet unmodified, it simply appeared anomalous.

Friedman's use of the paradigm-stretching model

Friedman used exactly this paradigm-stretching approach in several pieces of work, some of which we have already mentioned.

1. In his joint work with Savage (1948c), Friedman used a simple expedient to rationalize gambling behavior, supposing that certain individuals might be risk-loving rather than risk-averse, whilst nonetheless optimizing (Chapters 1 and 8).
2. In the still earlier study done with Kuznets on income from independent professional practice he had already started down that path, by introducing uncertainty of return as a factor over and above the usual equilibrating differences (such as length of training) which account for income differences, to account also for greater variability of income in certain professions. In his subsequent thinking about consumption the distinction between predictable and uncertain components of income was developed as the basis for his new theory of the consumption function (Chapter 9).
3. Then, in 1953, the two notions – uncertainty and a willingness by certain individuals to take a gamble – were combined to explain

skewness in the personal income distribution as a matter of rational choice (Chapter 8).

4. Finally, the difference between permanent or 'true' and transitory components in income was adapted in the fifties to account for the cyclical movements of measured velocity (Chapter 10).

We might note that in 2. and 4. especially there is considerable attention paid to data, both for identifying the nature of the problem to be solved and for checking the tentative hypothesis offered in explanation. This is very Marshallian and is true to Friedman's own precepts. (Marshall, in offering his account of the Giffen hint, pursued extensive if somewhat informal inquiries into household spending behavior. These enabled him to determine the possible empirical scope of upward sloping demand curves – he restricted his hypothesis to England, and noted that it would be undermined if maize were substituted for wheat flour in bread – and to identify the elements giving rise to them: see Pigou, 1956, pp. 438–9.) In 1. by contrast, Friedman and Savage seem content merely to find an explanation of a few well-known facts; and in 3. the facts to be explained – a certain peakedness and skewness – are not particularly striking, nor is any testing of the explanatory hypothesis attempted. All four examples do, however, show Friedman using the categories of accepted knowledge flexibly – they are not *given* in scope or number by existing theory. As Friedman himself characterized Marshallian economics at one point, it is a matter of constructing 'special tools for special problems' (Friedman, 1974*b*, p. 160).

The factors of influence model

The second of Marshall's strategies that we shall notice is one in which he tries to identify and ascribe a weight to the various factors (causes) producing an observed outcome. An example is the one already discussed above, his lengthy memorandum on the effects of an import duty. This, as he himself notes, is a search for the 'causes of causes'. Clearly in such an exercise we need facts: they supply the materials from which we try to infer causes; they are 'the bricks out of which reason builds the edifice of knowledge' (Pigou, 1956, p. 179; see p. 176). But the facts will not have done their work unless they suggest *all* the main causes at any one time that might have produced the effect (*ibid*. p. 176). And, finally, we must try to go beyond qualitative analysis if we are to offer policy advice; for 'mere qualitative analysis ... will not show the resultant drift of economic forces' (*ibid*., p. 301).

This three-pronged strategy is clearly something that impressed itself upon Friedman, for he adapted, to form a composite, quotations from

Marshall embodying much of what we have just said, in his essay on the Marshallian demand curve (1949c in 1953e, p. 90). And it is easy to find other instances in which he virtually mouths Marshall's sentiments, without actually citing him: see, for example, the statements he makes about the importance of being able to predict the consequences of changes in circumstances, which he uses almost as a definition of 'positive economics' ('Positive economics': see 1953e, p. 39; also 1968b, p. 15).

Friedman's use of the 'factors of influence' model

Friedman adopts the 'factors of influence' strategy in most of his empirical work. Thus, it informs his search for the causes of changes in the level of economic activity – the aim of his extended monetary studies, starting in 1948 (Chapter 10, below). It underlies his wartime work on the 'inflation gap'; for Friedman this meant investigating the channels by which a shift in the composition of production (towards war output) will show itself. In other words, it meant looking for the causes of causes (see Chapter 9). It guides his comparison of the effects of an income versus an excise tax (1952a in 1953e), a piece of work that he viewed as a footnote to his account of the Marshallian demand curve (Chapter 1, above). It summarizes what he saw as the next stage of research in consumption studies, once there is tentative acceptance of the permanent income hypothesis. Thus: 'The principal task in this area at the present stage of knowledge is to find the major determinants of k [the ratio of permanent consumption to permanent income] and to measure their influence' (1957c, p. 231). It governs his studies in the determinants of the cyclical versus the secular behavior of velocity (1959b and 1963b, Section E); and it supplied the impetus for his never satisfactorily developed studies in the transmission mechanism (see 1963b in 1969c, p. 222; and 1982, pp. 57–8).

Perhaps it should not surprise us to find such pervasive use of the 'factors of influence' model in Friedman's work. After all, it is very close to the standard multiple regression model beloved of all economists. There are nonetheless at least five things about Friedman's use of this model that are distinctive. By spelling these out we shall identify more precisely the emphases of his own research practices.

1. One is the degree to which he pursued the combined approach of letting the facts suggest tentative causal connections while at the same time relentlessly interrogating them. His monetary studies exemplify the strategy in a positive way (see Chapter 10); although we might also note the paucity of standard regression analyses in Friedman's work even in

this area, which is strange for an able statistician unless it reflects his awareness of the critical role of specification in such work. Nowadays panel data sets and almost minute-by-minute tapes of transactions in certain markets are making it less unusual to find economic researchers doing something very like what Friedman practiced. Even so, the dominant econometric practice still involves an application of technique from a position of great confidence in economic theory, with relatively little attention given to the nature of the data involved (see De Marchi and Gilbert, 1989). And in the 1940s, when Friedman formed his style and began practicing it, it was in stark contrast to the dominant deductive mode, in which a few stylized facts were adduced and analytical possibilities sorted out according to some plausibility criterion.

2. A second distinguishing mark of Friedman's use of the 'factors of influence' model is his belief that appearances may be deceptive. This meant that he had to be seeking the causes of causes; the more directly obvious or proximate causes would not do. That is another reason that a detailed and wide knowledge of the facts was so important to him. Friedman and Schwartz' *Monetary History* and their *Monetary Trends* are perhaps the best examples of this belief at work; but the refusal to take first appearances as a stopping point comes through in Friedman's scepticism about measured income and measured velocity (for these see Chapter 9), and in his postulate that the true Phillips curve is vertical (or nearly so) (Chapter 10). We might interpolate that Friedman felt uncomfortable about using the word 'cause' lest he mislead himself and others into believing that he had identified the ultimate causal factor(s) (private communication to J. Daniel Hammond, 13 June 1985). Admissible interpretations are multiple and all hypotheses tentative.

3. A third characteristic, tying in with what we said under 1., is that in Friedman's hands the 'factors of influence' strategy stresses variable selection and (empirical) model specification to a much greater extent than run-of-the-mill regression analyses. In recent years we have been alerted afresh to the importance of specification, sample size, diagnostic testing and so on; and the sophistication of regression methods and reporting of results has increased enormously. But again, in historical context, Friedman's work stands out for his awareness of statistical pitfalls in the application of the 'factors of influence' approach. We see this in his early book review of Jan Tinbergen's study of business cycles in the United States, in which Friedman addresses the specification issue (though not in so many words) (1940, p. 659). It marks his work with Gary Becker on the dangers of regressing consumption on income – in effect, said Friedman, this is regressing consumption on itself (1957*a*, p. 70). It is reflected in his insistence in *A Theory of the Consumption*

Function and in the Friedman and Meiselman (1963*e*) comparison of the relative stability of the multiplier and of velocity, that analytically appropriate variables (e.g. 'autonomous' spending) be chosen, and data (e.g. income data for communities or homogeneous groups within urban areas) used that create a strong link between the regression analysis and the problem to be resolved. It lies behind his insistence in his discussion of the vertical Phillips curve (1975*b*, at pp. 24–5) that before a true test of the natural rate hypothesis could be performed an adequate specification of the expected inflation term in the equation must be found; a suggestion that Friedman himself was unable to pursue adequately, but which was taken up, with different – and for Friedman unacceptable – results it is true, in Lucas' rational expectations formulation (1972). Not that Friedman always got it 'right' or did all he might have (see Hendry and Ericsson, 1985). But he consistently stood for an awareness of variable selection and specification problems that marked his work as unusual.

4. Friedman used the Marshallian 'factors of influence' strategy to study processes of change, which he called dynamics, not to settle upon a correct description of influences in a static way. Instead of taking observed outcomes and seeking their efficient causes in the way that a logician might construct an argument, Friedman busied himself with the processes that intervene between potential causes and outcomes. We have cited instances already (his work on the 'inflation gap'; his analysis of the effects of an income tax versus excise taxes); but he sees dynamics as integral to the specification of the consumption function (1957*a*, p. 65 and Section IV); and it underlies all his work on the monetary transmission mechanism (see 1951*a*, pp. 113–14 and Chapter 10, below). Only an understanding, and if possible a quantification, of processes of change could enable the economist to advise the policy-maker.

5. Finally, we need to notice a new and very special use to which Friedman put the standard regression model itself. Instead of simply taking the disturbance term to reflect omitted variables or measurement error in the usual way, in a lot of his work Friedman drew a distinction between 'true' variables and disturbances as white noise. This set up data interpretation problems (for measured income, for regressions of consumption on income, for measured velocity, for observed Phillips-type trade-offs), in which the task of the econometrician was to extract the correct signal (see Sargent, 1987). By restricting the nature of the disturbances, and the relationship between 'errors' and 'true' variables, in various ways, Friedman was able to produce tests of hypotheses in place of doing regression analysis merely to discover 'best fit'. Compare,

for instance, his negative comments on Tinbergen (1940) with what he himself attempted in *A Theory of the Consumption Function* (1957c).

JUDGMENT SUSPENDED, BUT A LIST OF THINGS TO LOOK FOR

Caution

We have now set out in summary form the main precepts held by Friedman as methodologist; and we have also, by looking forward to his applied work and by drawing some parallels with Marshall, indicated much about the character of his positive economics. It should be apparent from the discussion, however, that not much purpose is served by simply trying to produce a checklist, showing all those instances in which Friedman did, or did not, fully adhere to his own methodological precepts. What he stands for, above all else, is a set of attitudes towards the research process. And it is anything but obvious that assessing on a scale of 1 to 10 whether in a particular instance he did or did not 'start with the facts' (for example) adequately captures the nature of the problem situation he was trying to deal with. Nor does asking 'did he test, or did he merely interpret data?' (see Diesing, 1985) reflect fairly the iterative process of inquiry he undertook. Our own summary of Friedman's precepts at the start of this chapter is, for that reason, right on the edge of being misleading; and it is crucial that it be read in conjunction both with our discussion of Marshall and the materials presented in Chapters 8 through 10, below.

That said, the reader nonetheless has a right to expect some clear guidance in approaching the chapters that follow. We offer this, but in the form of things to look for rather than as neatly packaged judgments. Note beforehand two important problems that fall outside our list. One is that Friedman at times goes beyond empirical analysis and intrudes his own political or value preferences into what is supposed to be positive economics. We come upon this in Chapter 8, where he suggests that it is worth analysing personal income distribution in terms of private choices. Is this a testable proposition, or an implicit plea, in line with his more popular protests against redistributive interventions as infringements on personal freedom (e.g. 1962c, p. 9)? It is not clear, though it ought to be. We encounter it too in Chapter 9 (p. 192) where, in discussing the 'inflation gap', Friedman inserts the judgment that the price mechanism is the least undesirable allocative mechanism among those available. On a host of other issues, however, where Friedman himself acknowledges that his conclusions might be viewed by some as foregone, he is adamant that he had been swayed by empirical evidence and not value judgments (see 1968*b*, pp. 9–10). We take up this whole vexed area for separate study in Chapter 12.

The second problem is that Friedman is not able to come up with predictions that are quantitatively accurate enough for positive policy advice. He can point to the 'key' elements in a problem, to the main factors of influence; and he is enabled thereby to *exclude* certain policies (monetary fine tuning, for example). But mostly he is not able to go beyond what philosopher Alexander Rosenberg (1989) aptly dubs 'generic predictions' (of direction of change only; relating to average occurrences rather than individual cases). We see this in Chapter 10, where for all his efforts to spell out the details of a monetary transmission mechanism, Friedman is unable to determine with fine accuracy the split of nominal income between prices and output; and where the time lags involved remain of frustratingly 'variable' length. This does not stop him from making forthright and specific predictions which seem to go beyond what his positive economics will support. This matter too is taken up for separate examination, in Chapter 11.

Characteristics to look for

With these major exceptions, and some minor ones to be noted on the way through, we would expect to find Friedman:

1. offering explanatory hypotheses that at a minimum suffice to account for known observations; where
2. what is observed is (empirical) relations holding under a variety of circumstances or institutional regimes (so that the relations seem to be more than casual); and where
3. the relations sought after in the first place are suggested by tentatively held theories.

We would also expect, and largely find:

4. a strong array of evidence *for* the theories tentatively held;
5. testing of the explanatory hypotheses abducted, according to the criterion 'do they "work"?' (i.e. do they predict reasonably well the consequences of changes?);
6. some discussion, in the context of specific problems, of what 'reasonably well' means.

We sometimes find, though in general we would not expect:

7. much interest in purely formal analysis (an exception here is the 1951*c* analysis of fiscal policy-induced instability);

8. nor in results of general scope, divorced from the particulars of concrete problems and situations;

9. nor in models or explanatory hypotheses of a speculative sort, not well-grounded in observation, but defended on grounds of common-knowledge 'plausibility' (an exception is to be found towards the end of the Friedman–Meiselman study (1963e: see Chapter 9, p. 212).

Because of the underdetermination of theory by data and the difficulties of experimenting in economics, we would anticipate, and do find to an uncommon degree:

10. care in keeping quite separate broad theory, or frameworks, or paradigms, on the one hand, and specific predictions, on the other; with a good deal of attention paid to the need to 'specialize' a theoretical model before it becomes a testable or empirical model; and

11. much effort devoted to assessing the *comparative* robustness of alternative explanatory hypotheses, where possible in the form of 'crucial' experiments. Note that this is complementary to 5. and 6. above.

Finally, as to overall style, we would anticipate, and find:

12. much more emphasis on reliable, cumulative results than on weeding out error (i.e. than on falsifying); and much more stress on tentative 'knowing' than on deductive demonstration.

8 · MODELLING CHOICE

We turn now from Friedman's views about how economic research should be done to see how he actually did it. We shall look at his modelling of choice, at the inadequacies (from his point of view) of Keynesian macroeconomics, and at his monetary thought. These last two obviously overlap. Our aim in each instance is to shed more light on the nature of 'positive economics' by looking at Friedman's practice as an economist.

THE OPTIMIZING FREE CHOICE PARADIGM

We start off with Friedman's efforts to model choice. This is an appropriate starting point for several reasons. Friedman's efforts in this area are in part an attempt to see how far important social phenomena such as occupational rewards and personal income distribution can be explained as the effects of individuals making free choices. As will be stressed in Chapter 12, for Friedman individual freedom is *the* touchstone of a desirable political environment. In addition, he sees economic freedom as being fundamental to political freedom. Claims are often encountered to the effect that individualistic societies involve greater inequality. One way for Friedman to rebut such claims has been to show that incomes and their distribution reflect individual choice to a greater degree than is normally assumed. Hence his success in extending the range of application of choice theory bears directly on the defense of his political beliefs. Furthermore, this area of research happens to embrace early and sustained empirical and analytical interests of Friedman's − in household budget data and in statistical models of behaviour, for instance − and that in such a way as to allow us to illustrate in a fairly straightforward manner certain characteristics of his economics.

In contrast to the hypothetico-deductive approach, there is a strong sense, as we have seen (e.g. pp. 124 and 136–7), in which the methodology of positive economics says that good research starts with the facts. Although this notion is quite broad, at a minimum any hypothesis to be tested must pass the preliminary check of being 'consistent with the evidence at hand' before we can know that it is worthwhile deducing from it new facts and checking these against evidence not in the original set (1953d, in 1953e, pp. 12–13). Research into the 'facts', appropriately, formed the first phase of Friedman's work on choice. That work, however, extended over many years and passed through three phases. It centered throughout on occupational choice. After an initial data-gathering phase in the late 1930s which included deriving a hypothesis to resolve one major issue, why there are differences in average income levels between occupations, Friedman did not return to the subject of choice for several years. In phase two he published, in 1948, together with L. J. Savage, a new and distinctive hypothesis, capable of explaining the consequences for occupational choice of the observed wide variability in incomes within occupations. In 1953, in a third phase of this research, Friedman applied this particular explanation to the question of personal income distribution. The treatment below will adopt this three-phase division.

Before beginning our examination of Friedman's work on choice, however, some further comments on our approach – and his – are in order. We treat Friedman's efforts to model choice 'as if' (!) they amounted to a conscious research program. More than likely they did not. Our treatment therefore should be seen as a convenient reconstruction. The research program construct carries with it certain connotations of an integrated set of techniques and guiding purposes. These should not be allowed to obscure the fact that the three pieces of work we look at are of very different character.

Thus the early joint study with Kuznets of professional incomes is a very good illustration of several of Friedman's methodological precepts. It involves close study of the facts and the development of an explanation that accounts for several quite specific features of the data. Broadly speaking, it seems to illustrate the Marshallian 'factors of influence' model for inquiry. It does not quite fall under the paradigm-stretching model because variability of income within a profession was not explicable by means of the inherited 'equilibrating differences' framework of analysis. Instead, it constituted a challenge to extend the free choice paradigm, but a challenge that Friedman saw ways to meet only over time, as he discovered how to view gambling decisions as rational, and how to make use of the distinction between 'permanent' and unpredictable components of income.

The second study – the Friedman–Savage work on expected utility – is a perfect instance of the paradigm-stretching model. But the observational basis for this work is much less extensive; moreover, no tests were conducted despite considerable attention by Friedman to render his expanded hypothesis testable.

The third and final piece of research in this 'program', Friedman's 1953 attempt to integrate uncertainty and risk-loving behavior as a way of explaining peakedness and skewness in personal income distribution, finds free occupational choice to be consistent with these features. But ability to account for skewness and strong peakedness is not discriminatory evidence of the explanatory power of the free choice hypothesis. Nor is there any examination of the constraints (e.g. inherited wealth, power) which might overwhelm free choice as a determinant of distribution. Moreover, there are scarcely any starting facts in this work: it is merely one suggested possible application of the paradigm of rational choice. In short, this third study is far from Friedman's ideals of good positive economics and may have been for him little more than an occasion for making a political point.

Bearing these things in mind we turn to the studies themselves.

INCOME DIFFERENCES AND THE MARKET MECHANISM

From 1937 to 1941 Friedman was occupied with an NBER study of incomes in selected professions. The work had been begun by Simon Kuznets in 1933 as an outgrowth of a Department of Commerce survey of national income in the United States for 1929–32. After he joined Kuznets on the project, Friedman enlarged the span and coverage of the data and assumed responsibility for the statistical analysis and economic interpretation of the samples. The final product dealt with the incomes of physicians, dentists, certified public accountants and lawyers for the period 1929–36, and of consulting engineers for the original study period, 1929–32. It bore the title *Income from Independent Professional Practice* and was published in 1945 under the names of Friedman and Kuznets, although its form and content were due in large measure to Friedman; so much so that the work could be submitted by him towards satisfying the requirements for a PhD at Columbia University.

Friedman noted in his 1953 essay ('Positive economics') that 'the so-called "initial stage"' of fact gathering is never strictly free from prior hypotheses: 'A theory is the way we perceive "facts", and we cannot perceive "facts" without a theory' (1953*d*, in 1953*e*, pp. 13–14, 34). Theory enters into the classification we use and determines the factors implicitly or explicitly said to be important to explain the phenomena being looked at. For this reason data gathering and analysis are not readily disentangled. The phenomena to be explained in this case were differences in the level of incomes between the professions and between these and other occupations, on the one hand, and characteristic features of professional income distributions, on the other. These features were found to be: 'considerable skewness, wide variability, and great peakedness' (1945, p. 62).

Most of the interpretation in *Income from Independent Professional Practice* had to do with average income differences rather than with these characteristics. It was only in phase two of his research on choice, as noted earlier in this chapter, that Friedman developed the technique necessary to begin an analysis of the effects of one of the characteristic features of the distributions, namely wide variability.

In explaining differences in the level of income between professions Friedman, using Marshallian price theory as paradigm, tried to specify separately 'supply' and 'demand' influences, and used these to account for *relative* net income differences. This enabled him to view the net income difference between any two occupations as the return to a deliberate choice. In the first instance individuals were regarded as being of equal ability and as competing freely. Then, given the demand for professional services, appropriately defined, the relative numbers in each profession may be regarded as the supplies called forth by and freely made available in response to the observed net income difference. The difference is thus treated as an equilibrating or equalizing difference.[1]

Proceeding by steps Friedman first looked at strictly 'actuarial' factors, involving a comparison of training costs and specific occupational expenses with expected net lifetime returns. These factors are what create the so-called equalizing difference. The expected probability distributions of returns were taken as 'given'. Initially, too, abstraction was made from differences in taste (for risk; for non-pecuniary rewards); from market imperfections; and from social stratification. These were analyzed in their turn, to account for portions of the net difference that could not reasonably be attributed to actuarial factors. At each step an effort was made to quantify the influence of the separate factors.

This research followed Friedman's prescribed pattern of a fruitful, 'positive' investigation. Data were first gathered and a hypothesis derived to account for what seemed to be interesting factual characteristics. In this case, the generic hypothesis proposed was that equalizing differences in average income reflect free choice of occupation.[2] A *limited* number of specific factors, including restrictions on competition, were adduced to give content to this broad explanatory hypothesis. The work was pursued with a certain awareness of yet another desirable characteristic of 'positive' inquiry, the need to test at each of the two stages noted above. Not only must the hypothesis describe the known facts, but it must stand up against new facts, or data outside the set used to derive it.[3]

This double check was accomplished in *Income from Independent Professional Practice* as a spin-off of the way the work evolved. Kuznets, in 1936, completed 'a tentative manuscript' covering data to 1932. When Friedman took over, it was a simple matter 'as questions arose concerning the validity of some conclusions in the original draft . . ., [to use] such of the data for more recent years as were easily available to see whether they confirmed or disproved the conclusions drawn from the data for earlier years' (1945, preface, p. x). Friedman was sufficiently satisfied with his classification and analysis of the explanatory factors to retain both in his discussion of wages in different occupations in the 1976 edition of his *Price Theory* (1976b, Chapter 13). The only significant change introduced was the additional factor of tax structure.

THE EXPECTED UTILITY HYPOTHESIS AND INCOME VARIABILITY

One striking feature of incomes within the professions studied, and a feature too that seemed to distinguish the professions as a whole from all other occupations, was great variation in the incomes received by different members of a profession. How does the likelihood of receiving an income that deviates more or less from the average affect labor supply? Friedman and Kuznets found that variability is greater in medicine than in dentistry, and they cited Adam Smith and Marshall respectively to the effect that a general 'overweening conceit' among the young plus the prospect of 'a few extremely high prizes' increases the attractiveness of an occupation with wide variability in income (1945, pp. 128–9). If these views are correct, then 'if *all other things were the same*, a difference in expected average income just sufficient to compensate for the extra financial costs incident to the choice of medicine, would mean that more individuals would choose medicine than dentistry as a career' (*ibid.* pp. 129–30).

This suggestion posed a puzzle for Friedman. We have encountered this in Chapter 1, p. 14, but a reminder is in order. If a taste for gambling can influence occupational choice in the way supposed, the explanation, however plausible in itself, had to be considered *ad hoc* from the point of view of conventional price theory. The reason is that utility analysis traditionally embodied an assumption of diminishing marginal utility; and under this assumption a preference for gambling is irrational, since an even chance of winning or losing some given amount means a negative expected change in utility. An effect of risk or uncertainty on occupational choice such as the one suggested, therefore, put it outside the scope of the hypothesis of utility maximization, as traditionally understood.

What is necessary before gambling behaviour can be reconciled with utility maximization? In a 1948 paper with L. J. Savage, 'The utility analysis of choices involving risk' (1948c), Friedman outlined the following route. Firstly, consider choices as being made, not between certain (definite) outcomes, but between probability distributions of possible outcomes. This is simply a way of defining choice under uncertainty (risk in Knight's terminology). Secondly, suppose that there exists a class of functions which provide consistent ranking of choices in the same way as indifference functions help us to do for riskless choices, but where the choices are as we have redefined them, namely between alternative probability distributions of outcomes. Thirdly, suppose that there is a class of functions which not only meets the requirements for consistent ranking but also attaches a number to each choice, so that we can speak, if we wish, of a transitive ranking of choices by amount of 'utility'.

To apply this to the problem of choice among occupations that involve variability of expected returns we need only regard the probability distributions as being those for incomes. But what we now have is basically a mathematical problem – to prove the existence of such a class of functions as has been supposed. The formulation remains too general to have much empirical content. It says only that the supposed functions display consistency and transitivity. We therefore need to define a more specific form of the general functions relating utility to objects of choice. Following Friedman's exposition of the problem in his *Price Theory*, let the object of choice B be a probability p_1 of income y_1, p_2 of income y_2, and so on. We may then postulate the *special* relation or hypothesis[4]

$$G(B) = \sum_{i=1}^{k} p_i U(y_i)$$

It must be shown that a U(y) exists which has the property that G(B) calculated according to this special relation yields the correct ranking of objects of choice (Friedman and Savage, 1948c, and Friedman, 1976b, pp. 77–8).

In 1944, Von Neumann and Morgenstern, in their *Theory of Games and Economic Behavior*, demonstrated the existence of a class of functions linking utility with expected (probable) outcomes and unique except for origin and unit of measure. In 1948, Friedman and Savage adapted this proof to their problem of occupational choice involving risk. Their own contribution was to point out that it is not enough to know that the first derivative of such functions is positive, which implies only that people choose more income rather than less. We need also to know the sign of $U''(y)$ for different ranges of the function. Then a utility function that is concave from below will have the property that the expected utility of income $- p_1U(y_1) + p_2U(y_2)$, for a specific two-income choice $-$ is less than the utility of expected income.[5] In such a case a person will not gamble: he or she will take a certain but somewhat lower income in preference to a small risk of a large reduction in income. The reverse will be true if the utility function is convex from below. Thus a utility function that is alternately concave and convex over certain ranges will capture *both* the phenomenon of insurance and the phenomenon of gambling.

This seems to be much ado for little gain. At considerable expenditure of effort the hypothesis of utility maximization has been shown to be capable of explaining a previously excluded set of behaviors. Judgments, however, will differ about the significance of this achievement for positive economics. In phase three of his work on choice Friedman himself makes direct use of the result just sketched to suggest 'that one cannot rule out the possibility that *a large part of the existing inequality of wealth can be regarded as produced by men to satisfy their tastes and preferences*' (1953c in 1976b, p. 277, emphasis added). If so, then this is useful, if negative, information to the would-be interventionist. In some more obvious ways too, the work of Friedman and Savage illustrates aspects of the method of positive economics that go beyond what we learned in phase one of this program of research on choice.

The first of these is that Friedman displays a keen sensitivity to the need for a hypothesis to have empirical content. This shows itself in his concern to derive 'a special theory' to give substance to the very general notions embodied in the function $G(B)$ (1976b, p. 77; see point 10 in Chapter 7, p. 173). It also emerges in another place. In his derivation of the utility function $U(y)$, Friedman imagined subjects gambling with specified probabilities being attached to the outcomes. To generalize the derivation $-$ that is, to be able to predict additional choices using it $-$ it is necessary to specify the probabilities attaching to each new possible choice. He points out that hypothetical experiments with subjects allow us, in principle, to establish detailed personal scales of probabilities. This is necessary to make the expected utility hypothesis refutable, in principle. 'The combined hypothesis that each individual acts as if he assigned a personal probability *and* a utility value to any hypothetical event and chose among alternatives available ... in such a way as to maximize expected utility is now a hypothesis that in principle contains no unobservable elements' (*ibid.*, pp. 83–4, emphasis added).

A second feature stems directly from this last point. Friedman is careful not to leave an impression that the expected utility hypothesis is a realistic description of individual psychology. In line with Dewey, he refuses to build his economics on the presumption that we possess the necessary inside information to describe motives. This, as we have seen, became one general ground for his rejection of the idea that we can test merely by seeking plausibility – inherent, or widely acknowledged empirical good sense – in our assumptions. A special reason is hinted at in Friedman and Savage (1948c). In postulating 'that individuals act *as if* they assigned personal probabilities to all possible events', Friedman points out, we are *not* asserting that questions put to individuals about how likely they regard various hypothetical occurrences will always yield meaningful answers (1976b, p. 84). This fits Friedman's observation about humans' superior capacity to rationalize, and leads him to conclude in 'Positive economics' that we do better to trust 'what they [businessmen] do rather than what they say they do' (1953d, in 1953e, p. 31, n. 22). Notice that this feature means that we do not in fact have a *directly* testable hypothesis.

A third feature of Friedman's method, which is illustrated by the Friedman–Savage work on expected utility, is a direct implication of the remarks just made. Since the expected utility hypothesis – for good reason, in Friedman's view – embodies only the notion of individuals acting 'as if' they calculate and compare probabilities and expected utilities, there is only one test of the validity of the hypothesis that makes sense: not, is it plausible according to received wisdom but, how well does it predict?

OCCUPATIONAL CHOICE AND INEQUALITY

The final phase of Friedman's work on choice is his attempt in 1953 to apply the expected utility hypothesis to explain personal income distribution. This is to be found in a paper entitled 'Choice, chance and the personal distribution of income'.

In outline, Friedman took over the results of his work with Savage, with the one change that the utility function is now said to link cumulative wealth, rather than income, with utility. In a hypothetical world of identical individuals each of whom faces identical courses of actions and prospects, income inequality would reflect deliberate choice, the amount of 'inequality' depending to some degree on the shape of the utility function shared. If this function is convex from below, individuals would be willing to sacrifice some expected income for increased variability. This preference, in turn, would produce greater 'inequality' than if the function were concave downward (as in the hedging, or insurance range: see the diagram in note 5).

Using the same formulation as in Friedman and Savage (1948c) (i.e. linking expected utility to expected wealth – standing in, here, for income – where expected wealth is measured by the weighted sum of wealth prospects, the weights being the probabilities of each prospect) Friedman is able to show that, given a plausible restriction on the relation between wealth prospects and highest expected wealth for each individual and assuming costless redistribution, 'the *ex post* distribution of wealth depends only on the shape of the utility function and the maximum expected wealth per person for the society as a whole and not at all on differences in the prospects available to different [individuals]' (1953*c*, reprinted in 1976*b*, p. 270). Alternatively, 'the opportunities offered man by "nature" [e.g. inheritance] determine only the mean value of the realized distribution of wealth; the inequality of wealth is entirely a man-made creation' (*ibid.*, p. 269). This result is somewhat weakened when the costs of redistributive arrangements are allowed for.

But Friedman's main purpose is to show that distribution may reflect both individual choice among risky prospects and 'joint advance agreement' on some redistributive arrangement. The latter may be implemented by private enterprise or 'government' (*ibid.*, p. 267).

To incorporate redistributive arrangements, divide each individual's wealth into a component not accessible to such arrangements and a component that is modified by such arrangements. The final wealth distribution is then the probability sum of two distributions. One redistributive arrangement supposes that each individual buys a share in a lottery, for which sum he or she receives some specified chance of a prize. The effect of the lottery is to shift the overall distribution towards the low end, since the aim of the redistributive scheme is to provide some minimum for those who do not win a prize. It will also reduce the variability of expected receipts, since individuals are supposed to pay for chances in such amounts as to offset differences in the prospects they originally enjoyed. In any event, the net effect of the lottery is to create two component distributions, one for winners and one for losers, which in turn are superimposed upon the wealth outcome that is not subject to any redistributive scheme. If winners are very few the overall distribution will be skewed to the low end of the wealth scale. Adding the winners' component distribution may not introduce a second distinct mode, but may merely move the mode of the overall distribution a little to the right and flatten and extend the tail of that distribution. The overall distribution will then display relatively great peakedness, with an exaggerated tail at the high end of wealth (*ibid.*, p. 276).

We may note in passing that the idea of representing wealth and income distributions as the sum of two distinct distributions occurred to Friedman in the course of modeling the burst of rockets fitted with proximity fuses during a stint with Allen Wallis' war-time Statistical Research Group from 1942 to 1945 (Wallis, 1980, p. 323; Friedman, 1976*b*, p. 277, n. 19). This is an early hint of Friedman's peculiar aptitude for using statistical notions and properties in the development of economic hypotheses which we have noted above (Chapter 7, p. 170, point 5.).

Now great peakedness and skewness, it will be recalled, are precisely the features displayed by distributions of incomes from independent professional practice (p. 127, above). According to Friedman, observed distributions of wealth, and incomes from other sources too, display similar features. Hence, he concludes, 'the distribution function to which our theoretical analysis leads meets at least the initial test of being able to reproduce the more outstanding features of observed distributions of wealth and income' (1976b, p. 277).

The political relevance of this piece of analysis has already been noted. We should stress, however, that if it were to be used for policy ends that would mean going beyond positive economics; for it falls short of yielding a generalization about economic phenomena 'that can be used to predict the consequences of changes in circumstances', which is the avowed aim of 'economics as a positive science' (1953d, in 1953e, p. 39). The problem is that meeting 'the initial test' is something very many hypotheses may do. As Friedman says in 'Positive economics', 'observed facts are necessarily finite in number; possible hypotheses, infinite' (ibid., p. 9). This difficulty is frankly acknowledged in the 1953 paper: 'of course, the fact that [the analysis sketched above] is not patently inconsistent with observed distributions of wealth or income does not mean that it is consistent with them or that the model on which it is based isolates the central elements accounting for existing distributions of wealth or income' (1976b, p. 277). The general lesson to be drawn in this case is one that is stated in 'Positive economics': positive economics comprises only tentatively accepted hypotheses, or those which have not yet been disproven (1953d, in 1953e, p. 9).

Friedman was inclined to see much more in his analysis. Apart from an underlying plausibility in the hypothesis – he is not averse to using this to add confidence (see Chapter 1, p. 15; and Chapter 9, p. 213) – he saw in it too a justification for further empirical study; and he was pleased with the wide scope of his preferred explanation: 'many common economic and social arrangements – from the organizational form of economic enterprises to collectively imposed and enforced income and inheritance taxes – can be interpreted as, at least in part, devices for achieving a distribution of wealth in conformity with the tastes and preferences of the members of society' (1976b, pp. 277–8). This last, as noted above, is a weak reed because of the numerous alternative interpretations possible. Friedman's argument is hypothetical, and we may regard it as a novel theoretical advance but very far from the quantified, reliable predictions that are said to be the aim of positive economics.

THE PROGRAM IN REVIEW

This reminds us that the whole program of research on choice was motivated by a desire to see in how far distribution could be accounted for by individual choice. That is clearly stated in the preface to *Income from Independent Professional Practice*: 'this approach treats professional activity as taking place in an economy best described as a free enterprise system in which the production of goods and distribution of incomes are regulated primarily by the impersonal mechanism of the market' (1945, preface, p. v.). The 1953 paper on choice, chance and distribution fits closely with this intention, although it ultimately stressed the importance of (socially) chosen rather than governmentally or naturally imposed distributions. It is somewhat lost sight of in the original work (Friedman and Kuznets, 1945), which is preoccupied with data collection, analysis, and presentation. The basic interpretative framework, and its key notion, the equilibrium net income difference, however, are outworkings of it. In terms of its approach, *Income from Independent Professional Practice* involves finding a simple hypothesis that adequately accounts for the data, and attempting to quantify the effects of a limited number of explanatory factors, whose predictive power is checked against data outside the original set. This captures much of the method and the purpose of positive economics.

The intermediate step in the program, represented by Friedman and Savage (1948c), reinforces the idea that positive economics comprises empirically testable hypotheses rather than formal analysis as such. The 1948 paper also furthers the intention of the program by incorporating risky behavior into the theory of free and rational choice. But it does nothing for demonstrated predictive power, which is after all the relevant test of a positive theory.

Finally, to come back to the 1953 paper applying the expected utility hypothesis, we see an attempt to show that the role of institutional or 'external' factors in personal income or wealth distribution may be 'less direct and simple than is generally supposed' (1953c in 1976b, p. 278). Turning this negative conclusion on its head, the hypothesis of utility maximization *can* explain much even of what has often been regarded as the result of legal arrangements (e.g. inheritance taxes) or 'acts of God'. To repeat our word of caution from the start of this chapter, however, while this result is fraught with implications for policy it does not have much in it that could be called positive economics.

Thus this program did not end with a great deal in the way of firm predictive content which might be checked and applied in policy analysis. That element was present in the Friedman–Kuznets study to some extent. The later inquiries were more a matter of special analysis designed to extend the range of application of the starting hypothesis or paradigm. Analytically, what was new in the whole approach was the replacement of determinate models by weighted prospective outcomes, the weights being probabilities; and the use of specific properties of distributions to give empirical content to general economic hypotheses such as utility maximization. In this narrower context, we can view Friedman's contribution as an example of devising novel ways to 'specialize' a generic theory; in other words, as one step towards testable hypotheses.

NOTES

1. The model of equalizing differences was part of Marshall's inheritance from classical economics.
2. Friedman felt that he could not account for the relative height of physicians' incomes by equilibrating differences, and resorted to a non-competitive element, the monopoly power of the American Medical Association. This, however, became a matter of disagreement among the board members of the NBER and led to a long delay in publishing the Friedman–Kuznets study, and there is only a very muted reference to the AMA's exercise of power in the final manuscript. For further details of this episode see Silk (1976), pp. 54–6. Note that non-competing groups was also part of the classical inheritance, a supplement to the equilibrating differences notion, due to Cairnes.
3. As Friedman put it in 1948 in a request to the Rockefeller Foundation for support for a Study of Monetary Factors in Business Cycles:

   It is clear that the first stage of this study is to compile and put into systematic form some quantitative data that will provide the chief basis for whatever inferences we can make about the behavior of monetary and banking phenomena during business cycles and about their role in generating, or determining the character, of business cycles. At a later stage, of course, these data will need to be supplemented by others to test tentative inferences, and to explore channels of monetary influence not now recognized.

4. For cumulative distribution function $F(y) \equiv$ [probability $(\tilde{y} \leqslant y)$] for random variable $\tilde{y}$, assume that there is a preference function $V(\cdot)$ representing a ranked set of preferences which are complete, transitive and continuous. If $V(\cdot)$ is a linear functional of $F(\cdot)$ then $V(F) = \int U(y)dF(y)$ (or the expected value of $U(\tilde{y})$ for some function $U(\cdot)$ over income levels y); $U(\cdot)$ is the Von Neumann-Morgenstern utility function for an individual (see following paragraph in the text). If y can take values y_1 to y_n with probabilities p_1 to p_n, then

$$\int U(y)dF(y) = \sum_{i=1}^{n} p_i U(y_i)$$

See Machina and Rothschild, in Eatwell, Milgate and Newman (eds) (1987), vol. 4, p. 202.

5. In Figure 8.1, commonly used to illustrate this point, let y (income) take value y_1 with probability $\frac{2}{3}$ and y_2 with probability $\frac{1}{3}$. Then the expected value of this chance or lottery, for the special form of preference function normally assumed (note 4 above), is $\tilde{y} = \frac{2}{3}y_1 + \frac{1}{3}y_2$, located two-thirds of the way

towards y_1 on the horizontal axis. The expected utility of this lottery – i.e. the value $E[U(\tilde{y})] = [\frac{2}{3}U(y_1) + \frac{1}{3}U(y_2)]$ – lies between $U(y_1)$ and $U(y_2)$ on the vertical axis, two-thirds of that distance towards $U(y_1)$. Since $\tilde{y}$ is a random variable, it is less risky to take a certain payment of $\tilde{y} = E(\tilde{y})$, which will yield utility $U[E(\tilde{y})]$ than to bear the risk of $\tilde{y}$ and obtain expected utility $E[U(\tilde{y})]$. If the utility function is convex from below the riskier option will be preferred.

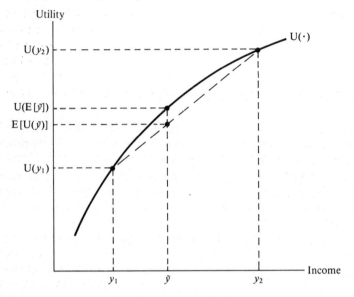

Figure 8.1   Expected utility: the case of risk-aversion

See Machina and Rothschild, *ibid*.

9 • THE SHORTCOMINGS OF KEYNESIAN ECONOMICS

THE EARLY ORIGINS OF FRIEDMAN'S ANTI-KEYNESIANISM

We pass now to Friedman's preoccupation with and rejection of Keynesian economics. One of the ironies to be borne in mind as we proceed is that Keynes, on Friedman's view, was 'a true Marshallian'.[1] To some extent, as this might suggest, Friedman is opposed to Keynesian economics rather than the economics of Keynes. It is also true that he criticizes Keynes' own analysis, but not until the 1970s and almost as an afterthought.

Friedman's opposition to Keynesian economics is well known, but it is familiar to most only in the context of his efforts to bring about a monetarist counter-revolution. This suggests two related possibilities. It may be that Friedman's is a straw-man version of Keynesian economics. Perhaps too his opposition only dates from his own rediscovery of the quantity theory in the late 1940s or early 1950s. Both suggestions are wide of the mark. Friedman's opposition had its origin, if not its clearest expression, in work he did on household spending in the 1930s and, more directly, in research on the 'inflation gap' in the early 1940s. And the reasons for his dissatisfaction at first had nothing to do with monetarism, but much to do with the sorts of reasons why Marshall was deemed superior to Cournot.

We distinguish two phases in Friedman's growing dissatisfaction with Keynesian analysis. The first runs from 1942 through 1963, beginning with a critical note on 'inflation gap' analysis and ending with the Friedman–Meiselman effort to establish that velocity is more stable than the autonomous expenditure multiplier. This phase will be our concern here. Phase 2 is so integrally connected with the monetarist counter-revolution that it is treated separately in that context, in Chapter 10.

In the period 1942–63 there is little evidence that Friedman took Keynes as his point of departure. He was concerned primarily with the poverty, both from an analytical and a policymaking perspective, of the then-common Keynesian models.

Friedman began by questioning the empirical basis of the Keynesian system and progressed to the conviction, expressed in *A Theory of the Consumption Function* (1957c), that 'I do not myself accept [the] income-expenditure theory as a valid and tested interpretation of experience' (1957c, p. 236). The last publications in Phase 1, Friedman and Becker (1957a), and Friedman and Meiselman (1963e), are attempts to bolster this judgment statistically.

Two of the things that Friedman valued in Marshall were categories moulded to the data of the problem at hand, and analysis that represents an appropriate level of abstraction – simple enough to manage, yet detailed enough to yield precise answers to concrete questions (1953d in 1953e, pp. 14, 35; 1974b, pp. 145–6, 159–60). Quantification is very important here. Theoretical categories must be related to *measurable entities*; and the ultimate aim is to get *quantitative estimates* of the effects of causal factors so that the analysis can be used to shape policy. These characteristics of good economics are stressed in Friedman and Wallis (1942), 'The empirical derivation of indifference functions',[2] long before Friedman started calling them 'Marshallian'. We also encounter them in a volume published in 1943 (1943a) embodying significant contributions by Friedman, although they are presented in the form of things lacking in 'the Keynesian analysis'.

'INFLATION GAP' ANALYSIS

The 1943 volume is a book authored by Carl Shoup, Friedman and Ruth Mack (SFM), entitled *Taxing to Prevent Inflation*. It contains the results and the methods developed by a team directed by these three to estimate the amount of extra taxation necessary to avert a wartime inflation. The senior author, Shoup, acknowledges in the preface that the basic framework for analysis of the problem is due to Friedman.[3]

The concrete problem with which the group began was to assess what kinds and degrees of changes in taxation would be necessary to reduce private disposable income to non-inflationary proportions in a situation where the government is drawing more of the nation's resources into war production. Two distinct aspects of the problem can be distinguished. First, what kinds of possible responses in the economy to the government's action are there? This is a question about the channels through which the implied 'inflation gap' might be closed. Second, granting that an increase in spending will initially call forth extra output but will also, at some point, induce higher prices, we desire quantitative methods of predicting *when* prices will begin to rise. We have Friedman's contribution towards answering the first question in his (invited) reply to a paper by Walter Salant, 'The inflationary gap: meaning and significance for policy making', which was somewhat critical of the SFM method of gap estimation. Both paper and reply are printed in the *American Economic Review* for June 1942 (1942*b*). Friedman's efforts in the second direction are contained in Part 3 of *Taxing to Prevent Inflation*.

The problem of a wartime diversion of resources is that consumers will have the means to go on spending as before while a smaller share in output will be made up of goods available for consumption. In Keynesian terminology there is an inflationary gap.[4] How is this gap closed? The very adjective 'inflationary' suggests that the main, or sole, method is a price rise.[5] Friedman dissented strongly from this interpretation:

> [T]his implication is in many ways misleading. The mere revaluation of goods available for sale does not by itself close the gap; it is the redistribution of income and the change in spending-saving habits accompanying a price rise that closes the gap. Moreover a price rise is not the only way in which the gap may be closed (1942*b* in 1953*e*, pp. 251–2).

One of the things that may happen as prices rise is that nominal incomes too increase. At higher prices and incomes consumers, wanting to maintain constant real spending, may be willing to disburse larger monetary amounts and the nominal gap may therefore actually widen. On the other hand, redistributive effects may narrow the gap. A price rise will tend in the first place to increase profits. Those who receive profit incomes, being used to fluctuations in their receipts, will tend to spend a disproportionately low fraction of this windfall gain. This may raise the ratio of saving to spending and so help close the gap. How much prices will have to rise will depend, among other things, on how quickly trade unions react to the increase in profits, and whether consumers assume that the initial inflation will continue. Moreover the final outcome may be quite different if consumers baulk at higher prices and boycott price-inflated goods, or if supplies can be supplemented by drawing on accumulated stocks.

The possibilities for closure clearly are numerous. But in that case, of what value is a simple estimate of the gap itself? Friedman's answer is disarmingly frank. Of the primary consumer expenditure gap – likely expenditure at base prices compared with available consumer goods and services at base prices – Friedman said that it is worth estimating only to show how far the statistical estimate of voluntary savings would have to err for the gap to be wholly due to statistical error; or at best to show how large is the task, if we desire to close the gap via an increase in 'voluntary' savings. He even rejected the idea that the gap measured the amount by which taxes would have to increase to prevent inflation. In line with the comments cited above, he noted that just how much taxes must be increased depends on spending-savings habits as well as on such considerations as the kind of taxes imposed. In other words, 'an analysis directed toward policy should not stop with an estimate of the primary expenditure gap. It should take as its function the evaluation of the quantitative aspects of the alternative measures that might be taken to close the gap' (1942*b* in 1953*e*, p. 260).

In this welter of sceptical comment Friedman seems to be doing little more than agree wholeheartedly with the paper by Salant which, nominally, he was to criticize. His purpose, however, was to show that even if one approaches gap analysis and its application to policy with the same caution and awareness that Salant displayed, the effort is of mainly negative value. Why? Because (as could be inferred from what has been said already): 'to estimate the gap, and the consequences that will flow from it, requires precise and quantitative knowledge of the process of economic change – of how impulses are transmitted throughout the economic system, of lags in adjustment, technical possibilities, and human reactions' (1942*b* in 1953*e*, p. 262); and this is knowledge of which we simply do not have very much in hand (*ibid.*, pp. 261–2).

This is in fact an indirect attack on Salant. Salant had surveyed two approaches to gap estimation: one, the SFM method, used estimates of component changes in capital formation, residential construction, and so on, to get at civilian demand. It ignored what Salant referred to as 'secondary' effects – presumably multiplier effects stemming from the primary expenditure changes. An alternative method, employed in a study done for the Office of Price Administration (OPA), was viewed by Salant as conceptually more satisfactory because it estimated demand using an explicit system of interdependent behavioral equations and thereby captured both primary and secondary effects.[6]

If we read Friedman's contribution in the Shoup, Friedman and Mack volume, we find there a clearly expressed set of objections to Keynesian models; but it is not difficult to see in his more muted response to Salant objections of an exactly comparable sort. What he says in direct response to Salant is (a) that we know little about 'the quantitative interrelationships of the economic system' – a use of words so specific as to suggest a reference to the OPA's demand system; and (b) that useful estimates of the inflationary gap are possible at all only because of wartime circumstances, which enable us to know the direction and even the magnitude of demand changes in a way that cannot be presumed in peacetime (1942*b* in 1953*e*, pp. 261–2). In other words, gap analysis as a piece of abstract theorizing has not added to our knowledge of economic dynamics (the cycle) and simply cannot be regarded as a useful tool of policy except in highly specific circumstances. It is therefore scientifically sterile for the most part.

In *Taxing to Prevent Inflation* Friedman made his criticisms more detailed. If one wants to forecast the increase in income that will accompany an increased armaments programme, it might seem reasonable to take investment, in the sense of 'offsets to savings', as the strategic variable determining changes in income. Once estimates of total investment or categories of investment are made, this could be translated into a change in income simply on the basis of historical information. But what exactly is contained in that information? If it is a correlation between past changes in investment and in income, and nothing more, the whole approach seems like seeking a 'refuge in empiricism' (1943a, p. 114).[7] Alternatively, if there is a supposedly causal analysis lying behind this way of viewing investment and in turn accounting for the correlation, it is presumably 'the Keynesian analysis' (*ibid.*, p. 141). The question then becomes, how empirically reliable is this Keynesian analysis?

Friedman offered the following brief account of Keynesian thinking.[8] Let changes in income be the result of discrepancies between *ex ante* saving and investment. While we cannot measure *ex ante* saving and investment, we might infer discrepancies from changes in inventories – provided we knew what portion of any such change were speculative. Without this information, the Keynesian analysis can be applied only with the help of heroic assumptions. Assume, for example, that *ex ante* saving is the same as *ex post* saving this period. In other words, assume *ex ante* saving is equal to current investment. Estimate next period's investment and compare this with current investment. A difference between the two may be interpreted as the difference between *ex ante* investment and saving. Friedman concluded with two obvious criticisms: 'the links between the statistical estimates and the *ex ante* concepts are extremely loose'; and 'the [supposed underlying] relation between income and *ex ante* investment can be considered stable only under equilibrium conditions'. Since the analysis gives no reason to believe that this relationship will be stable in the face of shocks to the system, 'the validity of the procedure should ... be judged on a largely statistical level' (1943a, pp. 141–3). Friedman made one additional comment, at the statistical level, that correlation indisputably exists between income and investment. He suggested that a safer comparison would be that between the two components of income, investment and consumption (*ibid.*, p. 146).

This last comment foreshadows some of the doubts about the estimation and predictive accuracy of Keynesian models to which Friedman subsequently gave expression in his later paper with Becker (Friedman and Becker, 1957a). But in 1942–3 his main concerns lay elsewhere. From a methodological point of view, we may notice three things of interest.

First, Friedman was negative about gap analysis in part because it compared unfavorably with fruitful problem-solving. If we may apply the lesson of our comparison between Cournot and Marshall in Chapter 7, gap analysis (as it was being used) smacked of the 'arithmetic and descriptive' rather than the problem-solving approach. Gap analysis had added nothing to our knowledge of change (dynamics), which was a first prerequisite to successful policy intervention (1942*b* in 1953*e*, p. 262). Moreover, the estimates were subject to such wide margins of error as to be almost useless (*ibid*., p. 261). And finally, they were being interpreted in such a way as to encourage would-be interventionists to impose strict price controls; whereas for Friedman the price system was 'the least undesirable method of allocating the limited resources that will be available' (*ibid*.). Hence, 'if they could be constructed, breakdowns [among broad classes of output] of the type suggested by Mr Salant would be desirable under alternative relative prices, *not for determining basic policy, but rather for estimating the relative price changes that would be likely to occur*' (*ibid*., emphasis added).

Second, if we ask, why these deficiencies? the answer will have something to do with our lack of knowledge. And if we know all too little about the interrelationships in the economy – behavioral relations, time lags, human reactions, and so on (see *ibid*., pp. 261–2) – then it is pointless to move to greater sophistication in model-building. Complexity and sophistication in models is no substitute for ignorance about how the economy actually functions. This seems to be the spirit of Friedman's comment on Salant, and if so it is an early hint of what he presently would find so wrong about Lange's analysis, with its 'formal models of imaginary worlds, not generalizations about the real world'; and a hint too of his criticisms of the Klein–Christ efforts to construct a simultaneous equation forecasting model for the economy. Fruitful economics must start with and be able to account for the facts.

Third, it is very clear that at this stage Friedman had not found a way to deal with non-empirical entities. His concern with the non-empirical character of the Keynesian analysis is in line with his negative judgment in the 1942 paper with Wallis on the possibilities for deriving indifference curves from data. Just how well supported were the supposed causal mechanisms and relations of the Keynesian system? This empirical concern was to preoccupy him for many years.

KEYNESIAN 'GOOD INTENTIONS' VERSUS USEFUL PRESCRIPTIONS

Friedman's next brush with Keynesian analysis came when he was asked to review Abba Lerner's *The Economics of Control*. The book appeared in 1944, Friedman's review only in 1947. We focus on just one segment of the review, dealing with Lerner's views on controlling unemployment and economic fluctuations.

Friedman expressed reservations of exactly the same sort as he had expressed about inflation gap work in 1942. Lerner's formal condition for a stable high level of output and employment is that aggregate demand be 'adequate'. But, 'this is nowhere spelled out in fuller detail, nor is there any systematic discussion of the criteria in terms of which "adequacy" is to be judged' (1947a in 1953e, p. 312). Even more serious, however, was Lerner's failure to turn his discussion of fiscal actions to maintain adequate demand from 'a logical exercise' – taxonomic and descriptive, again – into 'a prescription'. For it to serve as the latter we would need to know

> when there is 'insufficient total demand', whether this insufficiency is a temporary deficiency in the process of being corrected or the beginning of an increasing deficiency that, if left alone, will lead to drastic deflation ... what medicine to use when a diagnosis has been made, how large a dose to give, and how long we may expect it to take if the medicine is to be effective (1947a in 1953e, pp. 313–14).

This information, Friedman added, is not easily obtained. The reason foreshadows his later comment on the problem of interpretation facing economists when all they are presented with is outcomes (1953d, pp. 10–11). It is not lack of data that is the problem. It is the difficulty of identifying causal mechanisms in the movements of the important economic magnitudes that makes Lerner's comments into mere statements of 'good intentions' rather than a useful guide to action.

One response to the difficulties of identifying the current state, and of forecasting the future state of the economy is to argue that it does not much matter. If the government finds it has made a mistake, it can quickly reverse itself. This, Friedman insists, is a mistaken view. Lags exist between the need for action and government recognition of the need; between recognition of the need for and the actual taking of the necessary action; and between the action and its having an effect. Furthermore, these lags comprise 'a substantial fraction' of the duration of cyclical movements. Thus government may find its actions biting at just the point when they are no longer needed, with the result that fluctuations are exacerbated rather than damped by policy (1947a in 1953e, pp. 315–16).

Friedman's criticisms of Lerner's work thus mirror what he had to say earlier about mere identifications of the 'inflation gap'; except that in this last comment he goes considerably beyond his earlier insistence that we must take lags of adjustment into account in considering ways in which the gap may be closed.

In a 1951 article Friedman turned this point about lags possibly causing policy to worsen cyclical fluctuations into a logical demonstration ('The effects of a full-employment policy on economic stability: a formal analysis', 1951c). He is quite open about the nature of this particular contribution. It falls into the class of analyses which clarify the issues, and 'indicate in general terms the considerations on which an answer in any particular case depends. It does not attempt to answer them for any particular case' (1951c in 1953e, p. 117). In other words, it is logical analysis rather than an empirical hypothesis. And as such, we may add, it is more Millian than Deweyan.

Friedman's proof itself is not relevant to our purposes; but note that he there sets out, for the first time in his writings, an explicit though by then fairly common version of the Keynesian model. This enables him to stress that the Keynesian system is (a) timeless (without dynamics) and therefore cannot even address the problem which he identified in his review of Lerner; and (b) neglects price movements for all positions below 'full employment'. By contrast, recall that in his own discussion of the inflation gap price changes and responses to them formed an essential part of the transmission mechanism and adjustment process, which also, of course, took time. These themes were central to his rejection of Klein's early Keynesian econometric models, also published in 1951 (1951a, pp. 113–14).

To take stock, at this point Friedman had voiced concern at the non-empirical character of Keynesian concepts (e.g. *ex ante* savings); he had on two separate occasions reacted negatively to economists of Keynesian ilk who put forward as useful tools for policy simple notions or mere 'language' (e.g. the inflation gap derived from general aggregate demand analysis; and Lerner's 'adequate' aggregate demand) without the facts, the detailed analysis and the quantification of possibilities essential to arriving at genuinely usable prescriptions. He had also questioned the lack of an empirically secure theory to cause us to expect stability in the critical Keynesian investment-income relation. If the relation merely reflected a short span of historical data covering no unusual episodes, he added, one must consider that it might be unreliable.

None of these reasons for doubt, we repeat, had to do with monetarist propositions. They did not come in until later, although Friedman began his research on monetary statistics in 1948. His scepticism had a strong empirical thrust to it. If there is any single theme in these early criticisms of Keynesian analysis it is related to empirical dynamics, or stability: whether inflationary or deflationary gaps will widen or close; whether the government's stabilizing efforts will help or hinder; whether the investment-income relation and spending-saving habits are stable. But these concerns did not lead him to articulate an alternative theory. This having been stressed, it should also be said that of course, like any pragmatic researcher, Friedman approached problems with the best knowledge available. This includes the facts 'first', but it also meant for Friedman the Marshallian price theoretic analysis, including the maximizing paradigm (cf. Chapter 8, p. 177). Hence it is not insignificant that he insisted, in his one real criticism of Salant, that the purpose of gap analysis should be, not to base policy on restricting demand to potential output 'at ... *desired* prices', but to investigate the *likely relative price changes* that may *actually* occur as resources shift in response to demand (see 1942*b* in 1953*e*, p. 261, emphasis added). Who is to determine what prices are 'desired'? Some czar in the OPA? A political preference slips in here, for freedom from coercion, giving rise to the conclusion that the price mechanism is 'the least undesirable method of allocating ...' (*ibid.*; see further, Chapter 12, below).

Four more pieces of work must be noted in which the emphasis is on the empirical underpinnings of our attempted explanations. The first is *A Theory of the Consumption Function*, published in 1957 but in essentials already outlined by mid-1951. There Friedman developed hints that are present in his own earlier work on a testable hypothesis to the effect that consumption depends primarily on 'permanent' rather than current income. The work is perhaps the best known of Friedman's analyses aside from his reformulation of the quantity theory. That would perhaps argue for our noticing it only briefly. However, because the treatment embodies an intriguing approach to unobservables we dwell longer upon it than is necessary simply to show how it fits into Friedman's assessment of Keynesian analysis.

The other three pieces of writing devoted to fact-related doubts about the Keynesian analysis are 'Price, income, and monetary changes in three wartime periods' (1952*b*), 'A statistical illusion in judging Keynesian models' (1957*a*) and 'The relative stability of monetary velocity and the investment multiplier in the United States, 1897–1958' (1963*e*). These will be touched on briefly after a more extended look at *A Theory of the Consumption Function*.

FRIEDMAN'S 'PERMANENT INCOME' HYPOTHESIS

The problem context

In *A Theory of the Consumption Function* Friedman began by spelling out an empirical problem. Keynes' view was that current consumption expenditure is a stable function of current income. The form of this relation, moreover, was said to be such that the average propensity to consume declines with income. Early budget data and inter-war series initially seemed to confirm this hypothesis. But two post-Second World War findings proved troublesome. First, work by Kuznets suggested that the long-term savings ratio is constant. Furthermore, consumption on his reckoning proved to be not only a much higher fraction of income than had been suggested by earlier studies, but the long-term marginal propensity to consume seemed to be higher than in budget studies taken separately. Second, post-war experience was bothersome for the view that the consumption-income relation is reliably stable; for post-war savings proved to be much lower than commonly expected on the basis of estimates of the consumption function made with inter-war data. In terms of the methodology of positive economics Keynes' consumption function failed the basic test: it did not even satisfactorily rationalize known evidence.[9]

A plethora of explanations arose, including various suggestions to the effect that relative, not absolute income, is the appropriate independent variable to use. A second line of explanation adapted the Haberler–Pigou effect to argue that the low post-war saving ratio might be due to consumption's being a function of wealth as well as of current income. Friedman took up this latter notion, though it is interesting to note a much later comment of his to the effect that he never gave as much credence to the wealth effect as a way out of Keynesian under-employment equilibrium as he did to price changes and the resulting redistribution effects (see Friedman, 1976b, p. 317). Empirically wealth effects seemed to him to be less important than relative price effects (1976b, p. 231). This is consistent with the stress he placed on the latter in his early brushes with Keynesian analysis. General equilibrium challenges to the notion of under-employment equilibrium have occasionally been acknowledged by him in formal contexts – in particular, to argue that there is no basic flaw in the price system – but they seem never to have been of more than secondary interest (Friedman, 1976d, p. 16 and n. 6).

'Wealth' was the key notion in Friedman's own consumption hypothesis; but it entered in an entirely different way than merely as a variable to supplement current income. Thus:

> The designation of current receipts as 'income' in statistical studies is an expedient enforced by limitations of data. On a theoretical level, income is generally defined as the amount a consumer unit could consume (or believes that it could) while maintaining its wealth intact. *In our analysis, consumption is a function of income so defined* (1957c, p. 10, emphasis added).

Friedman used Irving Fisher's indifference curve analysis to illustrate what a wide gap exists between the statistical magnitudes consumption and income and the proper theoretical notions, 'permanent' (sustainable) consumption and its counterpart 'permanent' income. This could have led to further problems, of the sort that, as he pointed out earlier, plagued attempts to apply Keynesian theory to forecasting income. For 'the theoretical constructs are *ex ante* magnitudes; the empirical data are *ex post*' (1957c, p. 20). Friedman rejected the idea that adjustments be made to statistical magnitudes so as to yield closer approximations to 'permanent' income and consumption, preferring instead an indirect approach to operationalization that had served him once already (in Friedman and Savage, 1948c).[10] He chose to treat consumer units '*as if* they regarded their income and their consumption as the sum of two ... components' (permanent and transitory); and as if they consumed according to some optimizing-over-time strategy (*ibid.*, pp. 20–3). The permanent component of income was interpreted as reflecting the effect of factors which the consumer considers determine his or her wealth.

   This specification of the problem, in terms deriving from *Income from Independent Professional Practice* and using a modelling technique akin to the one adopted in 'Choice, chance, and the personal distribution of income' (income considered as analogous to an 'expected' value within a probability distribution, 1957c, p. 21), suggests how the analysis would be developed further. The hypothesis $C_p = k(i, w, u)Y_p$, where i is the set of rates for borrowing and lending facing a consumer, w expresses the relative importance of property to non-property income and u stands for relative preferences for consumption compared to additions to wealth, plus the definitional statements $Y \equiv Y_p + Y_t$ and $C \equiv C_p + C_t$, is so broad as to be consistent with any and all data. Friedman therefore chose one particular way of 'specializing' it: he supposed that there is zero correlation between the transitory components of income and consumption and of each with the corresponding permanent components (*ibid.*, p. 26). This makes the hypothesis testable by specifying certain characteristics of the relationship between random statistical components and between them and the (unobservable) permanent income component of the theory.

   This is methodologically very interesting. In line with the work we have described in Chapter 8, it implies that the presence of unobservables is not in itself a reason to reject the theory as purely formal and of limited use, so long as implications can be deduced which are empirical. Finding such implications is the ingenious achievement of *A Theory of the Consumption Function*. Evidently, when Friedman earlier complained about unobservables in the Keynesian analysis he did not see his way clear to constructing an indirect empirical test. Nor did he when he rejected indifference curve analysis, in Friedman and Wallis (1942a). The idea of indirect testing, however, plays an important role in 'The methodology of positive economics', (1953d in 1953e, p. 28).

Making 'permanent' income observable

Just how did the statistical restrictions imposed by Friedman on the transitory components of income and consumption enable him to construe his consumption function hypothesis as empirical? The answer is contained in *Income from Independent Professional Practice*, Chapter 7, said in the preface to be both 'the most novel part of the analysis' and also to be due to Friedman (rather than to Kuznets) (1945, pp. ix, xii). The kernel of Chapter 3 in *A Theory of the Consumption Function*, where the permanent income hypothesis is laid out, is taken over, with little change, from the earlier study.

To get at the argument we have to read backwards. At the end of Chapter 3 of *A Theory of the Consumption Function* Friedman says:

> Differences among various groups of consumer units in observed marginal propensities to consume may not reflect differences in underlying preferences for consumption and wealth at all; they may reflect primarily the different strength of random forces, including errors of measurement, in determining measured income. Fortunately, considerable evidence is available on the importance of transitory components of income from studies of changes over time in the relative income status of individuals or consumer units. One of the attractive features of our hypothesis is that it enables us to bring this independent body of evidence to bear on the interpretation of consumer behavior. (1957c, p. 37).

The reference here is to the evidence presented in *Income from Independent Professional Practice*. In analyzing that evidence Friedman admitted that 'there is of course no way of isolating the permanent and transitory components of the income of a particular man. We can measure only his actual income, and we can classify men only by their actual incomes'. But, 'while we cannot isolate the transitory component of the income of a particular man, we can isolate the average transitory component of the average income of an income class' (1945, pp. 326, 327). This is the link Friedman needed between an unobservable and an empirical construct; and the zero correlation restrictions noted above are his method of effecting it.

The significance of Friedman's argument goes far beyond our immediate concerns. Making theory testable by imposing certain statistical restrictions (e.g. measurable properties of distributions) creates a natural alliance between economic analysis and statistical methods. Friedman was an early user of identifying assumptions, which have long been part of standard econometric practice, and even in the 1940s were familiar to econometricians. Among economists, however, few of whom in the 1940s tried to find ways of testing their theory as Friedman did, he was a pioneer. The ingenuity of his efforts to bridge theory and testing bears comparison with that displayed by New Classical economists who have introduced cross-equation identifying restrictions. [11]

The Friedman–Kuznets data on professional incomes showed that if individuals in a profession are grouped into average income classes in any one year, the average incomes of the same classes in a later year are related linearly to the average incomes of the base year. This apparent linearity suggests stability of relative income status in a profession as a whole. If the same stability characterizes separate income classes then we may conclude that chance occurrences affect equally those who rank high and those who rank low in the professional distribution. If this were so it would suggest that high and low income rank are basically attributable to 'permanent' influences such as training, ability, personality; and the location, type and organization of practice. Technically, the problem comes down to finding a way of isolating the 'transitory' component of an income class. This, as noted above, cannot be done for an individual, but Friedman devised a way of doing it for the average income of an income class, on which he had data. The technique involved essentially assuming zero correlation between the permanent and transitory components of income (1945, p. 326).

For any income class in year 1, average year 1 income = average permanent + average transitory income for year 1. While base year transitory components help determine the initial actual classification of individual incomes, this grouping is random with respect to the transitory components in any later year. This randomness and the assumption of zero correlation between transitory and permanent components allows us to say that the average transitory component of any base year income will be zero in the later year, and that:

average income in year 2 = average *permanent* component of income in year 2.

Assume that in two years in which the permanent component is the same it is also the same for all individuals separately. Then:

average income in year 2 = average permanent component in year 1.

Hence, the difference between average incomes in year 1 and year 2 of a base year income class measures the average transitory component for the group in the base year. Expressing this as a proportion of the base year difference between average income for the class and for the profession as a whole tells us how much of that difference is due to transitory factors. And if the proportion is the same for all classes we may conclude that all are equally affected by accidental economic occurrences over time (1945, p. 328). In such a case average incomes in year 2, by classes, plotted against average incomes in year 1, would form a straight line, consistently with what was observed. This rationalization of the linear relations helps the analyst by isolating the 'permanent' factors and thus facilitates the search for an explanation in instances where the observed relation is *not* linear.

Applying this technique to the consumption function is basically only a matter of translating terms. We follow Friedman's own exposition. Hypothesize that consumption is some constant fraction of 'permanent' income, as suggested by the relation OC_p in the diagram below. Make the special assumption – for ease of exposition – that the mean transitory components of income and consumption are zero (1957c, p. 34). Classify consumption units by income. Both transitory and permanent components of income enter into this classification; but the classification is random with respect to transitory components, since C_t and Y_t are assumed to display zero correlation. 'It is primarily this assumption', Friedman notes, 'that introduces important substantive content into the hypothesis and makes it susceptible of contradiction by a wide range of phenomena capable of being observed' (1957c, p. 27). Transitory components of consumption for different groups will average out to the average for all consumers taken together; and this is assumed to be zero. For any measured income group, therefore, we are assured that average consumption is permanent consumption. For the measured income group Y_0 ($\equiv Y_{0t} + Y_{0p}$), for example, permanent consumption is AY_{0p} and the permanent income associated with $Y_{0(p+t)}$ is Y_{0p}. Note that consumption is AY_{0p} rather than $DY_{0(p+t)}$ because $Y_{0(p+t)}$ is not permanent income for that group but includes transitory elements as well; and Friedman assumes that high actual incomes are likely to be attributable in part to favourable transitory effects and vice versa for incomes that are low (1957c, p. 35).

For consumer units with average measured income, transitory components of both consumption *and* income will be zero. Hence for Y_a, $C = C_p$, $Y = Y_p$ and $C_p = Y_p$. This is represented by point E. Now $[Y_{0(p+t)} - Y_{0p}]/[Y_{0(p+t)} - Y_a]$, or AB/EF, is the proportion of the difference between average income $Y_{0(p+t)}$ and average income for all units Y_a, which is due to transitory effects. If this is constant, the line containing points E and B will be a straight line.

Standard regressions of consumption on measured income capture points like E and B; and a linear form captures the characteristics of consumption commonly assumed in Keynesian analysis, namely a constant marginal propensity and declining average propensity to consume. Thus Friedman's technique for rationalizing the observed linear relation between income classes in a profession through time also enabled him to account for observed findings from cross section regressions of consumption on measured income.[12] At the same time, by adopting the

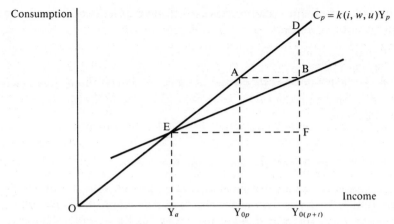

Figure 9.1 The 'permanent' income consumption function

Source: Adapted from Friedman (1957c, p. 34).

restriction of zero correlation between C_t and Y_t he was able to isolate the average transitory component of income in the average incomes of particular income classes in a profession, or of the average income of consumer units classified by measured income. This gave him a means of specifying a difference between observed relations such as EB and hypothetical relations such as OC_p. Since the hypothetical relation itself is broadly consistent with the findings of time series studies, he had thus also reconciled the conflicting empirical results noted at the outset. The reconciliation, it is important to recall, rests in part on the idea that measured income includes errors and random forces having nothing to do with underlying preferences for consumption and wealth.

Notice that the postulated zero correlation between C_t and Y_t, which allowed Friedman to reconcile the conflicting findings, is not itself open to test; its role was to provide points of contact between actual data and a hypothesis that was cast in terms of unobservables. The greater part of *A Theory of the Consumption Function* is devoted to confirmation of the hypothesis – the final stage of a positive economist's research. In particular, Friedman found:

1. that his hypothesis was consistent with a wide range of results from existing studies linking income and consumption; also
2. that it contained more implications than alternative though comparable (e.g. relative income) hypotheses; and
3. that it predicted precisely the effects of classifying consumer units by changes in their measured income from one year to another and was consistent with data not previously used in analyzing consumption

behavior, namely the data on measured income of individual consumer units in successive years.

Friedman regarded 3. as the most striking evidence in favor of his hypothesis (1957c, p. 225). [13] This, of course, was to a significant degree evidence available from Friedman and Kuznets (1945), indicating again just how important the earlier study was to *A Theory of the Consumption Function*.

Turning the new hypothesis against the Keynesians

The implications for Keynesian analysis are fairly obvious and Friedman mentions them briefly right at the end of *A Theory of the Consumption Function*. First, the secular stagnation thesis, or Keynes–Hansen thesis, in so far as it depends on the notion of a rising ratio of savings to income, is undermined. Second, introducing wealth into the consumption function and postulating that an increase in wealth (via price reduction) tends to raise the ratio of permanent consumption to permanent income implies that a Keynesian under-full employment equilibrium will not occur. Third, the permanent income hypothesis implies that a smaller part of consumption is induced by current income and a larger part is autonomous with respect to current income than the Keynesian analysis contends. Since, in that analysis, changes in investment cause movements in income, smaller induced changes in consumption mean a smaller investment multiplier. This in turn suggests that the economic system is more stable than the Keynesian analysis would have it.

The first of these implications was of no more than doctrinal interest, since the secular stagnation thesis had long since disappeared from the corpus of concerns of Keynesians. The second, Friedman noted, constitutes a challenge to the Keynesians, but more work needed to be done on the determinants of C_p/Y_p and their empirical significance. And the third, relevant to cyclical fluctuations, is offered not as an assertion about 'the actual empirical characteristics of our economy', but as a conditional hypothesis, 'dependent for [its] validity on the prior acceptance of the income-expenditure theory as an explanation of economic fluctuations' (1957c, p. 238).

At first sight the harvest of this effort seems rather scant. Friedman had repeated what he and Savage achieved with expected utility: by modifying existing theory in a certain way additional known facts had been incorporated. In the Friedman and Savage work, gambling and risk averse behavior had been reconciled. In Friedman's new consumption theory, cross section and time series stylized facts were jointly explained. In both cases the underlying paradigm of utility maximization was enlarged in its explanatory domain. And in both, too, the troublesome issue of unobservables had been addressed. In the Friedman and Savage work this was by the simple expedient of adopting 'as if' reasoning; but in the consumption function work this strategem was embellished in an important new manner. By postulating features of the covariance structure of permanent and transitory income Friedman had found a way to interpret the relation between measured consumption and measured income that would be true to theoretical considerations. Put in the more usual formulation, he had found a method for rendering theoretical variables part of a testable hypothesis. Without meaning to minimize this advance, in itself it only amounted to making testable a possible rationalization of some broader set of facts. The further testing of this new tentative hypothesis should have involved checks on data not previously available or at least not before used for this purpose. Friedman did this; yet one comes away from that evidence with the uneasy sense that confirmatory checks in themselves are not very convincing, that it would be more telling if in addition some *discriminating* tests with *alternative* hypotheses could be run, of the sort that Mayer, in an exemplary exhaustive examination, later undertook (Mayer, 1972).

Possibly Friedman sensed this himself. At any rate he seems to have turned almost at once (perhaps even concurrently with the work on consumption) to testable implications of the Keynesian or income-expenditure theory of fluctuations – unstable investment interacting with a stable consumption function – *and* to the elaboration of comparable implications for an alternative theory.[14] In this latter case, as we shall see, the work on permanent income played a critical role. It is to these comparative checks that we now turn.

EMPIRICAL INADEQUACIES IN THE KEYNESIAN ANALYSIS

Regression bias in the Keynesian consumption function

A fourth implication of the permanent income hypothesis, listed by Friedman as a subject for further research but not as directly challenging the Keynesian analysis, is that regressions of consumption on *measured* income capture not just income in a sense truly relevant to consumer behavior – Y_p – but 'a more or less arbitrary mixture of income in this sense and accidental elements' (1957c, p. 231). Such regressions unwittingly capture, as an influence on the ratio of consumption to income, a feature of income *distribution*, namely the relative dispersion of transitory components (*ibid.* pp. 231, 232).

In an article with Gary Becker, 'A statistical illusion in judging Keynesian models' (1957*a*), Friedman had already drawn attention to a similar statistical problem in regressions of consumption on measured income, namely the problem of regression bias. The article picks up on Friedman's 1943 suggestion that as investment and consumption are both components of measured income, correlating income and investment or income and consumption introduces a spurious element (p. 191, above). The problem can be skirted by correlating consumption with investment. This was turned into a test of the explanatory power of the multiplier, which Friedman held to be the key relation in the income-expenditure theory, by the suggestion that investment (a proxy for autonomous spending) should be able to explain consumption if the theory is valid. Friedman and Becker found, however, that consumption is better explained by its own past values than by investment. This is in line with the results of an earlier correlation that Friedman identified (1943*a*, p. 146) between changes in capital formation and consumption spending for the period 1919–40. He came up with a rank correlation coefficient of 0.62, lower than the 0.79 value obtained when changes in capital formation and national income were compared for the same period (*ibid.*, p. 143).

This presumably was part of what Friedman had in mind when he wrote in *A Theory of the Consumption Function* that 'I do not ... accept [the] income-expenditure theory as a *valid and tested* interpretation of experience' (1957*c*, p. 236, emphasis added). [15] A second element had to do with his growing conviction that 'the demand for money is highly stable – more stable than functions such as the consumption function that are offered as alternative key relations' (1956*b* in 1956*a*, p. 16). That comment was made in 'The quantity theory of money – a restatement', published a year before *A Theory of the Consumption Function*. What Friedman meant was that income velocity is more stable than the Keynesian multiplier. That is a strong statement since it implies very precise predictions and the necessary conditions for a crucial experiment.

It is sometimes suggested (e.g. Blaug, 1980, pp. 218, 223) that Friedman's monetary research turns the method of instrumentalism – Friedman's method, as Blaug would have it – on its head. Empirical predictions are made, but then successive variants of an explanatory theory are invoked because the predictive test fails to persuade. We disagree radically with Blaug's characterization of Friedman's methodology. Friedman's pragmatic approach in fact so integrates observation and theorizing that it is somewhat misleading to identify an order in the ongoing process of inquiry. This integrated approach is nicely illustrated in Friedman's early examination of three wartime episodes, where he both specified the quantity theory and the Keynesian theory in the form of 'empirical hypotheses' that are 'different and competitive', and 'tested' them against the history (Friedman, 1952*b* in 1969*c*, p. 166).

The first crucial experiment: quantity theory versus multiplier analysis

In 'Price, income, and monetary changes in three wartime periods', Friedman laid out the competing hypotheses in the following terms:

> the quantity theory asserts in essence that the velocity of circulation of money is the empirical variable that behaves in a stable and consistent fashion; the income-expenditure theory, that the propensity to consume, or the consumption function, is the empirical variable that behaves in a stable or consistent fashion. (*ibid.*)

In 1948 he had begun, with Anna Schwartz, an NBER study of data and conditions affecting 'the supply and rate of use of generally acceptable means of payment' (1949*d*, p. 80). In retrospect it looks as if he had seen by the late 1940s that he would not make an impression on the dominant Keynesian thinking merely by expressing methodological reservations about the system and its concepts. Something had to be offered in its place: an alternative that bypassed what he had long recognized as the key Keynesian element, the multiplier, and which performed better on the prediction front than it did. He chose the quantity theory as his candidate and probably began the NBER study with the aim of collecting data appropriate to testing the adequacy of a simple quantity theory hypothesis, to the effect that changes in money produce changes in activity. [16]

By 1952 he had enough evidence for a fairly convincing discriminating test. He chose three war-time experiences: the War between the States (the Civil War) in America, the First and Second World Wars. War-time data, he noted, 'are peculiarly valuable'; for in war-time 'violent changes in major economic magnitudes occur over relatively brief periods, thereby providing precisely the kind of evidence that we would like to get by "critical" experiments if we could conduct them' (1952*b* in 1969*c*, p. 157). And these particular war-time episodes 'offer an especially close approximation to the kind of critical experiment [we] would like to conduct . . . in all three cases the rise in prices was of almost precisely the same magnitude, so this critical variable is under control. Yet other crucial features varied, offering the opportunity to test alternative hypotheses designed to explain price changes' (*ibid.*, p. 158).

After examining the evidence Friedman concluded that 'price and income changes during the three wartime periods seem more readily explicable by the quantity theory than by the income-expenditure theory' (*ibid.*, p. 166).

Notice that in interpreting these data Friedman made no direct test of the relative stability of velocity and the multiplier. He found in divergent increases in the stock of money a proximate reason for similar divergences across episodes in income increases; and in a common behavior of money relative to real output for the common increase in prices across episodes. But he did not try actually to establish the behavior of velocity or of the consumption function. Nonetheless, this was a perfectly satisfactory if somewhat crude attempt to conduct a discriminating test and, together with the Friedman and Becker evidence, sufficient to warrant the negative judgment on the Keynesian theory expressed in *A Theory of the Consumption Function* (see above, p. 204).

There is one curious historical episode that may have a bearing on this judgment, although any connection is indirect and highly conjectural. To see it we need to go back to the work Friedman did for the *Taxing to Prevent Inflation* study. We mentioned earlier the two parts of the forecasting problem facing the investigator who wants to know at just what point increased armaments spending will cause prices to rise. One needs to know the flexibility of output (which will depend roughly on unemployed resources), and the likely increase in spending. Friedman noted that two methods were in common use to estimate spending: one was based on 'the historical relation between changes in the stock of money and changes in income' (1943*a*, p. 115). He surveyed carefully one existing study, by James W. Angell, which made use of the money-income relation. Angell had found what he called 'an extraordinarily stable relation' between changes in income and in the money supply for the period 1899–1929; but Friedman dismissed this as irrelevant: 'the long-time [*sic*] upward trend of both national income and the stock of money is bound to give a close correlation between the two totals' (*ibid.*, p. 119). He was more interested in year-to-year changes. When he used Angell's data to plot year-to-year changes for 1934–9, however, Friedman found the relation to be 'extremely unstable'.

That is how matters were left in 1943. On the face of it, Friedman could not have been encouraged by this finding to look to the quantity theory for an alternative to the Keynesian analysis. It cannot have escaped him, however, that the range of the ratio between changes in national income and changes in net capital formation was 1.4 to 7.6 for the period 1934 to 1939 (*ibid.*, p. 145, Table XVIII), whereas the range for the so-called 'extremely unstable' ratio between changes in income and changes in money was only 1.08 to 2.37, excluding an extreme figure for 'the confused year 1937' (*ibid.*, p. 119). At the time this may not have struck a chord, and we know that for several years thereafter Friedman concentrated his criticisms of the Keynesian analysis on other issues, including the proper form of the consumption function. But as a search for an alternative *framework* began to seem unavoidable, he may have taken his own earlier findings seriously and decided also to re-examine the period of the Great Crash and recovery. Certainly in later years (1968*b*, p. 13) he was inclined to say that 'more important than ... [post-war failures to keep interest rates 'low' and the elaboration of the wealth effect] for my own personal views ... was a re-examination of the evidence for the Great Contraction of 1929–33'. At the very least we can say that his inflation gap work shows that the notion of making a statistical comparison of key implications of the quantity theory and the Keynesian theory was present in embryo form and thus preceded any of his more detailed efforts in this same direction in the 1950s.

We might note, though this is a far cry from agreeing with Blaug's judgment, that Friedman does seem to start here by accumulating empirical knowledge. He began with only a rudimentary notion of a quantity theory to oppose to Keynesian theory. In Friedman's version of the two competing empirical hypotheses, quoted above, it is significant that he says 'the propensity to consume, or the consumption function', but he did not match this by saying 'the velocity of circulation, *or the demand for money function'*. In 1952 he evidently had not developed his later formulation of velocity as a function of the variables in a demand for money function, although work towards that end was proceeding; for the counterpart to the NBER study on money supply conditions and statistics was a Workshop in Money and Banking at the University of Chicago, where Friedman and students under his guidance pursued topics that were in effect tests of the stability of a demand for money function. This work came to fruition in Friedman's famous 1956 Restatement and in the student studies in the quantity theory of money in the volume of that title (Friedman, 1956*a*). There Friedman could declare both that 'the quantity theory is in the first instance a theory of the *demand* for money' and that 'There is an extraordinary empirical stability and regularity to ... income velocity [i.e. the demand function is stable and velocity determinate if not actually rigid] that cannot but impress anyone who works extensively with monetary data' (1956*a* in 1956*b*, pp. 4, 21). There is a sense in which Friedman already knew this last and in which his Restatement is a case of known evidence in search of a theory. Monetary regularities too, just like choices in favor of risky prospects, had to be brought within the purview of price theory and the utility maximization hypothesis. The Restatement did this for velocity.

Nonetheless, it should be stressed, Blaug's way of characterizing Friedman's research misses the point. Friedman had a paradigm – Marshallian price theory – and his monetary inquiries were *always* part of an attempt to strengthen and extend its domain of application to monetary phenomena (cf. paradigm-stretching). Thus of the studies being pursued in the Chicago Workshop in Money and Banking (and which issued in *Studies in the Quantity Theory of Money*), Friedman could write in 1953: 'these studies have a cumulative value in reinforcing one another. They derive from a common theoretical formulation and in turn contribute to its elaboration and confirmation. The result is in one sense [a] reaffirmation of the classical quantity theory of money; in a more important sense, it is a revised, improved, and more meaningful theory'.[17] Note too that in Friedman's original plan for pursuing his monetary studies, as outlined in a request to the Rockefeller Foundation for funding, he included a detailed statement of the need to go beyond 'technical considerations' relating to money as a mechanism of payments and to investigate money as an *asset*, an idea wholly in line with the Cambridge cash balances approach and with price theoretic considerations (Rockefeller Archive, GR, 200S, Box 573, Folder 4906: 10 September 1948). In other words, we see here precisely the sort of tentative hypothesis guiding data-related research, and ongoing refinement of theory in the light of empirical knowledge, that we would expect of a pragmatic researcher.

To carry this further at the moment would lead us too deeply into Friedman's monetary theory. We therefore close this section on his opposition to the Keynesian analysis with a brief look at the Friedman and Meiselman relative stability tests (1963*e*). This was work completed in the Chicago Workshop and offered to the Commission on Money and Credit established in the late 1950s by the private Committee for Economic Development, in response to their request for a submission.

THE FRIEDMAN–MEISELMAN COMPARATIVE TEST

In some ways Friedman and Meiselman (FM) is merely a continuation of the pursuit of a definite discriminating test, which began with Friedman's 1952 study of prices and income in three war-time periods. Because this is its origin it is easy to view it apart from *A Theory of the Consumption Function*, which may give rise to misinterpretation. The fact that he could say in *A Theory of the Consumption Function* that the permanent income hypothesis implies a *more* stable economy than the Keynesian analysis would suggest, and then go on to construct a test that hinged on velocity's being *less* volatile than the multiplier, for example, might be read as evidence of Friedman's inconsistency. It need not be: the statements that the multiplier may be less than originally believed and that autonomous expenditures are a relatively less reliable predictor of induced spending than money are not at all the same thing.

Friedman and Meiselman take as their test version of the income-expenditure theory the equation

$$C = a + k\text{A},$$

where A stands for 'autonomous' expenditure; C (standing for induced spending) is used rather than Y, to eliminate the statistical difficulty caused by A being a component of Y. A comparable quantity theory test equation is, then:

$$C = b + \text{VM}$$

This formulation of the test supposes reasonable constancy in both k and V; that is, stability in the consumption function and the demand for money function. At issue is the relative accuracy of forecasts of C. Three comparisons were made of the competing hypotheses that changes in autonomous spending and in the money stock determine changes in consumption, one in real terms, one in money terms (adding a price term to each of the equations) and one in terms of a comparison of the coefficients k and V when A and M are both included to explain C. For the period 1897 to 1958, using annual data, and for a shorter period using quarterly data, the quantity theory performed better, excepting the Great Depression years.

There are numerous points at which this test could be and has been criticized and it is not our concern here to survey these in detail.[18] Some of them are technical, dealing, for example, with the appropriateness of a consumption function specified in nominal terms, and the question whether there should be an intercept term in the strict quantity theory relation. Some are conceptual and measurement-related: for example, how to decide which classes of expenditures are 'autonomous'. A range of contemporary critics bothered about this (Hester, 1964; Ando and Modigliani, 1965; DePrano and Mayer, 1965). Then there is the question of the adequacy of the modelling procedure. Setting up the comparison of theories involved finding a common dependent variable. Choosing consumption as this variable required a transformation of the quantity theory, in which the dependent variable is usually income. This handicapped the quantity theory, according to Friedman and Meiselman (1965d, p. 770). But from the point of view of their critics, the whole approach – two simple equations compared according to some isolated statistical characteristic – was seriously deficient. It neglected interdependence and simultaneity; and the relation of the FM equations to structural equations for the system was ignored completely.

Friedman and Meiselman had their own reasons to worry about

complexity, and we shall turn to them in a moment. First, however, a word about the tests from a methodological point of view. Two contemporary critics who were disturbed about the issue of simple versus complex models were Ando and Modigliani (and, more recently, for similar reasons, Desai). After a lengthy discussion accusing Friedman and Meiselman of gross mis-specification errors, Ando and Modigliani elaborate on the meaninglessness of the FM tests. Here the argument runs in terms of claims that prediction cannot be the goal since the 'exogenous' variables are contemporaneous with those to be predicted; that neither can control be the aim, since the Friedman and Meiselman independent variables are not strictly defined as exogenous to the economic system, which is not even spelled out in their treatment; and that the supposedly competing means of stabilization, control of money or of 'autonomous' expenditures, are theoretically — in Keynesian general equilibrium models anyhow — parts of a single system (1965, pp. 714–16). The argument reflects the Cowles Commission approach to econometrics which was still dominant at the time; and it is worth setting out some of the FM responses, because this highlights just how unorthodox, and either how little understood or little accepted, was Friedman's research strategy among his contemporaries.

We concentrate on just three points, each of which brings out the very heavily empirical character of Friedman's economics. The first two points emerge as part of Friedman and Meiselman's response to the view that their two chosen test equations might be better portrayed as elements in a single larger system. At one level FM answer simply that this is irrelevant to their purposes: 'our aim is to compare the quantity theory with the income-expenditure theory, not with a joint theory' (1965d, p. 770). It is likely that the methodological substance in this answer is the position already stated in 'Positive economics'. There are so many empirical models that can be derived within a given general theory (so many cause–effect relations, or inversions of assumptions and implications, in a multi-equation system), and so many theoretical explanations consistent with given data, that focusing on overarching theories and theoretical models gives us little help in discriminating between fruitful and unfruitful hypotheses. (For an illustration of the former point see note 18 in 1965d, pp. 768–9. See also their comment on the impossibility of ascribing outcomes to the parts of composite models without first knowing the component parts in detail, in *ibid*. p. 770.) The implication of these views is that if one wants to see what really divides economist from economist one must look to empirical evidence bearing on alternative supposed causal relations.

How does one derive causal relations? Friedman and Meiselman refer (1963e, pp. 179–80) to criteria that are further worked out and applied in

Friedman and Schwartz' *A Monetary History* (1963*a*) and in their 'Money and business cycles' (1963*b*). These are so important that we outline them here, though we shall discuss them again in the next chapter.

1. First, one identifies statistical regularities which maintain their features across time and in the face of wide changes of an institutional and policy-related sort. These are proven-to-be stable relations.
2. Next, one selects a potential causal factor or factors, based on timing and analysis of those elements that could be necessary and sufficient to account for significant changes in the variable(s) judged to be dependent (see on this especially 1963*b* in 1969*c*, pp. 219–20).
3. Finally, one makes sure that the postulated cause(s) are in fact historically present and active in the way supposed (see further Chapter 10, pp. 229 and 231, below).

These criteria contain an answer at a second level to the critics' point about building a single encompassing theoretical model. A single overarching analysis involving many variables, FM point out, would necessarily be restricted to 'a narrow segment of space and time', because of the paucity of data covering many countries and long periods, and because of the time and effort involved (1965*d*, p. 761, quoting – incompletely – p. 168 of their 1963*e*). That, however, is just the opposite of what is needed to generate confidence in supposed causal relations derived by the three criteria just mentioned.

Third, and once again underlining the importance of the empirical in all this, Friedman and Meiselman defend the method they used for determining what expenditures were to count as 'autonomous' on the ground that it involved an admittedly far from perfect but at least 'specifiable and reproducible' procedure for making the notion of 'autonomous' empirical. FM contrast this with the appeals to plausibility – the invoking of accepted theory, intuition and that which is 'beyond reasonable doubt' – of their critics (1965*d*, pp. 764, 784). This is a particularly graphic instance of Friedman's opposition to plausibility appeals, the basis for which we discussed in Part I above.

Recall our purpose in spending time on these three responses to critics. We want to see Friedman's strongly empirical approach to economics which was also, in his own eyes at least, a mark and a measure of his unorthodoxy as an economist. More precisely, he felt virtually alone in exploring the comparative explanatory reliability of alternative hypotheses following the rise to prominence of Keynesian thinking. To cite his request to the Rockefeller foundation for funding for the Chicago Workshop once more, he there complains of 'economists who have been willing to accept generalizations on the basis of the flimsiest of evidence'

(Friedman to Willits, 13 November 1953, Rockefeller Archive, GR, 200S, Box 573, folder 4907). In 1957, in his *Theory of the Consumption Function*, we have seen him protesting that 'I do not myself accept [the] income-expenditure theory as a valid and tested interpretation of experience' (1957c, p. 236). And in FM he deplores the 'flabbiness' of a profession so many of whose members shifted from a high regard for money pre-Keynes, to an opposite position post-Keynes, 'on the basis of essentially no evidence'. Worse: 'we [still, in 1963] know of almost no systematic attempt to assess the relevant empirical evidence' (1963e, p. 169).

We turn back briefly to a problem of complexity that did worry Friedman. It arises out of the difficulty of interpretation that plagues economics (and, indeed, all science): the underdetermination of theory by data. The world facing Friedman and Meiselman was, as ever, more complex than their test hypotheses. Thus suppose a consistent and high correlation is found between changes in M and changes in C. We may infer from this that V is stable and, since V is a function of the variables in the money demand function (see Friedman, 1956b), that this function is stable. But that gives us no information as to *which* variables in the function are more and which less significant for V. If Y is important and *r*, 'the' rate of interest, is not, Friedman would be delighted, since that would confirm that the effect of changing the money stock on income is 'direct', bypassing the Keynesian interest rate-investment link. But this cannot be read out of a good performance by the test equation:

$$C = b + VM$$

Friedman and Meiselman recognize this and devote the final part of their paper to adducing plausible reasons why the elasticity of the demand for money with respect to interest is likely to be low. The argument hinges on the process by which changes in M are transmitted. Given that the variables in the money demand function include rates of return on all assets other than money, they can argue that the impact of a change in M on any one of these rates is likely to be small because the total impact will be diffused over many assets. Be that as it may, the fact remains that the empirical test, while it conforms to the criteria of a crucial experiment, does not itself yield an answer to the question '*why* is the quantity theory out-performing the Keynesian theory?' The black-box nature of the test laid it open to criticism. In addition, one might argue that the test is irrelevant given Friedman's own repeated stress on shocks to expectations and subsequent adjustment processes in his concurrent studies on how money affects output (Wood, 1981, Sections V and VI, makes this point and gives references). If money has its impact through unexpected changes in the *rate of growth* of the money stock; and if the transmission mechanism is so critical in distinguishing appropriate from inappropriate (i.e. Keynesian) models, then simple correlation between *levels* of variables and with no dynamics specified must be judged of no value.

In their defence it must be said that Friedman and Meiselman pointed out the need for a more sophisticated statement, complete with a discussion of the determinants of V, and containing explicit dynamics. They even admit that greater complexity in representing the competing theories might reverse the results of their tests on simpler versions (1963*e*, pp. 171–4). Their results, they stress, 'cannot be decisive' (*ibid.*, p. 174). They cling nevertheless to their simple test because of what 'seems a reasonable presumption [namely] that the relationship which explains the most in its simplest version is the relationship that will be the most fruitful to explore further and to convert into a more sophisticated form' (*ibid.*, a claim repeated in 1965*d*, p. 762).[19] Superficially this looks like a Popperian claim: the bolder a theory – the more it claims to explain – the greater its content because the more likely it is that events will be found that refute it. But Friedman, we remind the reader, is interested in relationships which work, that is, roughly speaking, in confirmation rather than falsification. The presumption rests rather on the notion that simple hypotheses lend themselves to being tested over the 'wide range of space and time' that is necessary for having confidence in supposed causal relationships (1963*e*, p. 170), and on the very limited nature of the test they undertake. Friedman and Meiselman deliberately limit themselves to assessing relative accuracy in the forecasting of induced expenditures. They admit that, had they wanted instead to determine autonomous spending, or to decide how large induced spending is relative to income for the purpose of forecasting income, a more complex model might have served them better (1965*d*, pp. 769, 770). In short, for their purposes the kind of models they chose were appropriate.

It remains true that for policy purposes – forecasting Y – their approach is not very useful. The critics state this and FM do not deny it. Yet despite an emphasis on interpretation (see their conclusions, 1963*e*, p. 188), they clearly want to move towards, and believe they have facilitated movement towards, better policy (see *ibid.*, p. 170, 213). How their tests help towards this end is not clear, however, since they acknowledge that the tests have to do with average and comparative performance, whereas what is needed is actual or absolute performance 'in the individual case' (*ibid.*, pp. 213–14). In the end then the exercise seems most useful for the doubts it might have raised in those holding the dominant faith in the income-expenditure theory as the correct explanatory framework.

A SWELLING LITANY: FRIEDMAN'S CRITICISMS IN REVIEW

Looking back over the works that we have treated under the general heading of Friedman's opposition to the Keynesian analysis, it seems useful to distinguish two groups. The first covers his comment on Salant and the 'inflation gap' analysis to his work on the consumption function, or roughly 1942 to 1957. This overlaps the second group of writings, which run from 1953 to 1963: from the historical analysis of price, income and money change in three wartime periods to the Friedman and Meiselman comparative tests and the *Monetary History of the United States*. This overlap is not a problem, for according to Friedman the first written version of the analysis contained in *A Theory of the Consumption Function* was completed in 1951 (see 1957c, p. ix); and we may use this to bolster our claim that that book belongs, in the way it is brought to bear as criticism of the Keynesian theory, to the sorts of points Friedman made in the 1940s.

The hallmarks of Friedman's comments on the Keynesian system in the first group of writings are as follows:

1. a concern with concepts with an empirical counterpart;
2. a rejection of statistical regularities not strenuously 'tested' (for stability, for example);
3. a concern with how short-run change is transmitted, rather than with concepts having a static and merely taxonomic character;
4. an insistence on the predictive value of analysis purporting to be of policy relevance; and
5. a careful attention to empirical knowledge, including measurement problems, and awareness of statistical biases lurking in inappropriate formulations of relations to be estimated.

Item 1: this refers to the need, in Friedman's positive economics, for analytical frameworks to be composed of entities and relations which are capable of being measured. Recall his disappointment with the indifference curve framework because, for example, taste and opportunity factors distinguished in the theory have no unambiguous empirical counterparts (Friedman and Wallis, 1942a, Section IV, which is ascribed to Friedman). He felt similarly frustrated with concepts such as 'inflation gap', to which he applied Lady Macbeth's words, 'I have thee not, yet I see thee still'. *Ex post* there can be no gap; and the notion, employed prospectively, serves us only if the analysis is carried to the point where we identify the things that change to close the gap. The Keynesian difference between *ex ante* investment and saving as the prime mover with respect to output presented similar problems, since we have no way of knowing how much of inventories is speculative. In his own permanent income hypothesis Friedman introduced unobservables, but like the good empiricist he was he also developed a statistical method for linking his unobservable notions with actual data. The same holds for his use of 'autonomous' expenditure.[20]

Item 2: the resort of those who despair of reaching quantitative answers by 'a direct analysis' of complex interrelationships, and who lack the wit or perseverance to pursue an indirect route such as Friedman mapped out in *A Theory of the Consumption Function*, is to seek 'refuge in empiricism' (1943*a*, p. 114). It is not entirely clear what Friedman meant by this phrase, since his own work – early and late – is on the whole uncompromisingly empirical. That stance, plus his rejection of plausibility, rules out an interpretation which stresses theory as an independently valid grounding for empirical regularities. His early concern with the stability of economic relationships, however, is in line with his insistence later in such works as the *Monetary History* that extensive checks must be performed on empirical regularities, to see if they stand up across long spans of time and widely ranging circumstances. That is the interpretation we adopt here. Such checking was exactly what was lacking in the Keynesian investment-income relation: the analysis, recall, 'gives no reason to suppose that it will be stable when the system is not in equilibrium' (*ibid.*, p. 142). In the absence of broad-based testing of the relation it is impossible to make confident predictions of the sort that are needed for policy. These are predictions of the effects of changes in one or more variables (1968*b*, p. 15). Without having identified and explored the possible relations between variables, however, to rely on a correlation between any two of them in a limited data set is to say (a) that we know the direction of causation; and (b) that we know the supposed independent variable to be the sole significant factor involved (i.e. no other changes in conditions are relevant). If this is not blind faith, then the case must be one so simple that extensive analysis is anyway unnecessary. But that is quite unlike the real world. For, in the real world 'there are no such things as unambiguous facts. They are always subject to more than one interpretation' (*ibid.*, p. 14). It might seem that Friedman's adherence to the importance of money stems from 'mere empiricism'. His 1952 paper on prices, incomes and money in three wartime periods, however, represents the exploration in the data of relations in several variables, to see which combinations and causal orderings hold under comparable circumstances but widely spaced periods of time. Moreover, his further work on money in the 1950s may be summed up as being largely an attempt to account for the observed behavior of velocity in a similar manner. In other words, it was exploration of precisely the sort lacking in connection with the simple investment-income relation.

Item 3: we have touched on this already. A deficiency in just defining the 'inflation gap' or stating that full employment requires 'adequate' aggregate demand (Lerner), is that unless we go further all we have are unquantified and unanalyzed assertions about deviations from equilibrium, with none of the dynamics to reveal how policy might take effect. In 1946 Friedman devoted a whole review article on Lange's *Price Flexibility and Employment* to the evils of such thinking without examination of the *actual processes* of short-run adjustment; for one is then forced to choose among possible processes according to their 'plausibility' (Friedman 1946*b* in 1953*e*, p. 284). This can be used as a way of avoiding the ultimate test: does it work in correctly predicting the consequences of change? Taxonomy can be a kind of descriptivism and falls under Friedman's condemnation every bit as much as unreflective acceptance of correlations. A theme of Friedman's monetary theory, but also of his early criticism of Keynesian analysis, is that too little attention is paid to relative price changes (including distributional changes) in the process of adjusting to shocks. (This criticism is more muted in the case of the demand for money, where it becomes: adjustment to money shock occurs as individuals purchase a succession of assets to get rid of any excess cash. The Keynesian analysis in terms of just money and bonds is thus too limited a framework for appreciating what is really a very wide-ranging process of substitution away from cash.) The methodological counterpart to this criticism is his oft-repeated distinction between conceptual frameworks (theory as language, scaffolding to facilitate logical analysis) and theory which embodies and generates fresh, enriched empirical hypotheses, the end of which is to obtain more, and more exact, knowledge of quantitative relations useful for policy. The one deals in categories merely, the other in actual processes of adjustment.

Item 4: no additional comment on this is necessary. It is the aim of positive analysis: 'the true test of a scientific theory ... is whether it ... correctly predicts the consequences of changes in conditions' (1968*b*, p. 15). Moreover, it informs Friedman's criticism of 'inflation gap' analysis and of Lerner on unemployment policy, as it does the FM search for the more stable relationship accounting for income fluctuations.

Item 5: this refers to Friedman's concern in his early criticisms of Keynesian analysis that problems such as regression bias be avoided (1943*a*, p. 146) and that misinterpretation of actual data be minimized through having a clear understanding of 'true' as distinct from measured relations (1957*c*, p. 231). 'True' here, of course, means both statistically appropriate (the 'true' empirical model) and also that we possess some prior framework in our empirical enquiry to help separate random variations from underlying, systematic effects. Technical statistical concerns occupied Friedman early on. The second sense of 'true' was to receive much more attention in his monetary studies (cf. 1952*b* in 1969*c*, p. 157) as well as in his theory of consumption.

After 1951 Friedman's criticisms of the Keynesian analysis became more strictly tied to the idea of finding ways of testing the relative strength of the Keynesian analysis and the quantity theory, as predictive tools. His efforts in this direction are contained in 'Price, income, and monetary change in three war-time periods' (1952*c*); Friedman and Becker, 'A statistical illusion in judging Keynesian models', (1957*a*) and Friedman and Meiselman, 'The relative stability of monetary velocity and the investment multiplier in the United States, 1897–1958' (1963*e*), plus an article which we will only mention here, 'The demand for money: some theoretical and empirical results' (1959*c*). In this article Friedman applied the permanent income hypothesis to formulate a 'true' demand for money function incorporating permanent rather than measured income. This enabled him to argue that while measured velocity tends to vary pro-cyclically, 'true' velocity and the corresponding demand for money function are nonetheless stable.

The empirical tests in these later writings are of two sorts. The Friedman and Becker study takes the Keynesian theory on its own terms, and finds that it does not predict very well. Friedman (1952*c*), and Friedman and Meiselman (1963*e*), set up discriminating tests, the one qualitative, the other numerical, in which the relative performance of the Keynesian analysis and the quantity theory is at issue. Friedman and Meiselman could not clinch matters with numbers, and especially not without a test incorporating dynamics. As noted above, they fell back on an appeal to plausibility that would have been unacceptable in their opponents.

Friedman continued to believe in crucial experiments, or discriminating tests (as we shall see in Chapter 10), but he very quickly retreated from the notion that they could do more than strengthen conviction. There were methodological and statistical reasons for this, reflected in a broad way in Friedman's own repeated insistence on the ambiguity of facts (e.g. 1968*b*, p. 14). Moreover, the idea of a conclusive test runs counter to his own convictions about monetary theory in particular. For monetary theory, he wrote in 1969, is

> like a Japanese garden. It has esthetic unity born of variety; an apparent simplicity that conceals a sophisticated reality; a surface view that dissolves in ever deeper perspectives (1969*c*, p. v.).

Definitely not material, this, to be summarized by one single statistical test. Except that its aims were very limited – to add to our tested knowledge of selected connections in the economy – the FM study could be regarded as a false step. Certainly in one sense Friedman's monetary writings of the 1960s and 1970s can be seen as a retreat towards more subtle, historical analyses.

NOTES

1. Keynes had different ideas. Reacting to an address by Harrod dealing with methodology, he noted (*Collected Writings*, vol. 14, p. 296):

   > It seems to me that economics is a branch of logic, a way of thinking; and that you do not repel sufficiently firmly attempts à la Schultz to turn it into a pseudo-natural science.

   Keynes too considered himself to be a Marshallian, though the term Marshallian had a different meaning for him. *Both* Keynes and Friedman are right in some respects and wrong in others. There is evidence supporting both interpretations (Hirsch and Hirsch, 1968, which supports the Keynesian view). Obviously, I (Hirsch) have changed my mind somewhat since writing that article, but not entirely.
2. Recall that in 1942 Friedman was inclined to reject indifference curve analysis because he could see no way to operationalize it. Much of what we called in Chapter 8 his programme on choice theory may be viewed as an effort to rethink this early rejection: to find indirect ways of rendering choice theory operational.
3. Friedman was responsible for the analytical framework of Part I, the national accounts-based concept of the inflation gap; and for Part III, methods of forecasting the onset of price rises.
4. The simple excess aggregate demand definition of 'inflation gap' appears in the first (1948) edition of Samuelson's *Economics* (pp. 272ff.); but Keynes himself used the gap notion in his analyses of Britain's wartime financial problems (*Collected Writings*, vol. 22, pp. 289ff.). See also the references in Friedman (1943*a*), p. 131.
5. This straightforward conclusion is to be found, for example, in the first quarterly report of the OPA (1942, p. 29). There we read of projected consumer spending for 1942 of $86 billion, and of available consumer goods and services worth only $69 billion. 'The difference − 17 billion dollars − would, unless controlled, inevitably be converted into higher prices ...'.
6. Unfortunately, we have not been able to examine the OPA study, so what is said here is based solely on Salant's none-too-complete statement. It is perhaps worth noting that for Friedman conceptual adequacy could not be independent of empirical adequacy: what variables are included in a model, and how they are related, should reflect our empirical knowledge. If Salant had in mind conceptual adequacy in the Walrasian formal or 'in principle' sense, this would be rejected by Friedman as mere language.
7. Friedman was willing to accept mere correlations, as we saw in Chapter 3, above, but only at the first (or early) stage of research. Here what was involved was forecasting for policy purposes where the best available knowledge should be used. Friedman clearly felt that better knowledge *was* available to do the job.
8. It is not clear that he has any particular version in mind, although he refers to

several US Government agencies relying on an investment-income relation whose underlying rationale 'is often claimed to be the Keynesian analysis' (*ibid.*).

9. This stylized history is false in various respects, detailed in Thomas (1989). It follows Friedman's own version of the history. For our purposes – understanding *Friedman's* problem context – it is Friedman's version that matters.

10. This was mainly because he rejected the idea of deciding in advance exactly what 'permanent' should mean. That determination, he felt, 'is best left to ... the data themselves, to be whatever seems to correspond to consumer behavior' (1957*c*, p. 23). Of course, in estimating permanent income to test his hypothesis Friedman was obliged to employ some proxy. He chose a distributed lag of past incomes (*ibid.*, pp. 142ff.; cf. 1963*g*).

11. This refers to Thomas Sargent and his students rather than to Robert Lucas, whose theory is the basis for Sargent's econometric work but whose own econometric forays tend to be of the reduced form sort and to neglect cross-equation restrictions. (We are indebted to Kevin Hoover for insisting on this distinction.) Interestingly, however, Lucas reminds one of Friedman in the ways he finds to build bridges between theoretical and empirical hypotheses. Lucas tries to test the natural rate hypothesis, for example, indirectly and in part by adopting auxiliary assumptions involving observable properties of distributions on prices and then linking these with rationality in price expectations (Lucas 1972 in 1981, pp. 90–103, De Marchi and Kim 1989). See too the discussion on 'permanent' versus 'transitory' income as a signal extraction problem, in which links are drawn between Friedman, Muth and Lucas, in Sargent (1987, pp. 2–4).

12. This seems to be an instance in which an 'assumption' (here the one about average income consumer units) becomes a means of generating testable implications from a hypothesis. In a sense it might be said that the assumption 'becomes' an implication of the hypothesis. Perhaps this is what Friedman had in mind in 'Positive economics' (1953*d* in 1953*e*, p. 28); although the inspiration for the notion that assumptions can become implications of a hypothesis probably was Haavelmo's (1944) distinction between open systems of causal relations for parts of an economy, and the closed mutual dependence model for the economy as a whole (p. 22).

13. A variety of tests (carried out by Mayer, 1972) seemed to lend support to a somewhat weakened permanent income hypothesis. A more recent survey of empirical consumption function research, Hadjimatheou (1987), concludes that some sort of wealth effect clearly is present, but agrees with Spanos (1989) in criticizing the statistical inadequacy of early tests, and notes that the vast variety of modified specifications possible simply does not lend itself to much more than the questioning of extreme forms of the permanent income hypothesis. The concomitant is non-rejection of a wide variety of weaker versions.

14. A comparative empirical test of sorts had already been conducted (1952*b* in 1969*c*), but the competing hypotheses and the notion of relative 'stability' (of the velocity of money compared with the propensity to consume) had not been spelled out at all precisely. See further discussion, pp. 205–6.

15. In an application to the Rockefeller Foundation for funds in support of his Chicago Workshop in Money and Banking, Friedman refers to the crucial experiment of the three wartime episodes (1952*b* in 1969*c*) as having shown

that 'a modernized quantity theory of money fits these experiences better than the more recently popular income-expenditure theory'. He goes on to say that this outcome 'led me to make further statistical tests', the preliminary results of which 'suggest that the quantity theory gives better predictions of changes in money magnitudes; the income-expenditure theory, of changes in "real" magnitudes'. Thus he had a basis for the sceptical claim quoted in the text, even although, at the time, he wondered if some marriage of the two approaches might not be useful. (Friedman to Willits, 11 November 1953, p. 3; and Appendix to Proposal for a Workshop in Money and Banking at the University of Chicago, n.d. but stamped 7 December 1953, p. 2. Rockefeller Archive, GR, 200S, Box 573, Folders 4904, 4907.)

16. There is some evidence that when he began his monetary studies Friedman had no dominant prior beliefs about whether monetary, or real factors, were the main causal elements in fluctuations. His application for support for these studies to the Rockefeller Foundation merely notes that monetary *responses* in the cycle are not as quick as was commonly believed, possibly implying a dominant passive money view from which he was at most merely expressing mild dissent. (See 'Outline of work in first phase of banking study', 28 January 1949, Rockefeller Archive, GR, 200S, Box 503, Folder 4906.) At the same time, one aim of those studies was to inquire into 'the causal role of monetary and banking phenomena in *producing* cyclical fluctuations' ('Monetary factors in business cycles', a proposal drafted by Friedman, Rockefeller Archive, GR, 200S, Box 573, Folder 4906: 10 February 1949; emphasis added). And it is clear from the further request made by Friedman to Rockefeller in November 1953, for funding for a proposed Workshop in Money and Banking at the University of Chicago, that he believed the quantity theory had already been shown to be superior, and that his inquiries were in fact only improving, extending, and making more fruitful a (monetary) tradition at Chicago. (See letters from Friedman, 13 November 1953, and 27 September 1955: Rockefeller Archive, GR, 200S, Box 573, Folder 4907.)

17. Friedman to Dr Joseph Willits (13 November 1953, Rockefeller Archive, GR, 200S, Box 573, Folder 4907).

18. In addition to the detailed contemporary criticisms mentioned in the text, below, Johnson (1971) and Chick (1973) contain useful summary discussions. A more recent econometric critique by Desai (1981, esp. Chapter 3), hammers home the charges of mis-specification in the FM paper, initially levelled by Ando and Modigliani.

19. 'Reasonable' is open to various interpretations. Here, it stands for an assessment of and degree of belief *in the evidence* (see, for example, Chapter 10, below, p. 228 and n. 9). Shades, here, of Keynes's concept 'degree of belief', in which rationality adheres to a belief if we know some evidence to support it, and weight is attached according to the strength of our convictions (see Keynes, *Collected Works*, vol. VIII, p. 59; and the useful exposition in Darity and Horn, 1988).

20. The reader interested in pursuing FM's operational method in detail should consult the exposition given in 1963e, pp. 181–5. Since the method involves assessing a succession of statistical constructs of autonomous and induced expenditures, each assuming knowledge of all but one (hence 'problematic') element, the exposition is best read in its entirety.

10 • THE PRIMACY OF MONEY

What to expect

This brings us to our third mini-study, covering Friedman's monetary inquiries. These date from 1948, when the NBER study on money supply with Anna Schwartz began, and continued for the next thirty years, ending with the publication of Friedman and Schwartz' *Monetary Trends of the United States and the United Kingdom* (1982*b*).[1] We include here Friedman's 'A theoretical framework for monetary analysis' (we shall refer to the 1974*b* version) and his expositions in the late 1960s and 1970s of the natural rate hypothesis. These might be thought to be more a part of his opposition to Keynesian analysis; but as will be shown below they fit more naturally into a search for what he had called in 1949 'the manner of action of causes ' (1949*c* in 1953*e*, p. 91, citing Marshall) – an empirical search that he conducted more seriously than anywhere else in his work in connection with the monetary transmission mechanism.

A word in advance about some limitations in our treatment. We do not test Friedman's own predictions, or inferences from his derived hypotheses. We have tried in Part I to place his methodology in perspective, and in this part to see how well he sticks to his own prescriptions. The logical next step in assessing Friedman's monetary economics in particular would be an examination of his data transformations; and the application of a coherent set of test criteria so as to enable a judgment to be made as to whether his empirical models – not his theoretical hypotheses, but the estimable relations said to support and capture inferences from them – are credible.[2] There is a growing body of studies on both the statistical implications of data transformations and on the theory of empirical model testing, including at least one major and critical application to *Monetary Trends* (Hendry and Ericsson, 1985, whose reference list provides a good guide to the testing literature; see also Desai, 1981). Since, however, we have chosen to focus on how Friedman works, not on assessing the acceptability of what he did as judged by outside standards, the reader should note that our discussion here does not offer an independent examination of the empirical basis of Friedman's monetarism. Then, too, we arrive here at terrain that is frequently traversed by commentators. We can afford therefore to concentrate on a broad but neglected theme, the problem of interpretation facing the empirical economist. Our goal, as in the preceding mini-studies, is to clarify the nature of Friedman's reasoning.

If Friedman's monetary research is true to the precepts of positive economics, we should expect to find in his writings on the subject 'a full and comprehensive set of observed and related facts' (1946*b* in 1953*e*, p. 283); a simple, fruitful hypothesis – 'a way of looking at or interpreting or organizing the evidence that will reveal superficially disconnected and diverse phenomena to be manifestations of a more fundamental and relatively simple structure' (1953*e* in 1953*f*, p. 33); and a range of testable and quantifiable – and dependable – implications 'that can be used to predict the consequences of changes in circumstances' (*ibid.* p. 39). In other words, we should find facts to be explained, an explanatory organizing theory, and testable causal mechanisms.

If, further, he is right in likening monetary theory to a Japanese garden, we should expect an evocative presentation, with constant movement between finely detailed miniature studies and stark, simple outlines on a larger scale. (Perhaps Friedman intended the process also to show what Marshall might have meant by 'The one in the many, the many in the one'.) Certainly, order will be displayed, but an overarching and formal deductive system might prove of limited value in conveying it.[3]

This by way of preparation; for some of the charges laid at Friedman's door in this area are that he fails to provide any general macro-model and seems satisfied with a 'black box' instead of explicit theory; and seems willing to try to explain everything, thereby emptying such explicit theory as he does present of empirical content (see, for example, the criticisms of Wood, 1981). To some extent this criticism has its roots in the supposed deductive-nomological character of satisfactory explanation.

The process of inquiry once again

The sort of inquiry that we find in Friedman's monetary economics simply does not fit with the Hempelian and Popperian notions of deductive explanation and deductive testing. As we have seen, in general his thinking parallels much more closely Dewey's process-view of inquiry. So too his monetary research. Friedman himself does not explicitly set out the steps, but even the sceptical reader will be hard put to deny that they are recognizable if the important article 'Money and business cycles', (1963b), is read in combination with the *Theoretical Framework*.

First, there is the identification of empirical regularities – things like the correlated movement of money growth and nominal income and prices, or the pro-cyclical behavior of velocity and interest rates. These data must then be 'prepared', to use Nancy Cartwright's term,[4] or made into 'facts of the case', as Dewey would put it (1938, extract in McDermott, 1981, p. 234). This involves modelling in two distinct capacities. On the one hand there must be an organized framework, to provide for possible links between rather general underlying theoretical ideas and the observed data. Friedman's preferred framework, as usual, is that of supply and demand; in this instance, an exogenous (and variable) money supply and a stable demand for money, or, to be somewhat more specific, a quantity-theoretic account of nominal income. Informing the theory is also the ever-present postulate of maximizing agent behavior. On the other hand, there is a need for a model precise enough to capture causal mechanisms, capable of accounting in detail for what is observed.[5] These two capacities correspond roughly to the sorting out, and production-of-substantive-hypotheses roles of analysis that Friedman distinguished elsewhere (1953d in 1953e, pp. 7ff.)

In Friedman's case the causal prime mover – so he fervently believes – is money. Establishing this is in principle a two-pronged process: identifying *sufficient* reasons, and *necessary* ones. He does not actually get beyond the former. His logic is that if any one of his arguments or pieces of evidence does not convince, conviction may be strengthened by two put together; or if not by two, then three, mutually reinforcing because they make the same point from a different starting position (cf. Boland, 1979, pp. 505–6).[6]

All these steps in Friedman's process of monetary inquiry may be thought of as stages, provided that we do not forget that the process is ongoing and the 'stages' interact in an almost recursive manner.

It will be helpful if we spell out the two aspects of the modelling process – giving substance to general theory and showing how it might link up with observed phenomena; and identifying precise causal mechanisms – in somewhat more detail. Friedman's organizing theoretical framework will be outlined next, his modelling of 'the manner of action of causes' on pp. 233ff.

A THEORETICAL FRAMEWORK

Basic theories in economics are so general as to be consistent with any and all data. They need to be made specific before they are even potentially falsifiable, let alone actually testable.[7] We have seen Friedman's concern with this problem in trying to apply the general theory of choice (Chapters 1 and 8, above). His restatement of the quantity theory, too, is a special application of very general theoretical notions: that money is an asset; and that optimization occurs over an extended time horizon with respect to a portfolio of assets, including money. Capital theory and the theory of optimal choice are thus combined and extended in particular ways to supply the framework within which the so-called quantity theory can be modelled so as to imply the sorts of observations noted above.

The idea that Friedman's reformulated quantity theory is just one specification within a more open or general theoretical framework is most clearly reflected in his 'A theoretical framework for monetary analysis'. There he introduces a common model form, to facilitate communication between monetarists and Keynesians. This model contains a consumption relation, an investment relation, the income identity, money demand and supply functions and a market-clearing condition for money (1974b, pp. 29–30). The model is underdetermined, having six equations but seven unknowns. How we choose to add 'the missing equation' says a lot about our theoretical preferences.

Friedman explores three alternative closings. A basic quantity theory approach would simply have real income determined outside the system; a Keynesian approach would take the price level as given from outside.

Friedman's preferred closing differs radically from either. He opts for a theory of nominal income, bypassing the problem of breaking down income into its price and output components. But this is just a simplification. More importantly, he introduces expectations explicitly into the model by postulating a '"permanent" or "anticipated" rate of growth of real income' as a sort of reference rate (*ibid.*, p. 36). This rate, and also the anticipated real interest rate, are not absolute givens, but changes in either are assumed to be small relative to changes in the expected rate of inflation. Expectations about inflation will reflect past experience and both actual inflation and nominal income will respond to autonomous impulses, one of which may be the money supply growth rate. Such autonomous impulses transmit their effects through adjustments to behavior (e.g. in money balances held) by individuals whose anticipations (desires) are disappointed.

This formulation is a caricature of the differences between Keynesians and monetarists but it captures the two central themes in Friedman's own monetary thought: the idea that monetary impulses are primary; and the use of an adjustment mechanism resting on expectations to show how a monetary impulse transmits its effects to other economic variables, such as output and prices.

Neither theme is very evident in his earliest attempts to formulate a monetary theory, his restatement of the quantity theory in 1956; however, it is quickly apparent that this is an effort to identify a stable demand for money function, in relation to which the effects of exogenous changes in the money supply might be traced. Expectations enter into the original formulation of the money demand relation, but their centrality is appreciated only as Friedman, in the early 1960s, began to explore a transmission (or adjustment) mechanism. Comparing the explanation of the terms in the money demand function in the *Theoretical Framework* (1974*b*) with the 'Quantity theory − a restatement' (1956*b*) we see clearly how the role of anticipations came to prominence in Friedman's thinking over the decade of the sixties.

Friedman's 1956 restatement of the quantity theory was designed primarily to differentiate his monetary thought from the dominant Keynesian macroeconomics of the day. There is nothing in the formulation that a Keynesian would have to disagree with. Nevertheless, it gives Friedman an opportunity to inject his own preferred emphases: that money is an asset; that there is a whole range of rates of return relevant to the decision to hold money; that anticipations of price level changes cannot be ignored. Friedman makes money demand a demand for the services of an asset. He writes:

$$\frac{M}{Y} = \frac{1}{V\left[r_m, r_b, r_e, \left(\frac{1}{P} \cdot \frac{dP}{dt}\right), w, \frac{Y}{P}, u\right]}$$

where r_m, r_b, r_e are the nominal rates of interest on money, bonds and equities,

$$\left(\frac{1}{P} \cdot \frac{dP}{dt}\right)$$

is anticipated inflation (which enters into a term like r_e), w is the ratio of income from non-human wealth to income from human wealth, and u stands for the technological conditions governing real output and for general preferences for adding to wealth as distinct from consuming (1956*b* in 1956*a*, p. 11). If w and u may be taken as fixed for short-run analysis and the demand for money is fairly inelastic with respect to interest rates; or, expressed differently, if a change in M does not alter any one interest rate very much, then changes in real income will be the *main* determinant of velocity. This reduces to a minimum the significance of the Keynesian investment-income relation. Moreover, if V_p (permanent velocity) is a function of permanent real income, this allows measured velocity to differ from 'true' velocity, with the variation attributed to random or transitory fluctuations in income. A stable money demand function is perfectly consistent with such variations in V (Friedman, 1959c).

Such an unspecific model is open to any number of specific uses. On one specific interpretation – that money demand is unresponsive to interest – the Keynesian theory is robbed of explanatory power. And by insisting that money demand, or velocity, is a function of *permanent* income, observed fluctuations in V can be reconciled with the desired quality of stability in the money demand function.

RESEARCH RESULTS, 1958–68

In stating the generic framework of Friedman's monetary writings we have jumped ahead and need to go back and look at the actual research results he published in the period 1958–1963. The most important articles are collected in *The Optimum Quantity of Money and Other Essays* (1969c), and all page references are to this collection.

In 'The supply of money and changes in prices and output' (1958b) Friedman reported briefly on the main results of his NBER inquiries with Anna Schwartz into US monetary history. They found in data stretching back to the early 1880s a clear one-to-one relation between fluctuations in the money stock and in prices. The relationship was looser in the short run and not 'precise or mechanically rigid' even in the long run. There are in general two factors that might disturb it: changes in output and changes in desired cash balances. The relations between prices and output turn out to be complex, and either mild inflation or deflation seems to be consistent with real growth. The ratio of desired cash balances to income – the inverse of income velocity – is, however, fairly stable over long periods.

Notice the emphases in this report. Although no clear relation between prices and output emerges from the data, output fluctuations nonetheless are classed as a 'discrepancy' (1958b in 1969c, p. 174). This implies that the statistical relation between changes in M and in P is already accepted as a meaningful and stable basic causal relation, and it is therefore not surprising to find Friedman devoting most of his attention to the evidence *for* the priority in a causal sense of changes in M. Output is in effect treated as exogenously determined. Or, as he put it, 'The mainsprings of growth are presumably to be sought elsewhere' (*ibid.*, p. 184). Clearly in the interpretative procedures used here there is a certain amount of question begging.

As to velocity, the stability alluded to is by no means absolute. Friedman noted that there is a secular decline evident from 1875 to the end of the Second World War – though not thereafter – and that the interest rate has a systematic effect on the amount of cash held. The apparent turnaround in velocity since 1945 is dismissed with the observation that 'it is yet too soon to judge whether this is a fundamental change or simply a reaction to the abnormally high ratio of cash balances that was reached during the war' (*ibid.*, p. 176). In other words, the reversal has no implications for stability. What an adequate test period would be, however, is left unspecified. The systematic interest rate effect for its part, while acknowledged, is also dismissed as being 'rather small'.

In other words, both the long-term and short-run movements in the data are here clearly being interpreted in terms of independent movements in M, taking place along a stable money demand function. This suggests independent evidence for the exogeneity of M – evidence Friedman and Schwartz tried to adduce in *A Monetary History of the United States* – and evidence that movements in real income dominate all other variables in the demand function in determining velocity.

In 'The demand for money: some theoretical and empirical results' (1959*c*) Friedman built on the finding that secular movements in velocity seem to be dominated by real income. He argued first that short-run changes in interest rates, in so far as they are pro-cyclical, seem not to be sufficiently regular nor important enough to be capable of offsetting income movements in the required way. He then attempted to find an explanation that would reconcile observed pro-cyclical movements in velocity with the observed secular rise in velocity (ignoring, as before, the post-Second World War trend), running entirely in terms of the permanent income hypothesis:

> Suppose that the demand for real cash balances were determined entirely by real permanent income according to the relation estimated in the secular analysis and that actual balances throughout equaled desired balances . . . *measured* velocity would tend to be lower than what we may call *permanent* velocity at troughs, because measured income is then lower than permanent income, and would tend to be higher at peaks (1959*c*, 1969*c*, pp. 119–20).

A complementary account, in terms of current and 'permanent' price levels, was devised to explain the behavior of measured real cash balances (*ibid.*, pp. 120–1).

These explanations were in no sense a test of the power of Friedman's reformulated quantity theory to account for monetary history. At most they state a new point of view, whereby much of the observed cyclical movement in velocity becomes 'spurious' and the residual movement – that which cannot be explained by differences between measured and permanent income – becomes all that interest rates or other variables are needed to explain. The changed viewpoint nonetheless carries important negative implications for those inclined to interpret the volatility of measured velocity as evidence that changes in the money stock are *not* the key to explaining cyclical change. If Friedman's point of view is correct and if cash balances are adjusted to permanent income, a rise in M will have to raise desired cash balances by (M × V), at given real income. In other words nominal income in the short run would be 'highly sensitive' to changes in the money supply (*ibid.*, pp. 138–9). This may be an important element in an attempt to persuade Keynesians to give more heed to monetarist accounts of the cycle, but Friedman has to admit that it is 'highly speculative and involves taking our findings more seriously in detail than I can fully justify' (*ibid.*, p. 138).

It is of interest to note that Friedman reverts to his old distinction between 'arithmetic' and 'substantive' concerns in his discussion of velocity. Identifying the spurious element in changes in measured velocity is merely 'arithmetic' or technical; what is 'substantive' is the explanation (*ibid.*, p. 120). In 'The lag in effect of monetary policy' (1961*d*), he addresses the concerns of some critics of his earlier reports in favour of a monetary theory of cycles and makes a similar distinction (1961*d* in 1969*c*, pp. 242, 244). Here difficulties with the National Bureau method of measuring short-run change in terms of reference cycles; statistical problems of timing and lags; and questions of whether one should relate levels or rates of change, are dealt with. These issues are all in their way 'arithmetic'.[8] The substantive issues for Friedman turn on the channels through which money stock changes might exert their influence. But this is indeed exploratory, even speculative: there are no restrictions imposed by the generic theory itself on which interpretations may count and which may not. The sole restrictions are that any acceptable interpretation must be consistent with things known – an empirical constraint – and that it be 'not prima facie implausible'; which is to say that it be 'consistent with what we *think* we know about economic interrelationships' (*ibid.*, p. 255), ultimately also an empirical constraint.[9]

CAUSALITY AND THE IMPORTANCE OF MONETARY HISTORY

This brings us to Friedman and Schwartz' *Monetary History* (1963*a*). What precisely was known in this area by Friedman at the time this work was published? Three lines of work, remember, had preoccupied him in the preceding fifteen years.

First, he had begun with the notion that Keynesian theory carried the empirical implication that velocity is passive and changes in the money stock do not influence the level of activity. It had seemed important to him to check which of V or k – the multiplier – is the more stable.

Direct testing proved to be impossible for the reason that measured V seemed to display considerable short-term variability. Measured velocity, Friedman concluded, must therefore be reinterpreted. A satisfactory reinterpretation proved readily available, using the notions of permanent income and prices. In other words, Friedman found himself going from troublesome observations to a new, broader interpretation involving non-observables. This is exactly the way expected utility and permanent income had come to be introduced earlier.

Second, Friedman had pursued statistical inquiries into changes in the money supply and other variables. These confirmed a close statistical relation between movements in prices and in the stock of money over long periods, but it was not possible to ascribe invariable (causal) priority to money. While 'substantial' changes in M could be shown to exert an independent influence on P, this did not exclude a reflex influence. And this reflex influence, Friedman admitted, 'is often important, almost always complex, and, depending on the monetary arrangements, may be in either direction' (1958b in 1969c, p. 173).

As to short-term changes, the dominance of money is still less clearcut: moderate movements in money and prices are not clearly separable in the short run from disturbances in the relation between desired money holdings, real income and interest rates (*ibid*., pp. 177–8).

These findings, which emerged while work on discriminating statistical tests of the Keynesian and quantity theories were in process, further lessened the significance of the latter. If the dominant causal role of money can be shown fairly clearly only in the long run and for 'substantial' changes in money, and if reflex influences are 'often important', then some independent role for non-monetary influences must frequently be allowed for. This, combined with the need to reinterpret measured values of V, makes the significance of estimates of the relative stability of V and k unclear. By 1963 it was plain that the careful analysis of individual historical episodes was unavoidable as a supplement to the search for a discriminating statistical test, as Friedman and Meiselman themselves noted (1963e, p. 179). Notice that the decision to look more closely into the details of (well-defined) experience, rather than to retreat into a priori analysis of possibilities is a peculiarly Deweyan one. In striking contrast is Tobin's (1970) exploration, *not* of the historical evidence but of 'the lead-lag timing implication of alternative theoretical models . . .'. Tobin was trying to demonstrate the fragility of any inference based on timing, but in that he was not teaching Friedman anything he did not know and admit to.

Third, Friedman had worked on a reformulation of the demand for money. It had become his hope that for the most part analysis of the historical record could proceed within the framework of movements along a stable demand for money curve. Once again, however, the need to reinterpret measured V made it unclear in how far success in 'capturing' (estimating) demand equations could be taken as independent evidence for stability.

What Friedman knew in 1963, therefore, was that the facts resisted attempts to dismiss Keynesian interpretations out of hand, that is, on the basis of estimates of parameters alone; and that the superiority of the quantity theory as an interpretative framework could not be taken for granted, but had to be established in each instance for which it was used. This meant that the *Monetary History of the United States* had to be an analytical history in the sense that *alternative* explanations of events had to be tried for separate episodes. This is exactly what the book became: a record of events and, at the same time, a series of counter-factual investigations.

Counter-factual inquiry – what would have happened if . . . , where the 'if' did *not* in fact occur – on the face of it seems very different from putting empirical propositions directly to the test. At best it can help persuade us of the possibility that a preferred account could be true; that is, that it is admissible. But the ambiguity of facts and the corresponding multiplicity of explanations means that this is also about all we can expect from confrontations between single empirical hypotheses and actual events. These, too, as Friedman's researches clearly show, are often indirect and involve non-empirical entities. Moreover, in economics, the boundary conditions necessary to predicting normally comprise not actual events but events which *might* occur. It seems unnecessary, then, to draw a sharp distinction between the direct and counter-factual approaches in the case of economics.

Friedman's stress on historical episodes was not a move away from the idea of discriminating tests as such, only from the notion that a conclusive statistical (numerical) test is attainable. While he still used the term crucial experiments, he meant something less than the words themselves connote. In one sense this is inevitable once it is also recognized that theoretical models in economics may be compatible with a whole range of empirical models. Friedman and Meiselman give a simple illustration of the point in one of their responses to criticisms (1965d, pp. 768–9, n. 18). Take the basic Keynesian model

$$Y = C + I + (X - M)$$

where X is exports and M imports;

$$C = a + bY$$
$$M = c + dY$$

If autonomous spending A is taken to be equal to I + (X − M) then C and M can be expressed in terms of A plus the parameters a, b, c, d. Clearly the basic model is compatible with various modified definitions of A (including or excluding consumer durables, and so on); but each definition feeds into the reduced forms and affects the empirical results. [10]

What grounded Friedman's still considerable confidence in his ability to persuade opponents? He makes clear in the *Monetary History* that where just two variables are involved, in this case M and Y, there *is* a way of telling whether observed close covariation is due to M or to Y or to some as yet unidentified third variable influencing both. This is to look at a wide variety of experience, where just about the only common elements are M and Y themselves. If, then, timing points to one rather than the other; and if, in addition, we know something about the detailed antecedent circumstances; then we may be able to point to variations in M as the 'cause' of variations in Y, or vice versa. [11] This, of course, is just a version of Mill's Method of Difference. That method can be represented as a syllogism (Klant 1984, p. 18).

1. All events E have a cause.
2. $A_1, A_2, A_3 \ldots$ are the sole events eligible to be causes of E_1
3. In a number of cases it has been observed that E takes place without the occurrence of $A_2 \ldots A_4$, but never without A_1.
4. A_1 is the cause of E_1.

This can never be conclusive, or result in universal causal statements, because we can never be certain that point 2 is complete (Losee, 1980, p. 156). Much of the listing of As is a matter of counter-factual analysis and depends on the wit of the list-maker. Friedman, however, adopted two aids to make his list more compelling. One was to take as wide a range of experience as possible, encompassing institutional and other changes which might reverse the causation but apparently did not. Whence the great scope of the *Monetary History*. The other was to point to special episodes, either dramatic (as with the three wartime episodes discussed in Friedman 1952b) or in which the antecedent circumstances are known from independent historical research. Such episodes both shorten the list of likely As and directly strengthen (or weaken) the conclusion, point 4. That was the purpose of Friedman's crucial episodes.

Also underlying the counterfactual side of the *Monetary History* is the belief that appearances may be deceptive and that there is a single hidden structure lying beneath apparently unrelated phenomena (1963a, pp. 10, 676; cf. 1953e in 1956f, p. 33). Friedman's deep structure is that defined by rational, maximizing 'individuals'. Hence portfolio preferences and equilibrium are guiding notions in his examination of actual episodes in the *Monetary History*.

CRUCIAL EPISODES AND THE EXOGENEITY OF MONEY

Vicissitudes versus stable relationships

In the best Marshallian tradition there are two blades to the scissors of Friedman's monetary theory. And, as with Marshall, so with Friedman, neither blade alone does the cutting. One, the more theoretical blade, was the 1956 restatement of the quantity theory, which made the demand for money a preference function in a few variables, among them income and interest rates. With some empirical evidence and a theoretical argument for the stability of this function in hand, it was time to bring the second, more empirical blade to bear. This was an argument for the exogeneity and primacy of the money stock. Hence the *History* opens with the statement: 'this book is about the stock of money in the United States' (1963*a*, p. 3).

Friedman had stressed in his 'Price, income, and monetary changes in three wartime periods' that 'experience in general proceeds smoothly and continuously', making it difficult to separate systematic from random variations 'since both are of much the same order of magnitude' (1952*b* in 1969*c*, p. 157). Recall that that was the reason he liked data for war-time periods: it is then that violent changes in key variables tend to occur over brief periods, making the task of testing hypotheses somewhat more fruitful. Similarly, the *History* largely eschews trends, except as background.[12] Recall, too, his early (1943) acknowledgement that it is only to be expected that M and Y will display close covariation in the long-term sense. For both these reasons Friedman and Schwartz announced in the *History* that 'it is with the vicissitudes along the way that this study is mostly concerned' (1963*a*, p. 5).

Certain long-term relationships are nonetheless identified and form the necessary basis for a discussion of the vicissitudes. These are relationships we have encountered before. Variation in the money stock is reported to be closely related to movements in the nominal variables money income and prices; much less closely related to movements in real income, except for violent changes (*ibid.*, pp. 676, 678). Friedman and Schwartz devote most of their *History* to arguing that these relationships are remarkably stable, given the wide variation in institutional arrangements over the century of experience they record; and they single out certain counter-intuitive results which they view as supportive evidence of just how remarkable this stability is.

In their 'summing up' towards the end of the volume Friedman and Schwartz draw special attention to three pieces of evidence relating to stability:

1. Velocity declined 'rather steadily' until the Second World War; and its (pro-cyclical) fluctuations about trend are consistent, vary in amplitude with the strength of the cycle, and anyway remain within a fairly narrow range (*ibid.*, pp. 681–2).

2. M and Y display a pattern of cyclical movements that approaches constancy; M rises faster than usual during expansions and more slowly than usual during contractions, and the rate of rise peaks before the peak in activity and speeds up before the recession trough (*ibid.*, p. 682).

3. Exchange rate-adjusted relative prices in the United Kingdom and the United States have varied within a narrow range over the long period 1871–1949 (*ibid.*, p. 679).

The stability here displayed is said to be remarkable in the light of the radical changes occurring in the external forces influencing the money stock (1963*a*, p. 686) and the variety of means adopted to achieve relative price changes (tariffs, exchange controls, etc.) (*ibid.*, p. 679).

Other evidence is also mentioned in passing (*ibid.*, p. 683), but these three pieces are not randomly selected for emphasis. Velocity is a key monetary variable. If its behavior is *not* steady then the desired stability in the demand for money function is open to question. The regularity of movement *and* timing between M and Y, given the variety of influences on M and on its components (the factors determining base money, banks' demands for reserves and the public's demands for deposits), is almost an ideal result in terms of the search for monetary causes via the Method of Difference. The third piece of evidence seems to point to some underlying constraining influence on nominal variables – an underlying real economic equilibrium (*ibid.*, pp. 678, 679).

Arguing the primacy of money from history

With stability 'demonstrated', Friedman and Schwartz turn to arguing 'causal' primacy for the money stock, selecting once again three main pieces of evidence to make their case. They take three episodes in which sharp contractionary movements in the money stock occurred, independently of any concurrent change in economic activity but resulting subsequently in contractionary movements in activity. Their three crucial experiments are the January and June 1920 increases in the discount rate; the October 1931 increase in discount rate; and the doubling of reserve requirements between July 1936 and May 1937. We choose the 1936–7 episode for closer examination.[13]

In the three years preceding June 1936 the money stock grew by 9.5 per cent a year or more; in the two years after the increase in reserve requirements was announced the rate of growth fell to 4.2 per cent and

−2.4 per cent. Friedman and Schwartz argue that the change was so sharp that the subsequent contraction was more severe than it need have been. That is, money influenced activity and in significant degree. In June 1936, however, cash assets alone held by banks totalled $12.5 billion, more than $9.5 billion in excess of required reserves (1963*a*, Table 19, p. 460). Cash as a percentage of total assets held continued to rise even after the imposition of the higher reserve requirements, but cash in excess of required reserves relative to total assets in excess of required reserves dipped temporarily, before rising again. Friedman and Schwartz interpret this dip as indicating genuine contraction. The view of the Federal Reserve System at the time was that the excess cash was truly surplus, the result of a lack of private demand for credit, and the tightening action would therefore have no current impact on activity but might help to prevent a subsequent inflationary surge of credit (*ibid.*, 517ff.).

Underlying the Friedman and Schwartz interpretation is a conviction that the excess reserves were accumulated deliberately by banks following the 1933 panic. In other words, the excess reserves represent a shift in portfolio preferences towards greater liquidity. So, too, they argue, did the accumulation after 1937. Thus the temporary dip mentioned really was a tightening; it ran against the preferences of the banks to hold increasingly liquid portfolios. The Fed's public announcements in explanation of its move, on the other hand, fit an alternative interpretation; that, in Friedman and Schwartz' phrase, 'there was no unique desired structure of assets, corresponding to given rates of return on assets, disturbance of which would prompt banks to seek to restore that same structure; they would be content to retain the new one' (*ibid.*, p. 461).

A desire for greater liquidity − a shift in preferences − is a postulate that cannot be directly tested. What evidence, then, would enable us to decide between these alternatives? Friedman and Schwartz adduce a great deal favorable to their interpretation. Much of it is indirectly acquired, in answer to counter-factual questions, confirming the importance of that approach. Another feature of their style of argument emerges here, too, namely that they rely on no single piece of evidence but on the cumulative force of numerous small pieces (see p. 223 above). They make an impressive case, as the following six points indicate:

1. Certain clear trends are evident in the changes in banks' portfolios over the decade of the 1930s: 'bankers took the opportunity ... to strengthen their cash position and to expand investments, and among them, governments [i.e. official bonds], more rapidly than loans' (*ibid.*,

p. 452). It is against the backgrounds of these trends that short-term movements like those relating to the 1936–7 doubling of reserve requirements must be interpreted.

2. Did the portfolio shifts reflect changes in the relative supplies of different assets taking place against passive demand, or do they reflect changed preferences? If the former, one would expect assets whose importance increased to show higher yields (so as to induce bankers to hold them). The portfolio changes were clearly towards short-term and more liquid investments; but the yields on short-term assets fell from 1929 to 1936, and the spread between short- and long-term yields rose – exactly the opposite of what one would expect had the changes been in supply and not in preferences (*ibid*., p. 453 and Chart 35).

3. This rate movement does not in itself explain the move into cash; but yields in general fell so that cash became relatively less expensive to hold, just as we should expect as a condition accompanying increased cash holding (*ibid*., p. 457).

Summarizing to this point, then, there is evidence on changing trends in bank portfolios; these are explicable as a change in preferences; and the changes are reflected in relative yields.

4. The shift into cash in the 1930s was larger than might have been expected on the basis of the general decline in yields alone. This emerges from a comparison of the 1930s with pre-1929 and post-1939 data (ibid., p. 458).

Points three and four together suggest a shift in preferences for cash assets (*ibid*., p. 455).

5. The 1936–7 increase in reserve requirements interfered with the banks' desire to accumulate more cash. This can be inferred from the fact that they accumulated still more cash thereafter, apparently as compensation and in order to restore their desired (trend) position (*ibid*., p. 458).

6. A first shift in preferences occurred as a result of the banking panic in 1933; but a second distinct shift resulted from the Fed's raising of reserve requirements in July 1936. The deposit/reserve ratio reflects these shifts. It declined from May 1933 through June 1936, at first sharply, but at a steadily decreasing rate, virtually levelling off by mid-1936. A renewed decline set in after the July 1936 change in reserve requirements, when allowance is made for a pause due to Treasury gold-sterilization, which kept the stock of high-powered money from rising for most of 1937. If there were no second shift in preferences, the deposit/reserve ratio would have displayed a temporary bulge, reflecting gold-sterilization, and then

returned merely to its early 1936 level instead of renewing its downward trend (*ibid.*, pp. 539–40; Chart 44, p. 337).

The inconclusiveness of historical interpretation

These pieces of confirmatory evidence do not suffice to give a clear-cut answer to our question. The reason is that even although several of them discriminate between the alternative explanations they do not all do so, or do not do so completely. The behavior of the deposit/reserve ratio, for example, does not exclude Keynesian interpretation. Banks in the mid-1930s could be regarded as having invested in short-term Treasury and commercial paper to the point where rates were almost zero, so that any additional reserve would naturally be held as cash. That is one way to explain the observed close negative correlation between the deposit/ reserve ratio and the growth of high-powered money (*ibid.*, Chart 44, p. 537). James Tobin, who offers this alternative, declares himself unconvinced by the suggestion in Friedman and Schwartz that this correlation is just 'a coincidence' (*ibid.*, p. 535), and finds it difficult to accept that shifts in preferences caused by discrete events should be followed by such a perfectly smooth adjustment process as Friedman and Schwartz imply in attributing the downward trend in the deposit/reserve ratio wholly to preferred behavior on the part of the bankers (Tobin, 1965, in 1971, p. 480).

Before proceeding we ought to note that Friedman and Schwartz are not as vulnerable on this point as Tobin's criticism implies. They insist as usual on separating the trends from the vicissitudes, arguing in this case that the longer-term inverse correlation is 'not an essential characteristic of the adjustment process'. What is essential, they claim, is the inverse correlation between short-term 'irregularities' – 'reflecting, as it were, departures from the desired' – in the deposit/reserve ratio and in high-powered money (1963*a*, p. 535). This merely shifts the argument back a stage. How does one demonstrate that certain evidence is or is not essential? In this instance Friedman and Schwartz can offer an independent argument for their claims. They correctly point out that the longer-term correlation between the deposit/reserve ratio and high-powered money was positive in the 1920s and the 1940s; hence the negative correlation of the 1930s may indeed be no more than a coincidence. This is a good example of the advantage that a wide range of experience can give in argument with an opponent such as Tobin, who excels at raising questions about individual episodes on grounds of general theoretical considerations but who is unable to press his points because they are too loosely attached to history. Friedman expresses this in somewhat more barbed language when he applies to some models

Tobin later constructed to demonstrate the causal ambiguity inherent in some of Friedman's cases of empirical covariation a comment taken from his methodology essay: 'observed facts are necessarily finite in number; possible hypotheses, infinite'. Friedman adds: 'his [Tobin's] examples are ingenious but largely irrelevant to [the] basic issue' (1970d, pp. 325, 327); this, because they dealt with theoretical possibilities only, and did not represent tentative hypotheses based on a study of the facts.

Questions there are, nonetheless, about the case put up by Friedman and Schwartz. In instances where other factors than the ones they stress may have played a role, they tend to admit these but pass on quickly. The reader is left up in the air because offered no framework for evaluating the relative influence of the factors involved. Two examples can be given in connection with the 1936–7 episode. First, Friedman and Schwartz allow that the 1937 contraction played an independent role in inducing a reduction in the deposit/reserve ratio – and leave it at that (1963a, p. 540). Their own emphasis remains elsewhere, on the postulated change in preferences. Second, the authors acknowledge that coinciding with the onset of the contraction was a shift in the government budget from deficit to surplus (ibid., pp. 543–5). Once again, no comparative evaluation is attempted and Friedman and Schwartz merely plead that while this has been the factor most stressed by the dominant (Keynesian) thinking surely the money stock must be allowed to have played 'an important role'. Such a conclusion is inevitably something of a let-down after the earlier case to establish the desired interpretation of portfolio changes in terms of a shift in preferences. For that argument virtually ruled out a Keynesian interpretation running in terms of a flat liquidity preference schedule, while suddenly a different sort of Keynesian argument is allowed to enter but no basis for assessing it is offered. Confidence is not strengthened when Friedman and Schwartz also add, as a virtual aside, that the gold-sterilization programme was 'no less important' than the doubling of reserve requirements in causing the observed slowdown in the growth of money (ibid., p. 544). It looks as if the important thing was to establish that the Fed's analysis of excess reserves was mistaken, and its intervention likewise. The discussion simply stops short of quantitative analysis of the relative importance of all the factors operating.

SUMMARY OF THE FRIEDMAN–SCHWARTZ MODE OF INQUIRY

So much of the secondary literature on Friedman's monetary theory attacks his alleged failure to test that it is worth stressing again the nature of the reasoning employed by Friedman and Schwartz. The explanations they offer in the *Monetary History* possess certain basic features.

1. They stress underlying – supposedly equilibrium – trends. A given change is more or less significant as it represents a radical departure from or a continuation of these trends (cf. *ibid.*, p. 527, n. 28)
2. Equilibrium also involves preferences, which are reflected in portfolio composition.
3. Interest rates – relative yields – are critical to changes in portfolio composition; they are, indeed, the means by which the effects of changes in the growth rate of the money stock are transmitted.

Notice that this way of arguing reflects the basic components of the generic theory modelled in outline above (p. 224–6).

Notice, too, that in explaining specific episodes the authors are fully aware that there will always remain room for doubt. A wide range of experience is an essential complement to any single episode. Different pieces of evidence, derived in answer to a range of – mostly counterfactual – questions, are assembled to strengthen a case that no one piece of evidence would make convincing. But even where the final case rests on 'a number of . . . bits of evidence that together are fairly decisive' (*ibid.*, p. 457), the authors stop short of claiming more than is warranted. Additional factors are admitted to have played a role (e.g. *ibid.*, p. 540) although no quantitative assessment of relative importance is made; the possibility of two-way causation is acknowledged (e.g. *ibid.*, p. 514); and the authors' preferred explanation or emphasis is frankly acknowledged as ultimately just 'our view' (e.g. *ibid.*, pp. 534, 538).

This reticence is entirely correct given the number of choices that have to be made at every stage of the analysis, from imposing a framework to first collect and organize raw data, to identifying certain covariations as basic (and being willing to regard them as reflecting preferences or expressing some kind of trend or equilibrium), to selecting those questions to ask whose empirical implications would try the strength of a preferred explanation of events. This is a subtle and somewhat personal process. Argumentation and persuasion also enter: it has to do with winning another to one's own point of view. Judgments, of a personal or 'standard group practice' sort, enter at every turn. It has very little to do with theory-data confrontations à la Popper of the sort that Friedman is repeatedly attacked for not having undertaken. Notice, too, that Friedman and Schwartz successfully shift the burden of proof on to the supporters of the opposing hypothesis. Opponents are given the task, not of falsifying the money-change hypothesis – that $(-M)$ occurred independently of economic conditions – in simple and direct form, but of dealing with a whole series of mini-hypotheses (points 1–6 above) which are not even logically derived from the money-change hypothesis. This is where the cumulative force of partial but complementary bits of evidence comes in: a whole series of independent and separately only somewhat convincing explanatory hypotheses confronts the would-be critic. The normal basis for 'deductive testing' is here severely weakened if not destroyed entirely (cf. Popper, 1959, p. 33). In this case the mini-hypotheses are kin, all of them being related to the contention that a shift in bankers' preferences occurred in 1936–7. But it is not true to regard them as forming a logical chain: an increased preference for cash is logically as well as empirically distinct from an increased desire for short-term interest-bearing assets, even though both sorts of assets are liquid.

More fundamentally, the issue giving point to the mini-hypotheses here is whether legally excess reserves were excessive relative to desired levels. This determines whether the Fed's action amounted to a monetary contraction and therefore bears only on the exogeneity of money, which is an empirical rather than a theoretical proposition. Friedman and Schwartz never suggest otherwise, as a careful reading of Section 3 of their summing up chapter in the *Monetary History* shows. Yet the exogeneity of money is significant only in the context of a stable demand for money; so there is theory at risk, but it is only weakly linked with the test context of the 1936 and 1937 Fed actions. As Friedman expressed it in a later interchange with Tobin and Buiter, 'the fundamental differences among us are empirical, not theoretical. But this does not mean that we all use the same theory' (Friedman, 1976a, in Stein, 1976, p. 315). At issue here is how we respond to the complexity of economic events. One response – Tobin's, to some extent as it was Mill's – is to retreat into theory, away from the complexity. Friedman's is to unravel events into their component empirical strands and to see how well these can be simply and coherently explained. But no certainty or finality is possible, and the preferred interpretation is not chosen a priori. It reflects instead the researcher's tentative best attempt to explain the facts, 'a tentative presumption subject to modification as either additional facts may be adduced that point in a different direction, or a different way of organizing the evidence may be developed that brings order and stability out of apparent chaos' (Friedman and Meiselman, 1963e, p. 213).

THE TRANSMISSION MECHANISM

What of the charge, oft-repeated, that monetarism is black-box economics? Friedman himself is fully aware of the need for 'an explicit and rigorously stated' transmission mechanism (1963b in 1969c, p. 223).

Thus:

> However consistent may be the relation between monetary change and
> economic change, and however strong the evidence for the autonomy of
> the monetary changes, we shall not be persuaded that the monetary
> changes are the source of economic changes unless we can specify in some
> detail the mechanism that connects the one with the other (*ibid.*, p. 229).

Nevertheless, he has never got beyond what he called in 1963 'a tentative
sketch' of the mechanism. Must we conclude then that Friedman's
monetarism is instrumentalist; that the explanation of how monetary
fluctuations work their effects is less important to him than the fact that
they do?

Recall the elements of a fruitful theory, according to Friedman. First,
'a meaningful scientific hypothesis or theory typically asserts that certain
forces are, and other forces are not, important in understanding a
particular class of phenomena' (1953*d* in 1953*e*, p. 40). Second, the test
of what is 'important' is predictive success (1968*b*, p. 15). Together,
these give us confidence that we can control. With respect to the
transmission mechanism the situation is that we have an outline of the
dynamics of monetary adjustment. We also have an order of adjustment:
output first, followed by prices. But we have only a rather flexible set of
statements with large margins for error as to the lags involved (see
Friedman's own summary in 1975*a*). Moreover, the detailed linkages
between money and a variety of economic variables have not been
provided in rigorous model form, despite successive efforts by Friedman
to this end since 1963 (most notably in 'A theoretical framework for
monetary analysis' (1974*b*) and *Monetary Trends* (1982*b*)). This has not
prevented him from making bold predictions (see Chapter 11, below).
Nor has it undermined his fundamental conviction, based on detailed
historical investigation, that 'the influence running from money to
economic activity has been predominant' (1963*a*, p. 695). But a consequence is also that he has had to concede that the monetary authorities
know too little to justify efforts to control, in the sense of intervening in a
counter-cyclical way (e.g. 1970*a*, p. 26).[14]

By way of reminder, the insight that undergirds Friedman's claims to
have improved our understanding of the role of money is the following.
Money is regarded as a stock in the portfolio of assets. A change in the
rate of change in the money stock causes a discrepancy between actual
and desired (real) cash balances; then, as portfolio holders try to adjust
their holdings to eliminate this discrepancy, other flows are altered,
causing changes in relative asset prices. The adjustment follows a typical
sequence, affecting first financial markets and the prices of financial
assets (stocks, bills, etc.), and later the flows of payments for real
resources (goods, factor services, housing, land, etc.) (1963*b* in 1969*c*,

pp. 231–4). Friedman acknowledges that the process is much the same as in a Keynesian analysis, only a broader range of assets is considered: not just financial assets, but also 'durable and semi-durable consumer goods, structures and other real property' (1982*b*, p. 58).

That this insight warrants careful consideration is based on the degree to which the mechanism of adjustment explains known regularities in business cycles, including, with the help of particular assumptions about changes in desired velocity in passing to a new equilibrium, the observed greater amplitude of variations in income than in money. But here Friedman is again brought face to face with the difficulty with which his methodological essay began, the fact that theory is underdetermined by data; or as he refers to it (1953*d* in 1953*e*, pp. 10–11), the problem of interpretation. For there are many adjustment paths possible, depending on the exact specification of the mechanism (1982*b*, pp. 70–1). Ultimately, theory preference must reflect those additional criteria – simplicity and fruitfulness – that Friedman also mentions in his 1953 essay on methodology. His insight in monetary theory is potentially simplifying in that it brings monetary issues under the aegis of a separate known body of hypotheses, the theory of capital; and – on his reckoning, at least – it is potentially fruitful because it supplies conjectures about many more elements of cyclical regularity than does its Keynesian competitor. Again, as to economy of formulation, the adjustment mechanism proposed is in principle simplicity itself, and can be captured formally by a set of simultaneous differential equations.

The upshot of all this is that, while it may be doubted whether Friedman has satisfactorily answered the complaints about a black box, it is simply mistaken to accuse him of having no serious interest in explanation because he has no explicit and fully formalized transmission mechanism. As we noted at the outset, and have seen repeatedly in his search for empirical connections, he has been preoccupied with 'the manner of action of causes'. It is just that there are so many candidate causes and so many ways to model them.

KEYNESIAN INADEQUACIES ONE MORE TIME

The centrality of expectations

It remains for us to consider Friedman's renewed concern in the 1970s with Keynesian analysis, in 'A theoretical framework for monetary analysis' and in the pamphlet *Unemployment versus Inflation? An Evaluation of the Phillips Curve* (1975*b*). Earlier we said that these pieces of writing fitted more naturally into a discussion of Friedman's monetary economics than into the category of criticisms of Keynesian economics. The distinction is perhaps a little pedantic, but lying behind it is the idea that Friedman's analytical locus here is the adjustments that take place following an unexpected change in money or in nominal demand; and the categories he uses – real versus nominal – and the mechanism he exploits – adaptive expectations – are central in his earlier monetary studies. We shall take a little space to argue this view.

The *Monetary History*, recall, built a case by comparing monetarist against alternative possible explanations of crucial historical episodes. The 'Theoretical framework' and *Unemployment versus Inflation*? merely continue that strategy. Friedman's concern is only in small degree the theoretical inadequacy of Keynesian analysis. He does not repeat his earlier criticisms about non-empirical and ambiguous theoretical entities (see Chapter 9, above). He does conclude that Keynesian analysis is an underdetermined system (1975*b*, p. 18); but in the common model outlined in 'A theoretical framework' (1974*b*, pp. 29ff.) this is simply cast as a matter of a missing equation which Keynesians and monetarists, each in their own way, must find and add. We may regard this as mere skirmishing since no effort is made to represent Keynesian thinking with any subtlety. Friedman's deeper concern we infer, is that the Keynesian analysis did not generate explanations of specific regularities such as those mentioned in the previous section. As Friedman notes at the end of 'A theoretical framework' (*ibid.*, p. 61), repeating a message found often in his monetary writings (e.g. 1963*e*, pp. 168–9; 1966*a* in 1969*c*, p. 155; 1976a in Stein, 1976, p. 315), 'One purpose of setting forth this framework is to document my belief that the basic differences among economists are empirical, not theoretical.'

Read in this light, 'A theoretical framework' is just a way of focusing on empirical consequences of a change in the growth of the money supply. The point of the work is certainly not to develop and display a static model whose functional relations show striking differences between Keynesian and monetarist insights. Critics who read it looking for this have been disappointed. Its focus rather is on the adjustments that might be expected to follow an unanticipated *change* in money and prices (see Friedman's discussion of his reasons for preferring his way of closing the underdetermined common model, 1974*b*, p. 40 and pp. 43 ff.). In other words, we are back at the transmission mechanism.

The key idea here, as in the 1963 sketch of the mechanism, is a distinction between actual and *expected* magnitudes, or between measured and long-run ('permanent') or equilibrium (desired) magnitudes. Expectations were reinserted by Friedman into macroeconomics after several decades of preoccupation by the profession with the Keynesian short run in which short-run expectations themselves play no critical role.[15] Friedman's interest in expectations has often been noted, although the usual reference is to his 1968 address as president of the AEA, 'The role of monetary policy' (1968a). In that address he developed the notion of a 'natural' rate of unemployment, and warned that if the authorities try to peg unemployment below this rate, they will forfeit control of the growth of money, and a rising rate of inflation will be the consequence. Here the natural rate of unemployment is that rate at which inflation is *non*-accelerating. A different way of stating the basic idea is that there is no long-run Phillips curve trade-off: the observed trade-off is not stable, its position reflecting expectations, which can and do alter. At the heart of this analysis lay the distinction between real and nominal magnitudes, anticipated and unanticipated values of variables. In the absence of money illusion, individuals may still be surprised by a policy change. They may even take time to adjust their expectations to reality. But after they have made the adjustment, the key real variables that policy sought to alter (output, unemployment) will be unchanged. Again, the true historical locus of this perspective is Friedman's earlier efforts to sketch a transmission mechanism in the context of a stable demand function for real cash balances.

SUMMARY

We have briefly traced Friedman's monetary thought from the restatement of the quantity theory through the *Monetary History*, which was meant to establish by close historical study whether money can be the prime mover in economic fluctuations, to the *Monetary Trends*, which complements the earlier history by exploring many of the testable implications of significant changes in money growth. Roughly speaking, the *Monetary History* shows *that* money matters; the *Monetary Trends* shows the ways in which it matters. In this sense, the *Monetary Trends* is the culmination of work on the transmission mechanism (see especially *Monetary Trends*, Chapters 5, 6, 7, 8, 10).

There is no doubt that the conception underlying all of Friedman's work in this area is the modern quantity theory. He uses it to organize his reasoning about the behavior and relations between real and nominal aggregates in the economy (cf. 1953d in 1953e, p. 7). As we have seen, however, it is not a hypothesis that he sets out to test in the Popperian sense. 'Testing' the idea of the primacy of money turns out to involve detailed historical study and, in particular, building a case which becomes more compelling as its elements are added together — like putting more legs under a chair, to use a metaphor of philosopher J. T. Wisdom. [16] The case cannot, in the nature of things, be conclusive, but it can be used to raise doubts about alternatives. This is all part and parcel of dealing with that fundamental difficulty in science, to which we have referred often, that theory is underdetermined by data. Proof, numerical or otherwise, is out of the question when we are engaged in interpreting empirical reality. Essentially what one does is to supply a plausible account of as many related phenomena as possible. Testability for Friedman turns out often to mean the ability to retrodict. The limitations are of exactly the same sort when the problem is one of trying to predict empirical consequences from a theory. Since the theory is never exclusive – the one unique satisfactory account of 'the facts' – and usually quantitatively imprecise, the major concern turns out to be how many detailed empirical consequences it is capable of supporting. This is what it came down to in Friedman's successive discussions of the transmission mechanism.

The picture that emerges from Friedman's monetary thought is one in which a rich appreciation of what is to be explained is crucial, as is a capacity for drawing out the implications of alternative modelling procedures. Dramatic and discriminating tests have almost no place; the marshalling of evidence to strengthen conviction is almost everything. Scientific disputes, for Friedman the monetary economist, are fought out by generating more, and more refined, questions to which there are in principle empirical answers.

This more subtle view of Friedman's practice emerges perhaps most clearly in a study of his monetary thought, although it is also present elsewhere. This seems at first glance ironic, since it clashes sharply with the popular view that his attachment to monetarism is merely dogmatic. Certainly, as we have recognized in several places, strong underlying convictions supply a thrust to the whole enterprise, but the invitation is basically to others to participate in an examination of the evidence supporting these convictions and the empirical consequences of adopting alternative positions. As Friedman and Meiselman put it: 'if ... [our] evidence is not the most significant for deciding between the two alternative views, what evidence would be?' (1963e, p. 169).

NOTES

1. A first draft of the *Monetary Trends*, dealing only with the US, was completed *before* the *Monetary History* (see 1982b, p. xxviii). The published work complements Friedman's extensive inquiry into cyclical regularities with a study of the relevant trends in the United States and the United

Kingdom. The earlier published studies, though ostensibly on cycles, incorporate the main findings on trends, and the theory in *Monetary Trends* is largely familiar to the student of earlier published studies. Since our focus is on Friedman's analysis it seemed reasonable to neglect a detailed separate treatment of *Monetary Trends*.

2. Work is only just beginning on spelling out the shifts and transformations that economists go through in moving from theory to empirical model. The indirect route taken by Friedman in rendering his permanent income hypothesis testable is a relatively simple illustration of the process (Chapter 9, above). For a similar exposition of Lucas' moves in developing a test of the natural rate hypothesis see De Marchi and Kim (1989). An excellent and much more detailed account in the job search literature is given by Kim (1989).

3. We have in mind here the deductive-nomological model of explanation, according to which observed events are deduced, with the help of very specific initial conditions, to be instances of true general laws.

4. See *How the Laws of Physics Lie*, p. 157: 'when we present a model of a phenomenon, we prepare the description of the phenomenon in just the right way to make a law apply to it'.

5. This, however, really comprises two separate activities: a theoretical modelling procedure − the derivation and specification of precise, refutable propositions; and an empirical modelling procedure. To illustrate the difference, theoretically deviations from constancy in velocity might be ascribed to differences between 'desired' and actual velocity, and modelled accordingly (for example, using a constant money demand function and an adaptive mechanism for demanders off the demand curve). The empirical model of velocity, however, might be a regression of velocity on a constant (to take one simple possibility, suggested by Hendry and Ericsson, 1985). This empirical model represents *one* testable proposition consistent with the theory chosen. But there may be numerous others.

6. Logically this may not be very compelling, but Friedman's evidence is empirical, not logical, the role of theory or analysis being only to show the links between the pieces of evidence, in the usual kind of situation where we do not have knowledge of the whole (*or* where the knowledge we have is fragmentary or in bits and pieces).

7. Friedman was enough influenced by Popper to be concerned about falsifiability, although in general he thought (and wrote) in terms of testability. The difference is not significant for understanding his work, so long as it is borne in mind (a) that he is mostly concerned with actual testing, not just falsifiability; and (b) that for him a refutation did not mean the rejection of a theory but an indication that it must be improved and checked again; and so on, in an extended sequence.

8. However, as Hendry and Ericsson (1985) show for *Monetary Trends*, the transformation of 'raw' data by data-based phase averaging is not statistically innocent; hence technical measurement issues cannot always be viewed as unrelated to the explanation one wishes to offer.

9. In other words, 'plausibility' here means consistency, not with some common notion of what is true, but with those tentative hypotheses that capture our knowledge of the facts.

10. Or, to give a familiar illustration of the point from monetary theory, in the IS-LM version of a macro-economic system a 'monetarist' can be defined as one who holds that the LM curve is vertical. Taking this as a hypothesis, it

has the empirical implication that the measured interest elasticity of the demand for money is zero. But as Friedman later pointed out, a horizontal IS curve would serve the monetarist just as well (1976a in Stein, 1976, p. 311). And as he wrote in 1966:

> In my opinion no 'fundamental issues' in either monetary theory or monetary policy hinge on whether the estimated elasticity [of the demand for money with respect to interest rates] can for most purposes be approximated by zero or is approximated by -0.1 or -0.5 or -2.0, provided it is seldom capable of being approximated by $-\infty$. (1966a in 1969c, p. 155).

This can be read as saying that the connection between the slope of the LM curve and the defining characteristics of monetarism is just too loose: too many other elements remain to be specified, so that this particular empirical distinction is by no means definitive. Note that this example is purely illustrative of the point made in the text. The characteristic propositions of monetarism, having to do with absence of money illusion, are related more to a vertical long-run supply curve than to any particular shapes of IS and LM curves.

11. Cause is a word Friedman largely avoids, but he does talk about 'antecedent circumstances', 'direction of influence', and consequences (e.g. 1963a, pp. 686–7). This comes very close to what is normally understood by causal analysis.

12. Long-term empirical relations are, of course, the subject of *Monetary Trends*.

13. The 1920 episode is in any event less telling, as the authors implicitly acknowledge, because 'price and output movements of the post-World War I years in this country were, of course, part of a worldwide movement' (*ibid.*, p. 236) and because 'the business cycle from 1919 to 1921 was the first real trial of the new system of monetary control introduced by the Federal Reserve Act' (*ibid.*, p. 529). Apart from this, Friedman and Schwartz note that 'in economic aspects, the years 1937–8 are strikingly reminiscent of 1920–1' (*ibid.*, p. 529), and they draw parallels too in terms of the Fed's behavior. Together these considerations suggest that any lesson of the earlier experience can be subsumed under the later episode.

The October 1931 episode, for its part, has become inextricably bound up with the larger question of what precipitated the events of 1929–33. In this enlarged context, and from an IS-LM standpoint, the events of 1929–33 pose problems for the monetary interpretation. Active changes in the deposit-to-currency ratio were occurring and real balances increased; a striking decline in velocity took place; and interest rates behaved perversely, in that they did not rise in response to a negative monetary shock. All of these things require separate explanation before the main work can begin. It might be thought that more complex and adverse evidence would better test the ingenuity of proponents of the primacy of money, but there is a real danger too that we will become distracted by the larger events surrounding the increase in discount rate. For recent discussion of the events of 1929–33, see papers by Schwartz, Temin, and others in Brunner, (1981).

14. It may be objected that this is a happy result for Friedman since a monetary authority operating by rule rather than discretion is likely to save us from those forms of implicit taxation – loss of wealth, lowered real wages, higher tax bills imposed when we are pushed into higher tax brackets – often associated with inflation. At the same time, he has complained that it is not

knowledge of the dynamics that is lacking, but the political will to apply a steady hand (1975*a*, p. 178).

15. Keynes himself implied that short-term expectations (those relating to the intensity with which existing capacity is utilized) may be thought of as a continuous time-moving average. To isolate and reformulate them separately at any time is not only complicated but largely unnecessary, since entrepreneurs in practice proceed as if the immediate future will be like the immediate past. See *General Theory, Collected Writings* vol. VII (1973), pp. 50–1. An excellent account of the respective roles of short- versus long-term expectations in Keynes' thought is given by Darity and Horn (1988).

16. The metaphor is taken from J. T. Wisdom, 1944/45, p. 203.

PART III

PREDICTION AND POLITICAL ECONOMY

11 • FRIEDMAN'S PREDICTIONS

' ... WHETHER IT WORKS ...'

Prediction, we need hardly remind the reader, is for Friedman 'the true test' (1968*b*, p. 15) or 'the only relevant test' of a hypothesis (1953*d* in 1953*e*, p. 8), as he variously describes it. We have looked at Friedman's positive economics, which involves internal applications of this test. But Friedman has also made a lot of predictions on the basis of his own work, and going beyond it; many for popular consumption. Here we try to get a feel for the claims these embody and reflect on how well Friedman has followed his own precepts in this area. Firstly, however, some additional reminders, about what for him lies behind the making of a prediction.

What is needed to make a prediction

Recall, to start with, that no hypothesis can be exclusive. It is never the case that 'a single possibility alone [is] capable of being consistent with the finite evidence' (1953*d* in 1953*e*, p. 10). Predictive tests therefore determine only that a theory yields predictions that are 'good enough', or that are 'better than predictions from alternative theories' (*ibid.*, p. 41). The latter criterion is clear, but what is 'good enough'? The more complete phrase from which we abstracted it is: 'good enough *for the purpose in hand*' (emphasis added).

This qualification is crucial. It means that predictive adequacy is always conditioned by the problem to be solved. The problem, Friedman makes clear, determines two things: the class of phenomena for which the theory is supposed to offer explanations (*ibid.* p. 8; see also Chapter 3, p. 80); and whether the empirical model in which we instantiate our theory for purposes of testing is a close enough approximation to the real world (1953*d* in 1953*e*, p. 15).

Now we have introduced a distinction between theory, or hypothesis, and empirical model. It has entered into our exposition before (e.g. Chapter 10, p. 221, p. 245, n.5), but not centrally. Here, however, we must make clear just what the difference is. The distinction actually is Friedman's. He seems to separate theoretical models (e.g. perfect competition; pure monopoly), which are idealizations (*ibid.*, pp. 35–6), from some version of these which is estimable or otherwise checkable against the facts (*ibid.*, p. 24). We prefer to say theoretical models and empirical models. What links the two? In the first place, theoretical models contain theoretical terms, which are unobservable. These need to be related to something measurable. A second connection that has to be clarified results from the fact that theoretical models are idealizations. The set of real-world circumstances that will count as a relevant test case for the theory needs to be defined (*ibid.*, p. 24) – for each problem to be resolved. We might note parenthetically that in handling theoretical models themselves we may engage in both tautological manipulation (the 'language' or logical function of theory) and the generation of 'substantive hypotheses' (*ibid.*, p. 7). Friedman himself stresses the latter, as we have repeatedly had occasion to point out. This distinction is not the same as the theoretical-empirical model distinction and we shall say no more about it in this chapter.

The two sorts of links that must be forged between theoretical and empirical models may be thought of as 'rules' (*ibid.*, p. 24). This is Friedman's own term, borrowed from the Positivists. It suggests bridge principles or correspondence rules, but for Friedman there is also an essentially tacit component involved. One learns how to make 'right' judgments about what to include and what to neglect, in trying to solve actual problems, and under the 'right' influence from mentors (*ibid.*, p. 25). Be that as it may, the links constitute conditions that must be specified as part of the formulation of any empirical implication or prediction. The 'specification' – econometrician's language – Friedman insists, is not separable from the testable hypothesis, but integral to its statement (*ibid.*, p. 18).

Some difficulties

Two key difficulties now confront us in assessing Friedman's predictions. First, if the testable hypothesis is a closely conditioned proposition (conditioned on the 'specification' – what we might think of as auxiliary hypotheses, but inevitably involving choice of functional form, approximation, estimation technique and so on), what is 'the true test' testing? Clearly we have here some mixture of theoretical proposition(s) and test conditions that are jointly subjected to testing. This is the Duhem–Quine problem of old. One implication is that even an untoward outcome does not directly challenge the theory. The only way to be serious about using the predictive test is to spell out all the shifts and transformations that must be made between theoretical and empirical model and examine each in turn.

Second, however, if some of these cannot be stated – they are part of the internalized judgments of a school of researchers – we cannot lay them out for such examination.

This rather removes Friedman's predictions from the possibility of proper assessment. That is bad enough for economic science, but there is an added problem in Friedman's case. Like a good Marshallian or Deweyan, Friedman wants his predictions to be useful to policy makers. The policy maker probably has a preference for simple, unconditioned predictions, since these (provided they are well tested) are of the sort that can be turned into a rule, and one does not have to engage in a painstaking examination of each case that comes up. To some extent, too, the policy maker is influenced by the state of opinion. Shaping the public debate involves quite open efforts to persuade; moreover, the public at large possibly does not want and certainly is not fully able to assess the appropriately qualified predictions that an academic audience requires. Friedman has engaged energetically in persuasive writing for a non-academic public; and many, perhaps most, of his predictions are made in that context and bear the marks just identified.

In what follows we shall look at a selection of Friedman's predictions, drawn from his columns in *Newsweek* (citing those reprinted as *An Economist's Protest*, 1972*a*, and *There's No Such Thing as a Free Lunch*, 1975*c*). We shall try to sort out the 'specification' involved and ultimately to answer the questions whether Friedman did all that might reasonably be expected to make his predictions testable and to make the test conditions apparent to his readers.

A SAMPLE OF FRIEDMAN'S PREDICTIONS

We may distinguish various forms of statement made by Friedman, all of which might be associated with prediction. Here are some sample types, drawn from his early columns in *Newsweek*:

1. 'The most likely pattern for the year [ahead, 1970] is a mild recession ...' (1972*a*, xiii).
2. 'Inflation is always and everywhere a monetary phenomenon' (*ibid.*, p. 29).
3. 'Changes in monetary growth affect the economy only slowly – it may be six or twelve or eighteen months or even more before their effects are manifest' (*ibid.*, p. 42).

4. ' ... a system of floating exchange rates would eliminate the balance-of-payments problem ...' (*ibid.*, p. 95).
5. 'The result [of a 1966 increase in the minimum wage] will be and must be to add to the ranks of the unemployed' (*ibid.*, p. 144).

We can characterize these selections readily enough. The first is a typical conditional prediction. The only problem with it is that the model used to make the predictions, including the initial conditions assumed and the elements in the inevitable *ceteris paribus* (or 'specification') pound, remains largely in Friedman's head. That is a little unfair, however. The prediction comes in answer to an interviewer's question; and in other answers, and taking the interview as a whole, it must be said that Friedman spells out a whole lot of the background knowledge and 'other things equal' kinds of conditions (auxiliary hypotheses) that he wishes to invoke. The whole text in which this prediction is embedded therefore clearly is crucial to understanding it.

Statement 2 may be read in two ways. It might be meant as a statement of logical necessity, namely, that a general price rise cannot be sustained unless monetary conditions enable it. Alternatively, it might be read as an historical generalization. There is some evidence to support both interpretations.

In 'What price guideposts?' (1966*b*), predating by four years the *Newsweek* piece from which we have quoted, we find the same assertion made; and in the former article Friedman makes a case for both interpretations. On the one hand, wage increases can create 'at most a temporary general price rise, accompanied by unemployment', *unless* accompanied by a monetary expansion (1966*b*, p. 101). This is an argument that draws on the nature of the price system and its presumed tendency, via price-induced substitution, to shift demand away from higher-priced products. On the other hand, Friedman says that the assertion (2) above, 'is not an arithmetical proposition or a truism, and it does not require a rigid relation between the rates of rise in prices and in the quantity of money ... The monetary character of inflation ... is an empirical generalization ...' (*ibid.*, p. 98). This too is the way the assertion is presented in the *Newsweek* piece.

Probably, then, we are meant to understand the assertion as Friedman's summing up of the historical record, with added plausibility from an appeal to the underlying forces of the market. That appeal, however, is one which, as we have seen in our discussion of his arguments for the maximization postulate in 'Positive economics', Friedman does not attempt to bolster with evidence.

The third statement may be thought of as picking up on the idea just encountered, that no rigid relation between money and prices is deemed by Friedman to be an essential part of his overall statement. The statement itself simply alludes to some of the test conditions involved in assessing typically monetarist sorts of predictions. The conditions seem to be very loose indeed, and their looseness effectively removes such predictions from the realm of the refutable.

But what, then, is their status? Basically, they are statements of conviction about the importance of money, reflecting past experience, investigated in two ways: by the analysis of crucial historical episodes; and by tests of the comparative efficacy and reliability of monetary impulses versus autonomous spending multipliers. We have looked at these forms of investigation in Chapters 9 and 10. The point to be made here is that it looks as if much of what passes as forecasting or predictive assertion in Friedman's work cannot be properly understood apart from his methods of investigating the significance of money. The history, as he sees it, establishes a strong presumption for a lot of background knowledge, on which predictions might be based; and at the same time, it throws up a wide variety of circumstances to help test whether money really remains a fairly constant influence.

Statements 4 and 5 are similar to 2, in that their validity rests on the operation of the price system. They may be read as inferences about what we may expect from a well-functioning market system, in the ideal case; that is, excepting interferences. There was very limited evidence to support (4) − the effects of moving to flexible exchange rates − at the time it was made (15 May 1967), though crude evidence is usually adduced by Friedman when he talks about the impact of increased minimum wages (see, for example, 1972b, p. 145 and 1975c, pp. 6−8).[1] In a quite distinct context, Friedman once wrote:

> It is important to distinguish between the logical implications of a theory and the statements about observable phenomena that a professed adherent of the theory may make. As Keynes says, 'We can keep "at the back of our heads" the necessary reserves and qualifications and the adjustments which we shall have to make later on' (1974b, p. 143).

These two statements − 4 and 5 − blur the distinction quite blatantly; and presumably Friedman sees it as the responsibility of his audience to do the necessary keeping 'at the back of ... [their] heads'.

To sum up what can be learned by looking at the sorts of forecast-related propositions Friedman makes: clearly the underlying paradigm (agents optimize; markets work) is important, as is his reading of the historical record on the subject at issue; and equally crucial is that the reader is expected to be actively and intelligently involved, knowing enough to introduce the necessary reserves and qualifications. It is worth driving these lessons home by looking in somewhat closer detail at

Friedman's monetarist predictions, since that is the area in which his statements have created the most reaction.

FRIEDMAN'S MONETARIST PREDICTIONS

We deliberately ignore the numerous bits and pieces of monetarist forecasting in which Friedman has engaged over the years, in order to concentrate on just two 'episodes' of assertion or prediction that capture the thrust of his monetarism but at the same time lend themselves to more detailed analysis. The importance of this analysis will become clear as we proceed.

The two 'episodes' are a *Newsweek* article, 'Higher Taxes? No' (23 January 1967; in 1972*a*, pp. 69–70), and the extended exchanges it spawned between Friedman and Tobin; and the series of apparent setbacks to monetarist doctrine in the period 1981–6, when the links between money growth and GNP, and money growth and inflation, appeared to the press and to some non-monetarist observers to have broken down. The first episode involved a *denial* that fiscal policy is 'a sensitive and powerful device to control the short-run course of income and prices' (1972*a*, p. 70). The second involves a period (from October 1979) during which the Federal Reserve System proclaimed itself – albeit in an on-and-off way – to be attempting to follow monetary targets, but when financial deregulation raised questions about using M1 as *the* monetary aggregate on which to target;[2] and when velocity suddenly stopped rising steadily and reversed its direction, and also behaved with unusual volatility. Here was a period that, superficially at least, could hardly have been better designed as a test period for monetarism: the monetary authority embraced the doctrine, yet changes in circumstances threatened to undermine the predictive value of monetary growth figures.

Fiscal policy is unlikely to matter

In *Newsweek* for 23 January 1967, Friedman questioned 'whether higher taxes would necessarily be contractionary' (1972*a*, p. 68). His position was that 'To have a significant impact on the economy, a tax increase must somehow affect monetary policy – the quantity of money and its rate of growth' (*ibid.*, p. 70). James Tobin, in a criticism of Friedman's later *Theoretical Framework for Monetary Analysis*, challenged this view. Tobin set out a number of what he called 'characteristic monetarist propositions', translated into IS-LM terms. One of these reads: 'in particular, a shift in the IS locus, whether due to fiscal policy or to exogenous change in consumption and investment behavior, cannot alter Y [real income]' (Tobin in Friedman, 1974*b*, pp. 77–8). In a subsequent paper, by Tobin and Willem Buiter (in Stein, 1976), this was combined with another of the 'characteristic propositions': 'if Y is supply-determined, the M/p is determined and both the price level p and money income pY are proportionate to M' (Friedman, 1974*b*, p. 78). The combined proposition read: ' ... pure fiscal policy does not matter for aggregate real demand, nominal income, and the price level' (Stein, 1976, p. 273).

Friedman took exception to Tobin's 'characteristic propositions' (1974*b*, p. 138) and refers the reader (p. 138, n. 5) to his *Counter-Revolution in Monetary Theory* (1970*a*, pp. 22–6), where his own 'key propositions of monetarism' are stated in full. Friedman nonetheless takes up a variant of the Tobin propositions cited above, discussing at length, and in an IS-LM framework (for ease of communication), what he calls 'a truly characteristic monetarist proposition', the prediction that a tax increase is unlikely to have a braking effect (1974*b*, p. 139). In other words, he gives us an IS-LM translation of his *Newsweek* article. (The discussion is to be found in 'Comments on the critics' (of his 'Theoretical framework for monetary analysis'), in Friedman, 1974*b*, pp. 139–42; and in his comments on Tobin and Buiter in Stein, 1976, pp. 312–14).

Here is Friedman's analysis, paraphrased and stated as briefly as possible. First he presents the case *for* a tax increase having a braking effect.

Postulate: an increase in tax receipts.

By way of auxiliary assumptions, add the following:

1. money and the growth rate of money are unchanged;
2. government spending is unchanged;
3. there are no price level changes;
4. previous lenders to the government do not in their role as taxpayers spend what the government no longer borrows;
5. previous lenders to the government do not lend to businesses or individuals at a lower interest rate.

Then, after the tax increase there will be a shift leftward in the IS schedule, interest rates will be lowered and so too will real income (see Figure 11.1). In this 'strong' result, clearly there *is* a braking effect of the tax increase.

Friedman next assumes, alternatively, that auxiliary assumptions 4 and 5 are reversed, so that private spending offsets the decrease in government borrowing (no net shift in IS). There is still a possibility that a net spending decrease will occur, since while lower interest rates prevail more cash will be held. Moreover, people take time to adjust their own spending to a reduction in government borrowing.

According to Friedman, however, these net effects on spending will be

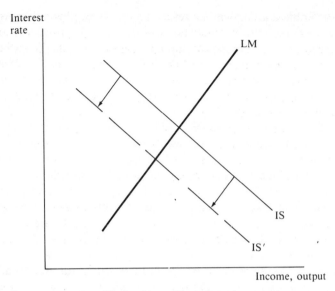

Figure 11.1 Possible braking effect of tax increase

'temporary' and, in all likelihood, 'minor'. Why? Temporary, because
the possible decrease in spending is a one-time thing. As the monetarist
sees it, at a lower interest rate velocity will be reduced. During the
transition to lower velocity, spending will be reduced for a given money
supply; but once the new, lower velocity is reached this effect will cease.
Minor, because the lower interest rate induces not just investment,
defined as plant and equipment, buildings and inventories, but a shift
into other assets, including money, and extending also to inventories of
clothing, consumer durables and perhaps even to the acquisition of skills
(cf. Friedman, 1969c, p. 231). Any and all such purchases will weaken
the net reduction in real income reflecting a change in velocity.

We are still assuming that the price level is unaffected (auxiliary
assumption 3 above). But should it fall, the LM schedule would shift to
the right and real income thereby *increase*.

So far, then, there is little ground for thinking that real income would
fall because of the tax increase. This, presumably, is a prediction 'good
enough for the purpose in hand'.

Friedman however, is interested mainly in 'the effect of nominal
magnitudes on nominal and real magnitudes' (1974b, p. 138), so he
introduces, finally, a combined case, involving both tax increases *and*
money supply changes, to demonstrate the superior potency of money.
This analysis is to issue in a prediction presumably 'better than' the
predictions yielded by fiscalists (Keynesians). If the government borrow-

ing, now replaced by higher tax revenues, had been financed previously through money creation, then the now-reduced borrowing allows a reduction to occur in the money supply. LM therefore shifts to the left. But this effect is ongoing, year after year, for every year that there is a reduced need for money creation. Hence the IS shift, which it has already been determined is likely to be temporary and minor, is swamped by the monetary effect (*ibid.*, p. 141). If, in addition, the price level falls with the money supply, then real income might actually increase, though *nominal* income would be lower.

If one assumes instead that the government's previous borrowing requirement had been met by bond issues, rather than money creation, Friedman still doubts whether there would be any significant net spending decrease; for privately issued bonds would now be held in place of Treasury issue. Moreover, there would be expectations of a lower future tax liability (hence of more disposable income) and an increase in private productive assets.

Now let us take stock of exactly what Friedman is claiming in all this. He deliberately uses a common language – IS-LM – to stress that the differences between him and neo-Keynesians such as Tobin are not as much analytical as had often been thought. Certain differences remain: how narrowly one interprets 'investment', for example (1974*b*, p. 140); the distinction between money and credit; whether one believes stock-flow relations (e.g. money and income) to be more reliable than flow-flow relations (such as embodied in Keynesian multipliers); whether one believes that relative price effects dominate wealth effects (see the list in Stein, 1976, pp. 316–17). These are not to be minimized; and they will be reflected in different theories. But what Friedman maintains, over and over, throughout this discussion, is that these are matters for empirical judgment. In some instances they start out as empirical 'presumptions' (*ibid.*, p. 315); but in every case they are open to empirical check, in the sense that the consequences to which they lead may be examined.

Thus, while Friedman acknowledges that words like 'temporary' and 'minor' are 'highly imprecise' (1974*b*, p. 141), he also claims that they are not hedges to take monetarist predictions out of the realm of the refutable (as Tobin and Buiter at one point suggested). Rather, such terms highlight the fact that the issues are not theoretical in some inexorable way; they *are empirical*: 'what we really differ on are precisely what effects are and are not "minor", not on whether an effect is precisely zero [as an *analysis* which postulates a precisely vertical LM curve would require]' (Stein, 1976, p. 312).

But what is the relation of all this to prediction? Friedman set out only to put doubt in the minds of those who were convinced in early 1967 that a tax surcharge would necessarily contain inflationary pressures. He did not set out to make a prediction. His subsequent analysis led him to suggest that a surcharge would be unlikely to have a strong braking effect; and he went on to assert that monetary effects might well dominate fiscal effects should they occur together in the circumstances under which the surcharge was introduced – were it to be introduced. In 1967 any analysis was necessarily counterfactual; the surcharge finally was imposed only in 1968. Friedman found himself making a prediction by default as it were. In the process of countering distorted depictions of monetarist predictions, given later by Tobin and by Tobin and Buiter, Friedman ended up leaving the impression that his original 1967 *Newsweek* statement was also a prediction, in this instance one of fiscal impotence.

It is necessary to put the record straight on that point, because in the process of answering Tobin, and Tobin and Buiter, Friedman ended up engaging in a theory-as-language discussion of hypothetical possibilities scarcely distinguishable from the Lange approach that he had so roundly attacked in the 1940s. To make predictions, recall, three things are important in the approach of the Marshallian positive economist: a detailed knowledge of empirical regularities; a model to help separate out relevant from irrelevant factors in the problem situation presenting itself; and a close discussion of the circumstances of the time, to ascertain whether these match the conditions of the model and of past experience. There was a good deal of prior experience with tax rate changes; so the first of these conditions could have been met, though Friedman did not in fact invoke this experience. On the other hand, the surcharge had not been imposed but was merely being discussed when he first addressed the matter; so the third condition was an empty box. This also rendered past experience directly useful only for constructing a relevant model. All that remained then was to discuss the model (hypothetical) possibilities.

This is not unimportant, however; for we got into this examination of Friedman's monetarist predictions in order to see more clearly the role of 'specification', or how the conditioned hypothesis looks when the conditions themselves are separated out. And Friedman's analysis does at least bring the conditions into sharp relief. In this context, two further points may be made.

First, it remains curious that Friedman allowed himself to be drawn into debate with Tobin, in effect allowing his initial query about the efficacy of a specific fiscal action to be turned into a monetarist assertion about the relative impotence of fiscal policy in general. Friedman no doubt felt confident about the monetary side of the equation, monetarist predictions being based on extensive work in all three of the stages prior to prediction which were just listed above. Nonetheless, when the debate finally was joined, in the early seventies, the tax surcharge had been put in place, and later suspended, and Friedman could have based his discussion on the effects of that experience instead of on a more detailed analytical defense of his original scepticism. That he did not do so is disappointing in the same way and for the same reasons as his not returning to his predictions about flexible exchange rates and minimum wage increases once considerable evidence had been garnered.[3]

Second, our purpose here being to see what gets packed into the 'specification', it is startling to realize just what an amount of convoluted analysis was necessary in this instance for Friedman to clarify exactly what underlay his original apparently simple and straightforward *Newsweek* comments. Can readers of that sort of commentary really be expected to intuit all of this and keep it at the back of their heads? Even if one argues that comment by an authority in *Newsweek* is to be taken on faith, the very notion of 'an authority' implies that it is not mere personal opinion that is offered but something carrying the stamp of a scientific consensus. We expect of 'experts' entering a controversial opinion to indicate that it is disputed and to give an idea as to the grounds for the differences in judgment that are possible.

Monetarism has failed?

We turn to the second episode, involving popular perceptions that in the early eighties monetarism had been exposed by events as a predictive failure.

The events are basically two: an apparent break in the money growth/inflation link between 1982 and 1986; and sharp changes in the magnitude and direction of trend in velocity from early 1981. Numerous factors have been suggested to explain these breaks, ranging from a strengthening of the dollar to changes in the components of the M1 monetary aggregate following financial deregulation. While the events are still imperfectly understood, it is clear that changes in velocity must be involved in both, hence some discussion of those changes is offered here, though the discussion is offered by way of background only and without any pretense at completeness even in that limited area. The details of the alleged breakdown are captured sufficiently for our purposes in Figures 11.2 and 11.3, below.

Financial deregulation in the US has been embodied in two pieces of legislation, the Depository Institutions Deregulation and Monetary Control Act of 1980, and the Garn–St Germain Depository Institutions Act of 1982. These Acts legalized changes in the way thrift institutions did business, permitting altered types of lending and asset holding, as well as allowing all depository institutions to offer Negotiable Orders of Withdrawal (NOW). The former Act also modified interest rate ceilings

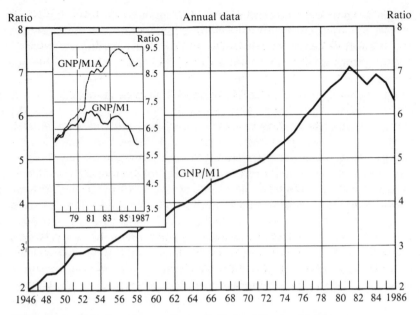

Figure 11.2 Velocity (*Source*: St Louis Federal Reserve Bank)

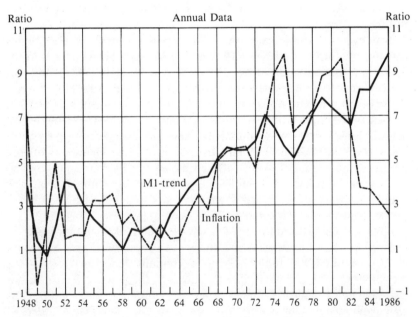

Figure 11.3 Inflation and M1-trend growth (*Source*: St Louis Federal Reserve Bank)

and established the Depository Institutions Deregulation Committee to oversee the phasing out of such ceilings altogether.

From our perspective what matters is that, with the inclusion of interest-bearing NOW and Super-NOW accounts and with savings subject to automatic transfer within M1, this narrow money aggregate came to include a savings component. This had possible consequences for the GNP/M1 relationship (velocity) and the M1/inflation relationship. Thus a given M1 may represent different amounts of 'transactions' money. Changes in the 'savings' portion of M1 might be expected to have a looser connection to prices and output than the strictly 'transactions' portion, hence the links between overall M1 and inflation or GNP might be expected to be modified. Moreover, as happened immediately after the introduction of NOWs (in the first quarter of 1981), there may be periods of rapid upward movement in the velocity measure using currency and non-interest bearing checkable deposits, a movement produced by a shift into NOW accounts. (The inset in Figure 11.2, showing a divergence in the path of M1A and M1 velocities – M1A measures currency and non-interest bearing deposits – captures this effect.)

The interest-sensitivity of the new M1 is also at issue here. Since interest is an opportunity cost of holding money, the interest-sensitivity of the new M1 might be expected to be greater than before. A decline in interest rates, for example, as occurred from 1981 onwards in a trend sense, should have induced more cash holding than when no interest was paid on M1 components, causing a rise in M1 relative to GNP, and a decline in velocity, relative to the situation before deregulation. Note, however, that this effect is uncertain. It was to be expected just after the introduction of NOW accounts, but as NOW accounts moved towards being subject to no interest rate ceilings (over a six-year transition period ending in 1986), the interest-sensitivity of NOW accounts should in principle have decreased. Experience with NOW accounts during our 'episode' was simply too new to say with certainty exactly what their impact on velocity was at the time.

Other factors, too, were involved. Studies have shown that GNP is not a good proxy for total transactions when its growth is strongly affected by inventories and exports, as happened in the early 1980s; but since swings in these elements – exports and inventories, though also in interest rates – are themselves not easily predicted, the negative conclusion from such inquiries was that velocity itself can at best be explained *ex post*. An additional distressing conclusion is that efforts to account for the error in reduced form equations explaining velocity, even after allowing for changes within M1, suggest that there may have been a basic change in the cyclical behavior of velocity. To date no convincing accounts of this apparent shift have been offered.[4]

The changes captured in Figures 11.2 and 11.3 were taken by many to be evidence that monetarism had lost its predictive power.[5]

How did Friedman react? Remarkably *unlike* a monetarist whose predictions had been upset. Not only was he not upset by predictive failure, but he seemed to think that the failure strengthened his position. How is that? Whereas monetarism has been widely interpreted as a new kind of policy activism, Friedman is repeatedly and consistently to be found making the point that we cannot make accurate predictions about the relationship between money and inflation or GNP, and that *therefore* policy activism by the monetary authorities is inappropriate. His monetarism is a combination of two opposite elements. On the one hand, there *is* a relationship between money and nominal GNP – 'substantial' changes in the one are 'almost invariably followed' sooner or later by changes in the other.[6] This must be accepted as a sort of 'environment' constraint on the practice of monetary policy. On the other hand, the short-run ability of the authorities to control the monetary aggregates is uncertain,[7] and the relationship between money and output or prices involves lags that are not only 'highly variable',[8] but reflect 'many forces other than monetary growth'.[9] As a result, Friedman's 'monetarist' message is simply this: 'We still have nothing like the knowledge of short-term relations that would be necessary to use monetary policy for fine tuning the economy'.[10] Or, as he put it back in 1969: 'I believe monetary policy is being oversold; I believe fiscal policy is being oversold. What I believe is that fine tuning has been oversold'.[11]

When it comes down to specifics, Friedman sometimes displays a confidence that masks the complexity of the problem of interpretation. Thus, on the 9 per cent decline in velocity relative to trend from the first quarter of 1981 through the second quarter of 1983, he simply denies that this is 'out of line' with experience or that the change reflects 'an erratic shift in the demand for money'. On the other hand, the decline 'is readily accounted for' by a systematic cyclical pattern of movement – that is, by stage-of-cycle effects – by interest rate changes, and by increased economic instability (hence uncertainty), *together* with 'of course, pure random variability'.[12] He would be the first to admit that there may be many alternative explanations that also suffice to account for the same facts; but presumably here he does not find them as plausible as his own. However, that may be, *ex post* sufficiency explanations do not constitute grounds for predicting with confidence, which, nonetheless, is just what Friedman proceeds to do. 'This analysis suggests that there is no reason to expect any further decline in leading velocity [measuring current GNP against a two-quarter lag in M1] unless there is a further sharp decline in interest rates. On the contrary, leading velocity can be expected to rise, following its usual cyclical pattern during an expansion'.[13] It did!

In instances such as this, it seems reasonable to expect the reader to understand that confident assertion should not be mistaken for a claim to foreknowledge. The tone is merely part of the effort to persuade.

The reader's scepticism, however, might be heightened when it is realized that the basic or underlying or constraining relationships in which Friedman puts so much trust are just so many 'prepared descriptions'.[14] Thus:

> During the past century, major changes have occurred in financial institutions, the role of government, the structure of the economy, the distribution of the people among occupations, the flows of international trade, and so on. Yet these charts demonstrate that no *appreciable* change has occurred in the relation between the quantity of money and the level of prices.[15] [Italics added.]

Much clearly depends upon what is meant by 'appreciable'. The relationship itself, however, is presented in several different forms in Friedman's writings, each leaving a distinct impression but none amounting to demonstration. He plumps repeatedly for an average inflation lag of two years; yet his graphical presentations vary in the other 'preparations' that lie behind the numbers shown. At times he shows M2 against the Consumer Price Index, with a two-year lag (*Newsweek*, 15 June 1981). At times, it is M1 against the GNP deflator (*ibid.*, 25 July 1983, using data covering roughly the same stretch of time). For a period stretching back prior to the First World War, the monetary measure used by Friedman and Schwartz in their *Monetary History* (broader than M1 but narrower than M2) is used, for historical consistency; but the money aggregate is divided by real GNP and compared with the GNP deflator. For long series, annual data are used, apparently without lags, and presented as percentage deviations from a period average (a century or a quarter century) (*Wall Street Journal*, 12 February 1987). For shorter periods, we may find M2 per unit of output against a concurrent price index, but with GNP lagging money by two quarters (*Newsweek*, 24 June 1974, in 1975c, p. 114). The closeness of fit is not at all the same in each of these representations.

One way to read these different prepared descriptions is that they all display the basic relationship, and that this fact alone − constancy in the face of numerous changes in definition or measurement − is further evidence for the existence of the supposed causal connection. That is clearly Friedman's view. For the very same reason, however, they all depend for their (monetarist) interpretation on the independent establishment of the causal primacy of money. Friedman, we have seen, is quite aware that covariation, and even timing, is not conclusive evidence for causation (see especially 1963b and his reply to Tobin, 1970d); and that he looks to the careful analysis of specific historical instances −

'crucial' episodes – to supply the needed evidence. All of that work must be taken as having been done, and as lying behind the simple connections he draws in his articles for the popular press. Yet at best it is misleading to suggest that varying visual impressions all amount to the same thing, and that they add up to demonstration. At worst it destroys confidence. As Hendry and Ericsson have put it: Friedman and Schwartz (in their *Monetary Trends*) make claims 'based on inferences from their statistical analyses' – claims about the exogeneity of money, the constancy over time of parameters in the money demand function, about the relative unimportance or interdependence of variables in using regression techniques, and about the appropriateness of their phase-averaging procedures for isolating long-run behavior – yet they do not actually present tests of the validity of these claims. As a result their work has the flavor of assertion without empirical basis. [16]

SUMMARY AND CONCLUSION

Summary

What are we to make of all this? It seems that in his popular writings – the ones in which we also encounter predictions – Friedman overstates his claim for the empirical evidence, stretching it to suggest unique causation, which elsewhere he denies is possible. Moreover, we encounter confident predictions, even adamant assertions of what *will* occur. On both counts one might want to complain.

Furthermore, Friedman's response to outcomes which go against his basic positions – we have in mind his monetarist views – is troubling. His views clearly include (a) a conviction that monetary effects dominate fiscal (or autonomous spending) effects; also (b) evidence that the monetary connection itself holds, though only given an allowance for considerable potential variation in time lags and in velocity itself. Given (b) the only evidence that would really upset Friedman is something that could be read as showing that the fiscal effects outweigh monetary effects. Even then, however, he might fall back on the claim that in the long run his framework is more useful for analysis, allowing as it does for both fiscal and monetary mechanisms but also generating more empirically testable implications than fiscalist approaches. Without assessing that claim, a question arises whether, if the connection between money and nominal income is as imprecise as it seems to be (on his own acknowledgement), Friedman should be predicting at all, let alone predicting with such confidence. For practical purposes we need to be able to measure all givens, whether functions (demand for money) or parameters, and to say whether their 'givenness' is something we may rely on. Friedman does not claim that we can do either. We are brought back to a point made earlier: if one actually wants a minimum of intervention then one does not need to forecast. Minimal intervention is what Friedman advocates (see Chapter 12, below). Hence he might actually draw strength both from disabling variability and from actual predictive failure.

Finally, this interpretation probably fits to some extent the whole range of his predictions, and certainly applies to the sample we looked at earlier in this chapter. They should all be read with an appreciation for the background: and 'problem context' here surely must incorporate policy as well as the narrowly analytical. Thus attention to audience, the state of opinion, and rhetorical devices, is essential to a proper grasp of what is being said. Knowing that this is so can only enrich the reading. It also means that simplistic dismissals of Friedman's predictions on the ground that many have 'failed' (e.g. Brady, 1986) miss the point. At the same time, popular commentary most requires, yet also generally neglects, to alert the reader to just these things; and Friedman's popular commentaries are no exception.

Conclusion: Predictions and the methodology of positive economics

One would expect a pragmatist economist to make predictions as part of his work in positive economics. For practical purposes predictions *have* to be made in social life. Moreover, since prediction is the ultimate test, we would *not* expect this aspect of the work to be neglected. In addition, being wrong in making predictions is a learning experience for the pragmatist and therefore cannot legitimately be avoided. Thus, while the methodological purist might look askance at getting his hands dirty by going into the real world where predictions are made, the pragmatist economist would have no such scruples, even as economic scientist.[17]

Yet we have encountered difficulties in reconciling Friedman's ideas on the methodology of positive economics and *his* predictive activity. First, as noted, we would expect a positive economist to use prediction as a test of his *own* research work. Friedman does this, but he also goes beyond the area of his own research interest, and where he does so, he not infrequently argues on the basis of the 'realism' (plausibility) of assumptions. Second, even in the areas of his major research concerns the predictions he makes are often of a sort that one would not expect knowing the results of his work. For his research suggests that we do not have the knowledge to make very detailed or accurate predictions. For Friedman there is no basis in what we know for trying to achieve precise objectives like perfect stability or something close to it; the best we can do is to adopt very broad and simple policies – such as a money growth rule – which might avoid the worst experiences of the past. But these views suggest almost the opposite of the kind of predictions that Friedman has often made.

Friedman's attitude to untoward outcomes has also been disconcerting to opponents and sympathizers alike. In effect, he makes confident predictions yet argues at the same time that bad results are just what we should expect, given the state of our knowledge. This has made his work difficult to assess, leading some, among them a natural ally like Harry Johnson, to accuse Friedman of breaking the rules. In Johnson's words (1976):

> He has frequently trapped and sandbagged critics of reputation and integrity by the techniques of underdisclosure of analysis and evidence and apparent overstatements of the strength of his results.

Under the circumstances it is perhaps understandable that the real and important distinction in Friedman's claim that he is a Marshallian and his adversaries Walrasians, has largely been lost on an audience confused by the sort of thing Johnson complains of. That distinction is not important to the average reader of *Newsweek* or the *Wall Street Journal*, but Friedman's frustrating blend of stridency and reticence affects his readers negatively at every level.

One related observation is in order. Friedman's behavior as predictor is an instance where we see a difference between what he said as methodologist and what he did. We have been bothered throughout by Friedman's non-evidential defense of the maximization-of-returns hypothesis (above, Chapter 4, pp. 95–9). Yet another area in which the divergence appears is in his work as political economist, to which we turn next.

NOTES

1. A lot more evidence has accumulated on both questions, and it might be instructive to see Friedman assess his original statements in the light of it. See Williamson (1985), Chapter 2 and Obstfeld (1985) on exchange rates; Welch (1978) and Parsons (1987, vol. 3, pp. 476–8) on minimum wages.
2. M1 in the United States is the money supply narrowly defined. Prior to financial deregulation it comprised notes and coin in circulation plus demand (or checking) deposits. After deregulation it came to include certain interest-bearing forms of account, thought to reflect not just decisions to hold cash, but to save (see p. 263 of the text for details). M1 is defined somewhat differently in other countries but is everywhere the narrowest measure among the monetary aggregates in use. Friedman himself has always favored a broader aggregate *for research purposes*, because he is able to obtain a longer series.

3. There is a certain amount of this done in the second edition of *An Economist's Protest*, mostly in the sections on monetary policy and wage and price controls, and mostly not very destructive.

4. See on all of this Wenninger (1984), Radecki and Wenninger (1985), Stone and Thornton (1987) and references cited in all three articles.

5. See, for example, 'The monetarists scramble to explain low inflation', *Business Week*, 13 August 1984; article by Eugene A. Birnbaum and Philip Braverman, *Wall Street Journal*, 23 July 1981; 'Monetarism' (a three-part series), *The Economist*, 27 April, 4 May, 18 May 1985.

6. 'The Fed hasn't changed its ways', *Wall Street Journal*, 20 August 1985; cf. 'Money and inflation', *Newsweek*, 26 May 1969, in 1972*a*, pp. 50–1.

7. 'A memorandum to the Fed', *Wall Street Journal*, 30 January 1981.

8. 'A case of bad good news', *Newsweek*, 26 September 1983; 'M1's hot streak gave Keynesians a bad idea', *Wall Street Journal*, 18 September 1986.

9. *Wall Street Journal*, 20 August 1985; *ibid.*, 18 September 1986.

10. *Wall Street Journal*, 18 September 1986.

11. In *ibid.*, but citing 1969*d*, p. 47.

12. 'Why a surge of inflation is likely next year', *Wall Street Journal*, 1 September 1983.

13. *Ibid*.

14. Nancy Cartwright's expression: see her *How the Laws of Physics Lie*.

15. 'Monetary history, not dogma', *Wall Street Journal*, 12 February 1987.

16. David F. Hendry and Neil R. Ericsson, 'Assertion without empirical basis: an Econometric appraisal of *Monetary Trends in ... the United Kingdom*', Federal Reserve System, International Finance Discussion Papers, no. 270, December 1985, pp. 1, 2.

17. The physicist does not have to get into the practical arena because he can experiment. To the economist, getting proposals tried in the area of social policy, which involves making predictions on how things will turn out, is an important substitute, as Dewey saw it (see, for example, Dewey, 1931, in Ratner, 1939), and one that follows from his pragmatic orientation.

12 • THE METHODOLOGY OF POLITICAL ECONOMY

In earlier chapters we have been concerned with Friedman's views on the methodology of positive economics. In this one we turn to consider the nature of the underlying rationale of his approach to political economy as revealed in his writings. Our major objective is to try to determine how his approaches to the two disciplines relate to one another. Since this is our objective we do not consider it necessary to deal at length with the substance of Friedman's work in political economy. Our concern is not with the results arrived at but rather with the way he arrived at them. Where we consider Friedman's substantive results we do so only for the purpose of shedding light on his underlying views about the methodology of political economy.

In some respects it is even more difficult to ascertain Friedman's views about the methodology of political economy than it is of his positive economics. We say this, first, because as we will show in the beginning part of this chapter, Friedman's rejection of the appeal to the 'realism' of assumptions detaches him from the neatly worked-out framework which economists have traditionally adhered to. Second, Friedman has not written even one essay on the methodology of political economy, and he has said considerably less in his writings on this subject than he has about methodology in his work in positive economics. It is therefore not surprising that there should have been almost a total lack of critical reaction to his views in this area. The result is that we do not have the insights of others to build on here, as we do in dealing with Friedman's views about the methodology of positive economics. Third, when we try to piece together the bits and pieces of what Friedman has said or implied about his approach to political economy in various places, we find what looks like two very different views. Thus, it can be argued, as shown in the second section of this chapter, that the rationale of Friedman's approach to political economy is pragmatic, as is his approach to positive economics. But as we show in the third section, there is far more evidence that Friedman's views about the methodology of political economy are very different from those of his positive economics.

There are further difficulties. Where Friedman reveals non-pragmatic views, as he does quite often, the basis of his position is not easy to understand because his arguments are not very well worked out. Since Friedman suggests that he has been inspired by classical political economy it seemed worth while to try to read him in light of that tradition; but it turns out that this is not very helpful. On the other hand, following the lead furnished by Friedman's disclosure that in political economy he was influenced by his teacher Frank Knight turns out to be more fruitful. Both explorations are conducted in the third section. We conclude that reading Friedman within the context of Frank Knight's thinking makes the rationale of his position more comprehensible. But when we do this we run into yet another problem.

Knight rejected the kind of approach to positive economics which Friedman champions for reasons which Knight explains in great detail. It emerges that the reason Knight chooses to approach political economy the way he does is closely linked to the reason for which he *rejects* the kind of approach to positive economics for which Friedman stands. But how then could Friedman advocate the pragmatic approach to positive economics and at the same time hold Knightian methodological views about political economy? Trying to understand how Friedman could have gotten into this seemingly inconsistent position is the major challenge facing anyone who tries to explain how Friedman's methodology of positive economics and political economy fit together. We make an attempt at an explanation at the end of the chapter.

THE TRADITIONAL WAY OF THINKING

In the traditional way of thinking, the relationship between the methodology of positive economics and political economy is reasonably simple and straightforward as shown, for example, in Lionel Robbin's position. Thus Robbins tells us:

> Political Economy in my vocabulary is not scientific economics, a collection of value-free generalizations about the way in which economic systems work. It is a discussion of principles of public policy in the economic field; it also involves *assumptions* which, in the nature of things, lie outside positive science and which are essentially normative in character. (1976, pp. 3–4, emphasis added.)

Since Robbins had told us in his very well-known earlier work (1949) that the positive economist builds his theory on 'realistic' (plausible or acceptable) assumptions, it follows, as the quote shows, that to transform this work into political economy one need only add acceptable ('realistic') ethical premises. In a very broad sense the rationale of the latter is no different from that of the former. Political economy, like positive economics, develops implications from premises which are acceptable.[1] (For a more modern example of this procedure cf. Arrow, 1951.)

But what happens to the relation between positive economics and political economy if one rejects, as Friedman does, the notion that positive economics rests upon 'realistic' or acceptable premises? To our knowledge this question has not been asked. Friedman in effect gives two answers, one of which looks inconsistent with his position on the methodology of positive economics. In the last part of the chapter we consider the problems that arise because of this incompatibility.

EVIDENCE OF THE PRAGMATIC APPROACH

A suggestion in 'Positive economics' that political economy is pragmatic

In 'Positive economics' Friedman notes (1953e, p. 5):

> I venture the judgment ... that currently in the Western world, and especially in the United States, differences about economic policy among disinterested citizens derive predominantly from different predictions about the economic consequences of taking action – differences that in principle can be eliminated by the progress of positive economics – rather than from fundamental differences in basic values, differences about which men can ultimately only fight.

Were this statement to stand by itself it would be difficult to interpret.[2] But it appears in the introduction to an article which, as we have shown, reveals a way of thinking close to that of John Dewey. The rationale of Dewey's philosophy supports the spirit, if not the letter, of the quoted statement. It seems reasonable, therefore, to consider the hypothesis that Friedman's approach here too, might be similar to Dewey's. There is room in Dewey's scheme of things for political economy although its nature is as radically different from the subject as traditionally conceived as is his logic of positive economics. In fact, (pragmatic) positive economics and political economy fit very well together as we will show.

The nature of pragmatic political economy

Since political economy involves making decisions about what policies should be pursued, on the face of it it would appear that its rationale must differ in basic ways from that of positive economics since, as everyone agrees, normative conclusions cannot be derived from positive statements. But once one views this issue in a social context, where positions have to be defended – this policy is desirable *because* ... – then this difference disappears, at least partly because one way to justify one's choices is to show what the different possible consequences of alternative policies will be; and then the same logical issues confront us in political economy as in positive economics. All of this is not meant to deny that value judgments enter into the making of policy decisions. But as Dewey argues (1938, Chapter 11; 1950, Chapter 5), *all* decisions involve value judgments, including the decision of the scientist to proceed one way rather than another.[3] It does not follow from this, however, that it would be helpful to have a deductive *theory* of values interposed between the positive work and the making of judgments, such as a theory of science which lays down the law on how the 'right' evaluations should be made. One must distinguish between the need to make value judgments, and the possible helpfulness of the traditional kind of ethical theory for making them. Dewey does not deny the former; he does have doubts about the latter.

While Friedman in 'Positive economics' seems to lean heavily on the normative-positive dualism, if we were to judge from the quoted statement we would have to conclude that in his way of thinking this dichotomy is not very meaningful. As we have seen, in 'Positive economics' he seems to see little if any value in normative analysis, not only for the pure economic scientist (positive economist), but even for the political economist whose chief interest is policy. And in fact it is not too surprising to find him arguing this way because that is the way pragmatists generally do argue, as John Dewey shows. For Dewey dealing with an ethical problem involves inquiry, just as a problem in science does, and doing the kind of valuing that is involved in moving the inquiry process along is logically the same in both as well. This approach is a very unorthodox one, of course, and unless one recognizes that the very way one looks at problems is different, it is hard to understand. Dewey insists that in dealing with ethical (or policy) issues detailed observation of the specifics in particular instances is as important as it is in scientific investigation (e.g. 1938, Chapter 11; 1950, Chapter 5). How one broad value relates to another 'in general' is a matter in which he has little interest. In the Deweyan system people reveal their values in the process of choosing some consequences over others. These values evolve in the course of making such decisions and seeing their consequences. The important traditional systems of ethics have significance, according to Dewey, because they are the result of the kind of inquiry process which he champions, reflecting particular times and places in history. They are of little use as algorithms from which to derive the 'correct' value choices (see, for example, his 1950, Chapter 5).

An alternative approach

Dewey's way, of course, is not the only defensible one for approaching policy questions. One can attempt to find 'self-evident' (acceptable or plausible) propositions and from them deduce results which show that a particular policy course is consistent with them whereas others are not. Agreement can be achieved in this way if the 'self-evident' premises are evident to all individuals involved. In fact, traditional political econ- omists generally attempted to convince in this manner. Note, however, that one can reason in this way in positive (value-free) economics as well, the only difference being that in positive economics all of the 'self- evident' or acceptable truths are observations about the nature of the world (e.g. people follow their self-interest), whereas in dealing with policy questions (in normative economics) some of the 'self-evident' or acceptable truths have to do with desirable states of the world (e.g. freedom is preferable to tyranny). As we have tried to show in Part I, traditional methodologists like Mill argued this way about positive economics. Since Friedman rejects this way of reasoning for positive economics, we should not be surprised if he rejected it also for political economy. Thus, even though one cannot come to a firm conclusion about Friedman's position from the few words we have quoted from a single source, if we had only this source to go by ours would seem to be a reasonable interpretation.[4]

The relation between positive economics and political economy in the pragmatic context

What then is the difference, on the pragmatic view, between positive economics and political economy? It is one of subject matter. Economic policy actions have non-economic consequences and it is here, on this view, that political economy comes in. For example, government action in dealing with economic problems may have the effect of restricting freedom, which in turn can have a whole host of consequences, or it can have the effect of favoring some groups at the expense of others, thereby raising questions about justice, etc. Thus, on this view one cannot entirely depend for policy advice upon one who is a positive economist and nothing more, because his range of interest and knowledge will be too narrow.[5]

Does the pragmatic approach to political economy make sense?

Granted all of this, is knowledge of consequences enough to enable policy choices to be made? How is one to choose *which* consequences are desirable? Clearly we are back where we started. If there is no agreement about which consequences are desirable, we may try to determine the consequences of the consequences and hope that somewhere along the line agreement can be reached, or we may appeal to self-evident or acceptable 'truths' (values in this case). If we choose the former we are still in the area of Dewey's *Logic*, where no distinction is made between the rationale of decision-making in positive economics and in political economy. This raises the question whether if we argue on the basis of consequences we are not caught up in an infinite regress. Will not this process simply go on and on?

By way of answer we note that unless there are areas where people evaluate the specific situation in more or less the same way – e.g. reading a meter, observing what actually happens, etc. – agreement would be impossible, science would be meaningless, and all we could hope for would be to find ways of dealing with differences so that social life can go on. We do not mean to deny that there is a difference between agreeing about observations and agreeing about policy; the question is how great the difference is. If one sees this difference as being overwhelmingly large, as Frank Knight did, for example, not only does it preclude a consequential approach to political economy; it all but rules out the kind of approach to positive economics that is adopted in the physical sciences for anyone interested in policy since, on this view, even very reliable knowledge about consequences is of little use. At the same time, one need not feel that people have as much in common in evaluating what is desirable as they have in evaluating observational data to believe that the difference is not a qualitative but a quantitative one, and that the greatest hope for enlightened social policy lies in the consequential approach.[6] Friedman's statement quoted at the beginning of the chapter would seem to have behind it this belief.

The competitiveness of the two approaches

But is this Deweyan (consequential) approach to policy a more 'valid' one than its competitor, the one that involves showing the desirability of particular policies by deducing conclusions from self-evident or acceptable premises? It is not necessary for our purposes to try to answer this question generally; it is sufficient to point out that the two are not necessarily competitors. We say this, first, because there is as much need for 'language' in the field of political economy as there is in positive economics. All that is implied is that what is said is no more 'self-evident' in the former than in the latter. People are not, as is often pointed out, perfect logic machines; hence they might initially accept a policy which, once made aware of its meaning and significance, they then reject.[7]

Second, the approach which deduces conclusions about desirable policy from self-evident premises would have a greater chance of succeeding – at least in so far as it leads to agreement, if not to dealing adequately with other social problems – in a society which is strongly tradition bound and where people are likely to have a common *general* view about the ends of social existence. Of course, even in rigidly traditional societies disagreements might arise about the priority of values, if not the values themselves, and discussion then can become very involved and indeterminate. However, experience suggests that confusion can be diminished by postulating a *summum bonum*, or greatest good, so long as the movement from tradition has not proceeded too far.[8] But in the American environment, where people were forced to *create* a society, rather than just inheriting one, this type of thinking has been prevalent only among those who subsisted on an imported intellectual diet, a group well represented on the eastern seaboard of the United States.[9] The thinking of the University of Chicago group – which includes Wesley Mitchell, John Dewey and Frank Knight – in which Friedman's mature thinking seems to have had its roots, is not of this imported variety. We shall therefore say very little about it in the rest of this chapter.

What the analysis in this section shows is that for the practical purpose of achieving agreement about social policy action, whether the assumptionist or consequentialist approach is more persuasive depends upon circumstances. If the purpose is actually to come to grips with an ongoing economic problem, such as unemployment, depression, poverty, etc., the consequentialist approach would be superior *if* the discussants agreed that they would choose that policy proposal that showed the greatest promise of success when actually put into effect. But what if the discussants in this society do not generally make their policy choices on this basis? Then it might be good strategy to adopt a hybrid approach, where positive economics is used to determine possible choices, and after these are made an argument is adduced for selected policies by showing that they are consistent with values which most people could readily accept.[10] In that way agreement is reached through discussion and at the same time the best knowledge is used to actually deal with the problem.[11,12] As will be seen later in this chapter, Friedman can be interpreted (implicitly) to subscribe to some such hybrid strategy.

Strengths of the pragmatic approach

In previous chapters we showed that Dewey made a distinction between a way of thinking which appeals to plausible assumptions as a basis for theorizing and one which appeals to implications drawn from theory that is supported by what actually happens. Dewey argued for the latter because the method was self-correcting and therefore led to the accumulation of knowledge; and because this method involved itself with the details of what happens, and thus had greater potential for successfully dealing with concrete practical problems. It enabled one to see what there was actually to explain and did not, as did the rival approach, confine itself to solving problems 'in general'. The pragmatic approach showed up even more of these advantages, Dewey felt, in the area of ethics than in the sciences because it forced people to face facts and to take moral responsibility for the specific decisions they made or recommended (cf. for example, 1950, Chapter 7). Behind Dewey's stance, of course, is the view implied in Friedman's statement, quoted at the beginning of this section, that when people begin to approach problems in this way, stripped of the kind of ideological blinkers which are quite common among thinkers who derive decisions by deducing them from 'obvious' values, they can learn to understand each other well enough to take effective action in dealing with pressing social problems.[13]

Pragmatic political economy as the 'in-between' approach

One can postulate the same tripartite classification of approaches to political economy as Friedman did of positive economics (cf. Chapter 1, above). On the empirical end in this classification the investigator confines himself to observing what policy choices people have actually made under different circumstances. At the other end the investigator is concerned with working out the implications of various value positions. The 'in-between' or pragmatic approach in such a classification would involve trying to determine how desirable outcomes could actually be achieved. What this shows is that the pragmatic approach to political economy stands in the same logical relation to the extreme empirical on the one hand and the extreme theoretical on the other as does pragmatic positive economics to the empirical and theoretical approaches to positive economics.

SIGNS OF INCONSISTENCY

We argued in the last section that the passage quoted at the outset suggested that Friedman's approach to the methodology of political economy is of a piece with his approach to the methodology of positive economics. Other evidence too can be cited to support this contention. Again and again Friedman argues for one policy over another by suggesting that one policy choice gives rise to one set of consequences and alternate choices to others. This is especially the case in his *Free to Choose* (1980c). Further, he argues (in *Capitalism and Freedom*, 1962c, p. 22): 'to deny that the end justifies the means is indirectly to assert that the end in question is not the ultimate end, that the ultimate end is itself the use of the proper means'. And he tells us: 'in any *particular case* of proposed intervention, we must make up a balance sheet, listing separately the advantages and disadvantages' (*ibid.*, p. 32, emphasis added). In the same spirit he asserts: 'the choice between the evils of private monopoly, public monopoly, and public regulation *cannot . . . be made once and for all*, independently of the factual circumstances' (*ibid.*, p. 29, emphasis added). All of this supports our initial conjecture about Friedman's position on the methodology of political economy.[14]

Extensive observation and the pragmatic approach

Nonetheless, when one looks more closely one finds that there is far more evidence that contradicts this conjecture than supports it. For one thing, a Deweyan approach not only involves an appeal to consequences, it also involves a range of observation extensive enough to enable one to go beyond solving problems 'in general' to derive the kind of knowledge that makes it possible to achieve good predictions in particular instances. There is as much need in political economy to start with 'some set of observed and related facts as full and comprehensive as possible' (1944 in 1953e, p. 282) as there is in positive economics. Judging by the way he argues his case, however, Friedman does *not* think so. For example, in discussing Old Age and Survivor's Insurance in his most scholarly work on political economy, *Capitalism and Freedom*, Friedman tells us nothing about conditions that prevailed among old people before the passage of the Act; nor what the savings distribution looks like today among people who retire; nor what the probability is that those with pension rights will actually collect their pensions; nor what the dangers are that savings will be wiped out – through inflation, depression, fraud and the like – by the time individuals reach retirement age and how real these dangers are; nor what the factors are that might make it difficult for people to save enough for old age even if they try, and so on. His predictions about what would happen if Old Age and Survivor's Insurance were abolished are based entirely on very general assumptions which appear plausible to him, not on data – quantitative or qualitative – as to the behavior of relevant variables.[15] One cannot defend Friedman here with his own argument that the 'unrealism' of assumptions does not matter – which we saw in previous chapters serves him well in arguing for positive economics – because he does not offer any substantial number of facts, as implications, which his assumptions explain!

Arguing on the basis of 'realistic' assumptions

Friedman argues at one point in *Capitalism and Freedom*: 'true, the number of citizens who regard compulsory old age insurance as a deprivation of freedom may be few, but the believer in freedom has never counted noses' (*ibid.*, p. 9). The way Friedman arrives at this rather curious conclusion is interesting. His major premise is that *any* government action constitutes a deprivation of freedom whether the people feel that way about it or not. It follows from this that government functions are to be kept to a minimum and Friedman tells us what he considers these minimum (legitimate) functions to be, basically, to protect freedom; preserve law and order; enforce private contracts; foster competition (*ibid.*, p. 21). Since old age insurance programs are not included within these functions, it follows that the deprivation of freedom which they entail is 'bad' because they are not in conformity with what is postulated at the outset as acceptable, regardless of how the vast majority of the people may feel about them.[16]

It would appear that in this instance Friedman's position on the methodology of political economy is different from that of his positive economics. He reveals broader commitment to this position very directly when he speaks elsewhere of his 'conviction that economics is a positive science capable of predicting many of the consequences of public policies with a fervent belief in individual freedom as a criterion by which to judge the desirability of those consequences'.[17] In the Deweyan system, in contrast to this, a complete separation of the realm of values from that of facts is the strongest negative heuristic.[18] Dewey is opposed to such separation because it cuts off inquiry; it tells us what is 'right' and what is 'wrong', and that is the end of the matter. Once one begins to ask *why* some functions of government and not others are 'right', a whole new process of inquiry is set in motion. The same function which might be 'right' under one set of circumstances might not be under another. This involves a very detailed examination in every instance as to what is appropriate and what is not. If any tentative generalizations are to be made about the appropriate role of government generally it would seem as necessary to have detailed knowledge in this area of experience as it is in positive areas if one is to act intelligently. In some places Friedman almost seems to agree with this, as when he argues, as we saw in the last section, that what role the government should take with regard to monopoly 'cannot ... be made once and for all, independently of the factual circumstances'. But then why does he not need to consider factual circumstances when trying to determine the desirability of old-age-pension systems; or consumer protection and discrimination legislation; or social welfare measures?

How doing political economy differs from doing positive economics

Another way to make the same point is to say that Friedman's way of doing political economy differs radically in some ways from his way of doing positive economics. This difference does not manifest itself in every aspect of the work; Friedman's choice of a general theory, or paradigm, seems to be the same for the two. Thus we saw that in arguing for the maximization-of-returns hypothesis – which functions here as a surrogate for neoclassical economic theory generally in positive economics – Friedman tells us that be believes that there is substantial evidence for this paradigm although he does not produce it. In other words, while to some economists – perhaps to many – it is telling that generations of economists support this paradigm, the fact that he does not present evidence suggests that he has chosen on the basis of plausibility. The major paradigm Friedman uses for political economy is a slightly modified form of Smith's 'invisible hand' hypothesis, and it is a reasonable conjecture that he believes as strongly that there is evidence to support it as he does the maximization-of-returns hypothesis.[19] By the same token, he does not present any substantial evidence in support here either. In this sense, Friedman chose a paradigm for political economy in more or less the same way that he did in positive economics.

The difference between the two methodologies, judging by what Friedman *did*, lies in the way the respective paradigms in the two studies are *used*. This difference is very great. In political economy he directly deduces from the broad theory, or paradigm, general answers to questions about right and wrong policy. In positive economics, on the other hand he uses the paradigm as a starting point in the kind of complex process of inquiry which we have talked about in previous chapters. Thus, in positive economics, it is not only possible but likely that one will come up with partial theories (or models) which give very different answers from what one would arrive at by directly deducing implications from the paradigm. An instance is Friedman's early work on risk-loving behavior. The difference is created by the process of inquiry which intercedes between the paradigm and the implications *in every instance*. Even so, of course, the starting paradigm has a substantial influence on the kind of results one comes up with. But one is constrained by the test of implications at every step of the inquiry and this imposes a discipline that is substantive. In Friedman's political economy, by contrast, the only substantive constraint generally is the plausibility of the assumptions behind the argument.

There are thus elements of Friedman's methodology of political economy which do not readily fit with his methodology of positive economics and, as we have seen, there are implicit suggestions for two very different kinds of political economy. An apparently ambivalent Friedman tells us, on the one hand, that 'the end in question is not the ultimate end'; but he tells us too of his 'fervent belief in individual freedom as a criterion by which to judge the desirability of those consequences [of economic policy]'. Why is only individual freedom considered a separate value? Friedman answers by telling us that the late eighteenth- and nineteenth-century liberals, with whom he identifies, 'emphasized freedom as the *ultimate* goal' (1962c, p. 5, emphasis added). Thus there apparently is an ultimate end or value in his way of thinking.[20] Friedman confirms this when he explains in another place (1965e, p. 20) that while 'from one point of view, freedom is not itself an end; it is a means', yet 'in social relations, in relations among people, freedom can be described as an end'. But this way of thinking is at odds with that of a pragmatist who does the kind of work in positive economics that Friedman does. In the next section we will elaborate on this unexplained non-pragmatic side of Friedman's approach to political economy.

NON-PRAGMATIC ASPECTS OF FRIEDMAN'S POLITICAL ECONOMY

The classical liberals

Since Friedman's approach to the methodology of political economy is for the most part different from that of his positive economics, certain evidence to the contrary notwithstanding, the question arises as to what his views of the methodology of political economy really are. Friedman himself is not very explicit so an answer must be inferred. He is clear that freedom is something like a *summum bonum* for him, but why he has chosen his particular conception of freedom and, more broadly, why 'freedom', however defined, should be given priority over every other social value he does not say. He does suggest, as we have seen, that he is following the policy ideas of the classical liberals, such as Adam Smith, who 'emphasized freedom as the ultimate goal' (1962c, p. 5). But this does not get us far because, as William Grampp has argued (1982), freedom was *not* in fact the *summum bonum* of the liberal economists.[21]

Grampp sums up his findings as follows:

> I cannot say in just what order of importance the economists placed each
> of these objectives. [Power, wealth, freedom, etc.] But I am reasonably
> sure that freedom did not come first to any of them. Power and wealth
> came before it at the start of the classical period; and at the close, justice
> and betterment came before it. (p. 5)[22]

This clue then is not very helpful. We cannot expect much aid from the
classical liberals in interpreting this side of Friedman's political economy,
because his way of thinking is simply not congruent with theirs.

Using Knight as an aid

Following another clue, however, gets us much farther. In the preface to
Capitalism and Freedom (1962c) Friedman acknowledges the influence
of his teacher Frank Knight on his thinking in this area, and pursuing this
lead turns out to be helpful. Knight devoted most of his later years to
formulating a somewhat idiosyncratic conception of political economy,
traces of which, once one looks for them, are readily found in Friedman's political economy. While there are some important differences
between Friedman's views and Knight's, there are enough similarities in
basic orientation for Knight's more carefully crafted work to help us to
come to grips with Friedman's basic notions about the methodology of
political economy. Without a knowledge of Knight's subtle formulations
of the methodology of political economy the rational basis of Friedman's
political economy would remain obscure.

Knight in a Deweyan context

In order to make good use of Knight, however, we must first relate his
way of thinking to that of his antagonist at Chicago, John Dewey, to
whom we have devoted a great deal of attention in our chapters on
Friedman's positive economics. This connection is not difficult to make
once it is recognized that the particular nature of the American environment seems to have had a great deal to do with influencing the thinking
of both philosophers, though each in a different way.

What impressed Dewey (and other pragmatists) the most was that
because of the diverse origins of the members of American society, an
appeal to any established ideology, cultural pattern, or accepted view of
life was impossible. [23] Given these origins it is understandable that Dewey
should urge that people get rid of what random bits of ideology they had
brought with them because these might act as impediments, and instead
face the likely consequences of specific courses of action designed to
overcome the particular problems which the new society faced. The

common core in the make-up of individuals would then come to the fore, as it does among individual scientists in reading meters or looking at the results of experiments. Society then would be better able to deal effectively with its problems. In other words, on this view there is no need to interpose an ethical theory of social policy between people's reactions to common problems and their attempts to cope with them; such a theory would only get in the way. Value judgments will sort themselves out in the course of making decisions though no *summum bonum* or accepted hierarchy of values is made use of. Certain common conceptions might be generated, but that is quite another matter.[24]

Frank Knight's philosophy has its roots in the same American environment, and as a result he, like Dewey, rejects the notion of developing a rationalized value position to which all people in the community may be expected to subscribe. But Knight does *not* foresee a measure of consensus emerging in the process of dealing with common problems. He views value differences as between individuals, rather than ideology, as a likely cause of social strife. It follows that Dewey's reliance on some common view emerging through consequentialist thinking will not work. Neither will rule by majority, if this is to be a truly ethical society, without coercion – one where decisions are made by consensus reached after discussion – because where there is disagreement social action coerces some individuals to go along with others and to do what they do not want to do. To Knight such compulsion is a monster to be avoided at almost any cost, a reflection perhaps of an attitude found in a frontier community.[25]

There is only one way, according to Knight, to avoid such compulsion and yet maintain a community, and that is to negotiate through discussion. As a result of such discussion no one group will wind up with everything it wants but all will recognize that the concessions they make are essential if society is to survive. But it is not easy, as Knight recognizes, to resolve disagreements via discussion among individuals who are very different from one another. For that reason the area of discussion must be minimized. This can be achieved by keeping the area of social action to an absolute minimum; that is, no political action should be undertaken unless its need for the whole group is beyond dispute.

'Freedom', as conceived by Knight, consists in not being coerced into doing what one does not want to do; or, as a disciple puts it (Grampp, 1982, p. 5), it is the avoidance of forcing an individual to do 'what he would not do if he was left to himself to do with his own as he would like'.[26] Since almost all social action if not all, involves coercion of those who disagree, an absolute minimum of social action is desirable on this view. In other words, the maximum of 'freedom' compatible with the continued existence of society is a more important social value than any other because the more 'freedom' there is the more individuals can adhere to their own values and pursue their own purposes. Thus, 'freedom' in the Knightian way of thinking, which on this point is also Friedman's, is the *summum bonum*; but it is a *summum bonum* that is very different from the traditional sort;[27] or, perhaps better put, it is a distinctive American type of *summum bonum*.[28]

It should be apparent that in Knight's conception of things the social sciences – a name, incidentally, which he was very wary of (see, for example, 1956, V) – play a much smaller role than that postulated by most others, particularly by those who hold a Deweyan point of view. After all, if social action is to be kept to a minimum, the amount of knowledge needed for social policy purposes would not be very great. Further, while Knight is not entirely consistent about this, his view seems to be that because of the nature of the material with which the so-called social scientist deals, the contribution he can make towards the prediction of consequences is very small.[29] Yet Knight sees a vital role for the traditional kind of economics in the political process.

The role of traditional economic theory

The major role of neoclassical economic theory, and the reason that it is so vital, according to Knight, is that in the discussion of social issues as part of the process leading to compromise in a truly democratic society *some frame of reference is needed*; without it agreement even on a compromise basis would be impossible.[30] Economic theory provides such a framework. It shows what the government does not have to do and thereby cuts down the area of contention, and it gives us a framework for talking about alternatives in the process of making compromises where action is essential.[31] Focusing on this side of Knight, his disciple James Buchanan tells us (1968) that on Knight's view 'economic theory is ... an idealized construction, a logical system, not an explanatory science'. And he observes further that according to Knight 'economic theory can help in the understanding and explanation of behavior, but not in the scientific prediction of behavior'.[32] Whether this puts Knight outside the mainstream of political-economy methodology is debatable, but there is little question that if he is part of this tradition he is certainly at the extreme. Knight was scathingly critical of any attempts to apply the methods of the physical sciences to economics (cf. for example, Knight, 1940); whether they in fact succeeded in doing so is another matter. In his work in the methodology of positive economics Friedman, as we have shown earlier, was critical of some mainstream economists for the very reason that, on his view, they only *thought* that they were following the methodology of the physical sciences whereas in fact they were not.

The Knightian foundations of Friedman's political economy

There are, as we have already noted, differences between Friedman's political economy and Knight's. The invisible hand, for example, plays a much more conspicuous role in Friedman's than in Knight's, while Knight's strong emphasis on the special nature of social problems is not as conspicuous in Friedman's. Yet it is only with the help of Knight, we suggest, that one can derive a coherent approach to political economy from Friedman's writings. But whereas seeing the Knightian components helps us to understand Friedman's approach, it at the same time points up difficulties. We consider them next.

THE RELATION BETWEEN THE METHODOLOGIES OF POSITIVE ECONOMICS AND POLITICAL ECONOMY

Reading Friedman's political economy within the context of Knight's helps us with one problem. But it creates another, which has to do with reconciling the two sides of Friedman's thinking about economics, positive and political.

The problems of relating the two

The problem has to do with whether one could consistently hold both positions. Knight's methodology of political economy raises some profound questions about social policy, and questions too about how one can go about trying to find answers to them. Here the differences Dewey points up on ways of thinking, which we spoke about in the first part of the chapter – relying on implications deduced from acceptable assumptions or on implications that coincide with what happens – can be very helpful. It suggests that in dealing with Knight's kind of problem one does not have to reason out on the basis of acceptable assumptions, as he does; one might try to determine consequences by using the tools of positive science, i.e. try to determine what the consequences of different kinds of government actions are likely to be at different times and places, including how people feel about these measures. But Knight rejects this kind of approach; the only kind of consequences he is interested in are those which derive from logical argument. Detailed observation of specific experience has little place in his system since he does not believe that it contributes to political discussion.[33] Quite consistently, he had little use for positive economics.

Friedman, for his part, is a fervent advocate of positive economics on the one hand and yet an advocate (for the most part) of Knight's political economy on the other. Since he obviously disagrees with Knight about the potential of positive economics there is no inconsistency in his defying Knight's negative heuristic and devoting most of his energies to this subject. But the fact that he shares Knight's views of the nature of social problems makes his pursuit of positive economics puzzling. The reason is that in the Knightian context it is not predictive power which is most useful for dealing with social problems but rather rational discussion; and for this purpose what is most needed are good 'languages' and not substantive hypotheses. (Cf. the quotes from Buchanan, above.)

It could be argued that the inconsistency we have uncovered is not primarily in Friedman's position but in life itself! Perhaps if we studied consequences, and consequences of consequences, long enough we would eventually reach agreement, and this would clear the way for social action that effectively contributes to the maximization of social welfare. But for practical purposes we have to act *now*, so that if we take the best positive knowledge that we possess and 'ground' it in values – values which might change with time as positive knowledge accumulates but have to be taken as given at the moment – we might be able to achieve the 'best' results.[34] Such a resolution might not be entirely compatible with the extreme Knightian view, but might it not be reconciled with a more moderate type, perhaps of the kind to which Friedman might subscribe?

A resolution of this sort may be possible but we do not think it is consistent with Friedman's position. The reasons are, first, that Friedman does not even hint at[35] the need for, let alone encourage, positive work on the non-economic aspects of political economy, for example, the need to study which conditions lead to the growth of freedom and which tend to diminish it.[36] Second, one who holds such views would not likely consider himself authority enough in the area of politics to make recommendations about values; Mitchell is a good example of this. After all, what credentials does the economist have to make such recommendations? Philosophers have traditionally claimed this province as their own because it is an area which transcends specific disciplines and it takes reason to deal with such questions. They are the experts on reason. It is they who are most skilled in deriving valid arguments from true premises.[37] Socrates argues this way and so long as we try to answer value questions 'in general' his argument makes a great deal of sense. In other words, so long as the positive economist considers himself different from a philosopher whose interest is in reasoning out conceptual answers to complex puzzles – not the kind whose answers yield predictions – his competence to lay down the law about judgments which involve values may be questioned. Knight, of course, was very much a philosopher in economics as in ethics; and he did not practice nor, as we have seen, did he have much interest in, the positive economics which is Friedman's major professional interest as an economist.[38]

Vining's attempt to reconcile Knight's views with positive economics

We get some insight into the kind of problem we are up against in trying to reconcile the positivist and political Friedmans by looking at remarks made by two economists, both of them sympathetic to Knight. The first one we consider is Rutledge Vining (1950, 1951), who seems to have been troubled by the fact that the charge could be made that Knight's views were not consistent with important recent positivistic trends in economics to which Vining was sympathetic, as he was to Knight's views. :

Vining was able to reconcile Knight's views with positivist economics by making it and political economy two very different subjects, not at all as close to each other as they are generally taken to be, arguing that neoclassical economic theory belongs in the political economy realm only and not in scientific economics. As Vining saw it (1950, p. 107):

> The men who perform, as economists, various professional tasks for corporate enterprises ... are not handicapped at all ... by not having at hand the kind of theory or knowledge that makes important the better known books on 'foundations' or 'fundamentals' of economic theory ... such as Marshall's *Principles of Economics*.

Expressing the Knightian view, he argues further that it is the character of economic theory as a logical system which is of central importance. On this basis Vining avoids open conflict, but this type of reconciliation will not work for Friedman, of course, because he has very different notions about the character of neoclassical economic theory and its major role.[39]

It should not be difficult to see why we have run into this problem of reconciliation. In considering any social problem – be it economic stability, equity, security, efficiency, etc. – if one approaches it in the Knightian manner one moves in an entirely different direction than if one approaches it in the positive economics (or social science) manner. Friedman gives us an example of this. In *Capitalism and Freedom* (1962c, Chapter 3) after telling us how badly the Federal Reserve Board behaved during the 1930s, Friedman concludes (p. 51) that 'money is too serious a matter to be left to Central Bankers' and adds that what is needed is 'a government of laws instead of men ...'. This looks like a non sequitur, which results from Friedman's inability to integrate his very different methodologies. After all, we could by the same token cite some disastrous presidential decisions and urge that our chief executive should be limited to acting according to formulas, or argue the same way about medical doctors, or even professors. Friedman may be right, of course, in arguing that the adoption of his money rule would enable us over the long run to achieve relative economic stability; we judge him on this by assessing his work in positive economics. But this is quite independent of the question whether in giving the Fed discretionary powers we make our government one of men rather than laws. There is a choice involved. If the loss of freedom that results from the government controlling the money supply is more important than stability, then we ought to get the government out of the money business.[40] (Since discretion means a greater loss of freedom in Friedman's terms, then we might choose to follow a rule even if we believe that discretion is more likely to give us stability.)[41]

Buchanan's comments on Friedman

Even more revealing than Vining's comments are those of James Buchanan. Unlike Vining, Buchanan rejects using the physical sciences as a model for economics and is wholly in the Knightian political economy tradition. We consider three of his remarks. The first has to do with Friedman's attitude towards the subjectivist approach. He notes (1979, p. 90): 'Milton Friedman ... objects to the Austrian-subjectivist approach largely on the grounds that it implies conversion rather than gradual conviction by the weight of logical argument and empirical tests'. It is, of course, the positivist Friedman who has these objections. The (Knightian) political Friedman should welcome the subjectivist approach.

In another place (*ibid.*, p. 178) Buchanan refers to Friedman's Nobel Prize lecture (1977*b*) and notes that 'Friedman suggests, implicitly, if not explicitly, that "science" is all, that the refutation of hypotheses is all that we are required to do, that a demonstration of the "is" must necessarily lead to the "ought"'. Though we would question the accuracy of these comments, still they seem to us to be illustrative of the kind of deep-seated antagonism that understandably exists between those who hold Friedman's scientistic views as positive economist and Buchanan's Knightian political economy instincts.[42]

In still another place (1959, p. 124) Buchanan observes (after reading Friedman's 'Positive economics' (1953*d*)) that 'Milton Friedman has provided the clearest statement of the positivist position, and he has called for a distinct separation between the scientific and the non-scientific behavior of individuals calling themselves economists'. In reaction Buchanan notes (*ibid.*, p. 124):

The social role of the economist remains that of securing more intelligent legislation, and the incremental additions to the state of knowledge which 'positive' economics may make seems to shut off too large an area of discussion from this professional competence.

It is not difficult to see why Buchanan argues the way he does. For, as Buchanan correctly perceives, anyone who holds the kind of views which Friedman developed in 'Positive economics' would rule out Knightian kind of political economy as a professional activity. That Friedman does include it creates the very puzzle that we are grappling with.[43]

The classical synthesis

After having said so much about the problem of reconciling the approaches of the positive and the political economist one begins to wonder how it was possible for the classical economists to reconcile the two so well that they were considered essentially one and the same discipline. We have already partly answered this question. They did so by having essentially the same methodologies for both. But there is much more to it than that.

The classical economists achieved a measure of objectivity for their positive economics through their belief that via careful introspection one could find generalizations not only about one's own motives but also about the motives of people generally. It was in this way that economists derived the 'realistic' behavioral assumptions on the basis of which they could derive 'scientific' conclusions. By the same token, the classicals felt that through introspection the economist got to know not only what was good for himself but also, very generally, what other people would consider was good for themselves as well.[44] As a consequence they believed that their notions about policy were as 'scientific' and objective as those about how the economy worked. The methodologies of positive economics and political economy were not only closely related but also almost identical, and the two fields were for practical purposes the same. It was not even necessary to have a vocabulary to distinguish between the positive economist and the political economist.

Note that it is not necessary to be ignorant of the normative-positive distinction to hold such a position.[45] Anyone who believes that he has a way of determining what is in the interest of mankind, as did the utilitarians, for example, would be no more normative in making a policy proposal than the medical doctor who gives advice about how to deal with disease. The synthesis the classicals achieved between positive and political economy is deeper than is generally recognized.

Friedman shatters this neat synthesis when he challenges 'realism'-of-assumptions methodology in positive economics. He substitutes for it a methodology looking to implications. Now if we want to retain a real synthesis, as the classicals did, we have to put with this positive economics a political economy which also has pragmatic foundations. We saw that Friedman made some moves in that direction but that for the most part he chose a political economy resting more firmly on general reasoning from assumptions than was the political economy of the classicals themselves. It is this factor which creates the problem we have been considering. We see no way of truly resolving it other than by substituting the pragmatic type of political economy for Friedman's Knightian kind.[46] If we do that then we would, like the classicals, make political economy an objective study. Positive economics and political economy would be brought closer together. The positive economist would have credentials to operate in the area of political economy, and we would have a methodology which is the same for both areas of the study of economics. We see promise for such a rationale for economics, reflecting our belief that Friedman's Deweyan-Marshallian methodology of positive economics offers great promise.

A possible reconciliation

We have yet one other possible interpretation of Friedman's overall position to consider. James Buchanan has made us aware that if we have a strong interest in improving the world, as Friedman undoubtedly does, deriving even very reliable knowledge pertinent to serious social problems may not have much practical effect; to be effective one needs to have reliable knowledge about the way the political process works. In very recent times Friedman has subscribed to Buchanan's thesis (cf. his 1980c, preface, and especially his 1986), though one also gets the impression that if he were a young man starting out he might move in a somewhat different direction from Buchanan's by applying the methods of positive economics to Buchanan's insights, trying to derive further knowledge by these means. Friedman does not follow this rationale, of course, in most of his writings on political economy, but might he not have followed a related one which, it can be argued, is discernible in his approach?

That Friedman did not in the 1960s follow a public choice approach does not mean that he was not aware of the problem towards which it was directed. There is, as we noted earlier, at least one other approach possible to the same problem. Recognizing that people might not be convinced by the results derived from research in positive economics, and believing that the 'realism'-of-assumptions rationale is more effective in argument, one could adopt a mixed strategy where positive methods are used to determine what should be done and 'realism'-of-assumptions type of argument is used to persuade voters and legislators to act on this knowledge. Might Friedman's overall position be interpreted this way?[47]

Friedman's position

May we then conclude that this *is* the implicit position that Friedman holds on the relationship between positive economics and political economy? No in one sense, yes in another. We cannot say that this position is implicit in his practice because, except for the area of monetary policy, he does not present much in the way of positive economics evidence in support of his policy recommendations. Hence, unless we assume that for Friedman maximizing the degree of negative freedom is *always* more important than achieving other goals, his political economy turns out to be too insubstantial to enable us to conclude that we have correctly determined his position. At best we can say that a pattern of thinking which we have observed in another area suggests that perhaps this in fact *is* Friedman's underlying position.

We saw in examining Friedman's defense of the maximization-of-returns hypothesis that while expressing the belief that considerable evidence supporting this hypothesis existed, he declined to produce it. Instead he proceeded to argue on the basis of plausible assumptions. It seems to us that implicitly he may be doing the same thing in his political economy; he may believe that very solid evidence is available, but since he does not have it at hand he proceeds to argue in the traditional way. But note that even if this is the proper way of reconciling Friedman's methodology of political economy with his positive economics and of resolving the inconsistency problem, we would still find his overall position unsatisfactory, as we did his defense of the maximization-of-returns hypothesis. The reason is that if we were to attribute this position to him, it would mean that in this one area, as in the other, he takes a short-cut, and instead of presenting solid positive economics evidence, he instead relies (implicitly in this instance) on the kind of 'realism'-of-assumptions argument which he ostensibly rejects. On the other hand, if we do not accept this interpretation, then the positive and the political are left unreconciled.

That we should end up being critical of Friedman's methodology of political economy is not surprising. The kind of criticism we offer results from looking at his work as a whole within the context of his methodology of positive economics. Had we looked at it in a (Knightian) political economy context, as Buchanan does (1979, p. 179), we would have ended up being critical, too, but (like Buchanan) rather because Friedman does not pay enough attention to the problem of getting the 'right' policies adopted.

Looked at in this way it appears that perhaps the major weakness in Friedman's overall position is that he has tried to do too much. Positive economics is the area to which Friedman has devoted most of his attention and it is the one, both in terms of results and in terms of ideas about methodology, about which there is little question concerning the importance of his contribution. About his political economy we have doubts because it is hard to avoid the conclusion that his methodology there is not consistent with his views on the methodology of positive economics. And because when read as an attempt to persuade, we find it lacking because it does not have behind it the kind of evidence which those who are advocates of Friedman's methodology of positive economics would insist on as a condition for accepting his work in this area as a substantive contribution.

NOTES

1. Perhaps this is the reason that writers on economic methodology, while pointing up the distinction between normative and positive, do not find it necessary to say anything specific about the methodology of normative economics (e.g. J. N. Keynes, 1890). Friedman is in this tradition, though for him this omission is less defensible than it is for the others.
2. Friedman explains this position more fully in his 1965e, pp. 25–6; 1967d, pp. 87–8; 1968b, pp. 1–16.
3. Dewey's refusal to make a sharp distinction between pure and applied science derives partly from this notion.
4. As pointed out to us by Michael McPherson, by considering only two approaches we are oversimplifying. The philosopher John Rawls, for example, appeals to consequences but they are of a different sort and he approaches them in a different way than Dewey does. To consider this complication, however, would take us very far afield and would not, we believe, affect our main conclusions.
5. We seem to have arrived at the same conclusion as did Mill when he argued that 'a man is not likely to be a good economist if he is nothing else'. But there is an important difference. Mill did not want to put his faith in the political economist, since as economist narrowly understood he was unable to predict adequately. It took the 'statesman' to add the appropriate specific disturbing causes. What we are saying is that even if the positive economist could predict *economic* consequences he would generally still not be a reliable guide because non-economic consequences would have to be predicted as well in a practical situation.
6. Rachels (1977, p. 166), though he exaggerates, brings out this feature of Dewey's approach to ethics when he attributes to him the view that 'if we could always exercise our intelligence to the fullest, we could always agree on evaluations'.
7. A good bit of the debate about ethics and social policy has less to do with choice of the 'right' values than with what actions are logically consistent with generally accepted values.

8. Dewey argues this way in his (1917, pp. 183–216). The reader should be warned that here, as in many other places, Dewey uses the term 'scientific' in a much broader sense than it is generally used today.

9. A good bit has been written about this (e.g. Winn, 1965, pp. xvi–xvii) but by far the most perceptive and telling statement is still George Herbert Mead's classic article (1930).

10. As to how such choices should be made, the traditional political economist appeals to self-evident general principles (assumptions) whereas the pragmatist appeals to consequences of consequences *in a particular situation*, in a sense taking it for granted that the nth consequence (consequences of consequences of consequences to the nth degree) is a desirable one. In other words, he does not try to justify his choice by argument beyond this point.

11. Through the use of the right kind of rhetoric one may be able to get agreement. But unless the definition of the term rhetoric is stretched so entirely out of shape as to include methodology as part of its meaning, one could say that rhetoric would not go very far, except by chance, towards helping solve problems. Thus, using the traditional vocabulary, one could say that Friedman opposes the 'realism'-of-assumptions type of thinking in positive economics because, while it may help us to make convincing arguments, it does not point in the direction of results which are practically or scientifically useful (for empirical science).

12. Frank Knight seems to take it for granted that in the process of *arguing* about social problems solutions will be found not only to the problem of reaching agreement but also to getting rid of undesirable phenomena as well. Perhaps this is one of the reasons he saw so little promise in positive economics.

13. It could be argued that Friedman is merely saying that the facts will prevail among citizens and legislators, as in other places (e.g. 1968c, introduction; 1977b) he has argued that the facts prevail among economists. But *why* does he hold such views? Were people blindly to hold inherited ideologies which are not necessarily in line with their true values, could facts prevail, even if in their feelings they do not differ to any significant extent?

14. Friedman is also being pragmatic when he argues (in 1967d, p. 86) that 'no objectives are really fully defined. They are partly revealed in their consequences'. But he goes on to argue that the aim of discussion about values 'is to see what the implications of our value judgments are, [and] whether they are internally consistent'. The two objectives are very different and involve different methodologies. Friedman seems to overlook this.

15. Friedman's expectation that such advice will be helpful is akin to expecting that one can cure a drinking problem by arguing with the drinker that his behavior is not in his own self-interest, against a background of what the critic perceives to be generally accepted truths, both about the way the world is, and values.

16. We find it difficult to reconcile Friedman's contempt for those who suggest that consumers may often not make the best choices in markets (cf. for example, 1977d), with his very strong feelings that the deprivation of freedom by such measures as the passage of the social security laws is 'bad' whether people feel that they are being deprived of freedom by these measures or not. He more or less repeats his position from *Capitalism and Freedom* in Friedman and Cohen (1972e).

17. Perhaps Friedman means here merely that before choosing we take into

account not only economic consequences but also how each of the consequences will affect the freedom of individuals in society. But the way it stands it sounds as if he does not believe that the choice of economic consequences is done on the basis of valuation and that from all possible economic consequences we should *always* choose the one which interferes with freedom the least. Any society that did that would run the risk of having its people starve to death.

18. Dewey opposes this dualism partly because it leads one, for no good reason, to put some values (in this instance maximum output) into one category and others (freedom in this instance) in another. Do we not need positive knowledge about freedom as well, and do we not also need to make normative judgments about how much to produce? If so, why this artificial separation for policy purposes?

19. While he talks a good bit about the bad effects of government intervention, what ties the whole together and makes the bad results meaningful is the possible alternative as represented by the invisible hand. An interesting exception (1962c, Chapter 3) is control of the money supply. We say that this is an exception because on the basis of the paradigm alone one would expect Friedman to urge the government to get out of the control-of-money business entirely, as advocated by members of the Austrian school. Friedman's money-rule policy suggestion may sound conservative to interventionists but to true believers in the invisible hand theory it is a radical departure, a result stemming from his work in positive economics. One wonders how many deviations there would be were Friedman to rely in other areas on the kind of positive economics inquiry that he does in the area of money.

20. We do not see a difference in this context between an ultimate 'goal' and an ultimate 'end'.

21. Cf. also Robbins, 1976, p. 175.

22. While freedom is a most important value for Smith, it is not the *summum bonum* that it is for Friedman. The difference manifests itself in various subtle ways. For example, while it is true that Smith in some places seems to envisage an even smaller role for government than Friedman does (cf. Smith, 1937 [1776], p. 651 with Friedman, 1962c, Chapter 2), in this context Smith is arguing for *efficiency* rather than freedom as Friedman does.

23. As we noted above (n. 9, this chapter), in Mead's essay one finds an excellent account of how the particular conditions in the American environment, particularly in the frontier communities, made this type of thinking the dominant one.

24. Louis Hartz (1955) shows how a specifically different type of liberalism evolved in the American environment.

25. That is why national planning is anathema to Knight. Knight asks: Planning for whom? Planning for what? Who is to control whom? (Cf. for example, 1947, Chapter 14.)

26. Friedman, too, as he shows in 'Economic libertarianism' (1965e, p. 10), is concerned with this very narrow type of freedom. In fact, his conception is even narrower than Knight's. The sole agent of coercion Friedman sees is government; for Knight the government is only the *major* one.

27. Those who argue on the basis of a *summum bonum* generally seem to believe that 'human nature' is fixed. Not so Knight or Friedman. In this respect both are pragmatic. Cf. Friedman's comments in Hook, 1967d, p. 92, where he talks about 'this process of searching for and developing values'.

28. Hartz (1955) stresses the fact that in America the middle class did not have a socialist lower class with whom to do battle or an aristocratic upper class that had to be answered. But what may have been equally important was the fact that the pioneer community consisted largely of unrelated individuals, come together from many places, who were therefore not ready to take responsibility for each other's well-being. As a result, any redistributive effort tended to be considered theft and great resentment could be generated against common actions that were not consistent with one's own values. 'The greatest good for the greatest number' did not strike a chord here; Pareto optimality with compensation was more congenial because it limits the government to maintaining the status quo. This attitude is manifest in Knight's political economy and this aspect is developed further by Knight's student, James Buchanan (e.g. 1959). Cf. also the interesting discussion between Buchanan and Samuels bearing on this issue in Samuels, 1975.

29. In one of his more moderate statements (1935, p. 132) Knight argues: 'We seem to be forced to the conclusion, not that prediction and control are impossible in the field of human phenomena, but rather that the formal methods of sciences are of very limited application. Common sense does predict and control, and can be trained to predict and control better: but that does not prove that science can predict and control better than common sense'. (This appears to suggest that we can do just as well without science for this purpose.)

30. To mainstream economists this may not look like much of a role for economic theory but to a Knightian, as Buchanan shows (e.g. 1979), this function is more important than any other because if it is disregarded those who call themselves economists cease being economists and become engineers.

31. Vining (1951) gives a very good account of this aspect of Knight's point of view. He bases himself on Knight's 1947, but this theme is found in almost all of his work.

32. Cf. Hirsch and Hirsch (in Samuels, 1980) for a discussion of Knight's none too clear views about prediction.

33. In some places (e.g. 1935, Chapter 4) where he sets up a taxonomy of approaches Knight does find a place for data used for making predictions, but this is so unimportant in his general scheme of things that one has the impression that he includes it only for completeness. In some places (e.g. 1935, pp. 133–4) he says that predicting economic behavior is more of an art than a science, which raises the question of how data are to be used in this art.

34. In *logic* one cannot derive an 'ought' from an 'is' proposition but the most fertile source of our values is what we have seen (and felt) happening in the course of our experience.

35. In some places (e.g. 1962*a*, Chapter 1) Friedman talks *very* broadly of the relation between political and economic freedom, but this merely skims the surface of this very complex subject, and there are, of course, very many more such subjects relevant to the problems Friedman deals with. (There appears to be a logical flaw in Friedman's discussion in the chapter noted because the bit of evidence Friedman presents shows only that political freedom is not found in countries which are not predominantly capitalist, not that government economic intervention of any kind leads to the loss of political freedom. In fact, some of the countries which he holds up as

paragons of political freedom have a great deal of the kind of government economic intervention which he is arguing against.)

36. The psychologist Erich Fromm (1965), to take an example of one who does explore the preconditions for freedom, argues that when conditions in a land are such as to make individuals feel very insecure they may very well opt for giving up freedom rather than retaining it. This is merely a hypothesis – though one rooted in a good bit of evidence from individual psychology – and much work would have to be done to have confidence in it. Yet such evidence as there is, inconclusive as it may be, gives one reason to doubt whether government interference is as important a cause for loss of freedom as Friedman supposes.

37. Friedman admits (1968b, p. 3) that he is only an amateur political scientist but argues this should not keep him from arguing about policy, because the public must choose and should therefore be given information about the range of professional opinion. But note that this would involve only making predictions on the basis of positive economics. Once the economist begins arguing what should be done, as Friedman does, his position is like that of the medical doctor who tells his patient that he *must* have surgery, instead of merely informing him that if he does not have surgery he runs certain risks which his expertise shows to exist.

38. Buchanan (1968) notes that 'Knight is the economist as philosopher, not the economist as scientist'. Thus Knight is rather an extreme, as we have seen, but even those who are more in the middle – Lionel Robbins, for example, – can give some justification for arguing policy positions as they do because as 'realism'-of-assumptions thinkers they are close to philosophy. Not so one who appeals to implications. (Note Mitchell's position about policy advice in Lucy Sprague Mitchell, 1953, pp. 552–3.)

39. Note Stigler's response (1951, p. 128) to Vining. It seems very likely that Friedman's reaction to Vining would have been similar.

40. J. Laurence Laughlin, whom Friedman has called the founder of the Chicago School, has argued for example (1920, p. 89) that deposit insurance is socialistic and therefore he was strongly against it. The pragmatic argument about stability meant nothing to him.

41. Very recently Friedman (in Dorn and Schwartz, 1987) has moved closer towards the Austrian position. He has done so for admittedly political reasons. The new position seems to us to be weaker than the old one because behind the previous position there is very solid – though, of course, not conclusive – evidence as to consequences. We know of no such evidence behind the new proposal. So far as political feasibility is concerned we do not see any evidence to suggest that the new has better prospects than the old.

42. On the one hand Buchanan expresses admiration for Friedman's positivistic work (1979, p. 90), on the other he rejects scientism in no uncertain terms (*ibid.*, p. 51). It looks to us that there is inconsistency in this.

43. Breit and Ransom (1982, p. 251) argue that 'to understand Friedman's contribution to economics, it is important that his philosophical ideas be separated from his scientific work'. We agree with this if by 'philosophical' we mean political, and if methodology is included with the scientific and not run together with the political. Breit and Ransom do not tell us *why* they think a separation needs to be made. This is a question we are trying to answer.

44. Young (forthcoming) shows how David Hume, the one who established the

is-ought dichotomy, could at the same time make the claim that his theory of *policy* was 'scientific'. Young also shows that Adam Smith held the same views as did Hume.

45. Hutchison (1964, Chapter 1) finds it strange that economists who understood the distinction between normative and positive should have clung to a belief in the 'science' of ethics, but there is nothing strange about it. As long as one believes that there is a way, through observation and reasoning, of determining what is good and bad for mankind, as the utilitarians did, an ethicist giving policy advice is being no more normative than a medical doctor giving advice about curing a disease.

46. Buchanan (1959) suggests a different kind of 'positive' political economy. In Buchanan's scheme, after the positive economist has derived from optimality analysis policies which are in the social interest, the political economist would predict what kind of compensations need to be made to achieve near unanimity in support of these policies. These predictions could then be tested objectively by seeing whether the near unanimity is achieved in fact when the policies are proposed for legislation. Such a political economy would not be consistent with Friedman's way of thinking because: Friedman wants to rely on his type of positive economics for making predictions and not the reasoning-out variety which Pareto optimality involves; and Friedman wants political economy to show us what is desirable (and undesirable) policy while Buchanan's type of positive political economy does not yield such answers.

47. If this is truly Friedman's position it would follow that he believes that voters and legislators will accept any policy which can be shown to be the one that minimizes the loss of freedom.

SELECT BIBLIOGRAPHY

Milton Friedman's Economic, Statistical and Political Economic Writings 1934–1987

* indicates reprinted in *Essays in Positive Economics.*
† indicates reprinted in *The Optimum Quantity of Money*
‡ indicates reprinted in *Dollars and Deficits*

1934 'The fitting of indifference curves as a method of deriving statistical demand curves', unpublished paper; summary and quotation in Chapter 19 of Henry Schultz (1938) *The Theory and Measurement of Demand*, Chicago: University of Chicago Press.

1935 'Professor Pigou's method of measuring elasticities of demand from budgetary data', *Quarterly Journal of Economics*, **50** (November), pp. 151–63; further comment, pp. 532–3.

1936 *a* 'Further notes on elasticity of substitution I: Note on Dr Machlup's article', *Review of Economic Studies*, **3** (February), pp. 147–8.
b (with H. Kneeland and E. H. Schoenberg) 'Plans for a study of the consumption of goods and services by American families', *Journal of the American Statistical Association*, **31** (March), pp. 135–40.
c 'Marginal utility of money and elasticities of demand II', *Quarterly Journal of Economics*, **50** (May), pp. 532–3.

1937 *a* 'The use of ranks to avoid the assumption of normality implicit in the analysis of variance', *Journal of the American Statistical Association*, **32** (September), pp. 675–701; Correction, **34** (March 1949), p. 109.
b 'Testing the significance of the differences among a group of regression equations' (abstract), *Econometrica*, **5** (April), pp. 194–5.
c Comment, *Studies in Income and Wealth* (vol. 1) New York: National Bureau of Economic Research (NBER), pp. 159–62.

1938 *a* 'Mr Broster on demand curves', *Journal of the Royal Statistical Society*, **101**, p. 2, 38; point 2, pp. 450–4.
b Comment, *Studies in Income and Wealth* (vol. 2) New York: NBER, pp. 123–30.

1939 Comments, *Studies in Income and Wealth* (vol. 3) New York: NBER, pp. 129–40, 463–7.

1940 Review of J. Tinbergen's *Business Cycles in the United States of America, 1919–1932, American Economic Review*, **30** (September), pp. 657–61.

1941 Review of Robert Triffin's *Monopolistic Competition and General Equilibrium Theory, Journal of Farm Economics*, **23** (March) pp. 389–91.

1942 *a* (with W. Allen Wallis) 'The empirical derivation of indifference functions' in Oscar Lange, Francis McIntire and Theodore O. Yntema (eds) *Studies in Mathematical Economics and Econometrics, in Memory of Henry Schultz*, Chicago: University of Chicago Press, pp. 775–89.
*c** Discussion of the inflationary gap, *American Economic Review*, **32** (June), pp. 314–20.

1943 *a* (with Carl Shoup and Ruth P. Mack) *Taxing to Prevent Inflation*, New York: NBER.
b 'The spendings tax as a wartime fiscal measure', *American Economic Review*, **33** (March), pp. 50–62.

1945 (with S. Kuznets) *Income from Independent Professional Practice*, New York: NBER.

1946 *a* (with George J. Stigler) *Roofs or Ceilings? The Current Housing Problem*, Irvington-on-Hudson, New York: Foundation for Economic Education.
*b** 'Lange on price flexibility and employment: a methodological criticism', *American Economic Review*, **36** (September), pp. 613–31.

1947 *a** 'Lerner on the economics of control', *Journal of Political Economy* (October), **55**, pp. 405–16.
b 'Utilization of limited experimental facilities when the cost of each measurement depends on its magnitude', in Eisenhart, Churchill, Hastay, Millard W., Wallis, W. Allen (eds) *Selected Techniques of Statistical Analysis for Scientific and Industrial Research*, New York: McGraw-Hill, pp. 319–28.
c 'Planning an experiment for estimating the mean and standard deviation of a normal distribution from observations on the cumulative distribution', in Eisenhart *et al.*, pp. 339–52.
d (with L. J. Savage) 'Planning experiments seeking maxima', in Eisenhart *et al.*, pp. 363–72.

1948 *a* (with Harold A. Freeman, Frederick Mosteller and W. Allen Wallis, eds) *Sampling Inspection: Principles, Procedures, and Tables for Single, Double, and Sequential Sampling in Acceptance Inspection and Quality Control Based on Percent Defective*, Columbia University: Statistical Research Group.
*b** 'A monetary and fiscal framework for economic stability', *American Economic Review*, **38** (June), pp. 245–64.
c (with L. J. Savage) 'The utility analysis of choices involving risk', *Journal of Political Economy*, **56** (August), pp. 279–304.

1949 *a* Discussion on liquidity and uncertainty, *American Economic Review*, Papers and Proceedings, **39** (May), pp. 196–9.
b Rejoinder to Phillip Neff (on 1948*b*), *American Economic Review*, **39** (September), pp. 949–55.
*c** 'The Marshallian demand curve', *Journal of Political Economy*, **57** (December), pp. 463–95.

d 'Money and banking' in Arthur F. Burns, *Wesley Mitchell and the National Bureau*, Twenty-Ninth Annual Report of the National Bureau of Economic Research, New York: NBER, pp. 80–1.

1950 'Wesley C. Mitchell as an economic theorist', *Journal of Political Economy*, **58** (December), pp. 463–95; reprinted in Arthur F. Burns (ed.) (1952) *Wesley Clair Mitchell: The Economic Scientist*, New York: NBER, pp. 237–91.

1951 *a* Comment (on 'A test of an econometric model for the United States, 1921–1947') in *Conference on Business Cycles*, New York: NBER, pp. 107–14.
b* 'Commodity-reserve currency' *Journal of Political Ecnomy*, **59** (June), pp. 203–32.
c* 'The effects of a full-employment policy on economic stability: a formal analysis' (in French), *Economie appliquée*, **4** (July–December), pp. 441–56.
d* Comments on monetary policy, *Review of Economics and Statistics*, **33** (August), pp. 186–91.
e Comment, *Studies in Income and Wealth* (vol. 13) New York: NBER, pp. 55–60, 119–22.
f 'Some comments on the significance of labor unions for economic policy', in David McCord Wright (ed.) *The Impact of the Union*, New York: Harcourt Brace Jovanovich, pp. 217–21.

1952 *a** 'The "welfare" effects of an income tax and an excise tax', *Journal of Political Economy*, **60** (February), pp. 25–33.
b 'Price, income, and monetary changes in three wartime periods, *American Economic Review*, Papers and Proceedings, **42** (May), pp. 612–25.
c Comment (on methodology) in Bernard F. Haley (ed.) *A Survey of Contemporary Economics* (vol. II) Homewood, Illinois: Irwin, for the American Economic Association, pp. 455–7.
d (with L. J. Savage) 'The expected-utility hypothesis and the measurability of utility', *Journal of Political Economy*, **60** (December), pp. 463–74.
e 'A method of comparing incomes of families differing in composition', *Studies in Income and Wealth* (vol. 15) New York: NBER, pp. 9–20.

1953 *a* Rejoinder (on economic advice and political limitations), *Review of Economics and Statistics*, **35** (May), p. 252.
b Research: discussion, *American Economic Review*, papers and proceedings, **43** (May), pp. 445–8.
c 'Choice, chance, and the personal distribution of income', *Journal of Political Economy*, **61** (August), pp. 277–90.
d 'The methodology of positive economics', in *Essays in Positive Economics*, Chicago: University of Chicago Press, pp. 3–43.
e *Essays in Positive Economics*, Chicago: University of Chicago Press.
f 'The case for flexible exchange rates', in *ibid.*, pp. 157–203.
g‡ 'Why the dollar shortage?', *The Freeman*, **4** (6) (14 December).

1954 *a*‡ 'Why the American economy is depression-proof', *Nationalekonomiska Föreningens Förhandlingar 1954*, pp. 55–72.

    b 'The reduction of fluctuations in the incomes of primary producers: a critical comment', *Economic Journal*, **64** (December), pp. 698–703.
    c 'A reply', *Journal of Political Economy*, (February), pp. 261–6.

1955   *a* 'Liberalism – "old style"', *Collier's Year Book*, New York: Collier and Son, pp. 360–3.
    b 'The role of government in education', in Robert A. Solo (ed.) *Economics and the Public Interest*, New Brunswick, New Jersey: Rutgers University Press, pp. 123–44.
    c 'What all is utility?', *Economic Journal*, **65** (September), pp. 405–9.
    d Comment on union strength, *Review of Economics and Statistics*, **37** (November), pp. 401–6.
    e 'Leon Walras and his economic system', review of W. Jaffe (ed.) *L. Walras' 'Elements of Pure Economics'*, *American Economic Review*, **45** (December), pp. 900–9.
    f Comment, (on input-output) in *Studies in Income and Wealth*, vol. 18) *Input–Output Analysis: An Appraisal*, Princeton: Princeton University Press, for NBER, pp. 169–74.

1956   *a* (ed.) *Studies in the Quantity Theory of Money*, Chicago: University of Chicago Press.
    b 'The quantity theory of money: a restatement', in *Studies in the Quantity Theory of Money.*

1957   *a* (with G. S. Becker) 'A statistical illusion in judging Keynesian models', *Journal of Political Ecnomy*, **65** (February), pp. 64–75.
    b 'Savings and the balance sheet', *Bulletin of the Oxford Institute of Statistics*, **19** (May), pp. 125–36.
    c *A Theory of the Consumption Function*, Princeton: Princeton University Press, for NBER.

1958   *a* 'Foreign economic aid: means and objectives', *Yale Review*, **47** (Summer), pp. 550–6.
    b† 'The supply of money and changes in prices and output', in Joint Economic Committee Print, *The Relationship of Prices to Economic Stability and Growth*, 85th Congress, 2nd session, Washington, DC: US Government Printing Office, pp. 241–56.
    c (with G. S. Becker) Reply to Kuhn and Johnston (on 1957*a*), *Review of Economics and Statistics*, **40** (August), p. 298.
    d (with G. S. Becker) Reply (on 1957*a*), *Journal of Political Economy*, **66** (December), pp. 545–9.
    e 'The permanent income hypothesis: comment', *American Economic Review*, **48** (December), pp. 990–1.
    f (and others) Discussion on wage theory and practice, *Industrial Relations Research Association*, Proceedings, **11** (December), pp. 212–21.

1959   *a* *A Program for Monetary Stability*, The Millar Lectures, no. 3, New York: Fordham University Press.
    b 'The demand for money: some theoretical and empirical results', summary, *American Economic Review*, Papers and Proceedings, **49** (May), pp. 525–7.
    c† 'The demand for money: some theoretical and empirical results', *Journal of Political Economy*, **67** (August), pp. 327–51.

1960 *a*† 'In defense of destabilizing speculation', in Ralph W. Pfouts (ed.) *Essays in Economics and Econometrics*, Chapel Hill, North Carolina: University of North Carolina Press, pp. 133–41.
b 'Comment on R. Bodkin's Windfall income and consumption', in *Proceedings of the Conference on Consumption and Saving* (vol. 2) Philadelphia.

1961 *a* 'Monetary data and national income estimates', *Economic Development and Cultural Change*, **9** (April), pp. 267–86.
b 'Vault cash and free reserves', *Journal of Political Economy*, **69** (April), pp. 181–2.
c‡ 'The demand for money', *Proceedings of the American Philosophical Society*, **105** (June), pp. 259–64.
d† 'The lag effect of monetary policy', *Journal of Political Economy*, **69** (October), pp. 447–66.
e 'Real and pseudo gold standards', *Journal of Law and Economics*, **4** (October), pp. 66–79.

1962 *a* 'The report of the commission on money and credit: an essay in *petitio principii*', *American Economic Review*, Papers and Proceedings, **52** (May), pp. 291–301.
b *Price Theory: A Provisional Text*, Chicago: Aldine.
c (with the assistance of Rose D. Friedman) *Capitalism and Freedom*, Chicago: University of Chicago Press.
d 'The interpolation of time series by related series', *Journal of the American Statistical Association*, **57** (December), pp. 729–57.
e 'Should there be an independent monetary authority?', in Leland B. Yeager (ed.) *In Search of a Monetary Constitution*, Cambridge, Massachusetts: Harvard University Press, pp. 219–43.

1963 *a* (with Anna J. Schwartz) *A Monetary History of the United States, 1867–1960*, Princeton: Princeton University Press, for NBER.
b† (with Anna J. Schwartz) 'Money and business cycles', *Review of Economics and Statistics*, **45** (February), pp. 32–64.
c 'More on Archibald versus Chicago', *Review of Economic Studies*, **30** (February), pp. 65–7.
d 'Price determination in the United States Treasury bill market: a comment', *Review of Economics and Statistics*, **45** (August), pp. 318–20; erratum (November), p. 424.
e (with David Meiselman) 'The relative stability of monetary velocity and the investment multiplier in the United States, 1897–1958', in *Stabilization Policies*, Englewood Cliffs, New Jersey: Prentice Hall, for the Commission on Money and Credit, pp. 165–268.
f 'Exchange rates: how flexible should they be?' statement, the US balance of payments; hearings, Joint Economic Committee, US; 88th Congress, 1st Session; Washington, DC: US Government Printing Office, pp. 451–68.
g 'Windfalls, the "Horizon", and related concepts in the permanent-income hypothesis', in Carl F. Christ *et al.*, *Measurement in Economics: Studies in Mathematical Economics and Econometrics in memory of Yehuda Grunfeld*, Stanford: Stanford University Press, pp. 3–28.
h‡ *Inflation: causes and consequences*, Bombay: Asia Publishing House.

1964 *a*† 'The monetary studies of the National Bureau', in *The National Bureau Enters its 45th Year*, 44th annual report, New York: NBER, pp. 7–25.
b 'Note on the lag in effect of monetary policy', *American Economic Review*, **54** (September), pp. 759–61.
c† 'Post-war trends in monetary theory and policy', *National Banking Review*, **2** (September), pp. 1–10.
d Comment on 'collusion in the auction market for Treasury bills', *Journal of Political Economy*, **72** (October), pp. 513–14.
e (with D. Meiselman) Reply to Donald Hester, *Review of Economics and Statistics*, **46** (November), pp. 369–76.

1965 *a* (*et al.*) 'The evolving international monetary mechanism', discussion, *American Economic Review*, Papers and Proceedings, **55** (May), pp. 178–88.
b‡ 'The political economy of international monetary arrangements', paper presented at the 15th general meeting (September) of the Mt Pelerin Society, Stresa, Italy.
c‡ 'The lessons of US monetary history and their bearing on current policy', memorandum prepared for Consultants meeting (7 October) Board of Governors, Federal Reserve System.
d (with D. Meiselman) reply to Ando and Modigliani and to DePrano and Mayer, *American Economic Review*, **55** (September), pp. 753–85.
e 'Economic libertarianism', in *Savings and Residential Financing*, 1965 Conference Proceedings, Chicago: US Savings and Loan League, pp. 12–29; discussion pp. 42–57.

1966 *a*† 'Interest rates and the demand for money', *Journal of Law and Economics*, **9** (October), pp. 71–85.
b 'What price guideposts?', in George P. Shultz and Robert Z. Aliber (eds) *Guidelines, Informal Controls and the Market Place*, Chicago: University of Chicago Press, pp. 17–39; and comment ('The case against the case against guideposts'), pp. 55–61.

1967 *a* *The Balance of Payments: Free Versus Fixed Exchange Rates*, debate with Robert V. Roosa, Washington, DC: American Enterprise Institute.
b† 'The monetary theory and policy of Henry Simons', *Journal of Law and Economics*, **10** (October), pp. 1–13.
c Panel, in *Money, Interest Rates and Economic Activity*, proceedings of a symposium of the American Bankers Association, New York: American Bankers Association, pp. 94–149.
d 'Value judgments in economics', in S. Hook (ed.) *Human Values and Economic Policy: A Symposium*, New York: New York University Press, pp. 85–93.

1968 *a*† 'The role of monetary policy', *American Economic Review*, **58** (March), pp. 1–17.
b *Dollars and Deficits*, Englewood Cliffs, New Jersey: Prentice Hall.
c 'Money: quantity theory', in *International Encyclopedia of the Social Sciences*, New York: Macmillan and Free Press, pp. 432–47.
d 'Factors affecting the level of interest rates', in *Savings and Residential Financing*, 1968 Conference Proceedings, Chicago: US Savings and Loan League, pp. 19–27; discussion, pp. 41–55.

1969   *a* (with Anna J. Schwartz) 'The definition of money: net wealth and neutrality as criteria', *Journal of Money, Credit and Banking*, **1** (February), pp. 1–14.
b 'The optimum quantity of money' in *The Optimum Quantity of Money*, pp. 1–50.
c *The Optimum Quantity of Money and Other Essays*, London: Macmillan.
d *Monetary versus Fiscal Policy*, debate with Walter W. Heller, New York: Norton.
e Roundtable on exchange rate policy, *American Economic Review*, Papers and Proceedings, **59** (May), pp. 364–6.
f 'Worswick's criticism of the correlation criterion: a comment', *Journal of Money, Credit and Banking*, **1** (August), p. 506.

1970   *a* *The Counter-Revolution in Monetary Theory*, Occasional Paper 33, London: Institute of Economic Affairs, for the Wincott Foundation.
b 'Controls on interest rates paid by banks', *Journal of Money, Credit and Banking*, **2** (February), pp. 15–32.
c 'A theoretical framework for monetary analysis', *Journal of Political Economy*, **78** (March/April), pp. 193–238.
d Comment on Tobin, 'Money and income: *post hoc ergo propter hoc?*', *Quarterly Journal of Economics*, **84** (May), pp. 318–27.
e (with Anna J. Schwartz) *Monetary Statistics of the United States*, New York: Columbia University Press, for NBER.
f 'The new monetarism: comment', *Lloyd's Bank Review*, (October), pp. 52–3.

1971   *a* 'A monetary theory of nominal income', *Journal of Political Economy*, **79** (March/April), pp. 323–37.
b 'A note on US and UK velocity of circulation', in G. Clayton, J. C. Gilbert and R. Sedgwick (eds) *Monetary Theory and Monetary Policy in the 1970s*, Oxford: Oxford University Press, pp. 151–2.
c 'Government revenue from inflation', *Journal of Political Economy*, **79** (July/August), pp. 846–56.
d *A Theoretical Framework for Monetary Analysis*, NBER Occasional Paper 112, New York: NBER.
e 'The Euro-dollar market: some first principles', *Federal Reserve Bank of St Louis Review*, **53** (July), pp. 16–24.

1972   *a* *An Economist's Protest: Columns in Political Economy*, Glen Ridge, New Jersey: Thos. Horton and Co.
b 'Have monetary policies failed?', *American Economic Review*, Papers and Proceedings, **62** (May), pp. 11–18.
c 'Monetary trends in the United States and United Kingdom', *American Economist*, **16** (Spring), pp. 4–17.
d 'Comments on the critics [of 1971*d*]', *Journal of Political Economy*, **80** (September/October), pp. 906–50.
e (and Wilbur Cohen) *Social Security: Universal or Selective*, Washington, DC: American Enterprise Institute.

1973   *Money and economic development*, the Horowitz Lectures of 1972, New York: Praeger.

1974 *a* 'A bias in current measures of economic growth', *Journal of Political Economy*, **82** (March/April), pp. 431–2.
b 'A theoretical framework for monetary analysis'; and 'comments on the critics', in R. J. Gordon (ed.) *Milton Friedman's Monetary Framework: A Debate with His Critics*, Chicago: University of Chicago Press.
c *Monetary Correction: A Proposal for Escalator Clauses to Reduce the Costs of Ending Inflation*, Occasional Paper 41, London: Institute of Economic Affairs.
d (*et al.*) *Indexing and Inflation*, AEI Roundtable, Washington, DC: American Enterprise Institute.

1975 *a* '25 Years after the rediscovery of money: what have we learned?' discussion, *American Economic Review*, Papers and Proceedings, **65** (May), pp. 176–9.
b *Unemployment versus Inflation? An Evaluation of the Phillips Curve*, Occasional Paper 44, London: Institute of Economic Affairs.
c *There's No Such Thing as a Free Lunch*, La Salle, Illinois: Open Court; also published as *An Economist's Protest* (2nd edn) Glen Ridge, New Jersey: Thos. Horton and Co.

1976 *a* Comments on Tobin and Buiter, 'Long-run effects of fiscal and monetary policy on aggregate demand', in Jerome L. Stein (ed.) *Monetarism, (Studies in Monetary Economics*, vol. 1) Amsterdam: North-Holland, pp. 310–17.
b *Price Theory*, (revised edn) Chicago: Aldine.
c 'Adam Smith's relevance for 1976', original paper, Los Angeles: International Institution for Economic Research.

1977 *a* (and Franco Modigliani) 'The monetarist controversy: discussion', *Federal Reserve Bank of San Francisco Economic Review*, supplement (Spring), pp. 12–22.
b 'Nobel lecture: inflation and unemployment', *Journal of Political Economy*, **85** (June), pp. 451–72; also published (with slightly altered title) as Occasional Paper 51, London: Institute for Economic Affairs.
c 'Time perspective in demand for money', *Scandinavian Journal of Economics*, **79**, (4), pp. 397–416.
d *From Galbraith to Economic Freedom*, Occasional Paper 49, London: Institute of Economic Affairs.
e (*et al.*) *The Business System: A Bicentennial View*, (with an introduction by Frederick E. Webster, Jr) Hanover, New Hampshire: Amos Tuck School of Business Administration.

1978 *a* 'The limitations of tax limitation', *Policy Review*, **5** (Summer), pp. 7–14.
b *Tax Limitation, Inflation, and the Role of Government*, Dallas, Texas: Fisher Institute.

1979 *a* (and Rose D. Friedman) 'The anatomy of crisis', *Journal of Portfolio Management*, **6** (Fall), pp. 15–21.
b 'Memorandum on monetary policy', in (UK) Treasury and Civil Service Committee, *Memoranda on Monetary Policy*, series 1979-80, London: HMSO.

1980   *a* 'Postwar changes in the American financial markets: the changing character of financial markets', in Martin Feldstein (ed.) *The American Economy in Transition*, NBER, a 60th Anniversary Conference, Chicago: University of Chicago Press, pp. 78–86.
 b (with Paul A. Samuelson) 'The economic responsibility of government', discussion, College Station, Texas: Center for Education and Research in Free Enterprise.
 c (with Rose D. Friedman) *Free to Choose*: *A Personal Statement*, New York: Harcourt Brace Jovanovich.

1981   *Market Mechanisms and Central Economic Planning*, the G. Warren Nutter Lectures in political economy, Washington, DC: American Enterprise Institute.

1982   *a* 'Monetary policy: theory and practice', *Journal of Money, Credit and Banking*, **14** (February), pp. 98–118.
 b (with Anna J. Schwartz) *Monetary Trends in the United States and the United Kingdom*: *Their Relations to Income, Prices, and Interest Rates, 1867–1975*, NBER Research Monograph, Chicago: University of Chicago Press.

1986   *a* 'Economists and economic policy', *Economic Inquiry*, **24** (January), pp. 1–10.
 b 'The resource cost of irredeemable paper money', *Journal of Political Economy*, **94** (June), pp. 642–7.

1987   *a* 'Quantity theory of money', in *The New Palgrave*: *A Dictionary of Economics* (4 vols) edited by John Eatwell, Murray Milgate and Peter Newman, Macmillan: London; vol. 4, pp. 3–20.
 b 'Monetary policy: tactics or strategy', in James A. Dorn and Anna J. Schwartz (eds) *The Search for Stability*: *Essays on Monetary Reform*, Chicago: University of Chicago Press.

BIBLIOGRAPHY OF WORKS CITED

Adelman, Irma, and Adelman, Frank L. (1959) 'The dynamic properties of the Klein-Goldberger model', *Econometrica* (October).

Agassi, Joseph (1983) Foreword, 'The philosophy and the psychology of learning', in W. Berkson and J. Wetterman (1984) *Learning from Error: Karl Popper's Psychology of Learning*, La Salle, Illinois: Open Court.

Alford, R. F. G. (1956) 'Marshall's demand curve', *Economica* (September).

Allais, M. and Hagen, O. (eds) (1979) *Expected Utility Hypotheses and the Allais Paradox*, Dordrecht: Reidel.

Ando, A. and Modigliani, F. (1965) 'Velocity and the investment multiplier', *American Economic Review* (September).

Archibald, C. G. (1959) 'The state of economic science', *British Journal for the Philosophy of Science* (May).

Archibald, C. G. (1965) 'The qualitative content of maximizing models', *Journal of Political Economy* (February).

Arrow, Kenneth, J. (1951) *Social Choice and Individual Values*, Cowles Foundation Monograph No. 12 (2nd edn), New York: Wiley.

Ayer, A. J. (1974) 'Truth, verification and verisimilitude', in Paul A. Schilpp (ed.) (1974).

Bailey, Martin, J. (1954) 'The Marshallian demand curve', *Journal of Political Economy* (February).

Bear, D. V. T. and Orr, Daniel (1967) 'Logic and expediency of economic theorizing', *Journal of Political Economy* (April).

Becker, Gary (1971) *The Economics of Discrimination*, Chicago: University of Chicago Press.

Berkson, W. and Wetterman, J. (1984) *Learning from Error: Karl Popper's Psychology of Learning*, La Salle, Illinois: Open Court.

Blaug, Mark (1974) 'Kuhn versus Lakatos or paradigm versus research program in the history of economics', in S. Latsis (ed.) (1976) *Method and Appraisal in Economics*, Cambridge: Cambridge University Press.

Blaug, Mark (1978) *Economic Theory in Retrospect* (3rd edn) Cambridge: Cambridge University Press.

Blaug, Mark (1980) *The Methodology of Economics*, Cambridge: Cambridge University Press.

Boland, Lawrence A. (1970) 'Conventionalism and economic theory', *Philosophy of Science* (June).

Boland, Lawrence A. (1979) 'A critique of Friedman's critics', *Journal of Economic Literature* (June).

Boland, Lawrence A. (1980) 'Friedman's methodology vs. conventional empiricism: a reply to Rotwein', *Journal of Economic Literature* (December).

Boland, Lawrence A. (1982) *The Foundations of Economic Method*, London: Allen and Unwin.

Boland, Lawrence A. (1983) 'Satisficing in methodology: a reply', *American Economic Review* (March).

Boland, Lawrence A. (1984) 'Methodology: reply', *American Economic Review* (September).

Boland, Lawrence A. (1987) 'Boland on Friedman's methodology: a summation', *Journal of Economic Literature* (March).

Boulding, K. E. and Stigler, George (eds) (1952) *Readings in Price Theory*, Chicago: Irwin.

Bowley, Marian (1937) *Nassau Senior and Classical Economics*, London: Allen and Unwin.

Brady, Michael Emmett (1986) 'A note on Milton Friedman's application of his methodology of positive economics', *Journal of Economic Issues* (September).

Brainard, W. C. and Cooper, R. N. (1975) 'Empirical monetary macro-economics: what have we learned in the last 25 years?', *American Economic Review*, Papers and Proceedings (May).

Braithwaite, R. B. (1953) *Scientific Explanation: A Study of the Function of Theory, Probability and Law in Science*, Cambridge: Cambridge University Press.

Breit, William and Ransom, R. L. (1982) *The Academic Scribblers*, (revised edn) Chicago: Dryden Press.

Breit, William and Spencer, Roger W. (eds) (1986) *Lives of the Laureates: Seven Nobel Economists*, Cambridge, Massachusetts: MIT Press.

Bronfenbrenner, M. (1966) 'A "middlebrow" introduction to economic methodology', in Sherman Roy Krupp (ed.) *The Structure of Economic Science*, Englewood Cliffs, New Jersey: Prentice Hall.

Brunner, Karl (1969) '"Assumptions" and the cognitive quality of theories', *Synthese*.

Brunner, Karl (ed.) (1981) *The Great Depression Revisited*, Boston: Kluwer Nijhoff.

Buchanan, James M. (1959) 'Positive economics, welfare economics, and political economy', *Journal of Law and Economics* (October).

Buchanan, James M. and Frank H. Knight (1968) in David L. Sills (ed.) *International Encyclopedia of the Social Sciences*, New York: Macmillan and the Free Press (vol. 8) pp. 424–8.

Buchanan, James M. (1979) *What Should Economists Do?*, Indianapolis, Indiana: Liberty Press.

Buchdahl, G. (1971) 'Inductive vs. deductive approaches in the philosophy of science as illustrated by some controversies between Whewell and Mill', *Monist* (July).

Burns, Arthur F. (1948) 'The cumulation of economic knowledge', in 28th Annual Report of the National Bureau of Economic Research (NBER), reprinted in Burns, *The Frontiers of Economic Knowledge*, Princeton: Princeton University Press.

Burns, Arthur F. (ed.) (1952) *Wesley Clair Mitchell: The Economic Scientist*, New York: NBER.

Butler, Eamonn (1985) *Milton Friedman: A Guide to his Economic Thought*, Aldershot, Hampshire: Gower.

Cahn, Steven M. (ed.) (1977) *New Studies in the Philosophy of John Dewey*, Hanover, New Hampshire: the University Press of New England.

Cairnes, J. E. (1875) *The Character and Logical Method of Political Economy*, (2nd edn), London: Macmillan.

Caldwell, Bruce J. (1980) 'A critique of Friedman's methodological instrumentalism', *Southern Economic Journal* (October).

Caldwell, Bruce J. (1982) *Beyond Positivism: Economic Methodology in the Twentieth Century*, London: Allen and Unwin.

Caldwell, Bruce J. (1988a) 'Clarifying Popper', paper delivered at the History of Economics Society (June).

Caldwell, Bruce J. (1988b) 'Hayek's transformation', *History of Political Economy* (Winter).

Cartwright, Nancy (1983) *How the Laws of Physics Lie*, Oxford: Clarendon Press.

Chick, Victoria (1973) *The Theory of Monetary Policy*, Lectures in Economics, London: Gray-Mills.

Christ, Carl F. (1951) 'A test of an econometric model for the United States, 1921–1947' in *Conference on Business Cycles*, New York: NBER.

Coddington, A. (1972) 'Positive economics', *Canadian Journal of Economics* (February).

Coddington, A. (1979) 'Friedman's contribution to methodological controversy', *British Review of Economic Issues* (May).

Cohen, Kalmon J. and Cyert, Richard M. (1965) *The Theory of the Firm: Resource Allocation in a Market Economy*, Englewood Cliffs, New Jersey: Prentice Hall.

Collins, Harry M. (1985) *Changing Order: Replication and Induction in Scientific Practice*, Beverly Hills, Los Angeles: Sage Publications.

Cournot, A. (1963 [1838]) *Researches into the Mathematical Principles of the Theory of Wealth: With Irving Fisher's Original Notes*, Homewood, Illinois: Irwin.

Cyert, Richard M. and March, James A. (1963) *A Behavioral Theory of the Firm*, Englewood Cliffs, New Jersey: Prentice Hall.

Darity Jr., William and Horn, Bobbie L. (1988) 'Rational expectations and Keynes' *General Theory*', *mimeo*.

Davis, Ken (1986) 'Boland on Davis: a rebuttal', *Journal of Economic Issues* (September).

Davis, Ken (1987) 'Boland on Boland: a further refutation', *Journal of Economic Issues* (March).

De Alessi, Louis (1965) 'Economic theory as a language', *Quarterly Journal of Economics* (August).

De Alessi, Louis (1971) 'Reversals of assumptions and implications', *Journal of Political Economy* (July).

De Marchi, Neil and Gilbert, Christopher (eds) (1989) *History and Methodology of Econometrics*, Oxford: Oxford University Press.

De Marchi, Neil and Kim, Jinbang (1989) '*Ceteris paribus* conditions as prior knowledge: a view from economics', *PSA 1988*, 2.

Dennis, Ken (1986) 'Boland on Friedman: a rebuttal', *Journal of Economic Issues* (September).

Dennis, Ken (1987) 'Boland on Boland: a further refutation', *Journal of Economic Issues* (March).

DePrano, M. and Mayer, T. (1965) 'Autonomous expenditures and money', *American Economic Review* (September).

Desai, Meghnad (1981) *Testing Monetarism*, London: Pinter.

Dewey, J. (1916) *Essays in Experimental Logic*, Chicago: University of Chicago Press.

Dewey, J. (1950 [1920]) *Reconstruction in Philosophy* (enlarged edn), New York: New American Library.

Dewey, J. (1972 [1929]) *Experience and Nature* (2nd edn), La Salle, Illinois: Open Court.

Dewey, J. (1929) *The Quest for Certainty*, New York: Minton, Balch and Co.

Dewey, J. (1938) *Logic: The Theory of Inquiry*, New York: Henry Bolt.

Dewey, J. (1939) 'Social science and social control', *The New Republic* (July); in Joseph Ratner (ed.) (1939) *Intelligence in the Modern World: John Dewey's Philosophy*, New York: Modern Library.

Diesing, Paul (1985) 'Hypothesis testing and data interpretation: the case of Milton Friedman', in Warren J. Samuels (ed.) *Research in the History of Economic Thought and Methodology* (vol. 3) Greenwich, Connecticut: JAI Press.

Dorn, James A. and Schwartz, Anna J. (1987) *The Search for Stability: Essays on Monetary Reform*, Chicago: University of Chicago Press.

Eatwell, J., Milgate, M. and Newman, P. (eds) (1987) *The New Palgrave: A Dictionary of Economics* (4 vols), London: Macmillan.

Fels, Rendig (1981) 'Boland ignores Simon: a comment', *Journal of Economic Literature* (March).

First Quarterly Report, for the period ended 30 April 1942, US Office of Price Administration, Washington DC: US Government.

Fisher, I. (1963 [1922]) *The Purchasing Power of Money: Its Determination and Relation to Credit, Interest and Crises* (new and revised edn), New York: Augustus M. Kelley.

Foucault, M. (1974) *The Archaeology of Knowledge*, London: Tavistock Publications.

Frazer, William J. (1984) 'Methodology: reply', *American Economic Review* (September).

Frazer, William J. and Boland, Lawrence A. (1983) 'An essay on the foundations of Friedman's methodology', *American Economic Review* (March).

Fromm, Erich (1965) *Escape from Freedom*, New York: Avon Books.

Galison, Peter (1987) *How Experiments End*, Chicago: University of Chicago Press.

Garb, Gerald (1964) 'The problem of causality in economics', *Kyklos*, **4**.

Garb, Gerald (1965) 'Professor Samuelson on theory and realism: comment', *American Economic Review* (December).

Georgescu-Rogen, Nicholas (1966) *Analytic Economics: Issues and Policies*, Cambridge, Massachusetts: Harvard University Press.

Gordon, Donald (1955) 'Operational propositions in economic theory', *Journal of Political Economy* (April).

Gordon, Robert J. (ed.) (1974) *Milton Friedman's Monetary Framework: A Debate with His Critics*, Chicago: University of Chicago Press.

Gordon, Wendell (1984) 'The role of institutional economics', *Journal of Economic Issues* (June).

Grampp, W. (1982) 'What became of liberalism'?, *The History of Economics Society Bulletin* (Winter).

Grunberg, Emile (1957) 'Notes on the verifiability of economic laws', *Philosophy of Science* (October).

Haavelmo, Trygve (1944) *The Probability Approach in Econometrics*, supplement to *Econometrica*, **12** (July), Menasha, Wisconsin: Banta, for the Econometric Society.

Hadjimatheou, George (1987) *Consumer Economics after Keynes: Theory and Evidence of the Consumption Function*, Brighton: Wheatsheaf.

Haley, B. F. (ed.) (1952) *A Survey of Contemporary Economics* (vol. 2), Homewood, Illinois: Irwin.

Hammond, J. Daniel (1986) 'Monetarist and antimonetarist causality', in Warren J. Samuels (ed.) *Research in the History of Economic Thought and Methodology* (vol. 4), Greenwich, Connecticutt: JAI Press.

Hammond, J. Daniel (1987a) 'Realism in Friedman's *Essays in Positive Economics*', Wake Forest Working Paper Series No. 87.9, *mimeo*.

Hammond, J. Daniel (1987b) 'Wesley Mitchell as a harbinger of Friedman's method', Wake Forest Working Paper Series No. 87.10, *mimeo*.

Hammond, J. Daniel (1988) 'How different are Friedman and Hicks on method'? *Oxford Economic Papers* (June).

Hands, Douglas W. (1985) 'Karl Popper and economic methodology: a new look', *Economics and Philosophy* (April).

Hartz, Louis (1955) *The Liberal Tradition in America: An Interpretation of American Political Thought Since the Revolution*, New York: Harcourt Brace Jovanovich and World.

Hausman, Daniel (1981) 'John Stuart Mill's philosophy of economics', *Philosophy of Science* (September).

Hausman, Daniel (forthcoming) *The Inexact and Separate Science of Economics*.

Helm, Dieter (1984) 'Prediction and causes', *Oxford Economic Papers* (November, supplement).

Hendry, David F. and Ericsson, Neil R. (1985) 'Assertion without empirical basis: an econometric appraisal of *Monetary Trends in ... the United Kingdom* by Milton Friedman and Anna J. Schwartz', Board of Governors of the Federal Reserve System, Washington, DC: International Finance Discussion Papers, No. 270.

Hester, D. (1964) 'Keynes and the quantity theory: comment on Friedman and Meiselman CMC paper', *Review of Economics and Statistics* (November).

Hicks, J. R. (1946) *Value and Capital: An Inquiry into Some Fundamental Principles of Economic Theory* (2nd edn), Oxford: Clarendon Press.

Hirsch, Abraham and De Marchi, Neil (1984) 'Methodology: a comment on Frazer and Boland I', *American Economic Review* (September).

Hirsch, Abraham and De Marchi, Neil (1986) 'Making a case when theory is unfalsifiable: Friedman's *Monetary History*', *Economics and Philosophy* (April).

Hirsch, Abraham and Hirsch, Eva (1980) 'The heterodox methodology of two Chicago economists', in Warren J. Samuels (ed.) *The Methodology of Economic Thought*, New Brunswick, New Jersey: Transactions Books.

Hirsch, Eva and Hirsch, Abraham (1968) 'The methodological implications of Alfred Marshall's economics', *Piraeus School of Industrial Studies Journal*.

Hollander, Samuel (1985) *The Economics of John Stuart Mill*, Oxford: Blackwell.

Hollis, Martin and Nell, Edward (1975) *Rational Economic Man: A Philosophical Critique of Neoclassical Economics*, Cambridge: Cambridge University Press.

Homan, Paul (1928) *Contemporary Economic Thought*, New York: Harper.

Hoover, Kevin D. (1984a) 'Two types of monetarism', *Journal of Economic Literature* (March).
Hoover, Kevin D. (1984b) 'Methodology: a comment on Frazer and Boland II', *American Economic Review* (September).
Hoover, Kevin D. (1988) *The New Classical Macroeconomics*: *A Sceptical Inquiry*, Oxford: Blackwell.
Hutchison, T. W. (1964) '*Positive*' *Economics and Policy Objectives*, Cambridge, Massachusetts: Harvard University Press.
Johnson, Harry G. (1971) *Macroeconomics and Monetary Theory*, Lectures in Economics No. 1, London: Gray-Mills.
Johnson, Harry G. (1971) 'The Keynesian revolution and the monetarist counter-revolution', *American Economic Review* (May).
Johnson, Harry G. (1976) 'The Nobel Milton', *The Economist* (23 October).
Jones, Evan (1977) 'Positive economics or what'?, *Economic Record* (September).
Katouzian, Homa (1980) *Ideology and Method of Economics*, New York: New York University Press.
Keynes, John Maynard (1973 [1921]) *A Treatise on Probability*; *Collected Writings* (vol. 8), editorial foreword by R. B. Braithwaite, London: Macmillan, for the Royal Economic Society.
Keynes, John Maynard (1938) letter to Roy Harrod, 4 July 1938 (*The Collected Writings of J. M. Keynes*, vol. 14), p. 296.
Keynes, John Maynard (1973 [1936]) *The General Theory of Employment, Interest and Money* (*Collected Writings*, vol. 7), London: Macmillan, for the Royal Economic Society.
Keynes, John Maynard (1973) *The General Theory and After Part II*: *Defence and Development* (*Collected Writings*, vol. 14), Donald Moggridge (ed.), London: Macmillan, for the Royal Economic Society.
Keynes, John Maynard (1978) *Activities 1939–1945*: *Internal War Finance* (*Collected Writings*, vol. 22), Donald Moggridge (ed.), London: Macmillan, for the Royal Economic Society.
Keynes, J. N. (1955 [1890]) *The Scope and Method of Political Economy* (4th edn), New York: Kelley and Millman.
Kim, Jinbang (1989) 'Discovery and testing in modern economics: the case of job search theory', Duke University PhD dissertation, *mimeo*.
Kitch, Edmund W. (ed.) (1983) 'The fire of truth: a remembrance of law and economics at Chicago, 1932–1970', *Journal of Law and Economics* (April).
Klant, J. J. (1974) 'Realism and assumptions in economic theory', *Methodology and Science*.
Klant, J. J. (1984) *The Rules of the Game*: *The Logical Structure of Economic Theories*, Cambridge: Cambridge University Press.
Klappholz, K. and Agassi, J. (1959) 'Methodological prescriptions in economics', *Economica* (February).
Knight, Frank H. (1935 [1951]) *The Ethics of Competition and Other Essays*, New York: Augustus M. Kelley.
Knight, Frank H. (1940) 'What is "truth" in economics'?, *Journal of Political Economy* (February).
Knight, Frank H. (1944) 'Realism and relevance in the theory of demand', *Journal of Political Economy* (December).
Knight, Frank H. (1947) *Freedom and Reform*: *Essays in Economics and Social Philosophy*, New York: Harper and Brothers.

Knight, Frank H. (1956) *On the History and Method of Economics*, Chicago: University of Chicago Press.

Koopmans, Tjalling C. (1947) 'Measurement without theory', *Review of Economic Studies* (August).

Koopmans, Tjalling C. (1957) *Three Essays on the State of Economic Science*, New York: McGraw-Hill.

Koopmans, Tjalling C. and Hood, William (eds) (1953) *Studies in Econometric Method*, Cowles Commission Monograph no. 14, New Haven: Yale University Press.

Krige, John (1980) *Science, Revolution and Discontinuity*, Brighton: Harvester Press.

Kuenne, R. E. (ed.) (1967) *Monopolistic Competition Theory: Studies in Impact*, New York: Wiley.

Kuhn, Thomas S. (1970) *The Structure of Scientific Revolutions* (2nd edn, enlarged), Chicago: University of Chicago Press.

Kuhn, Thomas S. (1974a) 'Logic of Discovery or psychology of research'?, in Imre Lakatos and Alan Musgrave (eds) (1974).

Kuhn, Thomas S. (1974b) 'Reflections on my critics', in Imre Lakatos and Alan Musgrave (eds) (1974).

Lakatos, Imre (1974a) 'Falsification and the methodology of scientific research programmes', in Imre Lakatos and Alan Musgrave (eds) (1974).

Lakatos, Imre (1974b) 'Popper on demarcation and induction', in P. A. Schilpp (ed.) (1974).

Lakatos, Imre and Musgrave, Alan (eds) (1974) *Criticism and the Growth of Knowledge*, Cambridge: Cambridge University Press.

Lange, Oscar (1944) *Price Flexibility and Employment*, Bloomington, Indiana: Principia Press.

Latsis, S. (ed.) (1976) *Method and Appraisal in Economics*, Cambridge: Cambridge University Press.

Laudan, Larry (1971) 'William Whewell and the consilience of inductions', *Monist* (July).

Laughlin, J. Laurence (1920) *Banking Progress*, New York: Scribners.

Leijonhufvud, Axel (1987) 'Whatever happened to Keynesian economics'?, in David Reese (ed.) *The Legacy of Keynes*, San Francisco: Harper and Row.

Leontief, Wassily (1971) 'Theoretical assumptions and nonobserved facts', *American Economic Review* (March).

Lerner, Abba, P. (1944) *The Economics of Control: Principles of Welfare Economics*, New York: Macmillan.

Lerner, Abba P. (1965) 'Professor Samuelson on theory and realism: comment', *American Economic Review* (December).

Liebhafsky, H. H. and Liebhafsky, E. E. (1985) 'Comment on "The instrumentalism of Dewey and Friedman"', *Journal of Economic Issues* (December).

Lipsey, Richard G. (1963) *An Introduction to Positive Economics* (2nd edn 1966), London: Weidenfield and Nicolson.

Lipsey, Richard G., Steiner, Peter O. and Purvis, D. D. (1984) *Economics*, New York: Harper and Row.

Losee, John (1980) *A Historical Introduction to the Philosophy of Science* (2nd edn), Oxford: Oxford University Press.

Losee, John (1983) 'Whewell and Mill on the relation between the philosophy and history of science', *Studies in History and Philosophy of Science*, **14**.

Lucas Jr., Robert E. (1972) 'Econometric testing of the natural rate hypothesis', in Lucas (1981) *Studies in Business-Cycle Theory*, Cambridge, Massachusetts: MIT Press.

Machina, Mark J. (1983) 'The economic theory of individual behavior toward risk: theory, evidence, and new directions', Technical Report no. 433, Center for Research on Organizational Efficiency, Stanford University.

Machina, Mark J. (1987) 'Choice under uncertainty: problems solved and unsolved', *Journal of Economic Perspectives*, 1 (Summer).

Machina, Mark J. and Rothschild, Michael (1987) 'Risk', in J. Eatwell, M. Milgate and P. Newman (eds) *The New Palgrave: A Dictionary of Economics*, London: Macmillan, vol. 4, pp. 201–6.

Machlup, Fritz (1964) 'Professor Samuelson on theory and realism', *American Economic Review* (September).

Machlup, Fritz (1978) *Methodology of Economics and Other Social Sciences*, New York: Academic Press.

Mackie, J. L. (1980) *The Cement of the Universe: A Study of Causation*, Oxford: Clarendon Press.

Maki, Uskali (1986) 'Rhetoric at the expense of coherence: a reinterpretation of Friedman's methodology', in Warren J. Samuels (ed.) *Research in the History of Economic Thought and Methodology* (vol. 4), Greenwich, Connecticutt: JAI Press.

Maki, Uskali (1987) 'How to combine rhetoric and realism in the methodology of economics', discussion paper, University of Helsinki, no. 252.

Marshall, Alfred (1961 [1890]) *Principles of Economics* (9th [variorum] edn with annotations by C. W. Guillebaud; 2 vols), London: Macmillan, for the Royal Economic Society.

Marshall Alfred (1960 [1923]) *Money, Credit and Commerce*, New York: Augustus M. Kelley.

Marshall, Alfred (1926) *Official Papers by Alfred Marshall*, London: Macmillan, for the Royal Economic Society.

Mason, Will E. (1980) 'Some negative thoughts on Friedman's positive economics', *Journal of Post Keynesian Economics* (Winter).

Massey, Gerald J. (1965) 'Professor Samuelson on theory and realism', *American Economic Review* (December).

Mayer, Thomas (1972) *Permanent Income, Wealth, and Consumption*, London: University of California Press.

McClelland, Peter C. (1975) *Causal Explanation and Model Building in History, Economics and the New Economic History*, Ithaca: Cornell University Press.

McDermott, John J. (ed.) (1981) *The Philosophy of John Dewey*, Chicago: University of Chicago Press.

McLachlan, Hugh V. and Swales, J. K. (1982) 'Friedman's methodology: a comment on Boland', *Journal of Economic Studies*, 9.

Mead, George Herbert (1930) 'The Philosophies of Royce, James and Dewey in their American setting', *International Journal of Ethics* (January).

Melitz, Jack (1965) 'Friedman and Machlup on the significance of testing economic assumptions', *Journal of Political Economy* (February).

Mill, J. S. (1973 [1843]) *A System of Logic Ratiocinative and Inductive*, (*The Collected Works*, J. M. Robson (ed.), introduction by R. F. McRae), Toronto: University of Toronto Press.

Mill, J. S. (1957 [1873]) *Autobiography*, Indianapolis: Bobbs-Merrill.

Mill, J. S. (1967) *Essays on Economy and Society* (*Collected Works*, vol. 4), Toronto: University of Toronto Press.

Mills, F. C. (1927) *The Behavior of Prices*, New York: National Bureau of Economic Research.

Mills, F. C. (1928) 'The present status and future prospects of quantitative economics', *American Economic Review* (March).

Mitchell, Lucy Sprague (1953) *Two Lives: The Story of Wesley Clair and Myself*, New York: Simon and Schuster.

Mitchell, W. C. (1910) 'The rationality of economic activity', *Journal of Political Economy* (February and March).

Mitchell, W. C. (1912) review of Irving Fisher's *The Purchasing Power of Money*, *Political Science Quarterly* (March).

Mitchell, W. C. (1927) *Business Cycles: The Problem and Its Setting*, New York: NBER.

Mitchell, W. C. (1950 [1937]) *The Backward Act of Spending Money and Other Essays*, New York: Augustus M. Kelley.

Mitchell, W. C. (1949) *Lecture Notes on Types of Economic Theory*, New York: Augustus M. Kelley.

Mongin, P. (1986) 'La controverse sur l'entreprise (1940–50) et la formation de l'"irréalisme méthodologique"', *Economies et sociétés, Oeconomia*.

Mongin, P. (1987) 'L' instrumentalisme dans l'essai de M. Friedman', *mimeo*.

Musgrave, Alan (1981) '"Unreal assumptions" in economic theory: the F-Twist untwisted'. *Kyklos*, fasc. 3.

Nagel, E. (1950) Introduction, in Ernest Nagel, (ed.) *John Stuart Mill's Philosophy of Scientific Method*, New York: Hafner.

Nagel, E. (1963) 'Assumptions in economic theory', *American Economic Review*, Papers and Proceedings (May).

Neumann, J. Von and Morgenstern, O. (1944) *The Theory of Games and Economic Behavior*, Princeton: Princeton University Press.

Newton-Smith, W. H. (1981) *The Rationality of Science*, Boston: Routledge and Kegan Paul.

Obstfeld, Maurice (1985) 'Floating exchange rates: experience and prospects', *Brookings Papers on Economic Activity*.

Parsons, Donald O. (1987) 'Minimum wages', *The New Palgrave: A Dictionary of Economics*, (vol. 3), pp. 476–8.

Pesak, Boris P. (1976) 'Monetary theory in the post-Robertson Alice in Wonderland era', *Journal of Economic Literature* (September).

Pigou, A. C. (ed.) (1956) *Memorials of Alfred Marshall*, New York: Kelley and Millman.

Piron, Robert (1962) 'On the methodology of positive economics: a comment', *Quarterly Journal of Economics* (November).

Popper, K. (1959) *The Logic of Scientific Discovery*, London: Hutchinson.

Popper, K. (1965) *Conjectures and Refutations: The Growth of Scientific Knowledge* (2nd edn), London: Routledge and Kegan Paul.

Popper, K. (1966) *The Open Society and its Enemies* (5th edn revised), Princeton: Princeton University Press.

Popper, K. (1968) *The Logic of Scientific Discovery* (2nd edn), New York: Harper.

Popper, K. (1972) *Objective Knowledge: An Evolutionary Approach*, London: Oxford University Press.

Popper, K. (1974a) 'Replies to my critics', in Paul A. Schilpp (ed.) (1974).

Popper, K. (1974b) 'Normal science and its dangers', in Imre Lakatos and Alan Musgrave (eds) (1974).

Popper, K. (1983) *Realism and the Aim of Science*, Totowa, New Jersey: Rowman and Littlefield.

Rachels, James (1977) 'John Dewey and the truth about ethics', in Steven M. Cahn (ed.) (1977).

Radecki, Lawrence J. and Wenninger, John (1985) 'Recent instability in M1's velocity', *Quarterly Review* of the Federal Reserve Bank of New York (Autumn).

Reder, Melvin W. (1982) 'Chicago economics: permanence and change', *Journal of Economic Literature* (March).

Robbins, Lionel (1949 [1932]) *An Essay on the Nature and Significance of Economic Science* (2nd edn), London: Macmillan.

Robbins, Lionel (1976) *Political Economy: Past and Present*, New York: Columbia University Press.

Rosenberg, Alexander (1976) *Microeconomic Laws: A Philosophical Analysis*, Pittsburg: University of Pittsburg Press.

Rosenberg, Alexander (1989) 'Are generic predictions enough'? *Erkenntnis*, **30** (March), pp. 43–68.

Rotwein, E. (1959) 'On the methodology of positive economics', *Quarterly Journal of Economics* (November).

Rotwein, E. (1962) 'Reply', *Quarterly Journal of Economics* (November).

Rotwein, E. (1973) 'Empiricism and economic method: several views considered', *Journal of Economic Issues* (September).

Rotwein, E. (1980) 'Friedman's critics: a reply to Boland', *Journal of Economic Literature* (December).

Salant, Walter (1942) 'The inflationary gap: meaning and significance for policy making', *American Economic Review* (June).

Salanti, Andrea (1987) 'Falsification and fallibalism as epistemic foundation of economics: a critical view', *Kyklos*, fasc. 3.

Samuels, Warren (1975) 'On some fundamental issues in political economy', *Journal of Economic Issues* (March).

Samuels, Warren (1977) 'Ideology in Economics', in S. Weintraub (ed.) (1977) *Modern Economic Thought*, Philadelphia: University of Pennsylvania Press.

Samuelson, Paul A. (1948) *Economics: An Introductory Analysis*, New York: McGraw-Hill.

Samelson, Paul A. (1963) 'Problems of methodology; discussion', *American Economic Review*, Papers and Proceedings (May).

Samuelson, Paul A. (1965a [1947]) *Foundations of Economic Analysis*, New York: Atheneum.

Samuelson, Paul A. (1965b) 'Professor Samuelson on theory and realism: a reply', *American Economic Review* (December).

Samuelson, Paul A. (1967) 'The monopolistic competition revolution', in Kuenne (ed.) (1967), pp. 105–38.

Sargent, Thomas J. (1987) *Some of Milton Friedman's Scientific Contributions to Macroeconomics*, Stanford: Hoover Institution.

Schilpp, P. A. (ed.) (1974) *The Philosophy of Karl Popper*, La Salle, Illinois: Open Court.

Schoemaker Paul J. H. (1982) 'The expected utility model: its variants, purposes, evidence and limitations', *Journal of Economic Literature* (June).

Schumpeter, Joseph (1954) *History of Economic Analysis*, New York: Oxford University Press.

Seligman, Ben (1969) 'The impact of positivism on economic thought', *History of Economic Thought* (Fall).

Senior, Nassau (1966 [1852]) 'Four introductory lectures on economics', in *Selected Writings on Economics*, New York: Augustus M. Kelley, 1966.

Silk, Leonard (1976) *The Economists*, New York: Basic Books.

Simon, Herbert A. (1963) 'Problems in methodology: discussion', *American Economic Review* (August).

Slovic, P. and Lichtenstein, S. (1983) 'Preference reversals: a broader perspective', *American Economic Review* (September).

Smith, Adam (1937 [1776]) *An Inquiry Into the Nature and the Causes of the Wealth of Nations*, R. H. Campbell, A. S. Skinner and W. B. Todd (eds), New York: The Modern Library.

Spanos, Aris (1989) 'Early empirical findings on the consumption function, stylized facts or fiction: a retrospective view', in De Marchi and Gilbert (eds) *History and Methodology of Econometrics*.

Stanley, T. D. (1985) 'Positive economics and its instrumental defence', *Economica* (August).

Stein, Jerome, L. (ed.) (1976) *Monetarism*, Amsterdam: North-Holland.

Stigler, George J. (1947) 'Notes on the history of the Giffen paradox', *Journal of Political Economy* (April).

Stigler, George J. (1951) 'Comment', *American Economic Review* (May).

Stigler, George J. (1965) *Essays in the History of Economics*, Chicago: University of Chicago Press.

Stigler, George J. (1981) 'A historical note on the short run: Marshall and Friedman', *History of Economics Society Bulletin* (Winter).

Stone, Courtney C. and Thornton, Daniel L. (1987) 'Solving the 1980s velocity puzzle: a progress report', *Review* of the Federal Reserve Bank of St Louis (August/September).

Suppe, F. (ed.) (1977) *The Structure of Scientific Theories* (2nd edn), Urbana, Illinois: University of Illinois Press.

Thomas, J. J. (1989) 'The early econometric history of the consumption function', in De Marchi and Gilbert (eds) *History and Methodology of Econometrics*.

Thomas, Vincent (ed.) (1956) *Essays in the Philosophy of Science of Charles S. Peirce*, Indianapolis, Indiana: Bobbs-Merrill.

Tinbergen, J. (1939) *Statistical Testing of Business Cycles, Vol. II: Business Cycles in the United States of America, 1919–1932*, Geneva: League of Nations.

Tobin, James (1965) 'The monetary interpretation of history', (a review article), *American Economic Review* (June); in (1971) *Essays in Economics, Vol. 1: Macroeconomics*, Chicago: Markham.

Tobin, James (1970) 'Money and income: *post hoc ergo propter hoc*'?, *Quarterly Journal of Economics* (May); in Tobin, *Essays*.

Tobin, James (1974) 'Friedman's theoretical framework', in Gordon (ed.) *Milton Friedman's Monetary Framework*.

Tobin, James and Buiter, Willem (1976) 'Long-run effects of fiscal and monetary policy on aggregate demand', in Stein (ed.) *Monetarism*.

Viner, Jacob (1917) 'Some problems of logical method in political economy', *Journal of Political Economy* (March).

Viner, Jacob (1924) *Canada's Balance of International Indebtedness*,

1903–1913: *An Inductive Study in the Theory of International Trade*, Cambridge: Harvard University Press.

Viner, Jacob (1928) 'The present status and future prospects of quantitative economics' (discussion), *American Economic Review* (March).

Viner, Jacob (1929) Review of F. C. Mills' *The Behavior of Prices*, in Raymond T. Bye (1929) *An appraisal of Frederick C. Mill's* The Behavior of Prices, New York: Social Science Research Council.

Viner, Jacob (1940) 'The short view and the long in economic policy', *American Economic Review* (March).

Viner, Jacob (1954) 'Schumpeter's history of economic analysis: a review article', *American Economic Review* (December).

Viner, Jacob (1955) 'International trade and its present day relevance', in *Economic and Public Policy*, Washington, DC: Brookings.

Vining, Rutledge (1950) 'Methodological issues in quantitative economics', *American Economic Review* (June).

Vining, Rutledge (1951) 'Economic theory and quantitative research: a broad interpretation of the Mitchell position', in *American Economic Review*, Papers and Proceedings (May).

Wald, Abraham (1940) 'The approximate determination of indifference surfaces by means of Engel curves', *Econometrica* (April).

Wallis, W. Allen (1980) 'The statistical research group, 1942–1945', *Journal of the American Statistical Association* (June).

Walras, Leon (1954) *Elements of Pure Economics* (Trans. William Jaffe), London: Allen and Unwin, for the American Economic Association and the Royal Economic Society.

Walters, Alan (1987) 'Friedman, Milton', in *The New Palgrave: A Dictionary of Economics* (vol. 2), London: Macmillan.

Webb, James R. (1987) 'Is Friedman's methodological instrumentalism a special case of Dewey's instrumental philosophy? A reply to Wible', *Journal of Economic Issues* (March).

Welch, Finis (1978) *Minimum Wages: Issues and Evidence*, Washington, DC: American Enterprise Institute.

Wenninger, John (1984) 'The M1–GNP relationship: a component approach', *Quarterly Review* of the Federal Reserve Bank of New York (Autumn).

Whewell, William (1967 [1847]) *Philosophy of the Inductive Sciences* (2nd edn, 2 vols), London: Cass.

Whitaker, J. K. (1975) 'John Stuart Mill's methodology', *Journal of Political Economy* (October).

Wible, James R. (1982) 'Friedman's positive economics and philosophy of science', *Southern Economic Journal* (October).

Wible, James R. (1984) 'The instrumentalism of Dewey and Friedman', *Journal of Economic Issues* (December).

Wible, James. R. (1985) 'Institutional economics, positive economics, pragmatism and the recent philosophy of science', *Journal of Economic Issues* (December).

Wible, James R. (1987) 'Criticism of the validity of the special-case interpretation of Friedman's essay: a reply to Webb', *Journal of Economic Issues* (March).

Williamson, John (1985) *The Exchange Rate System*, Policy Analyses in International Economics no. 5, Washington, DC: Institute for International Economics.

Wisdom, J. T. (1944–1945) 'Gods', *Proceedings of the Aristotelean Society*, New Series **XLV**, pp. 185–206.

Winn, Ralph B. (1965) *A Survey of American Philosophy*, Paterson, New Jersey: Littlefield, Adams.

Winter, J. R. (1988) 'Keynes versus Friedman: a question of methodology', paper presented at the History of Economics Society meetings, June.

Wong, Stanley (1973) 'The F-Twist and the methodology of Paul Samuelson', *American Economic Review* (June).

Wood, John H. (1981) 'The economics of Professor Friedman', in George Horwich and James Q. Quirk (eds) *Essays in Contemporary Fields of Economics*, West Lafayette, Indiana: Purdue University Press.

Yeager, Leland B. (1960) '*Methodenstreit* over demand curves', *Journal of Political Economy* (February).

Young, Jeffrey T. (1988) 'David Hume and Adam Smith on value premises in economics: is a "science of legislation" possible?', paper given at the History of Economics Society meeting, June.

INDEX